COMPARISON OF ECONOMIC SYSTEMS

COMPARISON OF ECONOMIC SYSTEMS

Theoretical and
Methodological
Approaches

Edited by

ALEXANDER

ECKSTEIN

UNIVERSITY OF CALIFORNIA PRESS

BERKELEY LOS ANGELES LONDON 1971

University of California Press
Berkeley   Los Angeles

University of California Press, Ltd.
London

Library of Congress Catalog Card Number: 79-118085
ISBN 0-520-01729-3
Printed in the United States of America

Contributors

ABRAM BERGSON   Department of Economics, Harvard University

MORRIS BORNSTEIN   Department of Economics, University of Michigan

EVSEY D. DOMAR   Department of Economics, Massachusetts Institute of Technology

ALEXANDER ECKSTEIN   Department of Economics, University of Michigan

ALEXANDER ERLICH   Department of Economics, Columbia University

ALEXANDER GERSCHENKRON   Department of Economics, Harvard University

ALBERT HIRSCHMAN   Department of Economics, Harvard University

LEONID HURWICZ   Department of Economics, University of Minnesota

SIMON KUZNETS   Department of Economics, Harvard University

TJALLING C. KOOPMANS   Department of Economics, Yale University

HERBERT LEVINE   Department of Economics, University of Pennsylvania

JOHN M. MONTIAS   Department of Economics, Yale University

BENJAMIN WARD   Department of Economics, University of California at Berkeley

Preface

This symposium volume is the product of a two and a half-day research conference on Scope, Method, and Theory of Comparative Economic Systems held at the University of Michigan in November 1968. The papers were circulated before the conference and a discussant was assigned to each paper. The discussant's comments then laid the groundwork for the lively debates at the conference.

The discussions greatly assisted the contributors to this volume in revising their papers. They all join me in expressing our appreciation to Kenneth Boulding, Martin Bronfenbrenner, Gregory Grossman, Thomas Marschak, Wolfgang Stolper and Peter Wiles for their contributions. Two of the discussants—Evsey Domar and Albert Hirschman—expanded their comments into papers which are included as separate chapters in this book.

The authors were also greatly aided by the written and oral contributions of the discussants-at-large. Thus we are deeply indebted to Jean Benard, Robert Dernberger, Branko Horvat, E. S. Kirschen, Oldrych Kyn, Harold Levinson, Siro Lombardini, Ivan Maksimovic, Alec Nove, Pavel Pelikan, Fred Pryor, William Shepherd, Knud Erik Svendsen, Shigeto Tsuru, and Ludek Urban. The conference and the writing of this volume was made possible by the Comparative Economics Program of the University of Michigan. The Program is, in turn, financed by a Ford Foundation grant for the support of international and comparative studies at the University. I want to extend our thanks to the Foundation, the University and the Program for their sponsorship, encouragement and support.

A. E.

Ann Arbor
August, 1970

Contents

Tables   *page*

Figures

I

Introduction

by ALEXANDER ECKSTEIN

1. Evolution of the Field

Comparative economic systems might be characterized as a field in search of a self-definition. This volume represents an attempt to contribute to this search by a) providing an analytical framework for the comparative study of economic systems, b) exploring alternative methodological approaches in the analysis of these systems, and c) probing some of the critical issues.

Comparative systems began to emerge as a distinct branch of economics with the crystallization of a new economic system in the Soviet Union.[1] John R. Commons taught a course on capitalism and socialism at the University of Wisconsin in the early post-World War I years.[2] Some of his students began to introduce courses in economic systems in several colleges and universities. The dominant *Problemstellung* of these comparisons—both in the courses and the textbooks—concerned the viability of the new economic system, its ability to function and to solve some of the critical questions and contradictions facing so-called capitalist systems. Courses developed at the time were often designed to demonstrate the weaknesses of the Soviet system and the corresponding superiority of our own. At times, and particularly under the impact of the Great Depression, the approach was reversed and the searchlight focused critically on the so-called capitalist system itself.

The emphasis was on the grand "isms," that is capitalism, socialism, communism, and fascism or variants thereof. The field was strongly influenced by the traditional comparative government approach, many of the analytical categories were political and ideological rather than economic.[3] At the same time, comparisons of economic systems tended to focus on their contrasts and polarities; that is, they principally dwelt on

[1] In this chapter and throughout this book the terms comparative economic systems, comparative economics, and comparison of systems are used interchangeably unless otherwise specified.

[2] See Calvin B. Hoover, *The Economy, Liberty and the State*, New York, 1959, p. 1.

[3] In their text, Hoot and Loucks state that "in the field of political science it has long been customary to compare and contrast political systems and forms of government." They go on to point out that enough information is now available to apply a similar approach to the study of different economic systems. (William N. Loucks and J. Weldon Hoot, *Comparative Economic Systems, Capitalism, Communism, Socialism, Fascism*, 3d ed. New York, 1948, p. 4.)

differences in kind rather than on differences in degree, on discontinuities rather than on continuities. Finally, the approach was preponderantly descriptive and institutional rather than theoretical or analytical.

The Great Depression and the profound problems of the prevailing order revealed by it stimulated a growing interest in this field. The sharp declines in levels of economic activity coupled with the rise of large-scale unemployment in many countries led to demands for the introduction of economic controls, of more centralized management of the economy, and of economic planning. In this context a number of questions arose concerning the relationships between freedom, economic planning, and socialization of the means of production. These controversies often suffered from a lack of clarity and rigor, both as to the meaning of the concepts and the definition of the issues. However the central concern emerged clearly enough: the compatibility of political democracy and macro-economic or central economic planning.[4]

Parallel with these public-policy oriented debates, a theoretical controversy developed of far-reaching importance in the study of comparative economics. This controversy revolved largely around the possibilities of rational and efficient resource allocation under socialism or, more specifically, in centrally planned economies with publicly owned means of production. The issues then posed by Von Mises, Hayek, Lange, and some others raised the technical and theoretical level of discourse in comparative economics and focused on a range of problems that had a profound impact on the development of the field as evidenced by some of the chapters in this volume.[5] This applies particularly to the questions posed by Hurwicz in his chapter on "Centralization and Decentralization in Economic Processes." The section on informational efficiency and decentralization, for instance, grapples with questions raised by Hayek in his discussions of bounded rationality. These same issues are also relevant to Levine's attempts to scale planned economies according to the attribute characterized by him as centralization of authority. Finally some of the issues raised in these controversies also contribute to an understanding of the differences in comparative efficiency between the United States and the Soviet Union explored by Bergson in Chapter VI.

[4] For instance these concerns are quite explicit in Barbara Wootton's book *Plan or No Plan*, New York: 1935. She argues that "the introduction of a socialized planned system of economics does not call for changes in the actual constitution or mode of election of Parliament itself" (p. 314). At the same time she asserts that "constructive national planning is impossible unless the instruments of production are owned by public corporations amenable to the direct orders of the planners" (p. 317).

[5] See F. A. Hayek (ed.), *Collectivist Economic Planning*, London, 1935, and Oskar Lange, "On the Economic Theory of Socialism" in B. E. Lippincott (ed.), *On the Economic Theory of Socialism*, Minneapolis, 1938.

The work on the economic theory of socialism, later developed by others,[6] has influenced the methodology of comparative economics in other ways as well. The introduction of model systems or system models as an analytical device can be traced to this interest in the economic theory of socialism. As a theory emerged for one model system, it stimulated work on the theory of other systems as well, facilitated in turn by extensive postwar research on the behavioral and performance characteristics of the Soviet and of other economies. This research undoubtedly played a crucial role for instance in the crystallization of a theory of the command economy.[7] These developments and the confrontation of system models and living economies contributed to a growing sophistication of the comparative economics field. They led to an increasing recognition that the preoccupation with comparisons based on "isms" were likely to yield overly simple and simplistic insights into the character of economic systems. In contrast, comparisons of models and realities tended to focus on the complexity and variety of living systems and their departure from the theoretical ideal.

Study of system models and of the behavioral and performance traits of national economies posed anew the question: "What is an economic system?" Does the concept refer to the theoretical models, to the system of economic organization characterizing an economy, or to the subsystems (e.g., institutions, firms, households) within it? Inasmuch as the definition will circumscribe the boundaries of the field and shape the criteria for the comparisons of economic systems, this is clearly a crucial problem.

Webster's International Dictionary (Second Edition) defines a *system* as "an aggregation or assemblage of objects united by some form of regular interaction or interdependence; a group of diverse units so combined by nature or art as to form an integral whole, and to function, operate or move in unison, and, often in obedience to some form of control; an organic or organized whole." Koopmans and Montias indicate in Chapter II that "depending on the comparison to be made, the comparor may feel that he can designate as *economic system* only that part of the total system, which directly or indirectly affects economic behavior and outcomes in at least one of the systems being compared." These are clearly broad definitions and of a high order of generality.

Kuznets uses a somewhat narrower and more specific definition in Chapter VIII when he refers to an economic system as "long-term

[6] For instance A. P. Lerner, *Economics of Control*, New York, 1944; Abram Bergson, "Socialist Economics" in H. S. Ellis (ed.), *A Survey of Contemporary Economics*, Philadelphia and Toronto, 1948, pp. 412–448; and Abram Bergson, "Market Socialism Revisited" in *Journal of Political Economy*, LXXV: 5 (1967) 655–673.

[7] See Gregory Grossman, "Notes for a Theory of the Command Economy" in *Soviet Studies*, XV: 2 (1963) 101–123.

arrangements by which various units within a society are induced to cooperate in production, distribution and the use of aggregate product— including means of control over productive factors, and freedom or constraint on individual units in the existing factor or goods markets." Grossman uses an even simpler and perhaps a somewhat more operational definition. According to him, "the set of institutions that characterizes a given economy comprises an economic system."[8] To complicate the problem further Koopmans and Montias point out that the boundary between system and policies is not sharp and may depend on the length of the period for which a comparison is made. For instance, a market economy with a fiscal policy of a balanced annual government budget may be considered as a somewhat different system from that of the same economy following a fiscal and monetary full-employment policy. If within a longer period the former system is succeeded by the latter, one may alternatively speak of a market system in which a policy change occurred at some point in time.

We are dealing here with such complex and multivariate sets of relationships that there are trade-offs in the usefulness of different kinds of definitions. These definitions can be general and comprehensive and at the same time probably less operational, or they can be more specific and operational, but then they necessarily have to be narrower. Ultimately, the usefulness or applicability of a particular type of definition will depend on the character of the comparison to be made. Nevertheless, the comparative analysis of systems of economic organization and their effect on economic behavior and performance would probably encompass the bulk of the field of comparative economics.

Approaching the comparative study of economic systems in these terms, how legitimate or valid is it to identify particular national economies with particular system models or "isms"? In what sense can the United States economy be regarded as a prototype of a capitalist economy, Britain as a socialist economy, and the Soviet Union as a communist one as outlined in most comparative systems texts? In terms of what criteria and of what kinds of indicators can the British economy or, let us say, the Swedish one be regarded as more socialist or less capitalist than the system of economic organization prevailing in the United States? Similarly, the Soviets refer to themselves as a socialist rather than as a communist economic system, because official doctrine requires that a number of conditions must prevail before communism can be attained.

How useful are these labels or categories in the study of economic system behavior and performance? Do they not serve to confuse rather than to clarify? Do they represent more than myths, programmatic pronouncements, or ideological labels? This raises a somewhat related

[8] Gregory Grossman, *Economic Systems*, Englewood Cliffs, N.J., 1967, p. 2.

question, namely what role does ideology play in shaping economic system behavior. In traditional approaches to comparative economics it was taken for granted that a study of Marxism was an essential and integral component of the subject matter in the field. However, very rarely if at all was this study coupled with an analysis of the specific interrelationships between Marxist economic theory and doctrine on the one hand and, let us say, Soviet economic organization and policies on the other. That these linkages existed was simply assumed without spelling it out. With this view Professor Gerschenkron takes sharp issue in Chapter IX, a problem about which more will be said below.

Under the impact of the developments referred to above, the character of the field has changed considerably in the last twenty years and as a result the traditional *Problemstellung* has been markedly modified. The approach is now less political, less ideological, more analytical and at the same time more operational. The focus has shifted somewhat from a holistic comparison of total systems to a comparative study of traits, institutions, and problems that cut across systems. This new approach may involve a comparative study of the consequences of industrialization, the impact of technological progress, the rise of large-scale organizations, bureaucratization of such organizations, and the dilemmas of decision-making inherent in the rise of these bureaucracies in different types of economies. It also signals a shift in preoccupations from questions revolving around the compatibility of planning and freedom to a comparative analysis of system performance in terms of certain explicitly stated criteria, such as economic growth, efficiency, or stability. *Pari passu* more consideration is given to system traits as a series on a continuum or a spectrum rather than as polar opposites, coupled with a recognition that all economies represent mixed rather than pure systems.

2. Some Critical Issues

The approach to the study of national economies as mixed systems with their distinguishing characteristics blurred rather than clear cut, requires a broader and rather different framework of analysis than might be called for in a more "ismistic" study of economic systems. This is the task we set for ourselves in this book.

Having discussed certain general methodological questions above, I would now like to turn to some of the critical issues. This section will first discuss and briefly appraise the criteria most frequently used in comparisons of economic systems. Some of these will then be subjected to more intensive analysis.

Variables and criteria in terms of which economic systems could be compared and classified are large in number as clearly outlined by

Koopmans and Montias. As they point out, the approach used will depend to some extent on the comparor and on the character of the comparison to be made. At the same time, if one concentrated on the central pre-occupations of the field as it has been crystallizing in recent years, one would find that, in one form or another, the work in comparative economics largely revolves around the following axes of comparison:

1. Property relations
2. Kinds of economic freedoms
3. The character of incentive systems
4. The character of the coordinating or resource-allocating mechanism
5. Locus and system of decision-making.

Property relations as a central distinguishing system characteristic loomed particularly large in the "ismistic" approach according to which capitalism, and the United States economy as its prototype, is based on private property holdings in contrast to socialist economies where the means of production would be at least in part nationalized as in Britain or Sweden, or wholly socialized as in the Soviet Union and other communist countries. To what extent does this view reflect the realities of the prevailing situation and what is the significance of property relations as a system characteristic?

The importance of property holding derives from its role as a source of control and a source of claims upon the product or the income produced by it. Individuals acting on their own behalf or on behalf of organizations, groups, or government organs may wish to exercise control for a multiplicity of motives, reasons, or ends, e.g., personal pursuit of wealth or power, growth or enrichment of the organization, or others. Koopmans and Montias refer to this as *custody* over resources and man-made means of production. In the case of owner-managed enterprises, the two aspects—control and claims—are automatically merged. However, in other forms of enterprise organization not only are control and ownership separated, but the control and claims function of ownership itself becomes divided as is richly attested by a vast literature on industrial organization. At the same time, custodial control also may, and often does, carry with it control over the distribution of claims. Property holdings therefore can provide power over the allocation and distribution of resources, output and incomes. That is why they have been one of the most important criteria in distinguishing and comparing economic systems.

This emphasis on property relations would be most useful in a world where forms of property holding and production organization would automatically invest ownership with the means for control and access to claims. In fact, this is not the case. In most contemporary systems forms of property holding become highly blurred in a complex criss-crossing of controls and claims. In many cases it is unclear where private ownership ends and public ownership begins. Wiles, for example, identifies ten ownership models ranging from private individual ownership of the means of production (primitive capitalism) to patterns which turn a whole nation into a commune (full communism).[9]

These polar forms represent the exceptions in contemporary economies, while actually prevailing property relations fall between the extremes. Thus corporate organizations—private and public—typify the modern industrial order with the two forms intermixed in most economies. Therefore in this respect, too, differences between systems represent differences in degree rather than differences in kind, although at the extreme ends of the spectrum the quantitative differences may become so large that they could be considered to be qualitative. Contemporary economies consequently, tend to be characterized by a "mixed" rather than a pure system of property relations.

The implications of this control and ownership problem have perhaps been most clearly worked out by Dahl and Lindbloom. They point to the vast number of possible forms in a continuum: At one end is an enterprise operated by a government department, at the other a small proprietorship, and in between a host of combinations involving varying degrees of public or private arrangements.[10] All of this is greatly complicated by the entry of each enterprise into a variety of relationships with other enterprises and organizations which may then further modify the type of control—public or private or a mixture thereof—over its activities.

For instance, if a private corporation operates a government facility on lease or contract to what extent can this activity be characterized as public or private? Similarly if a private contractor is engaged in research-and-development work for the Department of Defense, largely financed and controlled by it, is this public or private? How would one characterize the status of the RAND Corporation or of the Institute for Defense Analysis or other non-profit private research organizations primarily working on government contracts? Such examples, drawn from the United States and from other noncommunist states as well, could be multiplied manifold. Moreover, their counterparts could also be found in somewhat different forms and in varying degrees in communist states. Thus in every one of these states there are not only private plots in agriculture and private ownership in small-scale enterprises and under-takings, but in recent years various types of collaborative arrangements have been entered between private corporations from abroad and

[9] Peter Wiles, *The Political Economy of Communism*, Cambridge, Mass., 1962, pp. 4–12.
[10] Robert A. Dahl and Charles E. Lindbloom, *Politics, Economics, and Welfare*, New York, 1953, pp. 5–10.

domestic economic organizations involving foreign investment, licensing, and a variety of other types of joint ventures.

Socialists and free-enterprise advocates alike have tended to identify ownership in the past with locus and system of decision-making, the character of the coordinating or resource-allocating mechanism, and the character of the incentive system. Thus they tended to associate national-ization of the means of production with planning, centralized direction and control over resource allocation, and an egalitarian income distribu-tion to the point that the *former* was regarded as a prerequisite for the *latter*. Correspondingly, private ownership was considered a prerequisite to the market allocation of resources and to profit maximization as a major incentive and a criterion of enterprise performance.

This dichotomy and the more or less automatic association of certain custodial patterns with specified patterns of interaction represent a highly over-simplified picture of reality as detailed in Chapter III by Hurwicz and in Chapter V by Levine. The experience with national economic management since the Great Depression has taught us that centralized control over resource allocation is quite compatible with various forms of private ownership of the means of production as shown by our own wartime experience and the experience of Nazi Germany in both peace and war. One could correspondingly visualize an economic system with only minimal centralized control over resource allocation while the means of production are publicly owned. Yugoslavia is an example of an economy tending in that direction.

By the same token there is no necessary connection between macro-economic planning and ownership patterns—public or private; it is compatible with either as demonstrated by the post-World War II experience of countries both "West" and "East."[11] Similarly the relation-ship between planning and the institution of various types of government controls may be less direct and certainly more complex than would be suggested by the dichotomies mentioned above. As a general proposition one could say that planning requires the introduction of controls for its implementation, but that controls do not require planning.

Of course, in part this is a matter of definition. Thus if one regards a plan as no more than a projection or forecast, it requires no controls or implementing measures of any kind. The very concept of planning usually implies something more active. At a most general level, and according to the dictionary definition of the term, it involves "the deliberate pursuit of certain ends." That meaning requires that certain goals, targets or purposes be specified and that instruments (controls) be devised for their attainment. What about the reverse side of this coin: Does the introduction of economic controls necessarily imply the introduction of economic

[11] These refer to entities defined in Chapter II, p. 280.

planning? For instance, does the imposition of foreign exchange controls designed to stem capital flight represent an act of planning? If one follows the dictionary definition of the term, it does, because it represents a "deliberate pursuit of certain ends." However, if one identifies planning with national economic planning, which is the context in which it usually appears in comparative systems analysis, then these types of measures can be regarded as partial controls not in any way integrated or articulated into a plan. This view is certainly that adopted in Chapter V by Levine, who regards economic planning as "social control over an economy through a process which includes the drawing up of a picture of a desired state of an economy at a future point in time and the utilization of some instrumentalities to bring about this desired state."

The view of economic systems as a continuum along a scale is reinforced by a comparative examination of the resource- allocating mechanisms in different national economies with varying mixes of command and market allocation prevailing in the "East," in Yugoslavia, and in the "West." Distinctions and comparisons between economic systems are often based not only on the patterns of property relations, or decision-making, or types of allocating mechanisms but on the prevailing kinds and degrees of economic freedom and incentive systems. Following Grossman, it may be useful to distinguish three kinds of economic freedoms: freedom of consumer choice, freedom of occupations, and freedom of enterprise.[12] In respect to everyone of these, too, variations in actual national economic practice may be considered as differences in degree rather than in kind.

In principle free consumer and occupational choice is supposed to prevail both in the "West" and "East," in the "West" supposedly linked with consumer sovereignty. In fact, many constraints operate on free consumer choice in all systems. In all "Western" economies rationing of consumer goods and services was instituted during World War II. In the "East" rationing was also enforced during certain peacetime periods. In Communist China some form of rationing of consumer goods has prevailed since 1953 and to some extent from the advent of the new regime in 1949. The degrees of consumer choice in different economies may well vary significantly, but this cannot be determined by assumption, only by careful empirical investigation.

The issue is more subtle and complex in respect to consumer sovereignty. In a purely competitive system model, consumer preferences would govern the allocation of resources and the composition of the final bill of goods. In contrast, in the command economy of the ideal type, resources would be allocated by command and on the basis of the planners' rather than the consumers' scale of preferences. Consumers therefore could not

[12] Grossman, *Economic Systems*, pp. 8–9.

affect the resource-allocation bundle but could merely choose among the goods already produced without this choice having any impact on the composition of that bundle. In actual practice producers in the "West" can influence and manipulate consumer tastes and preferences, so that it could be argued that there too—at least to some extent—producers lead and consumers follow.[13] Of course, consumers have a veto power over what is produced, but this is true of the "East" as well. Consumer autonomy is also constrained in the "West" as it is in the "East" to the extent that the government appropriates resources for its own consumption. Again, this does not mean that there are no significant institutional differences between "East" and "West" which affect the role of the consumer in resource allocation. However, it is important to bear in mind the considerable variation among "Eastern" countries, particularly in recent years, even as among those in the "West." This differentiation, in turn, suggests that here too we are dealing with a continuum rather than a dichotomy.

This same general approach can be applied to a comparative study of incentive systems, and particularly to the role of profits and of wage and income differentials. As a number of studies of corporate behavior in the United States and other "Western" countries have shown, profit maximization as a criterion of corporate success and as a prime motive force for management performance tends to be qualified or constrained by a number of other objectives such as growth of the enterprise, corporate image, or prestige. Thus psychic incentives are substituted within certain ranges for material ones, and the material rewards themselves are a function of a complex of elements of which profits are only one, although in most cases still perhaps the most important single one.

On the other hand, important changes have been taking place in the "East" under the impact of economic reforms. In some cases these involve only small halting steps, whereas in others they entail an appreciable upgrading of the profit criterion as a success indicator for the enterprise along with some broadening of the scope of market allocation of resources. More broadly, wage and income differentials have served as major instruments for the allocation of labor both in the "West" and "East." Unfortunately although no satisfactory income distribution data are available for the Soviet Union and a number of other countries, such evidence as there is suggests considerable variation among countries without any significant correlation between egalitarianism in an income sense and location of an economy in the "East" or "West."

Similarly it is quite unclear whether significant differences can be

[13] This point has been developed at some length, and somewhat further than this writer would be prepared to go, by John K. Galbraith in his book *The New Industrial State*, Boston, 1967.

detected between individual countries or between "East" and "West" in terms of relative reliance on psychic versus material incentives as a means of motivating the actors in the economic system. Communist China, however, constitutes an important exception in this regard. The degree of reliance to be placed on psychic as compared to material appeals has been a major policy and ideological issue in China ever since the new regime came to power. At the same time, it has constituted a significant source of tension within the whole policy apparatus. The issue came to the fore with renewed force during the Cultural Revolution (1966–68), when Mao tried to impose once more the predominance of psychic appeals over material incentives. Similar controversies loomed large in the Soviet Union as well, but at an earlier stage of development.

Finally, it has been increasingly recognized that variations in co-ordinating and resource-allocating mechanisms and in systems of decision-making represent not only differences in kind, but differences in degree. Thus, modern industrialized economies tend to be dominated by large-scale organizations (enterprises, government bureaus, semi-public organs, and so forth). The typical decision-making dilemma of large bureaucratic structures—be they corporate or government bureaucracies—then becomes the reconciliation of efficiency with control. The decision-making dilemmas of these individual organizations also characterize economies as a whole and thus affect the character of the coordinating and resource-allocating mechanism used. Thus the different mixtures of market as against command allocation observed in different types of economies may be considered to reflect a continuing search for the optimal pattern of decision-making with the desired combination of efficiency and control.

What this brief comparative survey of certain system traits and its implications for the study of comparative economics suggests is: a) What Koopmans and Montias would consider environmental factors—e.g., stage of development, cultural and historical elements, the dominant ideologies or mythologies—could be significant in affecting economic behavior and performance irrespective of the prevailing systems of economic organization; b) such factors themselves may play an important role in the crystallization of particular forms of economic organization; or c) the differences in these forms are not as sharp or as wide as is frequently supposed. It would be beyond the scope of this introductory chapter to attempt a detailed analysis of these environmental factors. However two of these, stage of development and ideology, may require some further exploration—the first because it is so often neglected in comparative economic systems analysis and the second because it is frequently misused.

Accidentally or by design, implicitly or explicitly, economists have worked out a division of labor by which some of them study problems of economic development and others work on comparative economic systems. As a result, very little attention has been paid to the interrelationships between the two fields, specifically between stage of development or level of technology characterizing production processes and the prevailing system of economic organization. Thus in much of the economic literature, including the comparative systems literature, little interest is shown in the role of technology in shaping the form of economic organization or, conversely, the impact of economic organization on innovation, technological progress, and the techniques of production adopted.

These problems and interrelationships are explored by Professor Kuznets in Chapter VIII. He points up that marked changes in production forces require corresponding adaptations in institutions and forms of economic organization. For instance a large railroad or airline could not possibly operate within the framework of a family firm; or, conversely, it is most unlikely that a corporate form of enterprise would be engaged in handicraft methods of production.

In Kuznets' view the following four complexes have contributed to rapid shifts in the size and character of several parts of the economic system in older developed countries:

1. Shifts in production structure and the technology underlying these have altered optimum firm size with attendant tendencies toward monopoly, a few examples of which were cited above;

2. Increased international tension of the last half century has been associated with the spread of modern economic growth to more nation-states, particularly to the larger ones;

3. A complex of trends, associated with the first two, stems from the increasing recognition of the responsibility of the modern state for the juridical and the political equality of all its citizens, and also for equality of economic opportunity and most recently also for a minimum income base;

4. Some major discoveries (e.g., in atomic energy, space, and potentially DNA) threaten to have such far-reaching and overpowering effects on the fate of man that society has become reluctant to allow profit-oriented, private enterprise to undertake primary responsibility for it.

All of these developments have had a profound impact on the character of economic institutions in general and the role of the state in particular. The tendencies toward monopoly inherent in the first led to various forms of state regulation of enterprises and to the conversion of some to a quasi-public status. Major new discoveries, such as uses of atomic energy, have had a similar impact, except to a more marked degree; they have led not only to growing government regulation but to a significant enlargement in the scope of the state enterprise sector in the "West," and most particularly in the United States.

The first and the last of the developments cited in Chapter VIII have affected primarily the forms of production organization, particularly the extent and shape of public control over enterprises. At the same time, the second, third, and fourth has led to a marked rise in government consumption, primarily for defense and for health, education, and welfare. The latter really entailed a rise in private consumption but delivered to the household by the state. This change in turn had a far-reaching impact on levels of economic activity, patterns of resource allocation, household behavior, and forms of economic organization. In Kuznets' words, these four trends led to the formation of "the new industrial state, the new military state, the new welfare state, and the new scientific state, which are clearly significant variants of the free-market, individual enterprise state."

Technological change and the adoption of new techniques and methods of production create pressures for modifying prevailing modes of economic organization in all countries including those in the "East." In the "West" these changes have led, as pointed out in Chapter VIII, to a gradual narrowing in the scope of the market or a significant modification in its resource-allocating role. In the "East" on the other hand, technological pressures—associated with growing roundaboutness of production, increasing complexity and interdependence of production processes, and a growing information burden resulting therefrom—have led in recent years to a greater or lesser enlargement in the scope of the market and the role of the price mechanism.

As indicated above, ideology is another environmental factor that needs to be singled out for special attention. Its role in shaping economic system behavior or in affecting changes in prevailing systems of economic organization is an insufficiently explored and highly controversial issue as attested by Professor Gerschenkron's contribution in Chapter IX and Professor Hirschman's comments on it.

The linkages between ideology, human action, economic policy and economic organization are far from clear. Unfortunately this is not always sufficiently recognized. As a result, some of the economic systems literature tends to identify certain ideologies too simplistically with certain systems, e.g., classical liberalism and laissez faire with capitalism and orthodox Marxism with socialism or with economies of the Soviet type. However just as one cannot axiomatically assume that ideology plays a significant role in shaping economic policy behavior or in affecting systems of economic organization, one cannot rule out its relevance without investigating the character of these interrelationships and their relative importance as explanatory variables.

Hirschman stresses the need to distinguish between different kinds of ideologies in terms of their functions. Thus he points to the importance of

dominant versus insurgent ideologies. It may also be essential to differentiate between the various roles a particular ideology performs. Ideology
may serve as a guide to policy, as an element influencing policy, or as an
instrument for the implementation of a policy based on other considerations. Ideology may be an expression of certain beliefs, of a certain system
of values, of a certain faith, or it may serve only as a rationale, as a
propaganda weapon, as a false consciousness designed to justify or
buttress the institution and execution of certain policies.

In Chapter IX, Gerschenkron focuses his attention chiefly on the
instrumental and propaganda roles of ideology. In contrast, in his earlier
writings he emphasized the faith aspects of ideology indicating certain
definite relationships between relative backwardness, ideology, and the
emerging character of economic institutions in the process of industrialization.[14] One of the first steps on the road to further refining the concept
and its role in shaping or modifying economic policy and economic
organization may well be to develop a typology of ideological roles
encompassing the elements developed in Chapter IX, but not confined
thereto.

In this regard, it may be useful to think of a spectrum of roles with a
considerable overlap between them rather than sharp delineations. For
instance, government policy-makers and entrepreneurs might be genuinely
committed to laissez-faire while abiding by its principles in their conduct.
Alternatively they might firmly believe in it but at the same time use it
more or less unconsciously—perhaps by genuinely identifying the general
interest with their own self-interest—as a weapon for the propagation of
their special interests. Finally various individuals or groups might use this
ideology for purely manipulative purposes.

The role of Marxism as a significant factor in shaping economic
policies and institutions both in the "West" and the "East" may be
similarly ambiguous and complex. It would be hard to deny that socialist
movements and influences have significantly contributed to the rise of the
modern welfare state referred to in Chapter VIII. Of course, these
influences were themselves based on an amalgam of ideas and traditions of
which Marxism represented only one strand. Conversely, manipulation by
Lenin and his successors of Marxist doctrines to serve their own ends,
to serve as justifications for the execution of certain policies and the
creation of certain patterns of economic organization does not mean that
they themselves may not have been influenced by these doctrines. As
Alexander Erlich shows in the penultimate chapter of this volume,
Marxism did play a significant role in the Soviet Union not only in
providing a rationale for the implementation of policies but also in

[14] See Alexander Gerschenkron, *Economic Backwardness in Historical
Perspective*, Cambridge, Mass., 1962, Ch. 1.

affecting the choice among alternative policies in situations in which a number of possible courses of action might have been open to the leadership. After all, earlier Russian regimes equally dedicated to maintaining their rule and maximizing their power used instruments, institutions, and policies to accomplish these ends entirely different from those applied in the Soviet Union.

As Erlich shows, many fundamental features of the Soviet system can be traced to classical Marxist doctrine. This lineage certainly applies to public ownership of the means of production and less explicitly to the need for central planning. Marx, to be sure, considered a comparatively high level of development of productive forces a precondition for both. The introduction by Lenin and his followers of these institutions and elements in a backward country may have violated Marxism; but this does not mean that the institutions which actually emerged were not guided or influenced by Marxist doctrine. Similarly it could be argued that Soviet investment policies—most particularly the emphasis placed upon the development of capital-goods industries and the bias towards capital-intensive methods of production—could be traced to the two-sector model in the second volume of *Capital*. Whether in this case Marxist theory was the guide to policy or merely an ex post rationalization for decisions made in other terms can not be determined on the basis of presently available evidence.

In our brief survey of issues discussed in this volume, we have until now focused on certain system traits and on a few selected elements of the environment in which the systems function. Now we would like to consider the outcomes, the performance characteristics of these systems. This task requires first of all consideration of the norms, criteria, and desiderata in terms of which comparative systems' performance might be appraised.

Koopmans and Montias develop a long list of desiderata for this purpose. The most important of these, in the sense of most generally applied, may be considered the following five:

1. Attainment of high levels of per-capita consumption
2. Attainment of high rates of growth in output or in per-capita consumption
3. Maintenance and development of national strength
4. Equity in income distribution
5. Maintenance of full employment coupled with price stability.

Clearly different countries at different times may ascribe varying relative weights to any one of these objectives. Moreover, the "simultaneous pursuit of the (first) three desiderata, whatever their weights in the pertinent norm, implies a derived desideratum of *efficiency* in the use of resources."

By now—thanks to the work of Kuznets, Bergson and some others—a considerable body of data is available on the comparative growth performance of different economies at any one point of time and over time.[15] In contrast, the sample of comparative data available for measurements of equity and stability is much smaller and poorer. Exploration of factors and elements to explain variation in performance has gone hand in hand with the comparative measurement of such performance. However our understanding of these factors, particularly as they might relate to economic system variables, is still rather rudimentary. Therefore, Abram Bergson's study in Chapter VI is designed as a theoretical, methodological, and empirical contribution to a comparative-systems-oriented analysis of economic performance in the Soviet Union and the United States. It focuses on one major aspect of comparative performance, namely static efficiency.

According to Bergson, in order for a community to be perfectly efficient statically it must fully realize its production possibilities. The question explored in Chapter VI could be stated as follows: Assuming that the same level of technology was available to both the United States and the Soviet Union and given the resources (inputs) used in the two countries respectively to produce their outputs, what is the combined factor productivity differential of the latter as compared to the former. This differential is then used as an indicator of comparative static efficiency, especially in relation to the realization of production possibilities.

Domar on the other hand, argues that these productivity differentials are symptoms of a wide stage-of-development gap still prevailing between the United States and the Soviet Union, rather than of differences in efficiency. Bergson grants the importance of stage of development as a factor but considers it, along with the character of working arrangements or systems of economic organization, as one of several principal variables accounting for the observed differences in efficiency.

The problem could perhaps be illuminated by the following hypothetical example. Let us imagine an island economy and civilization completely isolated from the world and, as a result, relying on ancient techniques and methods of production. The economy may be fully realizing its production possibilities, but given the primitive techniques known and available to it, combined factor productivity is very low compared to that prevailing in a highly industrialized economy. In this case the productivity differentials reflect a wide divergence in stages of development rather than in efficiency. However, suppose that by some exogenous event—e.g., visits by foreigners, invasion, colonization—the island economy's isolation is suddenly

[15] See for instance Simon Kuznets, *Modern Economic Growth, Rate, Structure and Spread*, New Haven, 1966, and A. Bergson and S. Kuznets (eds.), *Economic Trends in the Soviet Union*, Cambridge, Mass. (1963).

brought to an end. As a result, the islanders will be exposed to a knowledge of production methods used everywhere, including in the most advanced countries. They will necessarily require some time to learn enough about the new techniques to put them to effective use. Moreover, the backwardness of the island economy, the illiteracy of its population, and other factors related thereto, hamper this learning process. As the learning process continues, new technological knowledge becomes available, and thus the production possibilities, with resources given, increase. Yet until this learning process is completed, one could not say that differentials in productivity between our island economy and those of a highly industrialized country represent a measure of inefficiency. Under such circumstances these differentials may represent some combination of stage-of-development and efficiency considerations.

In comparing productivity and efficiency in the United States and the Soviet Union, Bergson takes account of this learning effect but concludes that the Soviet Union has participated in the industrialization process for such a long time that for all practical purposes differences in access to the world pool of technological knowledge cannot be a major factor in explaining the observed productivity differential between the USSR and the United States. Thus the Soviet Union has had ample opportunity to borrow technology from abroad and to develop its own, so that recency of industrialization cannot be a significant factor in accounting for the combined productivity differentials. Moreover, if there was a learning lag in the Soviet Union under the circumstances, this in and of itself may be a symptom of inefficiency, though admittedly not of the static variety.

That this question cannot be satisfactorily resolved at the present state of our knowledge becomes evident when we compare the data in Table 1 of Chapter VII and of the table in Bergson's comment, both of which are based on the Fairless lectures.[16] They show that combined factor productivity in all industrialized countries is significantly below that of the United States. They also indicate that other factors must be at work besides stage of development. Thus using non-farm shares in labor force or GNP as indicators of development, the United Kingdom appears at least as developed as the United States, yet it has a significantly lower productivity. Moreover, the United Kingdom lags behind Germany and is about on a par with France, even though these countries have significantly lower non-farm labor and GNP shares. These comparisons would suggest the need for further research to clarify the sources of intertemporal and interspatial combined productivity differentials and the extent to which and the circumstances under which they can be said to be associated with efficiency.

[16] See Abram Bergson, *Planning and Productivity under Soviet Socialism*, New York, 1968.

3. About this Book

The point of departure for this symposium volume is provided by the analytical and methodological framework for the study of comparative economic systems found in the next three chapters. Chapter II outlines a broad and comprehensive framework, a series of empty boxes which, when filled with the relevant quantitative and institutional information, can serve as a basis for a comparative analysis of economic systems.

The theoretical framework developed in Chapter III omits a number of elements considered by Koopmans and Montias and focuses instead on the information and decision-making aspects of economic systems which constitute only a part of the former's more comprehensive scheme. Chapter III may thus play a roughly similar role in the comparison of existing or possible economic systems as do papers on models of economic growth in predicting and guiding growth in real economies. Professor Hurwicz seeks to clarify, by abstraction, the class of objects to which economic systems and their major subsystems belong. One may then look for conditions under which one system performs better than another. Ultimately propositions about relative performance, demonstrable under the simplifying assumptions of a model, could be translated into an empirically testable form and then checked for real economies.[17]

Hurwicz's concept of the adjustment process may also have a number of applications in comparative economics. It is a general concept which can easily accommodate all the fictitious resource-allocating mechanisms which economists have invented, such as the perfectly competitive system, the total command system, or the Lange-Lerner mechanism. In principle, it also accommodates the mechanisms actually at work in the daily resource-allocating decisions of a real economy. Environments are in fact observed, messages are sent, paper plans are arrived at, and physical actions are taken. All of these elements, and the response rules guiding them, are of course forbiddingly complex in the real world. Finally, Hurwicz considers centralization and decentralization, first with respect to authority, and second with respect to information.

While the two preceding chapters develop a particular framework, Ward in Chapter IV surveys a variety of methodological and theoretical approaches used, or potentially available, for systematic and systemic studies in comparative economics. Ward's main thesis is "that a more systematic study of the interaction between organization and the traditional economic variables . . .will produce a substantial increase in our

[17] These summary observations concerning Chapter III are largely based on Professor Tom Marschaks's comments delivered in his role as a discussant for the Hurwicz paper.

understanding of the economic process" along lines anticipated by the American institutionalists. The failure of institutionalists was not that they had nothing to say—on the contrary. Their failure can rather be ascribed to a total rejection of price theory without developing a substitute framework. Therefore "as an elaborative doctrine to hang on the traditional theoretical structure of economics the institutional approach might affect basic changes in that structure."

Proceeding on the basis of this criterion and general thesis concerning the interaction between organization and the traditional economic variables, Ward proceeds to test the value and usefulness of a number of studies in comparative economics under seven main headings.

1. "Intuitive groping" is based on a self-immersion of the investigator in a totality of culture, society, and economy to the point that he has internalized it. This internalization then provides him with a level of understanding such that he can develop propositions, more or less intuitively, about the relation between organization and economy. Thorstein Veblen's *Imperial Germany and the Industrial Revolution* is cited as an outstanding example of this approach.

2. "Adaptive failure" refers to studies which compare the actual performance of one or more economies in relation to some sort of ideal, whether normative or analytically simplified. Bergson's work on comparative static efficiency in his book on the *Economics of Soviet Planning*, much more fully developed and extended in Chapter VIII of this volume, represents a prime example of this approach. Another outstanding instance of this method is Grossman's work on the theory of a command economy.

3. "Neoclassicism" in Ward's usage encompasses three quite different approaches, namely what he calls "Marshallian analysis," "game theory," and "general equilibrium and stability." Under Marshallian analysis he considers micro-economic resource allocation ranging from competitive and monopolistic firms which are profit-maximizing units to organizations which maximize other variables such as participants' income per capita with the number of co-op members among whom income is to be distributed as one of the unknowns to be determined (Ward's Illyrian Firm).

The other "neoclassical" approaches appraised by Ward represent applications of game theory to simulated economies of different kinds, some of them including elements of bargaining between pressure groups, and studies of general equilibrium and stability in mathematically modelled or mathematically programmed economies optimized under various definitions and degrees of certainty.

4. "Adaptations to inefficiency" includes studies of adaptations to various forms of market failure and explorations of the "convergence hypothesis."

5. The "behavioral approach" embraces studies of comparative economic policy and economic decision-making behavior by various types of organizations such as enterprises or government organs.

6. One could raise some doubts as to whether this category, "adaptation to injustice," should be separated out or included under "adaptations to inefficiency." It refers to adaptations in legal and juridical practices designed to improve social welfare.

7. Studies exploring the links between ideology, doctrine, and ideas on the one hand and the behavior of economic organizations on the other are categorized under the rubric of "ideas and organization." These links are also the subject of Chapter IX and are discussed briefly in the preceding section of this introduction.

Ward, with his wide-ranging and comprehensive *tour d'horizon* in Chapter IV of a number of alternative methodological and theoretical approaches in comparative economics, rounds out the development and appraisal of analytical structures in the first part of this volume. It thus sets the stage for the contributions of Levine, Bergson, and Domar in the second part, in which they develop, investigate, and appraise different methodologies for comparing economic systems' behavior and performance. Levine undertakes a most complex but also most important task; he attempts to devise empirical measures or tests of the comparative degree of "plannedness" or "commandedness" in different economies. He suggests that "the basic scientific method used generally in economic analysis be used in the comparative study of planned economies, that from the various observations of different planned economies, relationships be drawn between different levels of the variable 'economic planning' and different levels of other variables which are deemed to be of interest."

In comparing the degree of "plannedness," Levine focuses on the exercise of authority by the center, on the measurement of the centralization of authority in a planning system. He outlines first a framework for studying the relationships between centralization of authority as the dependent variable and certain environmental (property relations, ideology, stage of economic development, size and resource endowments) and goal (e.g., rapid industrialization, catch-up with more advanced countries) elements as the independent variables. Then he points out the need to study the relationships between centralization of authority as an independent variable and certain economic performance characteristics such as growth, efficiency, and stability.

While Levine suggests a framework for the measurement of the degree of "commandedness" in different types of economies, Bergson develops a theoretical framework for a comparative analysis of efficiency and then applies it to measurements of combined factor productivity and static efficiency in the Soviet Union relative to the United States. He finds that with employment adjusted for labor quality, national product per unit of factor inputs in the Soviet Union in 1960 was at 34 per cent of the United States' level in terms of Soviet price weights and at 56 per cent in terms of United States price weights. The crucial question posed by Domar is whether this productivity gap is a symptom of inefficiency or of a stage-of-development differential. Assuming that the gap does indeed represent differences in efficiency, Bergson explores whether it can be traced to the character of the "working arrangements" (i.e., the character of the system of economic organization) or the stage of development. As indicated earlier, this particular range of issues must necessarily remain unresolved at the present stage of our knowledge and thus requires considerably more research.

Following the presentation of an analytical and theoretical framework in Part I, some of its concepts and the design of analytical and empirical techniques for measuring system performance based on these concepts are tested in Part II. Against this background the last part of this volume is devoted to an exploration of some of the "environmental" variables (in the Koopmans and Montias sense) which may affect the structure and functioning of economic institutions and some of the performance characteristics of economic systems. Two aspects of this environment affecting economic systems, namely those relating to stage of development and ideology, are explored in Chapters VIII, IX and X. Since the most critical issues raised in these chapters have been discussed in the preceding section, there is no need to deal with them at greater length here.

The volume concludes with an essay by Morris Bornstein in which he sets himself the task of integrating various approaches to the comparison of economic systems, including those presented in this volume. He deals with the concept of economic systems and the different bases of comparing them, followed by an appraisal of different methodological approaches. In conclusion, this synthesis tries to delineate the scope and boundaries of the field of comparative economic systems.

4. Concluding Comments

To increase our understanding of the economic process through systematic investigations of the interaction between organization and the traditional economic variables is the principal concern of comparative economic systems as a field of study. More specifically this involves studies of the interrelationships between economic institutions, or what Professor Bergson refers to as "working arrangements," and the behavioral and performance characteristics of national economies as a whole and certain sectors or subsectors thereof. For example this might encompass comparative studies of the relationships between property forms, incentive arrangements, fiscal and monetary institutions, resource-allocating mechanisms and the macro- or micro-economic behavior of particular economies. It might also entail studies of the environmental factors shaping economic institutions such as size, stage of development, character of the dominant and deviant ideologies prevailing in the country, and historical, cultural, social, and political factors. Some of the latter, however, may necessarily have to be left to interdisciplinary ventures as suggested by Bornstein, or to specialists in the other social sciences.

The interrelationships between organization, institutions, and economic variables have been explored most explicitly and systematically for the Soviet Union. This work needs to be extended and pushed further in several directions. The linkages between institutional and organizational variables on the one hand and economic variables on the other need to be investigated much more closely and explicitly. At the same time this study of interrelationships must be placed on a truly comparative basis.

Bergson's studies of comparative efficiency provide a good case in point. They serve to clarify and refine the concept and its theoretical underpinnings. Furthermore, they represent a major breakthrough in comparative measurements of the concept. Finally, they serve to highlight some crucial and as yet unresolved issues revolving around the sources of comparative efficiency differentials. These issues will require further investigation and the development of methods for partialing out institutional, organizational, system variables from stage-of-development or other variables and of measuring their weight in explaining the efficiency gap.

Major contributions to the further development of the field can undoubtedly be derived by testing and applying a) the general framework developed by Koopmans and Montias and b) more highly specified models such as those contained in Chapter III. At the same time, the development of new hypotheses and models linking institutional and economic variables—stated in testable terms—may represent another significant frontier for research.

More progress could also be made by further shifts in emphasis from holistic comparisons of total systems to a comparative study of traits, institutions and problems that cut across systems. This might entail for instance comparative studies of: stability conditions (e.g., in relation to price, income, and employment), problems of economic decision-making in large organizations in different types of systems, operation of labor markets, and so on.

Advances in the study of relationships between institutional and economic variables may also require a much more rigorous, empirical definition of the institutional differences between national economies. A good case in point may be Pryor's recent study of *Public Expenditures in Communist and Capitalist Nations.*[18] Along similar lines, the comparative role of the public sector in the ownership of the means of production, in the generation of national product for the economy as a whole and for the major sectors, and in capital formation, needs to be explored. Here then might emerge the basis for a more rigorous examination of the links, if any, between institutional differences, economic behavior, and economic performance in different types of economies.

[18] Frederick L. Pryor, *Public Expenditures in Communist and Capitalist Nations*, Homewood, Ill., 1968.

PART I

Analytical Framework for the Comparison of Economic Systems

2

On the Description and Comparison of Economic Systems

by TJALLING C. KOOPMANS
and JOHN MICHAEL MONTIAS

1. Introduction

The traditional comparison of economic systems starts from the trichotomy of capitalism, socialism, and communism. It goes from there to recognize a certain diversity of patterns within each of these three prototypes.

The last twenty years have seen a great deal of relatively independent experimentation with organizational techniques and institutional forms within each of the prototypes, and some borrowing of devices and forms between prototypes. In addition, the rather different institutional problems of less developed economies have received greatly increased attention. As a result, a rich and, indeed, somewhat bewildering variety of organizational forms and systems is now spread before us, which defies simple classification according to a few prototypes.

To the researcher the new situation offers a double advantage. Not only is the number of possible comparisons substantially increased, but, at the same time the greater variety of systems provides opportunities for comparison between economies that are alike in most respects and differ notably only in one or two of their critical traits or dimensions—a type of comparison that may permit the tracing of effects of specific traits on outcomes with greater chance of success. For instance, it may be more easily possible to compare the role of market prices and government controls in Belgium and the Netherlands, or of investment policies of Poland and Rumania—in both cases pairs of countries with many common traits—before proceeding to the more complex comparisons of the total systems of countries that are more widely disparate in their institutions, size, and resources.

In general, we believe the new circumstances invite approaches to the comparison of economic systems that altogether avoid prior classification according to the grand "isms" and instead start from comparisons of organizational arrangements for specific economic functions. Among these we should wish to consider the coordination of production activities by distinct organizations, the accumulation and utilization of means of production of new or existing types, the research and development for new methods and means of production, the distribution of currently produced goods and services among the participants and beneficiaries of the system, the maintenance of aggregate stability, and the protection of individuals from harmful effects of the economic actions of others.

Our decision to shun the "isms" as a basis for classification of observed economic systems does not preclude comparing models of admittedly hypothetical pure systems, representing one variant or another of one of the "isms" or of any other system proposed or contemplated. However, our decision leaves us without suitable terms for referring to categories of observed economies professing allegiance to the respective "isms." Reaching into geography for substitute labels, we shall occasionally and metaphorically use "East" for the diverse group of countries in which a communist party is the leading political organ; "West" for the developed "capitalist" and mixed "capitalist-socialist" countries; and "South" for the less developed noncommunist countries, regardless of their individual locations. It will then be understood that Cuba is in "East," while Australia and Finland are in "West." Yugoslavia, which does not seem to fit with either "East" or "West" in its economic institutions, will be mentioned separately when the need arises.

Although the conference to which this paper is a contribution is attended almost exclusively by economists, the importance of political and (non-economic) social factors, both in the realities of the systems to be compared and in the criteria (or "norms") entering into the comparisons, is apparent to all. Your authors herewith disclaim professional expertise in the socio-political sciences, but they have preferred the risk of making uninformed observations to that of not recognizing the crucial political and socio-logical aspects of the topic under discussion. Even so, our professional preoccupations may well have led us to follow some economic twigs while stopping short on some political limbs.

The main aim of the present paper is to suggest, without particular claim to novelty, one possible framework for the description and com-parison of economic systems. For an objective comparison the descrip-tions of the systems being compared should be couched as much as possible in system-free terms. It is in the nature of this undertaking that definitions and terminology take up an inordinate part of the paper. The ideal is that the *primitive* (undefined) terms entering into these definitions be few in number and universal in applicability and prior meaning. Preferably they should be drawn from fields such as engineering, psychology, physiology, that have a relatively system-free status. Terms such as "individuals," "preferences," "commodities," "production," "perception," "communication," "constraints on behavior," come close to meeting this requirement. Terms such as "price," "supervision," "organization," "decentralization," "planning," whose meanings may be system-bound or otherwise ambiguous, should then be defined for the purposes of the comparison, using the primitive terms.

We have not attained this ideal. Within the available time and space we have used more than a minimum of primitive terms in an exploratory attempt to block out what seem to us important aspects of both the conceptual and the statistical problems of system description and system comparison. We may well have neglected or dealt too cursorily with other aspects of comparable importance.

As a test of relevance, we do provide illustrative examples to convey contexts for the definitions and suggest possible uses for the concepts introduced. Finally, we rather liberally insert conjectures of regularities that more systematic empirical investigation might confirm or refute, again to suggest rather than demonstrate possible uses of the concepts.

2. A Conceptual Framework

2.1. Environment and System

Following Grossman[1] and others, we shall think of comparisons of economies or of their systems as being made via models of these economies or systems. That is, instead of comparing economies A and B directly, models M_A and M_B are abstracted from our knowledge of A and B, respectively, and are compared with each other as well as with the realities whose salient features they seek to embody. Of course, the choice of the models again depends on the particular purpose of the comparison to be made.

In the models here suggested for demonstration purposes, we distinguish (representations of) the *environment*, the (economic) *system*, *actions*, *outcomes*, and *norms* with respect to which the outcomes are evaluated and the systems compared. All of these are defined with reference to a particular time period to which the description or the comparison applies. Briefly, the *environment of the economy* includes *resources*, *initial technology*, *external factors* (including technology available from other economies), and the impact of *random events* on each of these. It also includes *initial preferences*, and *incomplete interactions* (as of the initial date of the period of comparison).

Resources, in turn, include *natural resources* proper (including climatic conditions), the *initial capital stock* (available means of production and goods in inventory or in process at the beginning of the period), and the *initial population*, its age distribution, health, skills, and education levels. Resources evolve over time by prospecting, investment, conservation or neglect of physical and biological surroundings of man, and also by

[1] G. Grossman, *Economic Systems*, Englewood Cliffs, N.J., 1967.

human reproduction, medical services, education, learning from experience, aging and death.

Technology (at any time) is thought of as a long list of commodity specifications, together with a long list of descriptions of possible activities. An *activity* is defined by its inputs (kinds and quantities), by its effects, and, if greater specificity is required, by the kind of repeatable *action* or sequence or combination of actions that, by the state of the arts at the time, is known to produce the effects whenever the inputs are available. The effects will be outputs (kind and quantity) in the case of production activities of goods and some services, maintenance of states of health or of satisfaction levels in the case of consumption activities, increases in the knowledge or skills of individuals in the case of instructional activities, and so forth. The inputs are efforts, the use of facilities or equipment, and in most cases other goods, services or resources. Technology evolves by the addition of new commodities and activities through research and development or through their introduction from other economies, and by the demise of old ones as a result of disappearance of demand or of requisite skills.

External factors are all traits of the rest of the world, other than of the economy in question, pertinent to economic processes in the economy. This includes the geographical position, resource endowment and purchasing power of important actual or potential trading partners, the existence and proximity of political or military rivals, protectors, or clients, and the systems in operation in each of these.

Random events give rise to uncertainty about the availability of resources, about the outputs (or even about the input or action requirements) of given activities, about the external factors, and may require definition in terms of subjective or objective probability distributions. Other kinds of uncertainty, arising from unpredictable aspects of behavior of economic agents within the economy, are characteristic of the system rather than of the environment.

The initial population has been included with the resources because of its productive potentialities. Its *initial preferences* must be recorded separately as a baseline from which subsequent preferences evolve. The standard description of preferences (at any time) associates with each individual a *preference ordering* (possibly represented by a *utility function*) of all alternative current and future consumption paths of that individual and possibly of his family ("private preferences"). The ordering can be thought extended to express also his "social preferences" concerning the consumption paths of others (living and as yet unborn) as well as more general system traits. The "social preferences" of central planners, for example, may be thought to guide their allocation decisions, which affect the welfare of the future as well as the present population.

However, the concept of preference ordering, whether it applies to individuals, to planners, or to other participants making allocation decisions on behalf of groups of system participants, does not require that the ordering of possible states be complete. How far into the future a decision maker attempts to discriminate among possible states or paths to these states and the efforts he may exert to specify and detail his preferences among these states or paths may also differ from system to system.

The term "utility function" is less appropriate for goals imputed to or proposed for organizations, including the economy as a whole. In those instances, we shall therefore use less specific terms, such as *goal function* and *norm*, to be introduced more fully below.

The representation of preferences by a goal function is normally associated with a model of consumers', citizens', organizational, or national choice that maximizes goal attainment among available alternatives. Progress in utilizing generalizations of that model to include realistic elements of habituation, of "satisficing,"[2] of random behavior,[3] of coping with uncertainty,[4] and of learning from experience[5] has been incomplete and uneven. Whichever model one adopts, the important implication it has for system description is the *decision rule* describing how consumer's choice or organizational or civic action depend on available opportunities and prospects. In particular, for statistical inter-system comparisons of consumers' behavior, studies of demand functions representative of entire populations or large subsets thereof will usually have to be substituted for a conceptually fuller description of choice. For these reasons, the skeptical reader may want to think in terms of "decision rules" wherever in the sequel we use the term "preferences," or "utility function," or "goal function."

Incomplete interactions include all orders not yet fulfilled (contracts to deliver goods or services, quotas in production plans) and commitments (repayment of loans, payment of pensions) required by, or compatible with, the system, which are outstanding at the beginning of the period to which the comparison applies.

The *system* is hardest to define because of the widely inclusive nature of the concept and because of the difficulty of separating economy from polity. In greatest generality, the *total system* includes all political, social

[2] H. A. Simon, *Models of Man*, New York, 1957, Ch. 14.

[3] D. Davidson and J. Marschak, "Experimental Tests of a Stochastic Decision Theory," in Churchman and Ratoosh, eds., *Measurement Definitions and Theories*, New York, 1959, Ch. 13.

[4] L. J. Savage, *The Foundations of Statistics*, New York, 1954.

[5] T. C. Koopmans, "On Flexibility of Future Preferences," in Shelly and Brian, eds., *Human Judgments and Optimality*, New York, 1964, Ch. 13, pp. 243–254.

and economic institutions, organizational structure, laws and rules (and the extent of their enforcement and voluntary observance), and all traditions, religious and secular beliefs, attitudes, values, taboos, and the resulting systematic or stochastic behavior patterns. The total system includes all these phenomena both as initially present and as evolving over the period of comparison through organizational change, new legislation or rulings, or new trends in attitudes and behavior. The provisions for creating or dissolving organizations, modifying relations between organizations, amending the rules, and influencing attitudes and behavior are themselves considered part of the system.

Depending on the comparison to be made, the comparor may feel that he can designate as *economic system* only that part of the total system, which directly or indirectly affects economic behavior and outcomes in at least one of the systems being compared.[6] So as not to prejudge this issue in general, we shall from here on use the term *system* in an open-ended way to refer to all or to the economically relevant part of the total system, leaving the burden of proof of nonrelevance with the comparor.

One may wish to extend the concept of the system to include perception of the environment, of the system, and of the interaction of its participants—as distinct from that environment, system, interaction taken by itself or as perceived by the comparor. This view recognizes the system participants' perception of the economy's environment and of their respective individual environments (defined below) as itself a system characteristic. Examples abound: A presumption of racial superiority may prevent an employer from perceiving the skills of a racial minority. A strong attachment to central planning may lead a planner to underrate the impact of random events in such industries as agriculture or fisheries. An entire literature on less developed economies deals with the obstacles that traditions, attitudes, and vested interests place in the way of the perception of technological opportunities.

In these examples the term "perception" is used in a sense somewhat broader than its primarily cognitive connotation in psychological parlance. Especially if we speak of the *perceived system*, we may think of an image of the system formed in the minds of its participants, which the comparor may infer or extract from expressions of views or opinions by these participants and from modes in which the participants address each other for purposes of persuasion. If we include in this discussion perceptions of one system by the members of another, it will be clear that such images, sometimes even caricatures, are formed under the influence of the observer

---

[6] Applying this notion symmetrically to the political comparor who designates as "*political system*" that part of the total system directly or indirectly affecting political behavior and outcomes, we must expect a very substantial overlap between the political and the economic system.

or critic's own institutional system and of information emanating from other observed systems. Where information about a system is manipulated by some of its participants for the purpose of influencing fellow-participants or participants in other systems, it is termed *propaganda*. Another closely related influence on an individual's perception of his or of other total systems is his *ideology*, a more or less stable pattern of frequently untestable ideas, symbols, and symbol clusters, usually expressed in widely disseminated printed, broadcast, or televised material, which supply him with a more or less coherent view or explanation of, and a definite attitude to, a broad range of the world's phenomena.

Actions differ from activities in that they are thought of as taken by a specific participant at a specific time, whereas activities are types of possible actions not dated or connected with a participant (though their possibility may be limited by time of inclusion in the technology or by skill requirements). Generally, an *action* changes the environment of the economy or of the participants or both in some minor or major way.

Taking actions as the elementary building blocks of economically relevant behavior, we may use the term *decisions* for commitments to several simultaneous or successive related actions and *policies* as classes of decisions adopted in order to economize on decision time and effort and, in many cases, made known in order to create stable expectations about future decisions.

The boundary between system and policies is not a sharp one and may depend on the length of the period for which a comparison is made. For instance, a market economy in which the central government follows a fiscal policy of a balanced annual government budget may be considered as a system somewhat different from that of the same economy in which a fiscal and monetary full-employment policy is pursued. If within a longer period the former system is succeeded by the latter, one may alternatively speak of a market system in which a policy change occurred at some point of time.

The policies, decisions, and actions of all participants other than a specific one, together with the outcomes of these policies, decisions, and actions, must be included with the environment of the economy to define the *environment of that specific individual*. The latter, in particular, includes both the technology available from outside the system and that generated by other participants within the system. That part of a participant's environment that he actually perceives is called his *information set*.[7]

Outcomes are all aspects or consequences of the system, and of the policies, decisions, or actions of all participants to which positive or

[7] Note that a participant may know about the existence of a technology, yet the technology itself may not be part of his information set, since it may be protected by patents or restricted by high communication or learning costs.

negative value is attached in at least one of the norms entering into a comparison. This may include any valuable or deleterious man-made changes in the environment during the period involved in the comparison and any "evolutionary" changes in the system that are made or come about in a manner compatible with it. It is also bound to include levels of consumption activities or of satisfactions and changes over time thereof, as well as aggregates, distributions, and possibly other functions of these levels or changes in levels. In Section 3 we give examples of important outcomes (there called "desiderata"), of which some are common to most systems, others are specific to one or more systems. In Section 4 we give examples of important categories of activities, ranging from some that are common to all systems to some others whose character or even existence is specific to the systems in which they occur.

Finally we come to the concept of a *norm* (criterion).[8] We believe that no meaningful comparison of economies or of their systems is possible without at least the implicit application of some norm. Even a seemingly entirely descriptive comparison must select from a vast multitude of traits that smaller number deemed sufficiently interesting (a value concept!) to be entered into the comparison. A norm may be implicit rather than explicit; it may be limited by the perception of the comparor; or its presence and nature may escape the perception of some or most of his readers. But the conscious and unconscious motivations of the investigator and the natural selection by which individual studies enter into the cumulative record of social science results tend to introduce, and make apparent over time, the underlying norms.

Norms become more visible when observed inter-system differences in various system traits are brought together and weighed against each other. We define an *explicit norm* (hereafter often briefly a *norm*) formally as an evaluation function (utility function, goal attainment function) of all outcomes which represents the preferences of some individual or group pertinent to the comparison.

The scientific character of a comparison is enhanced if any underlying norm is made explicit to the extent possible. Furthermore, it is instructive to make the same comparisons in the light of a number of alternative pertinent norms. These may include:

A. A norm perceived as a *prevailing norm* in any of the two or more economies being compared. This may be a norm explicitly adopted and imposed by a majority or minority enabled by the system to

[8] We choose the word "norm" without the connotation of disapproval of dissenters which sometimes adheres to it. While the term "criterion" is more value-free, it does not contain any hint that the interesting criteria are those to which at least some people attach a normative value.

make it the prevailing norm. If no such group exists, it may be a norm that embraces, or is explicit in, the outcome of the processes of adjustment of diverse interests inherent in the system.

B. A norm attributed by the comparor to groups of the population (minorities or majorities) whose preferences are given little weight in, or overruled by, the prevailing norm, in short, an *unavailing norm*.

C. Norms adduced by the comparor for purposes of discussion. This category may explicitly include (if he wishes) a norm he himself deems pertinent or even advocates. In regard to economies where a prevailing norm is imposed by a minority, or also where it is accepted by an inattentive and unreflecting majority, the category may further include a comparor's tentative but explicit estimate of a better balance of interests, possibly arrived at with the help of attitudinal surveys, legal documents, and more general past and current social thought. Finally, it may contain norms he explicitly attributes to groups of his readers, or to the intended beneficiaries of his knowledge and insights—regardless of the standing of these norms in the economies being compared.

2.2. Comparison of Economies and Comparison of Economic Systems

Differences in observed outcomes in different economies will in general reflect such differences as are present in all of the components of environment, system and policy we have distinguished. Symbolically, if e denotes environment, s system, p_s policies pursued by the participants under the system s, and o outcomes, then we may write

$$o = f(e, s, p_s)$$

for the grand relationships we would all like to know and understand. Even though our actual knowledge is pitifully small compared with the complexity of the relationships in question, writing them out in this explicit way may help in their discussion. The implied assumption is that the laws of physics, chemistry, technology, agronomy, human and animal physiology and psychology—the same fields from which the primitive terms are drawn—circumscribe what can be achieved by any given economic organization, in a manner subject in principle to objective inquiry and explicit description.

A system may be more suited to one environment than to another, in the sense that more desirable combinations of consumption, growth, and national security may be attained by that system in one environment than in another. (It may be argued that some systems may not even be viable unless certain environmental conditions are met.) The interdependence between the environment of the economy and the system is cited by

Wittfogel, who suggests that in certain environments special forms of hierarchic organization, run by bureaucracies with virtually unlimited powers over the participants in their system, may have arisen in response to the need for coping with drought (through irrigation), with floods (through flood control), and with other negative factors in their environment.[9] Another example, much discussed in the literature, is the strong influence of the mere size of an economy on the optimal degree of enterprise specialization.[10] A third example, perhaps more conjectural, is the tendency of a low level of skills in an economy to favor a more centralized system.[11]

But even if differences in environment were not to favor corresponding differences in system, a statistical comparison of systems under some given norm would still require that one allow for the inevitable effect of environmental variables on system performance under the norm. The initial capital-labor ratio, mineral wealth, climate and soil, the geographical location of other nations important for trade, national security or influence, are all examples of environmental variables that codetermine, say, the consumption-growth-security locus attainable with the "best" of systems. The use of observations on economies with markedly different environments for the empirical comparison of systems therefore requires the econometric estimation of the vector function f, or at least of the first and possibly second derivatives of important outcomes in f with respect to those environmental variables for which the data present important differences.

A similar problem arises with respect to the policy variables p_s. The very nature (as distinct from the numerical values) of these variables will in general depend on the system. This is particularly true for the policies of ruling organizations. It may well be true also for those of other participants. One may wish to compare systems under the policies actually or typically in use in each system during the period(s) of the comparison. In that case, separating the effects of policies from those of the system raises no new econometric problem. However, the principal reason for the distinction between system and policies is the greater ease of changing policies than systems. One may therefore also wish to compare systems on

[9] K. Wittfogel, *Oriental Despotism: A Comparative Study of Total Power*, New Haven: 1957.

[10] See, for instance, G. J. Stigler, "The Division of Labor is Limited by the Extent of the Market," *Journal of Political Economy*, LIX:3 (1951) 185–193.

[11] For pertinent comment, see A. Eckstein, "Individualism and the Role of the State in Economic Growth," *Economic Development and Cultural Change*, VI:2 (1958) 81–87; A. O. Hirschman, *The Strategy of Economic Development*, New Haven, 1958, p. 65; R. C. Wallich, "Some Notes Towards a Theory of Derived Development," in Agerwala and Singh, eds, *The Economics of Underdevelopment*, Oxford (1958) pp. 189–204.

the assumption that in each system, at least on the level of ruling organizations, the policies applied are the best available within the institutional and normative constraints of the system. In addition to estimation of the values $f(e_0, s_i, p_{s_i})$ of the outcome vectors f for some standardized environment e_0 and for the (s_i, p_{s_i}) combinations observed in the economies labeled $i = 1, 2, \ldots, k$, this would require the further estimation of first and second derivatives of important outcomes in f with regard to important components of p_{s_i} in those countries where policy is deemed clearly nonoptimal.

As in other relatively simpler problems in econometrics, the very limited opportunities for experimentation, the limited number of periods and of economies for which observations are available, and economic history's inherent selectivity in regard to the range of vector variables presented to view in any given economy and period do not permit such estimation without resort to *a priori* assumptions about the properties of the functions f and about their deduction from underlying, more autonomous, relationships. For instance, the activity–analysis model of production may be used in a first approximation as a source of mathematical constraints on the way in which important environmental variables enter into f. Likewise, ideas from organization theory may be drawn upon to spot crucial system and policy variables and to circumscribe the manner in which they enter into f. In Section 5 we seek to explore some possibilities in that direction with regard to system variables. As a third example that anticipates the "utility version" of the efficiency norm,

$$n(o) = n(f(e, s, p_s)),$$

a function of the outcome vector o to be introduced in Section 3.2, we need to draw on the theory of consumers' choice when faced with given market prices.

Whether these particular approaches are helpful or should be discarded for better ones is not the issue here. The main point is that the principles regarding the use of *a priori* postulates for the identification of economic relationships and for the tracing of causal chains, developed in connection with other fields of application of econometric methods,[12] also bear, *mutatis mutandis*, on the comparison of economic systems. In fact, in such comparisons, the dependence on *a priori* assumptions is the greater, the more numerous the differences between the economies to be compared.

---

[12] See W. C. Hood and T. C. Koopmans, eds., *Studies in Econometric Method*, New York (1953) especially Chs. I (J. Marschak), II (T. C. Koopmans), III (H. A. Simon); also Simon, *Models of Man, Op. Cit.* (n. 2) Chapters 1 and 3; and T. C. Koopmans and A. F. Bausch, "Selected Topics in Economics Involving Mathematical Reasoning," *SIAM Review*, I:2 (1959) 79–148, topic 11.

An ability to trace the effects of differences or changes in environment, system, or policies is crucial to the ultimate purpose of the comparison of economic systems: to find ways of improving the performance of any given economy or system in the light of some adopted norm. The use of models of the economies compared is therefore bound up in the normative character of the comparisons.

2.3. Organizational Structures and System Descriptions

We propose to describe a system for comparative purposes with the aid of the following terms and concepts in addition to those already introduced. We wish to stress that our ultimate purpose of facilitating the comparison of systems lies at the basis of our classification of institutions and of other system characteristics in the taxonomic material in this and in the following sections. We are mindful, for example, that the organizations, activities, actions and messages in a system may be subdivided into much smaller and more homogeneous categories than we suggest in this paper. Alternative classifications of approximately the same degree of "coarseness" also come readily to mind.

To demarcate a system, we specify a set of *participants* whom we identify as all individuals, and possibly groups of individuals acting with a specific group decision procedure (boards, committees, parliaments), that take economically relevant actions.

Participants' actions, including messages, may become part of the environment of other participants, who may respond to them if they so desire or if they are obligated to do so. This response is also an action.

We call *interaction* a set of actions, simultaneous, sequential, or of both kinds such that each participant in the interacting subset of participants directly affects the environment or information set or both of every participant in that subset. The relation is thus symmetrical: If person i interacts with person j, i's actions impinge on j and vice versa.

Orders are dated messages calling for a specific response (to act or desist) from the participant(s) to whom they are addressed; *rules* are messages stipulating or constraining the actions of a set of participants for an indefinite period and under specified conditions. The set of participants is explicitly defined in the message but not necessarily by listing them individually.

We conceive of participants as associating in organizations. An *organization* is defined with reference to a specific set of activities. It consists of a set of persons called *members* of the organization (which must include at least one participant of the system considered), who regularly interact with each other, by communication and possibly in other ways, in the process of carrying on one or more activities of the set. To be precise, for any two members i, q, of the organization, we require that there be a *chain* of interactions connecting them, that is, a sequence i, $k, l, \ldots, p, q$, of different members such that (i, k), (k, l), $\ldots$, (p, q) are interacting pairs[13] (not necessarily for the same activity or activities in the set). In particular, as we shall see below in Section 5.4.1, all participants form an organization in this sense for the set of all activities engaged in by at least one of them.

It will be convenient to use the word *entity* for either an individual or an organization.

To differentiate *associations*, *hierarchies*, and *quasi-hierarchies*, the three basic types of organizations we shall deal with in Section 5, we require the concepts of *supervision* and *superordination*.

A member of an organization *supervises* another member if he has the power to issue orders to, and exert significant influence on the actions of, that member with reference to one or more of the activities in which the organization is engaged or could engage.[14] If member i supervises member j who in turn supervises member k, and so forth, then i is said to be *superordinate* (or *superior*) to $j, k, \ldots$, and $j, k, \ldots$, *subordinate* to i, whether or not i actually also supervises $k, \ldots$. Note that a member may be superior to another for one activity and subordinate or neither-superior-nor-subordinate for another activity.

An *association* for an activity or a set of activities is an organization, none of whose individual members is superior to another member in carrying out any of these activities.

A *hierarchy* for an activity is an organization with the following properties:

1. For each pair of members of the organization *either* one member is subordinate (for that activity) to the other *or* both are subordinate to the same third member of the organization.
2. If one member is subordinate to another in the organization, there is a unique chain of successive supervisors (for that activity) connecting the two.

From this definition it may be inferred that a hierarchy has a unique head and that every other member in a hierarchy is directly supervised by precisely one member. These properties differentiate hierarchies as we have defined them from *quasi-hierarchies*, the third, residual, category of organizations, in which a supervision relation occurs between at least one pair of members, but where members need not be related to each other by a single chain of supervision, and more than one member may head the

[13] For an alternative, broader definition of an organization where the necessity for regular interaction *within* each pair of members (i, k), $(k, l) \ldots$, (p, q) in a chain is relaxed, see section 5.4.1.

[14] On the supervision relation, see also below, section 5.3.

organization. (Among modern nuclear families consisting of father, mother, and children such quasi-hierarchies are frequently encountered.) A hierarchy or quasi-hierarchy may itself be a member of an association, or vice versa, if all the members of the member-organization act according to or abide by the decision procedures of that organization.

This classification of organizations will be used in Section 5, where we put forward two conjectures on the efficiency of alternative organizations, including markets (which we conceive of as associations of a special type).

We call *ruling organizations* for a system certain organizations (usually structured as hierarchies) that have the power to issue *rules* or *orders* to some designated set of system participants to which they are addressed; these may include both members and non-members of these organizations. We shall call these rules laws. The *legal framework of the economy* is the set of all laws pertinent to the economic processes in the system.

We describe a system in terms of the patterns of interaction among its participants and in terms of the rules governing these interactions imposed by ruling organizations. A complete system description presupposes that an information set (see Section 2.1) and either a preference ordering (say, a utility function) or a decision rule can be attributed to each of the participants. If a utility function is attributed, the participant's *motivation* is then defined as a function that associates with each course of action open to him the utility of that outcome which, on the basis of his information set, he expects to result from that course of action.[15] If his information takes the form of a (subjective or objective) probability distribution of the outcomes of at least some courses of action, the term "expected utility" may be substituted for "utility" in this definition, or another model for choice under uncertainty may be employed.

The motivation for a participant's decision to comply or not to comply with an order from a supervisor in the organization of which he is a member depends, among other things, on his assessment of the loss or inconvenience he would suffer if he were forced to leave the organization—a possible outcome of failure to comply, once or repeatedly. Although the goals and policies of an organization are likely to constrain the actions of all of its members (with the possible exception of the head of a hierarchy if the goals and policies he is able to impose accurately reflect his personal preferences), we allow for the possibility of actions by members in conflict with the goals and policies of the organization as

[15] The behavior model suggested in this paragraph is in the tradition of the economist's theory of maximizing behavior already referred to in Section 2.1. A psychologist would note that changes in information would receive more attention than unchanged information. An organization theorist would note that the utilities of alternatives quite different from the one presently pursued would receive more attention when the participant's fortunes are strongly threatened.

interpreted by their superiors, as well as actions by members adversely affecting fellow members in terms of the latters' goals.

We shall find that the notions of price and of ownership, which will be defined when they are introduced in Section 5, can be fitted without strain into the conceptual framework we have set forth.

3. Norms (Criteria)

3.1. Outcomes, Desiderata, Indicators

We have defined outcomes as *all aspects or consequences of system, policy, decisions, or actions to which positive or negative value is attached in at least one of the norms entering into a comparison.* In turn, a norm was defined as *an evaluation function of all outcomes that represents the preferences held by some individual or group pertinent to the comparison.* The mathematical definition of a function then permits a norm to depend in fact on only a subset of all outcomes, indicating that the individual or group in question is interested only in some of the outcomes. We shall call *desiderata* for any given norm those outcomes on which the norm in fact depends positively. (Any *odiosa* can be transformed into desiderata by a change of sign.)

Before listing examples of important desiderata occurring in pertinent norms, we make a few more general observations.

The insertion of the word "aspect" in the above definition of an outcome entails that any trait of a system or policy can itself be a desideratum in some norm if value is attached to it in that norm, possibly because of presumed noneconomic effects. For instance, decentralization of economic decisions may be valued in itself because it is looked upon as strengthening the self-reliance of individuals. In contrast, in another system centralization may be valued in itself, because it is thought to help maintain central control over political and cultural decisions desired in the prevailing norm. In comparisons the fact that these system traits appear as outcomes valued in opposite ways in different norms must be taken into account.

The inclusion in a norm of, or the giving of extra weight to, a desideratum merely because of its presumed relation to some unnamed, perhaps noneconomic, desideratum introduces into the norm an assumption about causal relationships that may be mistaken. This element of speculation is present, to a smaller or larger degree, in almost all adoption and weighting of desiderata. It is enhanced by the fact that the more ulterior desiderata are often harder to quantify, and therefore proximate desiderata which are more easily measurable must represent the ulterior ends in question.[16]

[16] Cf. E. Kirschen and L. Morrissens, "The Objectives and Instruments of Economic Policy," in B. Hickman, ed., *Quantitative Planning of Economic Policy*, Washington D.C., 1964.

The use of statistical *indicators* as proxies for desiderata or odiosa raises problems of representativeness and comparability. Two countries may have a desideratum in common but may pursue different proximate goals to attain it. Most societies, for example, wish to minimize economic strife (for reasons related to desideratum y_5 to be defined in Section 3.2) and to preserve a reasonable degree of stability in the distribution of power and rewards. In some economies where labor is autonomously organized, man-days lost by strikes may be used as an indicator of strife and tension. But no such measure is available for economies in which strikes are illegal.

Another example concerns the volume of unfinished construction, an indicator likely to be relevant for comparing the intertemporal efficiency of alternative systems. Comprehensive data on this variable can only be obtained for the Soviet Union and for the East European economies. In market economies these data, if they are collected at all at the level of the construction enterprise, are generally not aggregated, presumably because neither the decision makers in the governmental hierarchy nor those in any nongovernmental organization have felt or articulated a need for them in reaching their decisions.

3.2. Common or Similar Desiderata in Various Norms

We begin our listing with some *common desiderata* that we believe to be present in the prevailing norms of most systems in the modern world. It is not implied that the relative weights given to the various desiderata are the same in the several norms in which they are held in common. Neither is a desideratum recognized as common necessarily expressible in the same form in regard to different systems. Nevertheless, a list of common desiderata is a first step toward a methodology of comparison of economic systems that may gain acceptance by economists living under different systems.

y_1 a high level of *per capita consumption* of goods and services desired by or for consumers.[17]

Although some individuals have sought a life of austerity and self-denial, as far as majorities of participants go this desideratum has a long history. It is practically universal in the modern world without any signs of an approach to saturation even in the wealthiest economies.

Currently almost as universal is the desire for

y_2 *growth* in the per capita consumption of goods and services through technical advances and through accumulation of physical and human capital.

[17] The words "by or for" allude to a system difference to be discussed further in connection with desideratum y*.

This is in part a matter of intertemporal distribution of consumption and of dissatisfaction with present consumption levels, especially in the less developed countries. It is also derived from another desideratum

y_6 to maintain or extend one's influence and power in the world,

which we mention here somewhat out of sequence while postponing further comment. Finally, especially in the more affluent countries with private property and enterprise, a given growth of population produces an at least corresponding growth in capital almost painlessly through the desire for continuity of income into the retirement period.[18] Additional sources of technical advance are the desire of the young to acquire skills and knowledge that have market value besides their personal value, the competition between business firms, nation-states, and systems in the technological race, and the pressure from scientists for funds to pursue their intellectual interests. One feels that in these circumstances, given the rate of population growth, a comparable all-over growth rate would have resulted in the most advanced countries of West even if growth had not enjoyed public and official acclaim as a national goal in itself—provided a full–employment policy was successfully pursued.

The three desiderata listed so far introduce the three major contenders for the aggregate use of resources in modern systems. The next three desiderata deal more with the apportioning of consumption by types of goods and by recipients. It is therefore appropriate here to make the point that simultaneous pursuit of the first three desiderata, whatever their (positive) weights in the pertinent norm, implies a derived desideratum of

y_* *efficiency* in the use of resources.

Perfect efficiency of an entire economy, an unattainable ideal, is defined, in the "commodity version" common to East, West, and South, as a choice of the kinds and levels of production activities in use such that within the bounds of the given resource availabilities it is not technologically possible to produce (or secure) more of any good or service (including leisure) desired by some participant except at the opportunity cost of producing less of some good or service desired by some participant. In another more inclusive "utility version," called Pareto optimality, or consumers' sovereignty, and rating higher in West than elsewhere, the definition says instead " . . . that . . . it is not possible to increase the utility

[18] J. Tobin has calculated that the United States capital stock corresponds in size to what would be implied in a life–cycle theory of saving that extends the suggestions made in F. Modigliani and R. Brumberg, "Utility Analysis and the Consumption Function: An Interpretation of Cross-Section Data," in Kurihara, ed., *Post-Keynesian Economics*, New Brunswick, N.J., 1954, pp. 388–436. See J. Tobin, "Life Cycle Saving and Balanced Growth," in W. Fellner et al., *Ten Economic Studies in the Tradition of Irving Fisher*, New York, 1967, pp. 231–256.

of any one individual without decreasing that of another." The former efficiency concept applies just to allocation of resources in production, the latter to distribution to consumers as well. The latter concept expresses the phrase "desired *by* consumers" in the definition of y_1. The former concept is implied in the latter (assuming nonsaturation), but standing by itself needs to be supplemented by a specification of the ratios[19] in which goods are "desired *for* consumers."

Neither the definition of efficiency nor the desiderata implying it go into the difficult organizational problems that are the main topic in the comparison of economic systems: How does one achieve or approach efficiency? Is its attainment harder and less complete if the growth rate is higher? What is its cost in terms of other desiderata yet to be mentioned? It is, therefore, desirable to have a measure of attainment of efficiency. Debreu has proposed such a measure for the utility version, which is not affected by ordinality of the participants' utility functions.[20] His "coefficient of resource utilization" is defined as the smallest identical fraction of all actual primary inputs that would still permit attaining the same utility level for each individual by a more efficient allocation and distribution. Even though hard to evaluate numerically, this measure may be a good starting point for the search for more easily determined measures.

Single-period efficiency (in either version) is obtained if all the inputs and outputs (or utilities) in the definition refer to one single time period.[21] In that interpretation, one must specify in the definition of efficiency that, in comparisons with other allocations (and distributions), the amounts of all goods to be held over for use in later periods be kept constant. *Intertemporal efficiency* is obtained if the same good available in different periods is interpreted as so many different goods, the while holding the initial and (for a finite horizon) terminal capital stocks constant. This concept implies single-period efficiency in all periods in question, but the converse is not true. Hence intertemporal efficiency is the stricter and indeed more meaningful desideratum of the two. For a sufficiently long horizon, it also reflects efficiency in choosing the size and composition of investment. However, it suffers from an implication of perfect foresight as regards technology, preferences, and actual allocation and distribution for $n \leq \infty$ periods ahead. A suggestion for a more flexible concept is made below.

[19] See, for instance, L. V. Kantorovich, *Ekonomicheskii raschet nailuchshego ispol'zovania resursov* (The Best Use of Economic Resources), Academy of Sciences of the USSR, 1959 (English translation, Cambridge, Mass., 1965).

[20] G. Debreu, "The Coefficient of Resource Utilization," *Econometrica*, July XIX:3 (1951) 273–292.

[21] This concept is also somewhat inaccurately named "static efficiency," a term better reserved for efficiency attained in a hypothetical stationary state with all variables constant over time.

While single-period efficiency in some sense implies maximal consumption y_1 in that period compatible with the stipulations in its definition, intertemporal efficiency is of course compatible with high or low growth, stationarity, decline, or fluctuation of per capita consumption. The growth desideratum y_2 adds to this a specific preference as regards *aggregate* intertemporal distribution of consumption.

A concern with distribution among individuals is expressed by

y_3 *equity* in the distribution of the conditions of living, or at least of opportunity in that regard, among contemporaries,

which is more strongly held in East and West than in South. The "conditions of living" include consumption levels (current as well as lifetime prospects), health care, opportunity for gainful employment, protection from adverse working conditions, absence of non-functional discrimination, and dignity in human interactions. We prefer the hard-to-define ethical term "equity" to the more definite term "equality," which ignores differences in need arising, for instance, from different states of health or from different numbers of dependents or providers. It also ignores the socially desirable incentive effect of income responding positively to productive effort. So what we mean is something like "fairness and efficiency modifying a desideratum of equality."

Particularly in West and South, social services and public goods are largely provided by mechanisms different from those by which other consumption goods are supplied. For this reason, we shall recognize a separate desideratum, which is a further stipulation within the consumption desideratum y_1.

y_4 provision of *social services and public goods*.

This desideratum rates higher, by and large, in East than in South and West, in relation to resources. However, the modern emphasis on increasing levels of widespread education, mentioned already in connection with the growth desideratum y_2, is almost universal. Likewise, the protection of the physical and biological surroundings of man from the adverse effects of economic activities, which we include under the desideratum y_4, is currently gaining strength in both East and West.

The following intertemporal aspect of the conditions of living deserves separate mention:

y_5 *stability* of employment and incomes.

In West policy makers use monetary and fiscal policy toward this goal. With respect to South, efforts are made to protect the value of exports against price fluctuations and overproduction by arrangements modifying the operation of markets in important raw materials. In East direct controls over investments and restrictions on short-term credits are used to maintain macroeconomic stability.

There remains the crucial desideratum y_6 already mentioned. We extend its definition here.

y_6 (*national strength*) to ensure the continuation of national existence and of national or ideological independence; where possible to extend national or ideological influence, prestige and power.

As between different countries or systems this desideratum is *similar* rather than common. It has the same definition, except that in each case a different name of country or system is written in.

The economic significance of this largely political desideratum is very great. It competes with all the foregoing desiderata by the absorption of resources in military preparedness and, if the case arises, in armed international conflict. A lesser but noticeable complementarity between y_6 and earlier desiderata arises from the benefits to production for civilian consumption thrown off by military research. A definite positive value for some of the other desiderata arises from some primarily nonmilitary activities motivated by y_6. This includes the emphasis on rapid industrialization in South and East and ventures in oceanographic or space research in the most highly developed countries.

Another important desideratum, similar in intent but possibly quite different in form of application as between different systems, is

y_7 *provision for orderly change in a system* to permit adjustment to changing circumstances without endangering its essential continuity.

System changes themselves were mentioned among possible outcomes in Section 2.1. Normally, system change desiderata differ considerably within one and the same economy as between prevailing and other contending norms. The prevailing norm tends to favor little or no change, while the contending norms favor a variety of not necessarily compatible changes. We return to these relationships in Section 3.5.

3.3. Desiderata Specific to Various Norms

As alluded to above, West favors and practices

y_8 *widely dispersed economic decisions* through inheritable private property, through individual and corporate enterprise, and through a legal framework enforcing contracts while permitting limited liability of corporations.

To different degrees in different countries of West and possibly South the concern for business enterprise is carried to the point of

y_9 *commercialism*, a tolerant attitude toward uninformative competitive advertising, sales pressure, and the influencing of essentially educational and cultural activities by business interests,

in some comparors' norms the tolerance of an odiosum rather than a positively valued desideratum.

The traditional desideratum of East,

y_{10} *centralized*[22] *decisions and control* over the composition of output and consumption,

has been abandoned in Yugoslavia and to a significant degree in Hungary, and is currently under hesitant and partial reconsideration in a few other countries because of its conflict with y_*.

3.4. Some Possible Comparors' Desiderata

The comparor may wish to improve the formulation of desiderata already recognized or to propose as pertinent some desiderata not previously formulated. An example of the former is

y'_1 *a flexible intertemporal efficiency* concept capable of recognizing uncertainty about technology at any future date, which will diminish as the date is approached, as well as similar uncertainty about future consumers' or planners' preferences.

The analytical difficulties in the way of such a conceptual refinement are considerable. An exploratory discussion of flexible preferences has already been referred to.[23]

An example of a newly proposed desideratum might concern the coexistence characteristics of various mixtures of economic systems. The comparor might wish to propose the study of unilaterally initiated or mutually agreed self-reforms of coexistent systems to

y_{11} *reduce both the cost of the balance of deterrence and the probability or destructiveness of armed conflict* between countries having similar or different systems.

The crucial importance of this (proximate rather than ultimate) desideratum for the future of mankind contrasts sharply with the difficulties of obtaining clarity and, if needed, agreement on policies promoting this desideratum. It is not even clear what bearing economic policies may have on its attainment, except for a general presumption that the increasing

[22] Again, "centralization" as understood in East.
[23] Koopmans, "On Flexibility" *op. cit.* (n. 5).

interdependence of economies in the modern world is likely to increase the importance of various system characteristics to coexistence problems.

Obviously, our list of desiderata could be extended indefinitely, and other authors might have regarded some other desiderata more important than some of those we have listed. Many proximate goals not specifically mentioned so far can be derived from our desiderata. For example, the defense of the balance of payments may be motivated by a desire for stability of employment and incomes, for growth in per capita consumption, for national strength, for equity in distribution, or for a combination of any of these desiderata.

3.5. Interaction between Prevailing Norms, Other Norms, and Systems

The very concept of what is a prevailing norm differs between systems. In a highly centralized system, the prevailing norm is essentially the norm of those who exercise power in the system. In a pluralistic society, where interest groups are clearly visible and in explicit competition through political processes, through collective bargaining, strikes, and threats of strikes, market strategy, persuasion through various media, demonstrations and other means, what we might call the prevailing norm can only be inferred from actual policies and decisions, rather than being read in declarations or programs. In such a society, the rules of the struggle for influence, power and wealth are an important part of the system. Knowledge of these rules, and of the contending groups and their specific norms, is essential for an understanding of the prevailing norms and their change over time. Undoubtedly similar processes take place in the more centralized systems in a submerged manner escaping any but conjectural and inferential contemporary analysis.

Systems and norms influence each other in many ways. The most important example concerns *system change*, which is itself included among the outcomes. System change tends to be resisted by those participants on whom the system bestows wealth, influence or power, a resistance aided by traditional values and the advantages of stability. The ideology of the dominant group, which may be spread among the participants through propaganda, advertising, proselytization, or other vehicles of persuasion, reinforces these conservative tendencies. It follows from this bias that comparison between two systems with similar environments on the basis of the prevailing norm of either will favor the system whose prevailing norm instructs the comparison. Even if the list of desiderata were to be the same in the two prevailing norms, any difference in the weights given to the desiderata in the respective prevailing norms will make either system bend the outcomes to its own norm, other things being equal. Total system change nevertheless occurs either when those in situations of power are dissatisfied with the performance of the system and are desirous of bringing about its reform or overhaul, or when a group of individuals who are not among the top power holders and feel disadvantaged or otherwise dissatisfied with the system can force a modification to give greater effect to their own norms. The pressure for change on the part of persons in and out of power depends on the information generated by the system about its performance, itself a system characteristic. It has been conjectured, for instance, that the amount and quality of information percolating to power holders will vary inversely with the political coercion and restrictions they impose upon society.[24] The change effected in the system is *evolutionary* if it takes place clearly within the framework and procedures recognized by the system. This requires that the prevailing norm give weight to y_7, provision for change in the system. A *revolutionary* change takes place if a group has ways to force a system change according to its norm which supersedes the previous total system outright. These are extremes of a scale, and intermediate forms of system change are frequent. In revolutionary change, the part of the system that changes most is the institutions, organizations, laws and rules. The regular patterns of behavior are not generally capable of abrupt change.[25]

As another, final example of an effect of system on norms, we refer to the observation by March and Simon in a discussion of ideas on organizational learning by Robert Merton: that system traits may over time become infused with value through a more or less unconscious process, called "goal displacement."[26] The authors cited state that the repeated choice of specific acceptable means to a valued end causes a gradual transfer of the preference from the end to the means adopted. The means itself may be a proximate goal, or an institutional device for reaching such a goal.

Finally, we note that the presence of one desideratum in the prevailing norm of a system may affect the meaning of another desideratum. In any system in which consumers' choice influences the incomes of managers in individual enterprises and in which advertising is a part of business operation, the very consumers' preferences that enter into the efficiency desideratum (utility version) are affected and at times distorted by advertising. To the extent that this happens, the tolerance of commercialism qualifies, and detracts from the merit of, the desideratum of efficiency in the utility version. Thus, the prevailing norm of that system (West) that attaches the greatest weight to consumers' sovereignty at the same time impairs its significance. Corresponding effects occur in the sphere of

[24] D. Apter, *The Politics of Modernization*, Chicago, 1965 p. 40.

[25] There is an analogy here with technological change. Important new knowledge can become available overnight. Its incorporation in new capital stock and a (re–) trained labor force takes much longer.

[26] J. G. March and H. A. Simon, *Organizations*, New York, 1958.

public goods and services. Observers, such as Eisenhower and Galbraith, have pointed to the influence that producers of military goods exercise on government expenditures.[27] The latter has also referred to the relative neglect of expenditures on those other public goods and services for which pressure from private producers is less pronounced or absent.[28]

4. Activities, Interactivities, Custody

4.1. Technological Activities

It will help in the discussion of organization in Section 5 if we insert here three brief, illustrative, and nonexhaustive lists of important categories of activities. The first list leans to the more purely technological activities, which at the same time are the more universal activities across systems. The sequence of categories within any one list is somewhat arbitrary.

A. *Categories of "technological" activities.*
Recognizing and locating natural resources (such as water, minerals, soils, forests, game, fish)
Specifying and/or designing commodities to be produced. We distinguish:
commodities not for final consumption, to be embodied or used up in production of other commodities, and means of production of some durability (including consumers' durable goods)
commodities for final consumption (including the services rendered by consumers' durable goods)
Producing all commodities of both types, choosing inputs and methods of production from among those available
Research and development of new methods of production
Transportation and delivery of output from producer to user or consumer
Maintaining inventories of storable goods
Labor force participation
Human reproduction, care of the young, education and training in the technological activities
The *rendering* of health services

With some flexibility of interpretation the activities in these categories can be fitted into the definition of activity given in Section 2.1. In all

[27] President Dwight D. Eisenhower, "Farewell Address to the American People," Jan. 7, 1961, *Public Papers of the Presidents of the U.S.*, 1960–61, Paper 421; J. K. Galbraith, *The New Industrial State*, Boston (1967), especially Ch. 27.
[28] J. K. Galbraith, *The Affluent Society*, Boston (1957).

economic systems there is some degree of functional specialization among participants in performing the technological activities, which is the more detailed the larger the scale of the economy. This specialization is due to the indivisibility of the human carrier of skill and expertise and to the greater productivity of a finer subdivision of specializations whenever scale permits full use of at least one individual of each specialized skill.[29] The resulting specializations are so similar in different modern economies or systems that, where languages differ, makers of dictionaries have had little difficulty in finding equivalent functional or occupational designations (often derived from the same root).

4.2. Interdependence of Activities

The second list contains activities arising from the technological interdependence of those on the first list. Two or more activities are called *interdependent* if efficient allocation of resources requires at least one of the following:

    i. the activities make use of the same indivisible input(s) (example: different tasks to be carried out on one lathe in the same day)

    ii. they contribute to the same indivisible output(s) (building a house)

    iii. they must be carried out jointly (one man holds the horse, the other shoes it) or simultaneously (individuals whose travel converges on a common meeting place)

    iv. they must be carried out in a certain sequence because an output of one activity becomes an input to another (transferring liquid iron from a blast furnace to a foundry)

    v. their levels must stand in a certain proportion, because two of their respective inputs originate from, or two of their respective outputs are required for, a single activity characterized by constant proportions of outputs or inputs.

The interdependencies i., ii., iii. are often absolutes. Interdependencies iv. and v. become a matter of degree if alternative sources of input or uses of output exist at moderate cost differentials. On the other hand, chains made up of pairs of activities whose interdependence is of type iv. or v. create secondary, tertiary, ... interdependencies of similar types that attenuate further as the number of links in the chain increases.

The coordination problems of production, transportation, distribution, consumption take their form in large part from the nature of the interdependencies between the activities involved. We believe that the literature

[29] See, for instance, G. J. Stigler, *op. cit.* (n. 10). By an indivisible factor of production we mean a factor that is not available for productive use in any quantity smaller than a positive smallest unit.

on activity analysis[30] can contribute elements to a formalization of these coordination problems that provides a background against which the solutions offered by different systems can be compared. Sections 4.3 and 4.4 contain further observations toward such a marriage of activity analysis and organization theory.

4.3. Custody and Transfers of Custody

We conjecture that in most modern systems almost any resource,[31] means of production, or good in process is at any time in the *custody* of some entity (operator, foreman, plant department, sales department, owner, manager, trader). In the case of a means of production or resource, the *custodial entity* controls its use in time and as between claimants. In the case of a material, good in process, or finished good, the custodial entity determines the next disposition of the good, such as leaving or placing it in inventory, continuing its processing, entering it into the next stage of processing, or making it available for consumption, in some of these cases while transferring its custody to another entity.

Transfers of custody tend to occur, for good and rather obvious efficiency reasons, in those states of each good between processing stages, to be called *transfer states*, in which one or more of the following applies:

a. the good is capable of being handled (automobiles) and/or stored (steel billets) and/or delivered (electric power) without serious loss of quality,
b. the specifications describing the transfer state are standardized, and
c. the transferrer or the transferee or both can expect to have a choice between more than one transferee or transferrer, respectively, who may belong to different entities engaged in the same production activities, or who may differ in the processing activity that preceded transfer,[32] or that is to take place after transfer (coal).

If a custodial entity is an organization, efficiency often requires that it be clear to all concerned to which member of the organization the custody

---

[30] See, for instance, T. C. Koopmans, ed., *Activity Analysis of Production and Allocation*, New York, 1951, and A. M. Manne and H. Markowitz, eds., *Studies in Process Analysis*, New York, 1963.

[31] There is one important category of resources not subject to specific custody. This category consists of generally accessible resources, with regard to which the use, the extraction and possible degradation are not easily controlled: air, the ocean and its mineral and biological content, inland water, in earlier periods land, increasingly in modern periods streets and highways. We return below (Sec. 5.4.4.) to the adverse effects on efficiency that may be connected with such absence or insufficient effectiveness of custody arrangements.

[32] For a description of an integrated steel plant simultaneously using steel obtained from different processes see T. Fabian, "Process Analysis of the U.S. Iron and Steel Industry," in Manne and Markowitz, *op. cit.*, Ch. 9.

of which good is delegated, even if subject to reversal by a supervisor for the custodial activity in the case of a (quasi-) hierarchy. For goods not in continual use (television set in the family) delegation may extend to all members of an organization on a first-come-first-served basis, again subject to reversal.

In any system in which one or more of the above types of goods or resources are privately owned, custody normally goes with ownership or is delegated by the owner.[33] For this and other reasons, forms of ownership of resources and of man-made means of production are usually regarded as a major system characteristic.

Transfers of custody or of delegated custody may take place between entities embedded in the same hierarchy or between entities not belonging to the same hierarchy for the activity or set of activities in question. Whether the transfer of a given type of good of similar specification in two systems falls in one or the other of these two cases will in general depend on the system. The relative frequency of transfers within, as against between, hierarchies is indeed an important system characteristic. However, we conjecture that there is a very substantial similarity and overlap between systems in the specifications, not only of finished goods and services, but also of the unfinished transfer states in the production of these commodities. We surmise further that the particular bundle of production activities taking place between two successive transfer states that two systems have in common depends less on system characteristics than on the scale of the economy or of the enterprise and, given a modicum of efficiency, on the environment. Among pertinent environmental factors, the relative scarcities of aggregate basic inputs, such as labor, resources, and capital, to the economy as a whole are particularly important.

We adduce three reasons for these conjectures. First, technology does not stop or change much in character at the boundaries between systems. Acceptability of technology is usually unrelated to the system of origin, and information on advanced technology circulates widely and is given constant attention. The second reason follows from the first. The economies inherent in the characteristics a., b., c. of transfer states listed above are rather apparent, and their perception is not much affected by system characteristics. Finally (the third reason), both scale and factor proportions are likely to enter into the bundle of production activities occurring between successive transfer states, scale because of the indivisibilities of human operators and pieces of equipment, factor proportions because even moderate efficiency demands reasonably full use of available factors.

Although the above reasoning has been given largely in terms of production of goods, similar reasoning applies, *mutatis mutandis*, to most

[33] Further remarks on the relation of custody and ownership are given in section 5.

industrial services as well, if performance of a service is substituted for transfer of custody of a good. This includes transportation, in which case only transport-relevant characteristics of the goods shipped need be taken into account.

4.4. Interactivities

We now list categories of activities, the need for which arises from the interdependence of activities in list A (Sec. 4.1). All the actions of which these activities consist are part of interactions and it is therefore natural to speak of *interactivities*.

B. *Categories of interactivities for the assignment and scheduling of technological activities*

Assigning, directing, or coordinating tasks for technological activities requiring simultaneous or successive actions by two or more individuals

Arranging the transfer of custody of a specific batch, quantity, or item of a specific good to the next using, processing, or consuming entity, which has a demand for it

Arranging for the use of a given resource or fraction thereof by a specific producer or household, during a given time

(Within the household) determining which quantity of which consumption good available to it is consumed by which member of the household at which time.

4.5. System-bound Activities and Actions

Although the activities of list B need to be performed under any system, their character depends on the organizational structure and operating procedures of the system more than do those in list A. However, in most systems the activities in list B are only a part of the organizational activities required by the system. One could, it is true, imagine a command system capable of perfect coordination, in which all the activities exemplified by lists A and B were implemented by commanded actions of individuals belonging to one large hierarchy. In that case, the commanded transfers of custody would themselves define the demands they meet and the supplies from which they are made. In all systems of record, many other activities intervene to determine these demands and supplies and to serve various other desiderata. The nature of these activities depends strongly on the system in which they occur. For that reason we are forced, in listing a few of these by way of examples, to use some terms which while perfectly familiar to the reader have not yet found a place in the framework of concepts developed so far, because they anticipate essentially organizational concepts to be introduced in Section 5.

C. *Examples of system-bound activities*

Activities determining capabilities to acquire custody of additional means of production through credit from financial institutions that absorb savings by individuals and organizations or from governmental credit institutions that may obtain their funds from tax revenues.

Activities that spread risk by pooling

Protection of individuals from ill effects of adverse conditions of labor (for instance, as provided by labor unions in interaction with employers)

Education and training for managerial and other system-bound activities

The *provision* of health services.

Additional more specific system-bound activities of an organizational character are discussed in Section 5, largely in terms of the kinds of actions and interactions they consist of. There is a good reason for this shift in terminology. We have defined activities as kinds of repeatable action, and the term "activity" is most serviceable where the action in question is in fact repeated in a rather routine manner. Organizations, however, the most system-bound aspect of an economy, are primarily concerned with coping with change, with the new and unexpected.[34] An organizational model for a stationary state, if at all conceivable, helps little in understanding the nature of organizational problems in any real-life system. For that reason, the expectation of repetition of an organizational action of precisely the same kind or form is generally much weaker, and the terminology of "actions" and "interactions" is more appropriate in an organizational context.

5. The Organizational Structure of Systems

5.1. Participants and Ruling Organizations

To be precise enough for both conceptual and statistical purposes, the description of each system entering a comparison should specify the set of its participants. For some purposes it may be useful to include in this set all the individuals located within certain geographical boundaries

[34] This applies particularly to economic organizations. Some other organizations, such as schools, churches, political organizations serve in addition to spread knowledge, faith or power, or to preserve any of these from attrition due to the predictable change arising from human aging and death.

during the period of comparison; another possible definition would include all individuals of a given nationality irrespective of their location; still another would include all individuals associated with organizations incorporated (or having their headquarters) in a certain nation or region. The definition of the set of participants in each system will determine the scope of the interactions that are considered to be "across systems," to be discussed in Section 6. In comparisons involving nation-states with dual economies, one may wish to treat each "economy" as a separate subsystem and consider the interactions between the subsystems as one would consider the external economic relations of any economy considered to be sufficiently homogeneous to qualify as having a single system.

As we saw in Section 2.2, ruling organizations set bounds to the actions of individuals and organizations. They also facilitate certain interactions, such as transfers of custody in exchange for a compensation, by sanctioning one or more means of payment (legal tender) for discharging all debts and obligations, and by supervising weights and measures used in defining the quantity of certain goods.

In most nations today, the diverse organizations known in their aggregate as the *government* are the only ruling organizations empowered to issue rules at least nominally binding on all participants in the system.[35] However, the power of these organizations to issue laws may be circumscribed by certain prior rules endowed with a higher status or by certain principles or values which may or may not be codified. Prior rules include compacts, constitutions, treaties, and collective agreements; principles and values include taboos, religious documents, ideological pronouncements and so forth that happen to be accepted as binding or restraining by the dominant group in the total system.

Within ruling organizations modern systems have developed specialized suborganizations for issuing laws, for inducing most participants to conform to these laws, for adjudicating disputes arising from conflicting interpretations of the laws, and for identifying entities that have violated laws and deciding on sanctions.

Whether or not all component organizations under a ruling organization are bound by the laws issued by competent organizations within this ruling organization may be a critical trait differentiating one total system from another. With regard to the economic system, a gain in efficiency is

[35] In the United States, Federal, state and local governments, together with the agencies whose powers emanate from them, are the only legally sanctioned ruling units. In the Soviet Union the Party is in practice a ruling unit alongside, and in some respects above, the government. In early modern times, the Catholic Church in Europe was a ruling unit emitting both rules (e.g., prohibition on interest–taking) and general orders (the tithe). Illegal ruling units include racketeering organizations such as the Mafia. In the process of modernization in West, the state gradually suppressed all competing legitimate ruling units.

likely to accrue from the settlement of disputes arising from conflicts of interests according to a regular, well-defined procedure, with the final adjudication conforming to certain durable principles, precedents, or both: Such a procedure will help define the limits within which decision makers may operate without fear of restraint or retribution and will foster expectations of regular behavior on the part of other participants in the system and thus reduce the risks of decision-making.

5.2. Actions and Interactions

To distinguish *informational* from *effective actions*, we require the concept of *message*, information conveyed by one or more participants to one or more other participants. An informational action changes only the environment of some other participants except for interactions associated with the process of communication itself. We call all other actions effective.

Informational actions comprise: 1. offers and acceptances, including, in particular, those concerning the transfer of custody of goods in transfer states, with or without payment in return; 2. rules and orders and responses thereto; 3. *communications*, messages containing information about activities, processes and preferences; 4. threats, appeals, and other messages aiming to exert influence.

Among the principal types of effective actions may be cited the actual transfer of custody of goods and the performance of services, financial transactions, the hiring or conscription of individuals for specific activities, strikes, sabotage, and production actions resulting in pollution (insofar as it affects other entities). An effective action may also carry a message. A gift may be bestowed or a service performed with the aim of creating an obligation on the part of the recipient to reciprocate the favor at some future time. Initiatives of this type are important in promoting commodity exchanges in pre-modern societies and in wielding influence in many modern ones. Similarly the information conveyed to invidious neighbors by the conspicuous display of clothing, furnishings, or cars may prompt them to purchase similar goods for the sake of keeping up.

In general, effective actions, once they have been registered in the information set of the participants they affect, have either a direct or an indirect impact on their utility function. Informational actions, in contrast, affect a participant's welfare only insofar as they influence his expectations of subsequent effective actions.

Effective actions may further be classified according to the presence or absence of mutuality in the interaction of which they are a part. *Complete mutuality* prevails in actions that require the consent of all parties affected (e.g., a sale prepared by an exchange of messages or by a jointly issued message known as a contract). *Partial mutuality* prevails in an interaction when an individual undertaking an effective action incurs some, possibly temporary, disutility in order (a) to forestall an action by one or more participants which would inflict on him an even greater loss in utility, or (b) to accumulate credits for future benefits, or in recognition of the legitimacy of certain claims. In all such cases, the interacting participants are involved in an ongoing relation, which they consider to be acceptable if not actually desirable (e.g., employees interacting with their employers, taxpayers with government officials). In all remaining instances of interactions, there is *no mutuality* among the interacting participants.

The same initiating action may belong simultaneously to one interaction, characterized by complete mutuality for some participants, and to another interaction characterized by partial or no mutuality for others. Thus the owners of a landsite near a highway, an advertising agency, and an outdoor display company may all agree to put up a billboard, whose sight may offend motorists traveling along that highway.

A two-way classification of interactions may be made according to the type of actions that initiated them and according to the degree of mutuality that characterized them. A number of instances of interactions are classified according to this principle in Table 1.

The exchange of messages may enable two or more participants to discover the mutually advantageous effective actions they might undertake without exposing them to the risk of the losses that a series of inferior effective actions might give rise to. Bargaining to reach a mutually acceptable price or a wage settlement is an example of such exploratory behavior in a market system. Planning procedures also usually call for exploratory interactions between members of the organization issuing the plan.[36] These preliminary explorations may involve contacts between members of different organizations, especially where the planning organization, as in France, for instance, is only empowered to issue an *indicative* plan (one which is not even nominally binding on the organizations concerned). Where the plan consists of a set of orders, as in the Soviet Union, the entities to which the plan is addressed normally belong to the same *complete hierarchy* as the ruling organization issuing the plan.[37]

Evidence about the degree of mutuality characterizing an interaction cannot be used mechanically to infer the presence or absence of Pareto optimality.[38] Although the sale of a good to a customer by a monopolist for example, may be accomplished with the freely given consent of both buyer and seller, the transaction does not lead to Pareto optimality for

[36] These remarks were inspired by Dr. Pavel Pelikán's comments on an earlier draft of this paper.

[37] See below, Section 5.4.3.

[38] For a definition of Pareto optimality, see section 3.2.

Table 1

Mutuality Basis of Some Interactions Touched Off
By Various Initiating Actions

| Initiating action(s) | Degree of mutuality characterizing interaction | | |
	Mutual agreement	*Pratial mutuality* based on legitimacy of claim or punitive sanction	No mutuality
Offer	Sale of a good	—	—
Rule or order calling for effective action	Payment of check by bank	Subordinate's compliance with an order in a hierarchy	Conscription of individual for military service
Communication	Sale of a patent	Repurchase of good by seller upon disclosure of misrepresentation	Unauthorized adoption of a process described in patent
Threat or other message aimed at exerting influence	—	Wage settlement on threat of strike	Performing forced labor for another individual on threat of life
Implicit message conveyed via effective action	—	Giving of present or favor in expectation or reciprocity	Sabotage, purchase and use of drumset in retaliation against neighbors' piano playing
Unilateral action unheralded by message	—	Traveling in a crowded subway	River pollution, theft

both participants, because there is some income transfer from buyer to seller, accompanied by a reduction in price and an adjustment in the monopolist's output and supply which would make both better off.

An action taken by one or more participants without the explicit consent of the other participants affected is likely to produce a situation deviating from Pareto optimality, whether or not the affected participants are made better or worse off by this action. "Transaction costs" and institutional obstacles may prevent the realization of the potential gains from mutually beneficial exchanges starting from such a nonoptimal situation.[39]

The relative importance of the differing degrees of mutuality and conflict underlying effective actions varies widely from system to system with putative, but not always ascertainable, consequences for the relative efficiency and equity of the systems compared. We have only one remark to make on this score: The effective actions based on orders involving partial or no mutuality as well as those based on complete mutuality all entail costs. No mutuality inflicts losses in efficiency due to the lower productivity of services rendered under compulsion (such as slave labor). In general, incomplete mutuality entails costs due to the necessity of assigning scarce labor to data-collecting, inspection, and control to ensure a close correspondence between orders and complying actions (and the morale effects of such control). In the case of complete mutuality, costs are incurred in making personal contacts, in information exchange and negotiations, in the persuasion necessary to achieve mutuality, in the verification of performance, and in actions to challenge nonperformance.

It may be noted that most effective actions based on mutual agreement involve participations in joint actions that are pairs, triples, or *n*-tuples of simultaneous and complementary single actions. Examples include transfers of custody within or between hierarchies, with or without simultaneous payment, and all loans and contracts for future delivery or performance. Certain rules issued by ruling organizations are designed to induce contracting parties to adhere to these agreements, even in the face of most random events but not of certain improbable events which, when they do occur, tend to be highly correlated and are therefore uninsurable. (These events are known in West as "acts of God.")

In modern systems, either transfer prices or exchange prices are an integral part of virtually all contracts. The *exchange price* offer for a good or service may be defined as an option for transferring to a different entity custody, other property rights, or both of one unit of a good or service against payment of a certain number of units of legal tender at a certain time. A *transfer* price differs from an exchange price only insofar as the option refers to a transfer between component entities of the same hierarchy or quasi-hierarchy rather than between separate entities, and in that actual payment may not be called for (e.g., bookkeeping transactions).

A message containing a price offer expressed in monetary units for a particular good will not generally call forth an acceptance by another

[39] On the relation between degree of mutuality and "externalities" see H. Demsetz, "Toward a Theory of Property Rights," *American Economic Review*, LVII:2 (1967) 347–359 and "The Cost of Transacting," Quarterly Journal of Economics, LXXXII:1 (1968), 33–53.

entity, unless the characteristics of the good have become part of the potential buyer's information set either through direct inspection or because its standardization has led him to expect predictable characteristics. The standardization of commodities effectively widens the intersection (the common subset) of the information sets of potential sellers and buyers and makes it possible for effective interaction to take place with significantly less prior transfer of information.[40] Standardization thus economizes on information costs and facilitates the transfer of goods, irrespective of other rules and patterns of interaction prevailing in a modern system.

5.3. Motivation

In the preceding section we briefly discussed the impact of messages on decision makers in terms of the mutuality that may or may not be required for the interaction to result in an effective action. Consent is, of course, a necessary but not a sufficient condition to be met if the message is to trigger an effective response, especially one consistent with the intent of the sender.[41] Even though, for instance, the legitimacy of a tax law may be recognized, the actual payment may fall short of and be significantly inferior to the amount actually due because of concealment of sources of income. A ministerial order to an enterprise in a centrally coordinated economy may not be carried out, in spite of possible sanctions. Likewise, a contract between two firms in a market economy may not be respected if its fulfillment eventually runs contrary to the essential interests of at least one of the parties. The precise response of a decision maker to an informational action will be conditioned by his motivation, which we have already defined as a function associating with each course of action the utility of the outcome of the probability mixture of expected outcomes.

Each individual in an organization may be presumed to apply his own utility function to the outcome of his actions, but in a hierarchy or quasi-hierarchy the preferences of superiors will tend to constrain the options left to subordinates. Constraints are more likely to be imposed whenever the preferences of superiors and subordinates diverge seriously and the fuller delegation of authority might lead to undesirable outcomes from the

[40] In the case of nonstandardized goods, price catalogues containing detailed information are normally circulated by potential suppliers. This routine, which presupposes experience leading to stable expectations on the part of potential buyers with respect to the accuracy of the information contained in these complex messages, also economizes on the costs of inspection and contact.

[41] Note, however, that under the hypothesis of perfect competition in a market economy, the entity quoting the price is assumed to be agreeable to any response or lack of response. Hence "intent" may not be strictly relevant in this limiting case.

superiors' point of view. The ability of superiors to impose on an organization such preferences as they hold in common will depend in part on the information they are able to collect about the outcomes of subordinates' decisions, as well as on the effectiveness of the sanctions they may administer to subordinates for deviant behavior. Because of the costs of obtaining complete compliance with orders mentioned in Section 5.2, we are led to suspect that a unique goal function cannot be invoked, let alone constructed, which would satisfactorily account for all the decisions made in an organization. Furthermore, in large complex organizations whose component organizations are engaged in different sets of activities, these divergent sets of preferences are likely to be important enough to engender conflicts between components or members or both. Where the size and complexity of organizations are themselves system coordinates, the presence or absence of these conflicts may be of considerable interest to the comparor.

Nevertheless, we shall occasionally refer to the putative goal function of an organization as if the managers were able to effect decisions on the part of their entire personnel consistent with a utility function acceptable to themselves.

To discuss one broad basis of motivation in organizations we shall need the term *profits*. This term applies when the inputs to an entity's activities are transferred from, and the outputs transferred to, the custody of other entities (for the set of activities under consideration.) The profits of an entity per period are then reckoned as the algebraic sum of the (negative) value of inputs and the (positive) value of outputs, both valued at transfer or exchange prices, whichever apply.

On the basis of rather casual observation or indirect reasoning, economic theorists in West have posited that decision makers—especially managers of "enterprises"—acted in such a way as to maximize the value of some outcome function, such as profits in market economies and the income from bonuses for fulfillment and overfulfillment of plan targets in the centrally coordinated economies.

Other economists have criticized these simple explanations of managerial behavior by pointing to the importance of other motives, which often conflict with profit maximization: Managers may wish to limit the time and effort they put into the job; they may prefer steady growth to higher profits; they may maximize their discounted expected utility accruing over time, a maximand that will not coincide with discounted profits if their utility-of-income function is strictly concave; they may choose outcomes that will be satisfactory without being optimal in any sense (as in the "satisficing behavior" described by Herbert Simon[42]); in a large hierarchy they may

[42] See Simon, *Models of Man*, Ch. 14 and 15, and the introduction to Part IV.

balance their immediate earnings against enhanced chances of advancement in the hierarchy, lowered chances of dismissal or punishment, or both.

To cite only one example, the offer of a license for a new technology is likely to be received differently depending on whether the recipient manager maximizes short-run profits, the enterprise's equity (if the system allows for a capital market), the growth rate of his enterprise, or its share of the market for his products over the next three years.

The rules governing the use and disposition of an economy's means of production—objects of a certain durability, capable of being used in a productive activity—usually place constraints on managers' actions and influence the objectives they pursue. Whether a manager of an enterprise maximizes short-run profits or the discounted sum of future profits may depend, for instance, on whether he owns part of the enterprise's means of production (on his "equity" in the enterprise) or at least on whether his income hinges in some way on their efficient utilization or disposition. Ownership refers to legally sanctioned rights of utilization and disposition by individuals or organizations over resources, goods in process, means of production or consumption goods, or over claims to shares in these rights. These rights may be exclusive, or hemmed in by legal or conventional restrictions, such as laws of entail forbidding the parcelling out of estates or their sale to unauthorized entities; or they may be abrogated under certain conditions in favor of the public at large or of ruling organizations (eminent domain, "fair housing" laws, collection of works of art "owned" by foundations that must make provision for the admission of the public).

Ownership normally implies custody, which may be delegated or separated in the case of organizations or individuals whose legal rights have been curtailed (e.g., due to the mental incapacity of an individual or to an enterprise's condition of receivership). In West the delegation of custody by the stockholders of a corporation to its managers may at times turn out to be irreversible, especially if the latter also own stock in it. In any case, ownership of means of production includes the right of the owner or his custodian to buy and sell them and to draw benefits from their productive use, an aspect with important consequences for equity which we shall not dwell on here.

The efficiency of resource allocation in any system must depend to a crucial extent on both the content of messages (e.g., in a market economy on whether prices reflect relative scarcities, or in a centrally coordinated economy on whether orders correspond to efficient input allotments and output targets) and on the responses of the makers of economic decisions to these messages (maximizing behavior in a market economy, compliance with orders implementing the principal production and allocation decisions in a centralized economy). In a competitive market economy, in particular, efficiency cannot be attained unless all resources and means of production are in the custody of some participant and are managed by these participants in such a way as to maximize the discounted stream of their future rents, corresponding to nondiscriminating rentals based on efficiency prices.[43] Access to resources held in common and not subject to such custody and management—pastures, forests, and even arable land in certain developing economies, crowded highways and city streets in developed economies, fishing grounds especially in international waters—is often not sufficiently restricted for their efficient utilization under a market system without the intervention of ruling organizations. Under unrestricted conditions, pastures tend to be overgrazed, timber overcut, land overworked, roads excessively congested, and species of fish threatened with extinction. In the absence of custodial entities restricting access to these resources or man-made facilities, directly or by an efficient rental charge, potential users are guided by the average costs they must bear—e.g., the average congestion delay on a road—which does not take into account the total additional costs imposed on other users by their decision to share in its common utilization.

5.4. Patterns of Interaction

5.4.1. Organizational graphs. In Section 2.3 we have defined an organization for a set of activities as a set of persons regularly interacting with each other in the process of carrying on one or more activities of that set. The theory of *linear graphs* offers a convenient device for representing the organizational structure of a system. Each participant is represented by a point (a *vertex*), each interaction by an *arc* connecting the vertices of the two interacting participants. For each category of interactions of interest, the corresponding graph contains the vertices of all participants engaged in such an interaction and all arcs representing instances of it. The category may be chosen to be strictly functional, such as making offers, accepting offers, supervising; or strictly substantive, such as interacting in truck gardening; or a combination of both, such as trading in vegetables. Figure 1 illustrates the device.

A graph is called *connected* if every pair of vertices in it can be connected by a chain (as defined in Section 2.3) that runs inside the graph. If the graph of all interactions in the system in a category of interest (such as the internal operations of truck gardening anywhere in the system) is not connected, each of its components (maximal connected subgraphs)

[43] For further discussion of the role of pricing in attaining efficient allocation See T. C. Koopmans, *Three Essays on the State of Economic Science*, New York, 1957, Essay I.

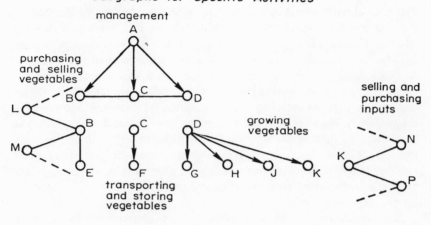

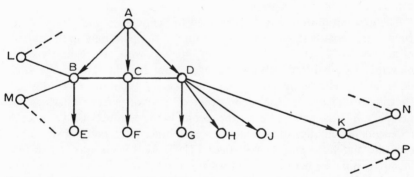

FIGURE 1: Graph for a quasi-hierarchic truck gardening enterprise in open ended association with several markets. Arrows indicate supervision, absence of arrows mutuality

represents a separate organization (a truck gardening enterprise) by the definition given in Section 2.3. If the category of interactions is enlarged (by the inclusion of trading in vegetables, say), a graph previously not connected may become connected.

By a sufficiently inclusive choice of the category of interactions, the entire set of participants in any modern system can be regarded as belonging to one and the same organization as defined. For, every participant is either a member of one of the following groups of interacting persons or belongs to a household that contains a member of one of these groups: 1. employees; 2. members of cooperatives; 3. self-employed or unemployed persons interacting through market relations; 4. institutionalized persons; 5. persons receiving pensions, gifts, or charities. Moreover, it may safely be assumed that there does not exist any subset of persons in the system no member of which interacts in some way with one or more members not in that subset. Thus we can represent and study every modern system through a connected graph generated as the union of the graphs corresponding to a given classification of all pertinent types of interaction.

Some interactions, such as supervision, are asymmetric. In Figure 1, this is represented by adding an arrow pointing from supervisor to supervisee to each such arc. A graph in which all arcs are given a direction is called a *directed graph* (briefly, a *digraph*). In particular, all hierarchies can be represented by digraphs.

The digraph notion may also be used to define an organization somewhat more broadly than we did in Section 2.3. Suppose that, in the pursuit of activities of a set A, person i either interacts with j or regularly sends messages to j without getting messages from him in return. We shall describe this relation by writing that i addresses j. We now draw a digraph showing a directed arc for each "ordered" pair of persons in which the first person in the pair addresses the second in the conduct of a given set of independent activities. If both address each other ("interact"), two arcs of opposite directions join their vertices. (This may, for instance, occur in a hierarchy if a member imparts information to his supervisor or to a higher superordinate, at the latter's request.) Call a *directed chain* a sequence i, k, l, ..., p, q of members (vertices) such that (i, k), (k, l), ..., (p, q) indicate directed arcs of the graph. An organization for a set A of activities is then represented by a graph such that each pair of vertices, say (i, q), is connected by a directed chain. (This implies that another chain for the pair (q, i) must also occur in the graph.)

For the study of the internal structure of organizations, especially hierarchies, engaged in several activities a slightly different interpretation of the organizational graph may be preferable, and will be used in Section 5.4.3. In this interpretation a vertex represents not a person, but the pairing of a person with an activity, which we shall call an *assignment*.[44] This device allows the same person to have different supervisors for different activities.

5.4.2. Organizational change. If we choose a period of time short enough to be able to disregard change in the number of participants in the system, we may represent the creation or dissolution of an organization merely as a change in the graph for the entire system. A complete system description, however, may have to keep a record of the organizations to which the members of a new organization formerly belonged, because they will contribute to the new organization information that would otherwise be unavailable to its members. For example, the reorganization of Soviet industry in 1957 involved the creation of new assignments and supervision relations and thereby brought into existence a new set of organizations comprising virtually the same set of participants as belonged to the old system. The chains of supervision that used to follow industrial lines (sets of industrial activities) now followed regional lines, at least for directors of enterprises and their superiors in the complete hierarchy for the Soviet economy. The members of the new organizations contributed their experience of previous activities and interactions in another organizational structure. These antecedents may have helped to smooth the transition to the new system.[45]

Every description of an organizational change in a system may thus be said to involve two sets of coordinates, one set belonging to the system before the change and one to the new state. The first set describes the procedures for modifying the system and identifies the persons belonging to one or more organizations of the old system who have the power to initiate or to carry out such changes or both. The second set describes the interactions between members of the new organizations and between them and persons still belonging to those old organizations from which they were recruited. Significant differences between systems may be detected in data pertinent to these coordinates. In particular, if the head of a new hierarchy remains subordinate to a member of one of the parent hierarchies, we may speak of the *centralized* creation of new organizations, a system trait with implications for attaining pertinent desiderata.

The creation of new and the dissolution of old organizations is also a crucial factor in the intertemporal efficiency of an economy in any system. New organizations usually are not confined to the activities of the organizations from which their personnel has been recruited. They are a vehicle for introducing new technologies and patterns of organization as

---

[44] The term allows an activity to be self-assigned.

[45] This interesting observation was made by Professor Arthur Wright in an informal talk at the Economic Growth Center of Yale University.

well as new modes of interaction with other entities. The dissolution of old organizations often does away with inefficient routines that cannot be eliminated without restructuring existing patterns of interaction. In East, ruling organizations have the exclusive responsibility for creating and winding up "enterprises on cost accounting," that is, economic organizations calculating their costs, receipts, profits and losses, and paying a part of their profits to, or receiving subsidies from, superior entities in the hierarchy. In part because rates of industrial growth are high in this group of countries and new supervisory personnel is systematically trained in educational institutions, the creation of such new enterprises can usually be effected without dissolving old ones, and rarely encounters effective opposition from vested interests.[46] In West (as well perhaps as in Yugoslavia) new enterprises frequently represent a serious threat to existing ones, especially if they compete for the same markets. To forestall such threats, existing enterprises may, and often do, resort to various devices to prevent newcomers from intruding on their territory, often with adverse effects on equity and on consumers' sovereignty. Access to the industry (the set of activities in which existing firms are engaged) may be restricted by the rules and orders of ruling organizations, or by barring potential newcomers either from their markets or from the resources required for their operations with the cooperation of banks, labor unions, railroads, and other organizations enjoying a protected status in their own industry. Attempts to engross trade to protect interests vested in existing organizations are not confined to privately owned enterprises. We conjecture that they will occur whenever 1) the interests of the managers of enterprises, whether publicly or privately owned, are bound up with the financial results of their enterprise's activities, 2) means to restrict unwanted entry exist, and 3) the heads of the threatened organizations do not perceive competition as being in the interest of the larger hierarchy of which they are a part. In Great Britain, for example, nationalized enterprises fend off competition from other nationalized enterprises, especially within the fuels and transportation sectors. Apparently no ruling organization is sufficiently mindful of the interests of the consumers of the products of these nationalized industries to defend them against the successful efforts of these industries to protect their markets.

5.4.3. Hierarchies and quasi-hierarchies. From here on we shall limit ourselves to a consideration of existing organizations, and resume our

---

[46] Where growth ceases or slackens, as happened in Czechoslovakia in the 1960s, the restructuring of organizations to promote efficiency presents acute problems, especially where it entails the dissolution of organizations in the less developed parts of the country.

discussion of hierarchies[47] and quasi-hierarchies. We now take the view that the supervision relation applies to assignments rather than to members. We stipulate in addition that supervision of a member in an activity implies that the supervisor is also (at least nominally) engaged in that activity.

To ensure the comparability of hierarchies embedded in dissimilar systems, the supervision relation should be broadly interpreted. An order issued by a supervisor may consist in the delegation of responsibility for certain tasks to a member of the organization or to a committee; a supervisor may also settle conflicts by arbitration, parcel out scarce resources, and so forth. Consultation of experts and mediation of conflicts, however, would not be covered by the supervision relation, because the advice or decisions of consultants and mediators usually have suasive rather than coercive power. In almost all hierarchies, subordinates may, under certain conditions, appeal to members of the organization standing above their supervisor for the activities connected with an order if they consider this order illegal (according to the rules of the organization or of the ruling organization to which it is subject) or if they deem the order extremely deleterious to their interests or to those of the part of the organization for which they hold or share responsibility. Subordinates may also kick upstairs problems that they are unable or unwilling to solve on their own. Although the simple conceptual scheme in Sections 2.3, 5.3, and 5.5 does not make explicit allowance for the right of appeal or for the referral of troublesome questions to higher ups for final decisions, it is flexible enough to encompass these variants of the supervision relation.

It follows from statements in Section 2.3 that the organization graph for the supervisory relation in a hierarchy for a single activity is what is called in graph theory a *tree*. The tree starts with the head of the hierarchy and, in the usual reproduction of an organization table, grows downward, ramifying at every vertex representing a participant supervising more than one other participant in the activity in question. A hierarchy in which all assignments involve one and the same activity is called a *hierarchy for a single activity*. It is called *complete* if 1) every branch of the tree has been traced down to the last participant supervised in the activity in question, and 2) if the head has no supervisor in the activity.

A *hierarchy for a set of activities* is a set of assignments and a supervision relation on that set, which can be thought of as obtained by joining (forming the *union* of) two or more hierarchies for a single activity, all of

[47] For a wide-ranging discussion of hierarchical structures in nature and in society, see H. A. Simon, "The Architecture of Complexity," *Proceedings of the American Philisophical Society*, CVI:6 (1962) 469–482.

which have the same person at the head. This head is then simultaneously engaged as ultimate supervisor in all the activities in which the hierarchy engages. Such a hierarchy is called a *complete hierarchy* if i) every component hierarchy is itself complete and ii) the hierarchy cannot be enlarged by admitting further hierarchies for additional activities. Under certain restrictions it can be shown[48] that, as a logical implication of these definitions, every assignment in the system belongs to precisely one complete hierarchy. (In the case of a self-employed person, this could be a one-man hierarchy.)

Examples for a market economy: The personnel of the blast furnace department in an integrated steel plant make up a hierarchy for activity a where a is the making of pig iron. The entire steel plant under one owner-head is a hierarchy for A, the set of all activities involved in the making of steel. The plant will be a complete hierarchy for A if the head of the steel plant is superior to every employee in the plant, irrespective of that employee's assignment in A (such as, for instance, the head of its medical service, whose assignment is an ancillary activity in A). However, should ownership rest with a body of stockholders supervising the head through a board of directors, then these two collective participants would need to be added before the hierarchy can be called complete for A. Finally, should the *same* body of stockholders also own and effectively supervise one other manufacturing enterprise, then this enterprise would have to be added in before the hierarchy can be called complete.

In a Soviet-type economy, the set of all persons either in the government supervising economic activities or in socialized economic sectors, together with the Communist Party hierarchy, including the Politbureau of the Central Committee, may be said to form a complete hierarchy. Under the above definitions, however, the use of this term is based on the presumption that no person engaged in a given activity is directly supervised *in the exercise of that activity* by both a Party member and by a different member of the government hierarchy. In other words, one-man leadership (*edinonachalie*) is assumed to prevail: Party channels are used to convey orders pertinent to Party activities (including control of the direction of economic activities exercised by members of the government hierarchy) and government channels to convey orders pertinent to the activities of the government hierarchy. To the extent that this principle is regularly violated, we should be dealing with one or more quasi-hierarchies. Yet we suggest that the fit may be close enough to warrant a discussion of the Soviet economy in terms of a complete hierarchy and its component hierarchies.

[48] For further details, see T. C. Koopmans, "Note on a Social System Composed of Hierarchies with Overlapping Personnel", *Orbis Economicus* (Organ of the Circle of Amsterdam Economists), XIII:3/4, (1969) 61–71.

Before the principle of one-man leadership was established and enforced in the Soviet system in the early 1930's, there were parallel lines of command, and many members of the quasi-hierarchy were subject to the orders of several immediate superiors—typically in the government, the Communist Party, and the trade unions—in the exercise of the same function.[49] The elimination of at least some of the overlapping or criss-crossing lines of command, particularly at lower levels, presumably made for greater efficiency in this case. Where objectives and priority among them are clearly defined for all decision makers, and where actions must be taken rapidly in response to orders, we suspect that quasi-hierarchies are less efficient than hierarchies. In other situations, including research and development activities, the case for a unique line of command is much less evident.

5.4.4. Two conjectures. We now define key attributes of hierarchies to be used in the conjectures. The *length* of any chain between two members i and j of the hierarchy is the number of members in the chain, including i and j. The *height* of the hierarchy is defined as the length of the longest chain extending from the head of the hierarchy to a member who is not superior to any other member in the hierarchy in any of its activities. A *tier* is the set of all persons related to the head of the hierarchy by chains of the same length (the head being the first tier).

The information drawn by superiors in a hierarchy from the information sets of subordinates, from their own environment, or from both depends on the activities that have been assigned to them (control, resolution of disputes within the hierarchy, coordination of interdependent activities, and so forth). To be carried out efficiently, the coordination by a superior of a sequence of interdependent activities requires detailed knowledge of each of the procurement, production, transportation, and transfer activities in the sequence as well as of the possibilities of substituting other activities for some of these wherever this may be efficient. To acquire this detailed knowledge himself, a superior might have to extract from his subordinates virtually their entire information sets. There are, however, limits to this information-collecting process: Information is expensive to collect; the capacity of superiors to process, store, and retrieve information is limited; and information that is not immediately communicated becomes obsolete as the participants' environment changes. With improvements in the technology and equipment for information–handling, these constraints have become less stringent. Nevertheless, whether information has been obtained from samples or aggregated from exhaustive reports, in transferring it from each tier to the next, losses and distortions in content and delays have remained unavoidable.

[49] See G. Bienstock, S. Schwartz and A. Yugow, *Management in Russian Industry and Agriculture*, Oxford (1944) 13 and 35.

A superior in a higher tier desiring to avoid such losses of information may send inspectors to the field (e.g., to the lowest tier) or try to see for himself. As we already pointed out in Section 5.3, however, inspection whether carried out by the highly placed member himself or by other members of his hierarchy[50] is expensive in terms of alternative uses of the personnel involved.

The interdependence between activities may hinge on the circumstances of a given moment, so that a particular assignment may be efficient for certain environments but not for others. In the face of this complexity, superordinates may not perceive the best opportunities for scheduling activities in a concrete situation. Thus the efficiency of assignment of activities, as well as their coordination, depends on the information available in the coordinating tier.

Let us now make the extreme assumption, which will later be relaxed, that no two members of a given hierarchy not in the same chain of supervision and responsible for different but interdependent activities can engage in informational interaction with each other. Coordination is thus effected exclusively through common superiors in the hierarchy. Suppose further that we take as given the quality of supervising personnel, the amount and accuracy of the information required by superiors to make effective coordination decisions, and all other variables affecting the efficiency of such decisions.

One would then seek to assign activities in a hierarchy in such a way that the most highly interdependent activities would be assigned to members with a common supervisor. When this assignment exceeded a supervisor's efficient span of control, it would become necessary to assign some still strongly interdependent activities to members whose nearest common superior was two (or more) tiers up the chain of command. Our presumption is that the number and degrees of interdependencies of activities in a modern economy are such, relative to the efficient span of control of supervisors, that even the best feasible assignment of activities from the point of view of efficient coordination through superiors would still leave pairs of activities of substantial interdependence to be coordinated by a nearest common superior many tiers up the chain. (Example: weaving fabrics for the upholstery of automobiles and making automobile bodies.)

Consider two hierarchies H and H', say, two plants initially engaged in disjoint sets of activities A and A' that have substantial interdependence between activities a, a' of the two sets, respectively. We conjecture that the

---

[50] The high-tier member normally is fully occupied with the information flowing to him through channels; attempts by that member to bypass them in seeking more precise or up-to-date information will usually entail delays in attending to current affairs.

longer the chains (for the interdependent activities) between the two heads of *H* and *H'* and their nearest common superior, the more likely it is that each of the two plants will initiate activities already belonging to the set of the other. Each will do so, we reason, because it will wish to ensure better coordination with its own activities of some of the activities initially carried on in the other plant. Furthermore, its incentive for this expansion will be the stronger, the more ineffective the coordination by the common superior in the initial situation. This ineffectiveness, we presume, will be the more serious the longer the chains separating the common superior from the heads of the two plants. How many common activities both plants will ultimately undertake will depend on variables other than the economies of information, such as the availability of equipment and other factors affecting costs of production (to the extent that costs matter).

Suppose that in the initial situation the two plants had been permitted and encouraged to interact directly, that is, to exchange information and to coordinate their own activities within certain limits set by their superiors. The incentive for *organizational autarky*—the phenomenon we have just described—would have been weaker. We conjecture that if complete mutuality were permitted, including the exchanges of goods or services at mutually acceptable prices, specialization between any two hierarchies in the system would be carried further than under a more restrictive arrangement.

We suspect that the phenomenon of autarky among hierarchies that may or may not belong to the same complete hierarchy occurs both in centrally coordinated and in market economies. We suggest that it might be instructive to study whether or not weaknesses in the coordinating functions of markets in these economies show up in the inefficient pursuit of an excessively wide range of activities in existing enterprises.[51] Or, to put the same point in a different way, we wonder whether the existence of small, highly specialized enterprises in certain developed market economies is not rendered possible by the presence of smoothly functioning markets for the inputs and the products of these enterprises' activities. In the case of the centrally coordinated economies of the Soviet Union and of Eastern Europe, evidence has frequently been cited of enterprises engaging in a very wide gamut of ancillary activities—such as maintaining inventories, facilities for producing crucial inputs, personnel engaged in procuring

[51] For example, it has been observed that the privately owned and operated railroads in the United States sometimes found it to mutual advantage to do classification work (assembling or reassembling cars into trains) for each other. However, if the need of railroad A for such work by railroad B lacked a reverse need, no trade took place because the practices of the industry did not include making money payments for such services.

inputs, repair facilities for machinery—the apparent or sometimes explicit aim being that of protecting themselves from the vagaries of an undependable centrally supervised distribution system. A verifiable implication of our conjecture is that plants belonging to different ministries would be more likely to take over each other's activities than those belonging to the same ministry, because their lowest common superior would be further up the hierarchy and there would presumably be less direct interaction between them.

We now set forth a related conjecture involving the conflicting interests of two hierarchies engaged in production activities which possess heads who are in the same tier of their complete hierarchy. We assume that both hierarchies have custody of their means of production and that the remuneration of at least some members with decision-making power in either organization depends on the outcomes of the activities of their respective organizations (such as volume of output, costs, sales proceeds, profits, and so forth).

Suppose now that some members of one of the two hierarchies, in the pursuit of its objectives and without prior agreement with the other, undertake an activity that adversely affects outcomes of the other. Suppose also that the decision makers in the adversely affected hierarchy cannot or may not obtain, through mutual agreement, compensation for the action that is fully equivalent in their preferences to its adverse effect. The action has thus given rise to an "external diseconomy."

If the heads of the two hierarchies involved on both sides of this action are supervised by the same member of a complete hierarchy, the conflict of interests will normally come to his attention. The common superior may or may not order that compensation be made, possibly depending on the effect of such action on the interests of the component hierarchy which he heads (strictly speaking, depending on the superior's interpretation of these interests). He will also have to decide whether a repetition of the action should or should not be prevented by a restraining order. If, however, this nearest common superior is several tiers up, the matter will be more difficult to resolve to the satisfaction of either organization, because the common superior will have less accurate information about the interests affected than a supervisor. We conjecture, therefore, that the likelihood of an efficient resolution of conflicts of this type will be the smaller, the longer the chain separating the parties in the dispute from their nearest common superior.

The conjectures on the efficient coordination of interdependent activities and on the efficient resolution of conflicts involving external diseconomies are clearly two facets of the same general problem of optimizing the interaction between two entities in a complete hierarchy when a mutually satisfactory cooperation is precluded by the rules and orders of superiors, by high transaction costs, or because the interests of the parties cannot be reconciled without such rules and orders (e.g., through mutuality).[52]

Indeed in a market system an entity inflicting damage on another will generally not feel compelled to compensate the latter for its losses or even to abstain from inflicting further damage. However, ruling organizations, through the issuance of rules restraining the behavior of private organizations, through nationalization orders followed by such restraints, or through the compulsory merger[53] of the conflicting entities, may be in a position to salvage some measure of efficiency in these situations. However, the serious pollution of the air over such cities as Chicago, Los Angeles, and Budapest suggests that those problems cannot easily be solved either in market or in centrally coordinated systems.

6. Interaction Between Systems

Since the boundaries between systems more or less coincide with boundaries between nations, interactions between nonruling entities in different systems cannot be discussed without at the same time considering interactions between governments pursuing political as well as economic objectives. One may take the view that the determination of the fraction of output allocated to military preparedness and other policy decisions that may affect the risk or the probable outcome of armed conflict are exogenous to economic systems but have to be taken into account as important environmental factors in studying both the operation and interaction of systems. One may alternatively regard both the political and economic interactions between systems as interdependent parts of a larger complex and consider the chain of causation *from* the economic and political traits of these systems, *through* their political and economic policies and interactions, *to* their presumed effects on pertinent desiderata such as the level of consumption, the risks of limited or large-scale loss of life, goods and resources, and the risk of impairment of national independence.

Whichever view one takes, the economic interactions between ruling

[52] It was argued in Section 5.2 that "externalities" create situations where mutually advantageous transactions are possible provided that all parties affected may freely interact and transaction costs are low. Restrictions on interaction may have complicated the Lake Baikal dispute in the Soviet Union between papermills polluting the water and the fisheries. There are also frequent cases where negotiations cannot take place because the perpetrator cannot readily communicate with the entities he adversely affects. How can people who would like to swim in a river, *if* it were not polluted, be compensated?

[53] A suggestion made by L. Hurwicz, "Conditions for Economic Efficiency of Centralized and Decentralized Structures" in G. Grossman, ed., *Value and Plan* Berkeley, 1960, pp. 162–175.

or nonruling entities belonging to two or more economies with similar or different systems reflect system traits, or rather traits of constellations of systems, which are of great interest in the present context.

Over the last century, the economic interactions between entities belonging to different nation-states have become ever closer and more intensive. These interactions may be classified into three groups. They may involve: 1) the transfer across state or system boundaries of goods, services, patents, licenses, franchises, news and weather information, and the movement of tourists consuming goods and services; 2) contacts between members of organizations whose membership or range of activities extends across these boundaries, including all interactions such as direct investments, transfers of know-how, and so forth, taking place within multi-national, privately or publicly owned companies and other international organizations; and 3) other informational interactions, such as exchanges of students or scholars in pertinent professions; informal contacts between members of labor unions located in different countries but not belonging to the same international union; exchanges of views between business or government leaders of different states who are not members of the same complete hierarchies, and others.

These more strictly economic interactions across systems may likewise affect every desideratum listed in Section 3. They have special relevance for y_1 and y_2, insofar as international specialization promotes the efficiency of allocation in each economy participating in trade and, withal, the level of living of its nationals and the economy's growth in per capita consumption. Since some of these interactions are often thought to interfere with y_5 (stability of employment and incomes) and y_6 (national strength and prestige), the governments of the nation-states responsible for regulating these interactions frequently evaluate their decisions in this area of policy in terms of a trade-off between the advantages they perceive in interactions across state boundaries through desiderata y_1 and y_2 and their disadvantages due to losses expected through y_5 and y_6.

The second group of interactions is of special interest in view of our emphasis on organizations. These interactions nowadays frequently take place within multi-national organizations, structured as complete hierarchies, embracing activities carried out in more than one nation or employing personnel belonging to several nations, or both. The executives situated at their apex impose more or less uniform rules, procedures, and patterns of organization over component organizations located in countries with widely disparate systems and levels of development. This relatively new phenomenon, together with the accelerated mobility of executives across national borders and the even more pronounced trend toward training executive personnel according to certain common precepts of business efficiency, in West, South, and also in Yugoslavia, has tended to diminish the differences between the patterns of organization prevailing in those groups of countries.

Private multi-national organizations are normally subject to the laws issued by the ruling organizations of the countries in which they have been founded or incorporated. In some instances, these laws govern the permissible actions of the foreign affiliates of the organization as well as of the components of the organization situated in domestic territory. These circumstances may produce jurisdictional disputes in cases where a component organization is nominally subject to the conflicting laws of two or more nations. It may also enable the ruling organization of one country to extend the reach of its strategic policies beyond its boundaries. For example, the United States has been able to impose certain restrictions on trade with Eastern Europe on affiliates of American enterprises incorporated in Western Europe.

In view of these possibilities, the government leaders of nation-states frequently look askance at the growth in their countries of the affiliates of multi-national enterprises. Among other reasons they fear that their foreign economic policies will be subverted by these organizations, which operate within their territories and thereby escape some of the provisions regulating across-system interactions. The protection of indigenous economic organizations, the advancement of nationals in preference to foreigners in the affiliates of multinational organizations situated on home territory, and the broad diffusion of available know-how and innovations are some of the areas where government leaders and representatives of multi-national companies have come into conflict.[54] When nation-states have been weak, as in some parts of South, it has at times been possible for multi-national companies to influence, if not to dominate, their governments, thereby resolving the conflicts in their favor. Colonialism and the dominant relation referred to in East, South, and some parts of West as neocolonialism are extreme versions of this same phenomenon.

Multi-national enterprises may, on the other hand, mitigate incipient conflicts between states because the web of common interests they have woven cannot be undone without palpable harm to all parties concerned. This statement applies especially to multi-national organizations that are under the joint management of several nation-states, such as the European Coal and Steel Community, or under the supervision of an international organization, such as the United Nations.

Governments in West have usually assumed at least partial responsibility for those economic activities of their nationals which transcend their state boundaries. It is usually up to the branches of the government dealing with foreign affairs to avert or to moderate the conflicts which these

[54] See, in particular, R. Vernon, "Economic Sovereignty at Bay," *Foreign Affairs*, XLVII:1 (1968) 114–117.

nationals, operating by themselves or within private or public organizations, may engender in conducting their activities abroad. The comparor can only note that the resentments aroused by certain types of economic interactions may not always be fully realized by all the governments concerned. For this reason, we have formulated a separate desideratum bearing on the co-existence characteristics of systems that would evaluate negatively characteristics that may jeopardize the political relations between states.

The authors are indebted to Gabriel Almond, Abram Bergson, Joseph Berliner, Albert O. Hirschman, Truus W. Koopmans, Janos Kornai, Charles E. Lindblom, Leon Lipson, Richard Loewenthal, Alan S. Manne, Thomas Marschak, Pavel Pelikán, Frank P. Penna, Frederic L. Pryor, Herbert A. Simon, Harvey M. Wagner, Martin Weitzman, and Arthur F. Wright for valuable information and comment.

3

Centralization and Decentralization in Economic Processes

by LEONID HURWICZ

1. Background

Interest in alternative economic structures can be traced to antiquity: Plato's *Republic* illustrates the possibilities of state planning, while Aristotle points out the disadvantages of collective ownership. Over centuries, humanity has resorted to a variety of institutional settings serving as background for the economic process. These settings, sometimes idealized into "economic systems," have been a subject of systematic comparative study, until recently primarily descriptive in nature.

Philosophers and scholars, however, have not had the field all to themselves. Those dissatisfied with their economic environment have often felt that the system itself is to be blamed and that it should be replaced by a different structure. Such views were implicit in the various "Utopias," of which Plato's *Republic* is a forerunner. In addition to More's imaginary island community which is responsible for the term, these included Bacon's *New Atlantis* and Campanella's *Civitas Solis*. But it is only in the early nineteenth century that the idea of replacing the existing economic system by a new one comes into full view in the writings, as well as actual experimentation, of the early socialists (Owen, Saint-Simon, Fourier). While some, at least, of the socialist schemes called for a measure of centralized control of the economic activities, an alternative direction of structural change—away from governmental power and toward voluntary association of independent units—was envisaged by Proudhon and his anarchist successors.

In a less radical form, the debate concerning the role of the government in relation to the economic process has been among the most striking features of the development of economic thought. This discussion occurred, for instance, during the transition from mercantilism in the direction of laissez-faire during the eighteenth century, with Adam Smith as one of the famous protagonists, and again, over a century and a half later, in the context of controlling, or at least moderating, the fluctuations in employment and prices.

2. The Issue

The early developments just sketched have in common two features of importance in the present context. First, they are largely normative in that they look toward a better economic system than that which prevails. In this respect, they are to be classified with modern welfare economics. True, much welfare economics deals with evaluation of alternative resource allocations or distributions, but—directly or indirectly—there is implied an assessment of alternative economic structures (e.g., perfect competition versus monopoly or oligopoly).

Second, a common dichotomy is at issue. The comparative merits of alternative systems are typically being debated under such labels as centralization against decentralization, social control or planning against free markets, or in similar terms. This dichotomy was present in the famous Mises-Hayek-Lange-Lerner controversy concerning the feasibility of socialism, and it persists today even in the distinction between two "socialist" economies, that of the USSR (the "command economy") and of Yugoslavia (the "socialist market economy").

A survey of the literature will show that issues concerning the proper internal structure of business and other large organizations involves similar dichotomies. Decentralization is a fashionable slogan in many corporations. Decentralization is a popular idea among advocates of "participatory democracy" as well as critics of present-day industrial society. Decentralization is also part of the cure proposed for the ills that plague our universities, witness recent events on many campuses. (Paul Goodman's discussion in *People or Personnel* is perhaps symptomatic.[1])

The current (though by no means universal) predilection for decentralization contrasts somewhat with the emphasis a few decades ago on the merits of (central) planning as against the dangers of (decentralized) chaos of "free" markets.

3. Analytical Approach

Even if one were tempted to conclude that the issue of economic centralization is subject to cyclical swings of fashion much like the length of feminine garments, clarification would be needed of the basic terms used in the debate. Contrary to a superficial impression, it is far from obvious what is meant by the statement that "the free market with free individual enterprises offers the well-known example of a complete decentralization of production decisions . . ."[2] Certain iterative procedures involving

[1] Goodman, Paul, *People or Personnel, Decentralizing and the Mixed Systems*, New York, 1968.

[2] Tinbergen, Jan, *Central Planning*, New Haven, 1964, pp. 84–85.

information feedback between a planning agency and producing units may be regarded as decentralized by some and as centralized by others.

Similarly, the terms planning and markets, so central in certain debates, have contradictory uses. Galbraith, in *The New Industrial State*, speaks of industrial "planning" in describing phenomena (price formations) which other economists might classify under market system, but which Galbraith regards as eliminating market influences.[3]

While there is leeway in the nature of definitions that one may wish to adopt, orderly discussion, and even description, is impossible without some definitions. It is perhaps characteristic of the state of the literature in this field that we may be provided with a definition of what it means to have a more or less centralized (decentralized) market economy and another definition of what it means to have a more or less centralized command economy, but no definition of "decentralization" to clarify the meaning of the statement that a market economy is decentralized in comparison with a command economy.[4]

But the need for conceptual clarification goes beyond a scholar's natural desire to bring verbal order into classical controversy. A discussion, conducted at least to some extent in a normative spirit, concerning both historically observed and nonexistent idealized economic structures must have an important analytical element. To make such analysis possible, we shall construct a model of rather general nature, so that a variety of economic structures can be regarded as its special cases. Once the model has been constructed, such concepts as centralization, decentralization, command, or planning, can be defined in terms of the properties of the model. It then becomes possible to proceed with analysis and to try to answer, within the framework of the model, questions about the feasibility of certain organizational structures in relation to assumptions concerning the economic environment. An example of such a question is whether decentralization without loss of optimal properties is possible in the presence of externalities.

4. A General Model of the Economic Process

We picture the economic process as consisting of two *phases*. In the first phase, the economic agents (producers, consumers, resource holders, government agencies) exchange "messages" (proposals, bids, plans, information about technology or preferences). In the second phase, these messages are translated into plans of action (production, exchange) for the various units and ultimately into decisions to be actually implemented.

[3] Galbraith, J. K., *The New Industrial State*, Boston, 1967.
[4] Grossman, Gregory, *Economic Systems*, Englewood Cliffs, N.J., 1967, p. 21.

For such a process to be well-defined, we must first specify the nature of the first phase. To begin with, we must specify the *language* in which communication takes place. For instance, in the conventional model of a (perfect) market, messages specify either points (vectors) in the commodity space (input-output vectors or commodity bundles being exchanged) or price vectors. But this type of language is inadequate for the sort of communication involved in planning. On the one hand, a planning agency may be specifying not just one input-output vector (as would be the case for an individual firm), but many—one for each sector or enterprise under its supervision; similarly it may specify not just one trade vector (as would be the case for an individual engaged in barter), but many—one for each entity under it. Messages of such multiple type can be regarded as special cases of *resource flow matrices*, which I have defined elsewhere.[5]

But even the language of resource flow matrices is insufficient to cover messages whose content describes the economic environment (technology, preferences, resource endowment). Yet in a planning system where individual producing units communicate their technologies to a central planning agency these more complex messages must be available. We see that the specification of the language to be used is a very important feature of model construction and may have decisive influence on the possibility of centralization within the given organizational structure. (The language will be denoted by M.)

The first phase, in general, is thought of as iterative in nature, i.e., it consists of a sequence of *stages*. A given stage is characterized by the messages emitted by various economic agents. The message emitted by agent i in stage s will be denoted by the symbol m_s^i. By definition, every message is an element of the language M. If the agents are labelled 1, 2, ..., n, there is produced in each stage a message n-tuple $(m_s^1, \ldots, m_s^n)$, written briefly as m_s. The iteration starts with an initial message n-tuple m_0, to be followed by m_1, m_2, ..., m_{T-1}, and the terminal message n-tuple m_T. (This notation is related to that in Malinvaud, but is not identical with it.[6] In particular, m_T does not correspond to Malinvaud's "plan" P^S, since in our model the "plan" is formulated in the second phase of the process.)

For the process to be well-defined, it is essential to specify how the message n-tuple of a given stage is formulated in relation to the messages of the preceding phases; also, there must be a rule to determine the initial

[5] Hurwicz, Leonid, "Optimality and Informational Efficiency in Resource Allocation Processes" in K. Arrow *et al.*, eds., *Mathematical Methods in the Social Sciences*, Palo Alto, 1959.

[6] Malinvaud, E., "Decentralized Procedures for Planning," in E. Malinvaud and M. O. L. Bacharach, eds., *Activity Analysis in the Theory of Growth and Planning*, New York, 1967, pp. 170–208.

messages. (These rules and relations may be probabilistic in nature.) The rule relating messages of a given stage to their predecessors are called *response functions*, the response function of the *i*-th unit at stage *s* being denoted by f_s^i. In general, the response depends not only on earlier messages but also on the unit's information concerning the *environment* (technology, preferences, resource endowment); our symbol for a complete specification of the environment is *e*. When the description of the environment can be split into separate descriptions e^i, pertaining respectively to the economic units, we may think of *e* as an *n*-tuple of the *individual environmental components* e^i, so that $e = (e^1, \ldots, e^n)$.

In the literature of the decentralization problem much emphasis has been placed on cases in which the *i*-th economic unit can only be presumed to know its own environmental component e^i (its own technology, preferences, resource endowment), at least in the initial phase (*dispersion* of information). Of course, the messages received in the course of phase one may provide at least partial information about environmental components of other units. This may be incidental to the nature of the process or it may be the purpose of certain stages of communication as in a planned economy where the central agency is assumed to collect technological information from units under its supervision.

The dependence of response on the preceding messages and the knowledge of the environment may be expressed by the equation system

$$m_s^i = f_s^i(m_{s-1}, m_{s-2}, \ldots, m_0; e) \qquad i = 1, 2, \ldots, n, \qquad s = 1, 2, \ldots, T.$$

The determination of the initial messages can similarly be written as

$$m_0^i = f_0^i(e) \qquad i = 1, 2, \ldots, n.$$

(Although stochastic *f*'s can and have been used, we shall primarily discuss the problem with reference to nonprobabilistic response rules.)

Two features of the response relations deserve comment. First, we have allowed for the possibility that the response at every stage may be based on information (messages) from *all* previous stages all the way back to the initial one. Malinvaud's model (in his Ch. V) calls for such accumulation of information obtained by the central planning agency from the various producing units concerning feasible input-output vectors.[7] On the other hand, many processes, as for instance the Walrasian competitive market process, can be formulated as first-order difference equations, so that the response function depends on the immediately preceding message but not on earlier ones. This type of a *first-order* process can be written as

$$m_s^i = f_s^i(m_{s-1}; e) \qquad i = 1, 2, \ldots, n, \qquad s = 1, 2, \ldots, T.$$

[7] *Ibid.*

The distinction between processes of finite order (such as first-order processes) and those that accumulate past information indefinitely is of considerable importance. We shall see that informational decentralization requires that the information available to any one participant in the process be limited. This limitation may be achieved with the help of restrictions on the nature of the message language M. Such restrictions, intended to preclude the possibility of a given unit completely communicating its environmental component (e.g., its preferences or technology) to a central agency, may however be rendered ineffective when indefinite accumulation of past messages is permitted. It is therefore essential to formulate simultaneous restrictions on the process both with regard to its language and its order (as a difference equation).

Second, we have also allowed for the possibility of varying the response rule as between stages; this is indicated by the subscript s (denoting the stage) attached to the response function symbol f_s^i. Processes free of such variability (i.e., where f_s^i is the same for all $s = 1, \ldots, T$), which may be called temporally homogeneous, are of particular interest. (Temporal homogeneity does not require that all the functions f_0^i be the same.) Again, the Walrasian process does possess this special property. However, certain formalizations of the market process, in particular those involving a "referee," as in T. Marschak's model, lack this homogeneity.[8] They resemble the type of dialogue envisaged by Malinvaud between the central planning agency and the individual producing entities. These dialogue processes exhibit a sort of cyclical homogeneity, in the sense that $f_s^i = f_{s-2}^i$. Basically, there are two fixed response patterns respectively for even-numbered and odd-numbered stages. Similarly, there may be two languages. In Malinvaud's terminology, one is called prospective indices and the second proposals.

The centralized process described by T. Marschak, on the other hand, lacks temporal homogeneity, because its early stages involve collecting environmental information by the center from other units to be processes by the center during the intermediate stages, with action commands to be transmitted from the center in the terminal stages through m_T.

The message n-tuple m_T produced in the terminal stage serves as the basis for decisions as to actions to be taken. The language of the terminal messages may or may not be that of possible actions. If not, one must, as it were, decode the terminal messages. Ideally, the decoded terminal message should provide for a feasible action plan. But in many cases it may turn out to be a set of mutually inconsistent action proposals, which we may call the *paper plan*.[9] For instance, the paper plan may specify the

[8] Marschak, Thomas, "Centralization and Decentralization in Economic Organizations, *Econometrica*, 27:3 (1959) 399–430.
[9] What is here for the sake of brevity called a "paper plan" may actually be an unreconciled complex of individual plans.

quantities demanded and supplied by the various units, although excess demand may not be equal to zero. It would then be necessary to make a transition from such a paper plan to a (by definition feasible) *real plan*. [This could, for instance, be done by scaling down (or up) all (paper plan) demands proportionately until they equal the supply available under the paper plan, if we assume that the only feasibility difficulty lies in the inconsistency of the plans (i.e., that all aspects of the paper plan are *individually* feasible) and that the scaling down or up does not destroy individual feasibility.] The transition from the paper plan to the real plan might also be iterative in nature, but we shall ignore this possibility. Our real plan corresponds to Malinvaud's "plan" P^S, which he explicitly requires to be feasible, as is true of the real plan in this paper. (He does not introduce the paper plan concept, but we have found it useful in discussing problems of planning. In fact, some sceptics may claim that the paper plan is a realistic concept, while the concept of a necessarily feasible real plan often has no empirical counterpart.)

The operation that transforms the terminal message into a (paper) plan is defined by what we may call the *decoding* function d; we thus have a relation

$$b = d(m_T)$$

where b denotes the paper plan. In turn, a transition must be made from the paper plan b to the real plan a, written as

$$a = r(b)$$

where the functional symbol r represents the realization function to remind us that a is to be a real (i.e., feasible) plan. (Note that neither $d(\cdot)$ nor $r(\cdot)$ involves knowledge of the environment e.)

Since m_T indirectly determines a, we may also write

$$a = \phi(m_T)$$

with ϕ called the *outcome* function. ($\phi = r_o d$ is a composite function.)

A plan specifies the prospective actions of all units and we may show this by writing

$$b = (b^1, \ldots, b^n), \qquad a = (a^1, \ldots, a^n),$$

just as

$$m_T = (m_T^1, \ldots, m_T^n).$$

A plan (whether "paper" or "real") may be thought of as a resource flow matrix, the i-th component of the plan being the i-th row of such a matrix. In a more complete treatment, one might want to allow for certain indeterminacies, and thus a plan might correspond to a set of resource flow matrices. In the terminology I have used, the choice of the language M, of the response functions f_s^i, and of the outcome function ϕ (involving the specification of the decoding and realization functions d and r) specifies an adjustment process, to be denoted by π.[10] To a considerable extent, the study of organizational structures involves the analysis of special properties of adjustment processes. This is true of the studies of the competitive mechanism, as well as of the contributions of Malinvaud, Kornai and Liptak, T. Marschak, J. Marschak, Reiter, Radner, and others.

5. On Choosing the Adjustment Process

Some of the historically important controversies involve not the analysis of a particular adjustment process but of the institutional framework that determines how the process itself is chosen.

Thinking now of the adjustment process π as a variable, one may consider that it will be chosen from some "natural" domain Π. To facilitate understanding, let us focus on the response function aspect of the adjustment process π while ignoring the outcome function. The responses of the i-th economic unit are governed by the $(T + 1)$-tuple of the response functions f_s^i, $s = 0, 1, \ldots, T$, to be denoted by $f^i = (f_0^i, f_1^i, \ldots, f_T^i)$. For the sake of brevity, we shall call f^i the i-th *behavior rule*. A domain from which f^i could conceivably be chosen will be denoted by $\mathscr{F}^i$.

It is often said that certain behavior rules would not be compatible with individual incentives. Since the notion of incentives is of fundamental importance in discussions concerning the possibility of a planned, centralized, or socialist economic system, it is advantageous to formalize it. This formalization can be accomplished, for instance, by using the concept of Nash equilibrium in non-cooperative games of strategy. We may think of f^i as the strategy employed by the i-th unit, with $\mathscr{F}^i$ as the domain from which the strategy could be chosen. It is further necessary to introduce some payoff (utility) function that represents the individual's motivation in choosing his strategy. We shall denote it by u^i. (The environment e will affect this utility, but we shall not go into the details of this admittedly important aspect of the problem. The effect of e, aside from the preferences of the i-th unit, might be treated probabilistically and integrated out through the computation of an expected value.)

The Nash-optimal n-tuple of behavior rules $\bar{f} = (\bar{f}^1, \ldots, \bar{f}^n)$ would be determined by the relations

$$\bar{f}^i = \operatorname*{maximizer}_{f^i \in \mathscr{F}^i} u^i(f^i, \bar{f}^{)i(}) \qquad i = 1, \ldots, n$$

where $f^{)i(}$ contains the $n - 1$ components f^j other than f^i. (It should be noted that the preceding discussion sidesteps the problem of coalition

[10] Hurwicz, *op. cit.*

formation which might occur when participants are free to determine their behavior rules.) An n-tuple $\bar{f}$ may be called (individually) *incentive-compatible* if it is Nash-optimal.

Similarly *group incentive-compatibility* may be defined in terms analogous to the concept of the core. More specifically one might introduce the concept of *admissible coalitions* (somewhat as in Luce-Raiffa ψ-stability) and define group incentive-compatibility as non-existence of admissible blocking coalitions. According to this definition, individual incentive-compatibility is a special case of group incentive-compatibility with the admissible groups each consisting of one individual.

A good deal of so-called positive economics attempts to see which behavior rules are and which are not compatible with individual or group incentives. The proposition that economic units will treat prices parametrically when these units are very small in comparison with the total market—but not otherwise—belongs to this category. (However, economics often chooses to focus on how a given process, e.g., the Walrasian mechanism, would work if its rules were followed, regardless of whether these rules are incentive compatible.)

On the other hand, the theory of government intervention in economic activities, whether in the form of zoning regulations, tariffs, or socialism, deals with restrictions on the choice of behavior rules by individuals. (Restrictions on behavior constitute a special case of restrictions on behavior rules.) The totality of these restrictions may be referred to as the prevailing *economic regime*.[11] Formally, the regime defines a *permissible domain* F^i from which the i-th unit is entitled to choose its behavior rule. The permissible domain F^i is a subset of the natural domain $\mathscr{F}^i$. The regime may be identified with the n-tuple $(F^1, \ldots, F^n)$. Two polar cases suggest themselves: The permissible domain F^i may equal the "natural" domain $\mathscr{F}^i$ for all units. One is tempted to call this condition the "true laissez-faire" regime; but of course no advocate of laissez faire would have advocated such an extreme solution. At the other extreme, each units's permissible domain might contain a single behavior rule (F^i a singleton set). Here the individual has no freedom of choice left, and the regime might be called "completely programmed" or automatized. (The reader should recall that, although the exposition is in terms of the f's, the concepts are meant to apply to other components of the adjustment process as well, viz., the outcome functions and language.)

If the permissible domains F^i are broad enough to contain the respective

---

[11] Frisch has used this term in a related but different sense, while J. Marschak speaks of a *constitution;* see R. Frisch, "On Welfare Theory and Pareto Regions," in *International Economic Papers*, No. 9 (1959) 39–92. See J. Marschak, "Towards an Economic Theory of Organization and Information," in R. Thrall *et al.*, eds., *Decision Processes*, New York, 1954, pp. 187–220.

Nash-optimal behavior rules $\bar{f}^i$, the regime itself may be called incentive-compatible. The critique of certain "decentralized socialism" proposals has focused on their failure to be incentive compatible. Similar observations apply to perfect competition when individual units are not sufficiently small.

The concept of permissible domains may deserve some attention as providing a tool for the formalization of the institutional framework of the economic system, including, in particular, the legal framework. It can also be applied to interpret two possible usages of the term "centralization," viz., as 1) a situation in which a decision maker determines the permissible domains for the other units, 2) a situation in which all but one decision maker has one-element (singleton F^i) permissible domains. In both cases the exceptional decision maker is the "center."

6. Structure of Authority

From now on we shall be studying situations in which a particular adjustment process has been chosen, and we shall explore those of its attributes that would suggest labeling it centralized or decentralized. In this section we shall deal with aspects of an adjustment process corresponding to structure of authority.

In defining centralization we want to cover a broader class of processes than (but including) that introduced by T. Marschak.[12] In particular, we want to accommodate the typical hierarchial decision structures observed in bureaucracies and certain planned economies. Marschak's case involves a one-person center which in the last stage tells everyone else what to do. This can be formally expressed as a property of the decoding function, viz., that

(1) $$b^j = d^j(m_T^i) \quad \text{for all } j.$$

Here i is the *(one-person) center*, the other units j in $)i($ are the *subordinates*. Thus (1) expresses a crucial aspect of one-person centralization. ("Person" may stand for an agency.)

In contradistinction, we will say that the *j-th unit* has *autonomy* if

(2) $$b^j = d^j(m_T^j).$$

In either definition we want to exclude the *trivial* case where

(3) $b^j = $ const. (independent of m_T) for all $j = 1, 2, \ldots, n$.

But the conditions (1) and (2) are not sufficient to provide correspondence of terminology with the intent of usage. In particular, we want to exclude from the definition of centralization the case in which m_T^i

[12] T. Marschak, *op. cit.* pp. 411–412.

(which other units must obey) was "dictated" to unit i by the other units at the preceding stage of the iterative process. Formally, this is expressed by the requirement that

(4) $\qquad\qquad f^i_T(m_{T-1}; e)$ be "sensitive to" e^i,

where

$$e = (e^1, \ldots, e^n).$$

With

$$e^{)i(} = (e^1, \ldots, e^{i-1}, e^{i+1}, \ldots, e^n),$$

the statement in eq. (4) means that, for a certain selection of the argument m_{T-1}, two distinct values of e^i (while $e^{)i(}$ remains the same) produce different values of m^i_T. Thus, by definition, *unit i is a one-person center when* (1) *and* (4) *hold and* (3) *does not*.

Similarly, to make autonomy of j meaningful, we wish to rule out the case where m^j_T was dictated to j by one of the other units. Formally, we require that

(5) $\qquad\qquad f^j_T(m_{T-1}; e)$ be "sensitive to" e^j

in the previously defined sense. Thus, by definition, *unit j is autonomous when* (2) *and* (5) *hold and* b^j *is "sensitive to"* m^j_T.

It will be noted that there can be no one-person center when more than one unit is autonomous.

We may wish to use the term "decentralized" (with regard to authority) when some autonomy prevails, so that there could be different degrees of decentralization (of authority).

The concepts of center and of autonomy can be generalized in several respects. For instance, to define the i-th unit as a (one-person) center we may replace (1) and (4) by the following requirements: that there exist some stage s' (possibly, but not necessarily, equal to T) such that, (1) for all j, $b^j = g^j(m^i_{s'})$, and (2) there does not exist a subset K of units not including i for which $b^j = h^j(m^K_{s'-1}, m^K_{s'-2}, \ldots)$ for all j. [In the earlier definition, for the special case $s' = T$, condition (2) of the generalized definition is satisfied by virtue of eq. (4), but it could be satisfied in other ways as well.]

The concept of autonomy can be generalized in a similar manner.

Another direction of generalization allows for the existence of a *directing group* instead of a one-person center. We shall only sketch this concept here. The actions of all units are determined by the messages of members of the directing group K; i.e.,

(6) $\qquad\qquad b^j = g^j(m^K) \qquad$ for all j

where m^K is the matrix of all m^k_s, k in K and $s = 0, 1, \ldots, T$. Furthermore group K is minimal in the sense that (6) is not true for any proper subset of K. (Under suitable assumptions K will be unique, although this is not obvious from the preceding definition. More generally, the set of all units $\{1, 2, \ldots, n\}$ might be partitioned into subsets each having its directing group.)

For some purposes one may wish to look at the hierarchical structure of the directing group. Unit 1, for instance, would be *directly under orders of* unit 2 *in stage s* if the following were true: $m_s^1 = f_s^1(m_{s-1}; e)$ is equivalent to $m_s^1 = g_s^1(m_{s-1}^2; e)$ where the range of g_s^1 is a subset of M ("the language") determined by m_{s-1}^2. The interpretation of this requirement is that unit 2 issues to unit 1 (at stage s) an order which specifies a restricted range of messages, say M_s^{12}, from which unit 1 must choose; the choice will be determined, according to a rule g_s^1, by the information unit 1 has about the environment e. In the limiting case where the set M_s^{12} is a singleton there is, of course, no latitude left to unit 1. It is easy to see how a tree type diagram of hierarchical structure could be constructed depicting the relation of directly taking orders when certain assumptions (e.g., asymmetry) are made.

These concepts could be used to represent a planning hierarchy of the following (one-step) type. For each economic sector (group of, say, producing units) there is a "sector supervisor," and he in turn directly takes orders from the "chief supervisor." In the initial stage of the process the producing units convey their production functions to the respective sector supervisors who aggregate them and inform the chief supervisor of the aggregate production functions of their respective sectors. The chief supervisor makes certain decisions in terms of these aggregates and other information available to him (say aggregate resource endowment) and sends to the sector supervisors messages in terms of sector aggregates. Finally, the sector supervisors determine the input-output vectors for their respective producing units. Here the directing group consists of the sector supervisors, but the hierarchy also includes the chief supervisor from whom they take (aggregate) orders. These orders can be interpreted as restrictive M-sets. The orders given by the sector supervisors to the producing units are singletons, i.e., the producing units lack autonomy. In fact, they have no influence on the choice of their input-output vectors, in the sense that, for a producing unit j, b^j not only is not determined by m_T^j but in fact does not even depend on m_T^j.

It might seem appropriate to couch a definition of command economy in terms of the authority concepts just developed.[13] Such an economy prevails when there exists a set of units constituting the hierarchy (the directing group being a subset of the hierarchy, and the units outside the hierarchy lacking autonomy or even influence on their own actions). The one-person-center economy described earlier is, therefore a special

[13] See Grossman, *op. cit.*, p. 15.

case of a command economy, whose hierarchy and directing group are collapsed into one unit—the center.

The exchange of information in a command economy need not be of the one-step variety sketched in the preceding paragraphs.[14] The producing unit, instead of conveying all (or, at least, all relevant) information in one iteration stage, may take part in repeated iterations between itself and members of the hierarchy. Malinvaud's formalization of Taylor's procedure belongs to this type, with the hierarchy being of the one-person (planning bureau) type.[15] (Of course, the planning bureau might have an internal hierarchical structure of the type described above, but Malinvaud ignores this aspect.) It is perhaps characteristic of the present state of terminology that while the term "command" seems appropriate as a description of such a process and has been so used by some workers in the field (e.g., Marglin), Malinvaud himself discusses the process as an example of a "decentralized procedure for planning." [16]

In a hierarchical structure it is possible to introduce concepts of centralization. In particular, a hierarchy is centralized when all of its members are under the orders of one member, either directly or indirectly. (Unit 1 is (indirectly) under orders of unit 2 if there exists a sequence of units, say $i_1, \ldots, i_p$ ($p \geqq 1$) such that 1 is directly under orders of i_1, which is directly under orders of i_2, and so forth, up to i_p, directly under orders of unit 2. The term "directly under orders" was rigorously defined above.) It is obvious that a 'one-person-center' hierarchy is centralized, hence the present usage is consistent with that developed earlier. It should be noted that the command economy, as here defined, may but need not be centralized. On the other hand, a centralized economy is necessarily a command economy. It should be clear that a Walrasian price adjustment

[14] T. Marschak's centralized process is of the one-step (no feedback) variety, with a one-person center.

[15] Malinvaud, *op. cit.*, Ch. IV.

[16] It may be natural to inquire about the meaning attributed by Malinvaud to the term "decentralized" in this context. In the absence of an explicit statement, the following elements seem to enter: the information concerning production functions is initially available only to the respective producing units (dispersion of information); the language of messages between the producing units and the planning bureau is of a simple nature, typically a vector of the dimensionality of the commodity space (or less); not all calculations are carried out by the planning bureau—some are done by the producing units. As noted above, one of Malinvaud's examples involves the accumulation of all the past messages, i.e., is not a difference equation system of finite order.

The fact that a given adjustment process may qualify both as command (in fact, of the centralized variety) and, at the same time, as a decentralized planning procedure points up the importance of the distinction between the authority aspects and informational aspects in classifying centralization phenomena. Malinvaud's procedures may be centralized with regard to authority structure but largely decentralized with regard to informational aspects.

economy is not of the command type, hence not centralized. In fact, in such an economy there is no directing group (hence no hierarchy) and all units are autonomous; thus the process is decentralized with regard to authority. (I have formalized an adjustment process closely related to the Walrasian under the label of the quasi-competitive process.[17] To relate the treatment there to the present work, certain details must be modified, since in the earlier paper the role of terminal messages m_T was not made explicit and there is no distinction between a paper plan and a real plan.)

7. Structure of Information

The now classic von Mises-Lange-Hayek controversy did not focus on the structure of authority in resource allocating mechanisms but rather on the informational aspects. In extolling the virtues of the market mechanism, Hayek stressed that its communication requirements, although minimal, were sufficient to provide the needed coordination between economic units.[18] By contrast, a (one-step) command economy would presumably require tremendous transfers of information from the individual units to the planning authorities as well as huge calculations to be performed by the latter, if efficient resource allocation were to be attained.

The need for calculation is obvious and its difficulties received particular attention in the early stages of the discussion when, following Barone, the planning authority was thought of as solving the Walrasian general-equilibrium equation system for the whole economy.[19] The Taylor-Lange remedy prescribed that the calculations be carried out by an iterative dialogue between the planning authority and the individual (producer) economic units, in a manner analogous to the operation of the market. In this fashion the calculating capacity of these units is enlisted to supplement that of the planning authority. If calculation is regarded as a sort of production process, this amounts to using several workers to accomplish a task that is excessive for one. The use of the calculating capacities of the individual economic units is an important aspect of the notion of decentralization of the resource-allocating mechanism in the context of this debate. (It also seems implicit in Malinvaud's usage.) In the light of recent developments in the field of giant high-speed electronic computers the merits of decentralizing calculations would deserve systematic consideration.

The problem of calculating solutions given the availability of relevant information is only one of the computational difficulties. Generally

[17] Hurwicz, "Optimality and Informational Efficiency," *op. cit.* (n.5).
[18] Hayek, F. A. "The Use of Knowledge in Society," *American Economic Review* XXXV:4 (1945), 519–530.
[19] Hayek, F. A. ed. *Collectivist Economic Planning*, London, 1935, 208.

speaking, extensive calculations (in addition to experimentation, and so forth) would be required for an individual unit to estimate, say, its complete production function as called for under a one-step centralized procedure. In the 'iterative dialogue' approach involving the individual units this burden is avoided by requiring the producing units to obtain (and transmit) at any given stage of iteration information concerning only a limited region of the production set.

Underlying the Hayek type of argument is the basic assumption that the information concerning a given unit's environmental component e^i (its production set, resources, tastes) can be obtained more easily and more accurately by that unit than by anyone else. In idealized form this assumption can be expressed by postulating that at the initial stage of the adjustment process each unit has complete knowledge of its own environmental component and no knowledge at all of other units' environmental components (dispersion of information).

This postulate can be formalized by specifying that, for a given set of incoming messages, a given unit's response function depends only on its own environmental component, but not on those of other units; i.e., we have

$$(6) \qquad \begin{cases} m_s^i = f_s^i(m_{s-1}; e^i) & i = 1, 2, \ldots, n \qquad s = 1, 2, \ldots, T \\ m_0^i = f_0^i(e^i) \end{cases}$$

where e^i has replaced the symbol e found in the general adjustment process formula.[20] (For the sake of simplicity, we are confining ourselves here to a first-order process.) The term *privacy* has been suggested to label processes of the type formalized by eq. (6). (The term I originally proposed,[21] "externality," turned out to be confusing by association with such phenomena as external diseconomies of scale.)

One implication of eq. (6) is that no one has (or can use) any information about other units at the initial stage ($s = 0$). Subsequently he only has such information as may have been conveyed to him through the messages. Thus, for instance, at stage $s = 1$, unit 2 only knows about unit 1 as much as was conveyed through the message m_0^2.[22]

In a first-order process with privacy [as in eq. (6)], given unit's knowledge of other environmental components is confined to that contained in their

[20] $e = (e^1, \ldots, e^{i-1}, e^i, e^{i+1}, \ldots, e^n)$.

[21] Hurwicz, *op. cit.* (n.5).

[22] In the present exposition we have ignored the possibility of using "addressed" messages, i.e., messages that are received only by some of the units. To some extent, the equivalent effect can be introduced by making, say f_s^3 insensitive to m_{s-1}^4; this could be interpreted as meaning that, in stage s, the message from unit 4 was not addressed to unit 3.

messages from the immediately preceding stage. More generally, one may consider a process

(7)
$$\begin{cases} m_s^i = f_s^i(m_{s-1}, \ldots, m_0; e^i) & i = 1, 2, \ldots, n \\ m_0^i = f_0^i(e^i) \end{cases}$$

in which information obtained from earlier messages can also be retained.

It is at this point that the nature of the permissible messages becomes crucial. If there were no difficulty in transferring complex messages, we might postulate that each m_0^i contains complete relevant information about e^i. Hence it could be assumed that one of the units, say unit 2, could become a one-person center in stage $s = 1$, because at this time $f_1^2(m_0^1, \ldots, m_0^n; e^2) = f_1^2(e^1, \ldots, e^n; e^2)$. Thus one-stage centralization becomes easy. (Commands would still have to be sent back to the individual units from unit 2, but that information transfer is simpler than the transfer of the environmental information.) The classic (Hayek-type) objections to such a procedure must be interpreted as implying difficulties in effecting such information transfers, at least in a single stage (one-step) of the process.

To formalize such difficulties one may proceed by imposing restrictions on the language M of the process, i.e., on the nature of permissible messages. It is natural, in the context of the present discussion, to make these restrictions severe enough to prohibit the transmission of complete information about production sets, indifference maps, and resource endowments, while still permitting messages of complexity comparable to those occurring in a Walrasian market process. To satisfy the latter requirement, one must permit the transmission of proposed input-output vectors as well as price vectors. As it happens, when the number of commodities is assumed finite, the dimensionality of the commodity and price vectors is the same, equal to the number of commodities (say m) in the economy. Hence, at the very least, the language M must be rich enough to contain messages specifying arbitrary points of an m-dimensional space. Formally, this could be accomplished by setting M equal to such a space. This would mean that a message is always an ordered m-tuple of real numbers.

In certain situations, it seems preferable to consider the effects of having a language M that is restricted, but not quite as severely. In particular, one may wish to permit messages specifying subsets, rather than merely points, of the commodity space. Such a language may appear overly rich since it makes possible the transmission of complete information concerning production sets. Nevertheless, this milder restriction on language would still make it impossible to operate a command-type process of first order [as in eq. (6)] in an economy with more than one producing unit. The

difficulty here would be not so much in transmitting technological information about the individual units to the center as transmitting the indi-
vidualized commands from the center to the separate units. For instance,
let the center be unit #1, the producing units #2 and #3. Suppose the
center has selected the respective input-output vectors, say x^2 and x^3, for
the two producing units. Obviously these could not be transmitted under
the assumption that the message emitted by unit #1 must be a single point
of the commodity space. But even if the center can transmit the set
consisting of x^2 and x^3, this ability would not resolve the difficulty as long
as the set transmitted was an unordered set, i.e., the two producing units
would not, in general, know which vector pertains to which producing
unit.[23]

An important relationship exists between the restrictions imposed on
the language of the messages and the number of lagged message n-tuples
permitted in the difference equations of (7) above. When more than one
lagged value of m_s is permitted, the effect is somewhat equivalent to
permitting a less restrictive language. Thus if m_{s-1} and m_{s-2} are permitted
as arguments of f_s^i for $s = 2, 3, \ldots, T$, and a message is restricted to a
point in the commodity space, the i-th unit can hold in its "memory" two
such points (from the two lagged messages); the result is similar to what
might have happened if there was only a single lag but it was permitted to
use two-point messages. The problem of issuing differentiated commands
discussed in the preceding paragraph, for instance, could be handled in a
two-lag (second-order difference equation) system by having, say, f_T^2
responsive to m_T^1 while f_T^3 is responsive to m_{T-1}^1. In particular, in systems
with unlimited memory, i.e., with f_s^i containing as arguments all the past
messages back to the initial stage, we come very close to obviating any
restrictions imposed on the language. It is therefore somewhat questionable
whether such processes constitute satisfactory formalizations of the
difficulties postulated in the informational decentralization debate.

Among other requirements to be considered in the present context is
that of "anonymity." [24] I shall not present it here in detail.[25] Suffice it to
say that this requirement is satisfied by the Walrasian process where
price adjustments depend on aggregate excess demand rather than on the
individual bids. On the other hand, the requirement is violated in a
command economy where it is essential to know the origin of a message.

[23] In my article on "Optimality and Informational Efficiency" (*op. cit.*), I
restricted messages to arbitrary subsets of the commodity space. In joint work
with Radner and Reiter, a stochastic adjustment process is used in which the
language is restricted to single points of the commodity space.

[24] Under "anonymity" the response to a message does not depend on its origin.

[25] See Hurwicz, *op. cit.* and also L. Hurwicz, "Conditions for Economic
Efficiency of Centralized and Decentralized Structures" in G. Grossman, ed.,
Value and Plan, Berkeley, 1960, pp. 162–183.

8. Informational Efficiency and Decentralization

Intuitively, an adjustment process is *informationally centralized* if, at some stage of the process, at least one of the participants comes into possession of all relevant information concerning everyone's environment and everyone's prospective actions. A process is informationally *non-centralized* if such concentration of information in one agent's hands cannot occur.

To rule out such concentration at all stages of the process, one must rule it out for the beginning and for the later stages of the process. To rule it out at the beginning, one can postulate initial dispersion of information (p. 93); this dispersion is reflected in the requirement of *privacy*[26] imposed on the response functions.

But even with initial dispersion, information might concentrate in one hand in the course of the adjustment process if there are no limitations on how much information is transferred and retained, at each stage. Such limitations are inherent in the attributes of *anonymity* and *self-relevance*,[27] as well as from the assumption that the process is (a difference equation system) of finite order. (The finite-order assumption limits the "memory" of participants.)

In my earlier work, I assumed the process to be of finite (first) order and defined *informational decentralization* in terms of privacy, anonymity, and self-relevance. Thus defined, informational decentralization constitutes a subcategory with respect to informational non-centralization. At present, partly under the influence of work done by Camacho, Radner, Reiter, and the Marschaks (J. and T.), I would be inclined to regard the concept of non-centralization as perhaps the more fundamental. However, the attributes of privacy, anonymity, and self-relevance, together with finite-order assumption, remain of particular interest. For on the one hand they are all present in the Walrasian competitive process which has served as the economist's inspiration for the notion of informational decentralization; on the other hand, they cannot all be present in the 'command' economy, the economist's standard example of informational centralization. If one thinks of different economic systems (adjustment processes) as points on a map, the aim in providing a definition was to draw a boundary line so as to divide the map into two regions, with the competitive mechanism situated in the "informationally decentralized" region and the command economy outside of it. Clearly, there are many ways of drawing such a line. Some writers have had a tendency to shrink the "informationally decentralized" region almost to the point of containing

[26] Previously called "externality."

[27] "Self-relevance" permits an entity to specify what would happen to itself only.

nothing but the competitive mechanism, others have been more broad-minded. (Typically, these concepts are only implicit in a writer's discussion rather than expressed through a formal definition or model.)

Why is it of importance how the line is drawn? One answer lies in the use to which the definitions are put. In the present case, the choice of definition affects the answer to the question as to how wide a class of environments is capable of (informational) decentralization without sacrificing the allocative efficiency ("performance") properties characteristic of the competitive mechanism. These properties may be formulated in terms of technological efficiency, or—somewhat more ambitiously—in terms of Pareto-optimality, or even in terms of social welfare functions. Elsewhere we settled on the complex of optimality properties arising naturally in the context of welfare-economics theorems concerning competitive equilibrium.[28] We defined a process as Pareto-satisfactory if its equilibria were Pareto-optimal and certain other properties were also present. Without going into formal definitions, suffice it to say that these are almost exactly the properties established by Arrow, Debreu, and Koopmans for the competitive mechanism when the environment satisfies, among others, the well-known conditions of absence of external (dis-) economies, absence of indivisibilities, convexity of production sets and of the preference functions, (we call these the "classical environments").

It is well known that equilibria may be nonoptimal or even fail to exist when some of these environmental conditions are violated. It then becomes natural to ask whether one can conceive of a system that would have the desired properties (Pareto-satisfactoriness) on the performance side. Now if the competitive mechanism will not do, what is the class of mechanisms that would be considered acceptable? If no restrictions were imposed on the informational nature of the mechanism, the problem could be solved by postulating an omniscient planner with infinite capacity to carry out computations within arbitrarily short time periods. To make the problem nontrivial, one must take into account some of the difficulties of handling information outlined in the preceding section.

Perhaps the simplest approach is to specify some of these restrictions under the label of informational decentralization (e.g., as at the beginning of this section) and ask whether it is possible to devise processes that are both informationally decentralized and Pareto-satisfactory (or, more generally, *performance-satisfactory*) in environments that violate some of the classical assumptions (e.g., where external (dis-) economies or indivisibilities are present). When the concepts used are rigorously defined, it is possible to answer such questions in certain cases. It turns out, for instance, that presence of indivisibilities can be overcome, but external

[28] Hurwicz, "Optimality and Informational Efficiency," *op. cit.* (n.5).

(dis-) economies may not be capable of informational decentralization without sacrificing performance-satisfactoriness.

At this point we become aware of the implications of adopting definitions of informational decentralization that are either too narrow or too wide. If the definition is very narrow (e.g., almost equivalent to that of the price mechanism), it will appear that environments other than the classical one are not (in the sense of such a definition) capable of decentralization without sacrificing performance. If the definition is extremely "lenient," practically every environment is formally decentralizable, but one may feel that such "decentralized" mechanisms are actually infeasible or excessively costly due to the difficulties stressed by Hayek and others.

At this stage of the discussion, it is possible to take two alternative, though not incompatible, routes. First, one may introduce the concept of *informational efficiency*. A process is said to be informationally more efficient than another if it requires, in some sense, less information for its operation. Properties such as 'privacy,' 'anonymity,' and so forth, may be regarded as specifying a certain minimum of information efficiency. Thus it may be interesting to know whether an adjustment process is performance-satisfactory (e.g., in the Pareto sense) without requiring more information than permitted by such restrictions as privacy or anonymity. This approach was explored by the writer and by others in a number of recent contributions.[29]

The alternative approach, whose merits have been stressed by both J. Marschak and T. Marschak in different contexts, takes explicit account of the technology, costs, and risks, of information processing that goes on when the economic mechanism (adjustment process) operates. A mechanism can then be defined as optimal if it is feasible (in terms of information processing technology) and provides the maximum value of outcomes, net of the costs of operating the system. For instance, one could determine, in principle at least, whether under specified circumstances a command or autonomous structure of authority would come closer to such 'net' informational optimality. (Here, as elsewhere in this paper, we abstract from the difficulties in enforcing the mechanism and also from values, such as freedom of decision, which are not explicitly included in the Pareto

[29] Camacho, Antonio, "Externalities, Optimality and Informationally Decentralized Resource Allocation Processes," to appear in *International Economic Review*.

Kanemitsu, Hideo, "Informational Efficiency and Decentralization in Optimal Resource Allocation," *The Economic Studies Quarterly*, XVI:3 (1966) 22–40.

Kanemitsu, Hideo, "On the Stability of an Adjustment Process in Non-Classical Environments," June 1970, prepared for presentation at the World Econometric Congress, Cambridge, Sept. 1970.

Ledyard, John, "Resource Allocation in Unselfish Environments," *American Economic Review*, LVIII:2. Papers & Proceedings (1968), 227–237.

ordering of outcomes, since they involve a valuation of the mechanism as such.)

In what follows, we sketch briefly a model that could serve as a common base for both approaches.

This model makes explicit that there are *error components* both in the perception and transmission of information pertaining to the environment and to messages received and that these errors are more or less serious and costly depending on the information-processing activities used. (A similar approach can be employed with regard to calculations, but we shall not introduce it here.)

We shall start with a very simple case. Perception errors will be denoted by generic symbols v, w, with a prescript denoting the perceiving unit. Thus $^iv^j$ will denote the error in perception by the i-th unit of the environmental component e^j; similarly, $^iw_s^j$ will denote the error in the perception by the i-th unit of the message m_s^j. [If the errors are thought of as random variables (obviously only a very special case), their variances indicate the obtainable accuracy.] The adjustment process can now be written as

$$(9) \quad m_s^i = f_s^i(m_{s-1}^1 + {}^iw_{s-1}^1, \ldots, m_{s-1}^n + {}^iw_{s-1}^n; e^1 + {}^iv^1, \ldots, e^n + {}^iv^n)$$

for all i, and $s = 1, \ldots, n$, with an analogous formula for $s = 0$. (The m's and e's are the true values, $m + w$ and $e + v$ the perceived values.)

Now the requirement of privacy can be justified, for instance, by specifying that the variance of $^iv^j$ is very large whenever $i \neq j$ and zero for $i = j$. A more realistic picture is obtained by introducing an informational activity variable x which describes the techniques involved in producing the perceptions used in the adjustment process. The information technology can then be described by specifying (1) the set X of feasible values of x, and (2) two groups of functional relations, associating respectively the error variances and costs with the values of x. Thus for instance, denoting the error variances by $\sigma^2(^iw_s^j)$ and $\sigma^2(^iv^j)$, we may write functional relations of the first group as

$$\sigma^2(^iw_s^j) = \beta_{w,i,j,s}(x),$$

$$\sigma^2(^iv^j) = \beta_{v,i,j}(x).$$

Covariances could also be assumed to depend on x in an analogous manner. Similarly, one might postulate informational cost functions written as

$$c = \gamma(x)$$

where c could be a resource vector, rather than monetary cost.

In such a model of informational technology we need no longer postulate that the error components have fixed variances. Instead, it might be postulated that one must use very costly technologies x to produce low variance values for ${}^i v^i$, $i \neq j$, while the cost of a technology x' that can produce a low variance ${}^i v^i$ is negligible in comparison.

Similarly, restrictions on the language M used in communication can be rationalized either in terms of feasibility or costs. Thus the variances of the w's may be relatively low when the message is simple (e.g., a single point of the commodity space) but high otherwise, unless, perhaps, one resorts to very costly methods of transmission of the messages. Certain correlations between the errors ${}^i w_s^1, \ldots, {}^i w_s^n$ may be used to explain the requirement of anonymity or aggregativeness of the process.

Clearly, the additive error model is very crude. More generally, one could define multi-dimensional random mappings from the spaces of true variables and so μ account for various limitations of perception in a more natural manner. The mapping representing i's perception of received messages will be denoted by ${}^i \mu_s$, that representing i's perceptions of the environment by ${}^i \varepsilon_s$.[30] The adjustment process can now be written as

$$(10) \qquad m_s^i = f_s^i[{}^i \mu_s(m_{s-1}); \; {}^i \varepsilon_s(e)]$$

where $m_{s-1} = (m_{s-1}^1, \ldots, m_{s-1}^n)$ and $e = (e^1, \ldots, e^n)$. In relation to the "mapping model" of (10), formula (9) represents a special case in which the range of the mapping has the same dimension as its domain, so that the dimensionality of the "true values" and of the "perceived values" is the same. More generally, however, these dimensionalities need not be the same: when we perceive only the sum or average value of the components of a vector, the true values are multi-dimensional, but the perceived values one-dimensional. A phenomenon of this type may occur with regard to the (message perception) mapping ${}^i \mu_s$, thus again justifying anonymity or aggregativeness.

As in the simpler error model, the nature of the mapping may be determined by the value of the informational activity variable x chosen from its domain X; variances and costs are again determined by functions defined on this domain.

Extreme assumptions (zero or infinite variances, costs, or both) lead to an analysis of a restricted class of adjustment processes (e.g., informationally decentralized) whose members are equally acceptable, while those outside the class are totally unacceptable. When knowledge about intermediate values of variances and costs becomes available, a more sophisticated analysis will be possible.

[30] The subscript s in ${}^i \varepsilon_s$ allows for informational activities, e.g., market research that would increase the i-th entity's knowledge of the environment through channels other than formal messages. (This generalizes the concept of the adjustment process beyond its formalization elsewhere in the paper.)

9. Open Issues

In the light of the preceding discussion, is there a meaningful problem of centralization versus decentralization of the economic system? Are we condemned to perpetual arguments about definitions, or are there substantive empirical or theoretical issues involved?

Perhaps not surprisingly, the writer feels that there are genuine problems, but also that these problems can be successfully tackled only within the framework of a formal model and with the help of rigorous definitions. One way of summarizing the complex of issues under discussion is in terms of the relationship between the structure of authority and the structure of information, taking into account performance-satisfactoriness on the one hand and the class of environments to be served by the system on the other. Figuratively, we may think of four variables ("axes") representing the structure of authority (command, autonomy), structure of information (privacy, anonymity), an indicator of performance-satisfactoriness (e.g., Pareto-satisfactoriness), environment class (e.g., free or not free of external diseconomies, indivisibilities, convex, continuous, etc.). Many of the questions raised can be expressed in the following manner: Which points (i.e., combinations of the values of variables) of this four-variable space are feasible, and among feasible ones which are preferable in terms of net performance (net in the sense that informational costs have been deducted)?

As an example, the market corresponds to a point in this space characterized by autonomy on the structure of authority axis, by privacy (and other components of what the writer has called informational decentralization) on the information structure axis, and by Pareto-satisfactoriness on the performance axis when the environment axis is chosen with the classical characteristics of divisibility, convexity, absence of externalities, and so forth. One hopes to establish impossibility theorems showing that certain points of the space are unoccupied, for instance combinations calling for informational decentralization, Pareto-satisfactoriness, and certain types of external diseconomies. When performance criteria are of the type specified by Malinvaud, it seems possible to devise command economies with partial informational decentralization, but so far for rather narrow classes of environments (e.g., Leontief-Samuelson economies).

Another important "axis" is that corresponding to individual or group incentive-compatibility. It may be conjectured that, in general, one cannot hope to achieve Pareto-satisfactoriness, informational decentralization, and individual incentive-compatibility even when externalities are absent. (If the conjecture is true in the form stated, it would *a fortiori* be true with group incentive-compatibility replacing individual incentive-compatibility, since the former implies the latter, an individual being regarded as a special type of group.)

When performance-satisfactoriness is required and the environment class is reasonably broad, there may be general relationships to be discovered between the structure of authority and the structure of information. Thus requirements such as privacy or anonymity might rule out command structure of authority, because privacy would make it impossible for the center to acquire enough information for optimal, or even feasible, decisions.

Among the so far unresolved controversial issues would be: What type of mechanism is appropriate for environmental conditions involving sharp transitions (e.g., war mobilization)? Traditionally it has been argued that conditions of this type require a command structure of authority.

Another important problem deserving investigation is the type of mechanism suitable, in the absence of operating markets for future goods, for investment decisions in economies where a great deal of complementarity results from separate investment decisions. Assuming that it is not feasible to create a market for the relevant future goods (which might conceivably take care of the difficulties), one may ask what combination of authority and information structure would provide performance-satisfactory results. Are some of the traditional arguments in favor of a command economy justified for such situations within the framework of the present analysis?

4

Organization and Comparative Economics: Some Approaches

by BENJAMIN WARD*

1. Introduction

Organization consists in habitual or frequently repeated behavior which requires coordinated action among several individuals. This definition seems to capture the primary elements of usage of the term, except for the notion that organized behavior is purposive. However, though organization is perhaps always created for a purpose, purpose is often very complex even in fairly simple organizations; also purpose tends to change over time, and an organization often contains conflicting behavior. Consequently, it seems more expedient to make purpose a possible subject of analysis in connection with organized behavior, rather than a defining characteristic of that behavior.

Three principal advantages may be claimed for organized behavior over unorganized behavior. In the first place, there are often economies of scale associated with organization. One manifestation of this is learning by doing, as Arrow has called it.[1] The repetition of particular coordinated acts may improve average performance up to some point. Machinery is often designed in anticipation of this effect, and learning curves may on occasion be empirically estimated. A second advantage consists in the stabilization of expectations of participants in an organization, and even of others not associated directly with the organization. This stabilization may of course contribute to the economies of scale of the organized, as opposed to unorganized behavior, especially through the information-saving that may result from confident extrapolation of aspects of the past into the future. But it also has other effects, notably the expansion of organized behavior. For example, the expectations of others, not originally

* The author would like to thank Joseph S. Berliner, Gregory Grossman, Herbert Levine, our esteemed chairman and other participants in the conference for critical comment, and the Project on Comparative Communist Societies, University of California, Berkeley, for a grant, both of which contributed to the improvement of this paper.
[1] Kenneth Arrow, "The Economic Implications of Learning by Doing," *Review of Economic Studies*, XIX:3 (1962) 155–173.

members of the organization, may become stabilized with respect to aspects of the organized behavior. Should this effect lead to frequent repetition of behavior by these others, the latter have, *ex definitione*, become organized. A final advantage that may accrue to organized behavior is inertia. To continue previous practice and not initiate a new decision process is often efficient behavior.

In practice of course a great deal of organized interaction takes place among organizations. And within any particular formal organization there are likely to be many suborganizations, i.e., relatively small groups of individuals who have established limited patterns of coordinated, more or less habitual behavior. The older school of institutional economists tended to emphasize precisely this organizational aspect of human behavior; but the institutionalists failed, at least in the sense that they have not reproduced themselves in the younger generation of economists. The superficial implication of the fact—that the concerns and approaches of institutionalists are not relevant today—is sufficiently destructive of the purpose of this paper, so that some comment seems necessary to explain the reason for that failure. This will be done by means of the following argument:

Let us think for a moment of the standard model of competitive capitalism and ask where in this model institutionalists would like to insert organized behavior. I think the following would cover the major claims of institutionalists:

1. For each good a market is institutionally defined; i.e., there is an organized way for any participant to make contact with dealers in any given good, including especially dealers in the factors of production. Thus a market is a complex group of organizations possessing inertia but also subject to rather frequent and perhaps steady change under the strong influence of organizational factors.

2. The selection of a partner in making a deal is not a matter of indifference to the participants, of more or less random pairing. Instead there is a good deal of habitual pairing, and this provides elements of friction, inertia, and change very different from the single-equilibrium-price model.

3. Emphasis on equilibrium rather than stability has led to undervaluation of the role of information in a market economy. It takes a lot of information to make an adjustment, very little to go on doing what you have been doing. Information is often structured so as to organize adjustment.

4. There is a teleological element in many adjustment processes. Expectations as to outcomes have an important bearing on the decision to make or to continue an adjustment, as do expectations as to the course

of the adjustment. For example, participants may choose not to make a Pareto-optimal adjustment, because they fear that the process may involve a change that will produce net costs for some of the participants. Because it is based on the analysis by participants of repetitive elements of behavior, the threat structure, an organizational feature of a market, thus plays an important role in determining market behavior.

5. The outcome of a movement from one equilibrium to another is not independent of the time path of adjustment, as comparative statics implies. On the contrary, the past sets strong informational limits on knowledge of the future and on the properties of expectations. Habitual response patterns to the relevant history play an important part in the behavior of organizations and individuals on markets.

6. The incentives of market participants are not a simple matter of profit- or utility-maximization with respect to quantities and mixes of goods but are conditioned by their position within the relevant organization: for example, whether you are a recent entrant into the market, a regular customer, a big customer, whether you have a favorably organized production, and so forth. These factors create a variety of organized behavior in markets which significantly influences the nature of equilibrium and adjustment to disequilibrium.

7. Equilibrium itself is a concept that, as usually interpreted, ignores organization. Homeostasis fits better, pointing as it does to the fact that an adjustment process tends to be dampened by such frictions as ignorance, fear, and inertia. Thus equilibrium more appropriately is a zone in which participants feel no overriding call to change their behavior, even though many participants recognize it as being not at equilibrium in the sense of current economic theory.

8. This in turn suggests that analysis of the stability of such hair-trigger adjustment mechanisms as the price-change-proportional-to-excess-supply models is largely irrelevant, stability in the small being essentially guaranteed by organizational frictions, and stability in the large being nonexistent.

The style of presentation of these "claims of institutionalists" was not designed to represent the kind of language an institutionalist himself would be likely to use. Instead it was designed to suggest by connotation the following two propositions: 1) The reason for the failure of institutionalism was not that institutionalists had nothing to say; on the contrary, they offered many pertinent and challenging criticisms of the received doctrine. The reason for their failure was rather their misinterpretation of price theory. As an elaborative doctrine to hang on the traditional theoretical structure of economics, the institutional approach might affect basic changes in that structure; but with price theory rejected more or less in its entirety, no substitute framework was established and the whole approach tended to collapse into a hopeless jumble of propositions with little discernible mutual relationship. 2) However, institutionalism did not really die, for much of its orientation has been given at least some limited and piecemeal representation in contemporary economics. Consequently it is not implausible that a more systematic study of the interaction between organization and the traditional economic variables—which define the kinds and amounts of inputs and outputs in an economy, the ways in which these are distributed over the participants (whether organizations or individuals), and the ways in which all these vary over time—will produce a substantial increase in our understanding of the economic process.

Comparative economics, involves—again by definition for the present purpose—analysis of the consequences of the interaction of different kinds of large-scale organization with appropriate economic variables. It is a major and perhaps one of the more promising areas of study within this general field. However it has been beset by what must be the major difficulty confronting students of the field, namely, the complexity of large-scale organization. To realize the problems that arise even in constructing a useful typology of organization, much less in developing useful theories of organization-economy interaction, it is enough to note that a large-scale organization is a collection of numerous overlapping patterns of organized behavior, and that organization changes frequently, and that many factors influence change.

Nevertheless the effort should be made, for large-scale organizations not only exist, they can be created, and the creator has some choice as to the sort of monster he will sire. Furthermore there is some stability in organizational behavior; indeed, this stability is part of the defining properties of organization, and relatively stable aspects of behavior are always promising as a subject of study.

In addition to inertia, scale economies, and stable expectations, there is another factor which tends to promote the persistence of organization; it might be called the principle of externalities. Organizational change almost inevitably produces externalities or consequences for some of those not initially participating in the decision to change. Those who expect to be hurt by the change will tend to resist it, which in turn raises the alternative cost of making the change. This is likely even when there are positive externalities because of the costs of negotiating. It is these features of organization, i.e., inertia, scale economies, and stable expectations which reduce the complexity of the problem and offer some basis for hope that the field of comparative economics, as rather restrictively defined, will be a promising one.

Complexity has an implication for research methodology: The more complex and the less well understood a field is, the less likely is it that anyone will be able to prove that a particular research technique will *not* be fruitful when applied in that field. In a sense the present paper is no more than a defense of eclecticism. I have constructed a half-dozen boxes, each of which purports to hold a set of studies in comparative economics with similar orientation and method, and of demonstrated usefulness. Each box is first very briefly described, then some aspects of one or two of the studies that belong in it briefly discussed, and finally the approach is briefly evaluated. The studies have been selected partly with a view to suggesting some of the more promising lines for future research, but subject alas to the constraint that they belong to that small subset of the universe of studies with which I have some familiarity. Each study is described in my words, not the author's, which means that much has been omitted that the author might consider relevant, and the style of language chosen, as with the institutionalist discussion above, may differ sharply from the author's. The aim is to get at propositions that fall within comparative economics as defined above and that illustrate the relevant procedure, regardless of the damage done to the author's context. In the final section the coherence of comparative economics as a distinct field is evaluated and some comments offered on its peculiar problems.

2. Intuitive Groping

In this approach the investigator first acquires an understanding of two or more distinct culture patterns and then uses this understanding to develop propositions about the relation between organization and economy. The term "understanding" may have several meanings in this context. In one, it refers to an investigator who has acquired a sufficiently profound appreciation of a culture so that he has internalized it, so to speak, and so that he may confidently make statements about the culture on the basis of no other evidence than his own feelings.[2] In a less transcendental meaning, the investigator does not forego the direct use of evidence but is perhaps a bit freer in assigning causal connections than would be the case if he had less confidence in his intuitions about the culture. The looseness of the methodology permits the investigator to rely on such evidence as the expressed views of sophisticated natives, views which have no more empirical support than that of a rather vaguely intuited judgment on one's own experience. Additionally, the investigator's views as to which aspects of human behavior are universal are likely to crop up as part of the theory.

Another feature of the approach is the mixture of theorizing and hypothesis testing. In a sense one can object to no process of generating

[2] This is an interpretation of "The Operation called Verstehen," a paper by Theodor Abel, *American Journal of Sociology*, LIV:3 (1948) 211–218, which contains references to the literature.

hypotheses, since the latter do not become "knowledge" until they have been subject to some verification procedure. But such separation is usually far from complete even in methodologically sophisticated studies. In the present approach the intuitive basis of the hypothesis, the simultaneous presentation of the theory, the evidence, and even the appeal to more than the cited evidence, is intended as a favorable test of the hypothesis. Though no rules of statistical inference can be applied, I think such hypotheses, if put forward seriously by a well-informed investigator and if plausible to the reader, have in fact been subject to a valid verification procedure. Unfortunately there is only a rather limited basis for establishing the degree of confidence that one might legitimately have in the truth of the hypothesis, but this is probably true of most statistical research in economics as well.

In his *Imperial Germany and the Industrial Revolution*, published in 1915, Thorstein Veblen presented an early convergence hypothesis, namely that Germany would in the long run come to behave more like England as its industrial plant aged, standards of conspicuous waste rose, and the cultural conditioning of modern machine technology had sufficient time to penetrate the German culture. Thus slower economic growth and a slower rate of application of new technology are associated with such organizational factors as the growing conservatism of business enterprises as they age, and with the increasing propensity to funnel profits into new consumption patterns instead of into further investment. These hypotheses rested in turn on an explanation as to why Germany had come to differ from England in important respects. Veblen's discussion of Germany's advantages from backwardness, aside from its emphasis on the ages-old high propensity of Germanic peoples to borrow technology without at the same time borrowing other elements of culture, has a modern ring in its emphasis on the role of the state and the relatively large size and young age of businesses. Its emphasis on the role of technology in both moulding and being moulded by society and on the role of human capital in determining the rate of progress and the speed of recovery from disaster are also familiar to the modern ear. The modern reader will no doubt be put off by Veblen's casual assertion of rather subtle facts important to his argument[3] and the extended treatment of such peripheral matters as the Scandinavian sagas and the British "gentry's" peculiar addiction to sports. But one advantage of the approach is revealed in Veblen's study: In competent hands the broad brush produces a good statement of what is

[3] T. Veblen, *Imperial Germany and the Industrial Revolution*, New York (1915), Ch. 4, p. 197. e.g., that steadily rising costs of production in Germany since the 1870s are the result of a "process of capitalization of differential advantages within the community, with the accompanying burden of fixed charges." The remark is offered without analysis or citation.

important; but in dealing with these great issues the more formal present-day ideals have not dramatically outstripped intuition. The latest treatments comparing the English and German experiences, though informed by two generations of research, are not so distant in either method or conclusions from this ancient work.

As a contemporary and perhaps more modest application of this approach I refer to a part of Nove and Newth's recent study of Soviet Central Asia and Transcaucasia.[4] They argue that Soviet organizational peculiarities partly explain the relatively much more rapid development of the Soviet Central Asian and Transcaucasian republics than that of their culturally similar neighbors during the Soviet period. To be sure there was an element of deliberate Soviet policy in this outcome. However, the basic rules of organization of the Soviet State and administrative apparatus also played an important role. For example the rules of organization called for national wage scales, which automatically meant a reduction in income differentials between these republics and Russia. Also the tax system tended to bring relatively more into the all-Union budget from the more developed areas, while most capital investment was financed out of that budget. The Middle Eastern republics received a greater-than-proportional share of investment as a matter of policy, but the financing rules, partly inadvertently, insured that the more developed areas would bear a substantially greater-than-proportional share of resource diversion. Other factors, such as the relatively more favorable treatment of the crops of the area in assigning delivery quotas and prices, also had a partly unplanned character.

Unfortunately the hypothesis suffers from a defect rather common to hypotheses in comparative economics in that its importance relative to other possible causal explanations is virtually impossible to establish. Even intuition is likely to be a rather weak guide here because of the inability of Western students closely to observe Soviet administrative practices, and of the limited published accounts of those practices by the Soviets themselves.

As a final example of this genre I have chosen a paper which intuits some comparative organizational hypotheses for Greece and Yugoslavia in recent years.[5] One of these hypotheses, which is not supported by citation of any statistics, is that profit-sharing in Yugoslavia plus a somewhat primitive capitalism in Greece combine to produce a more egalitarian

[4] *The Soviet Middle East, A Communist Model for Development*, New York, 1966.
[5] B. Ward, "Capitalism vs. Socialism: A Small Country Version," in G. Grossman, ed. *Essays in Socialism and Planning in Honor of Carl Landauer*, Englewood Cliffs, N.J. (1970).

income distribution in the middle reaches in Yugoslavia than in Greece[6]—surely a plausible argument even so (and *eo ipso* somewhat verified?). In addition there is a rudimentary attempt to deal with the "tendencies" problem (i.e., the ability of this approach to isolate likely causal connections, but its inability effectively to evaluate relative strengths of causes) by producing a sort of distribution of explanatory patterns instead of selecting merely the most likely one. The hypothesis assumes that virtually no fundamental differences between the two economies are a necessary consequence of the existence of capitalist forms of organization in one country and socialist forms in the other. One or two scenarios of possible future outcomes are designed to show how the two countries might become much more similar while preserving the central organizational difference as to the ownership of the means of production; another suggests that substantial differences may persist and be attributable in part to organizational differences.

This study should perhaps not be held up as a shining example; among other things, the scenario given most attention preserves and even strengthens democracy in Greece—the paper was written three months before the military coup. It has been inserted partly to indicate my sympathy for the approach and partly to suggest that there are ways of dealing with complexity short of waiting for the generation of data sufficient to satisfy an econometrician. Indeed I suspect that studies of this kind, though their results are certainly subject to revision should better data appear, produce results in which we can have more confidence than current statistical methodology would be prepared to grant. It is an approach widely practiced in neighboring disciplines where problems rather similar to those of comparative economics are faced.[7] In particular this approach seems well suited to situations in which the relevant data have not been given careful attention and where causal patterns are sufficiently uncertain so that the failure to consider an important causal factor is a major research risk. Successful work makes heavier demands on the breadth and common sense of the investigator than on his technical acumen.

3. Adaptive Failure

In this approach some sort of ideal, whether normative or merely analytically simplified, is taken as a standard, and the discussion centers around

[6] Meaning something like: The percentage of income going to the middle third of the population, when ranked by income, is closer to one-third in Yugoslavia than in Greece.

[7] See, for example, Dankwart A. Rustow, "Modernization and Comparative Politics: Prospects in Research and Theory," mimeo., 1968.

the deviations of an organization from that ideal. This device is of course a standard of economic polemics, but it has also been usefully applied by authors with an essentially scholarly purpose.

We may begin with an abstract of a rather broad-gauge application of the method by Gregory Grossman to the Soviet Union's complex of economic organization.[8] The balancing of supply and demand, it is argued, tends to be taken for granted by Western economists, but is of great importance for the administration of a Soviet-type of economy because it must be achieved by deliberate and conscious effort. But even with heavy resource commitment to its achievement, balance requires some decentralization because of the inability of the central authorities to deal in detail with the balancing of every commodity in the economy. The consequence of this is a partial loss of control by the center and the generation of unwanted results, in particular of various kinds of inefficiency. It is true that some parts of the economy may be separated out from the command sector and left to operate as markets, thereby reducing the load on the center. However, the requirements of coordination between the two regimes set strict limits to the areas of the economy in which market operation is feasible. Consequently a command economy of the Soviet type is constrained to operate with a rather high level of inefficiency.

The standard formally set by Grossman is that of an economy in which supply and demand are in balance.[9] However, there is some difficulty in providing a clear picture as to what constitutes empirical evidence of balance; and frequent references to inefficiencies throughout the paper suggest that in fact a conception of economic efficiency is being applied, probably a static conception.

Two types of constraints are claimed to set limits to the efficiency of the Soviet-type economy: 1) those stemming from the unwanted consequences of decentralization within the command framework, and 2) those stemming from the limited ability to mix command and market sectors. Western students of the Soviet Union widely believe these constraints to be in fact operative. No attempt is made to compare these inefficiencies with those associated with a market economy. However, the paper's aim was not to produce such evidence but only to make plausible an argument as to the location of sources of inefficiency in a Soviet-type economy. In this I believe it succeeds.

A second study along similar lines has been made by Abram Bergson.[10]

[8] "Notes for a Theory of the Command Economy," *Soviet Studies*, XV:2 (1963), 101–123.

[9] "Balance" is used instead of "equilibrium" to eliminate the connotation of stability that many seem to associate with the latter term. Balance has a homeostatic connotation, and though "homeostasis" too seems often to carry a connotation of stability, "balance" neatly escapes this connotative trap.

[10] *The Economics of Soviet Planning*, New Haven, 1964.

Bergson clearly specifies his intent to compare the actual working of the Soviet economy with the ideal of static efficiency. He bases the comparison on efficiency rules that are a sufficient condition for an efficient equilibrium and, taking a number of them in turn, asks how the rules of the actual economic game as played in the Soviet Union differ from the efficiency rules. Rules appropriate to many sectors of a modern economy, such as communal consumption, are not discussed. An example of the approach is the counterpart to Grossman's notion of balance, the rule that "prices should be at clearing levels" in consumers' goods markets. For a variety of reasons, including the administrative costs of frequent price changes and of taking into account variations in the price and income elasticities of different goods, there has been a pronounced tendency to price at retail below clearing levels. Evidence in the form of directions of change of prices and the existence of queues is used to support the conclusion of deviation from the standard. After considering a number of these rules and the likelihood and extent of deviation therefrom in practice, a comparative factor-productivity study of the United States and the Soviet Union is presented to measure the relative magnitudes of deviation. This study points clearly to less inefficiency in the United States as does Bergson's study reported in the present volume, but unfortunately neither permits judgment as to the principal causes of the difference.

A major purpose of Bergson's presentation was to provide a survey of Soviet economic institutions within a framework familiar to Western students. This seems to be an especially apt reason for choosing the adaptive failure approach. Furthermore, despite the data problems, a survey of this kind carried out by someone with obviously detailed knowledge of the institutions and with experience in interpreting the data, produces some partial verification of the hypotheses regarding deviation from the efficiency standard. Some areas, such as choice of technology, are less satisfying than others, but this is a matter essentially of data problems. General conclusions, however, are very hard to justify because of the incompleteness of the approach. The difficulties of measurement associated with public goods and the great data limitations in areas of key importance in the Soviet leaders' goals, such as military and space production, leave one skeptical of any general conclusions. Finally, the incompleteness of the specification of the ideal is troubling. Deviations from a merely sufficient condition for efficiency may only be an indication that a different sufficient condition is being met. The peculiarities of the Soviet price system are the most frequently cited basis for this objection; for example, some at least of the putative adaptive failures may really be fairly efficient adaptations to the rigidity of the existing price system.

As an example of the adaptive-failure approach applied to the contemporary welfare state we may take J. N. Wolfe's recent paper, "Planning by forecast." [11] Wolfe is concerned with the justification, in terms of economic theory, of indicative or toothless planning. Toothless planning occurs when the planning board has no authority to enforce its forecasts. There are several ways in which, even so, it may serve to make the economy operate more efficiently. For example, adjustment processes from a state of disequilibrium may at times be too slow or even in the wrong direction. The process of reaching equilibrium might be hastened if a planning bureau were to compile and publish estimates of the equilibrium prices, which if they were believed might prove to be self-justifying, thereby producing swift adjustment. Another possibility, which assertedly may be of more importance than has previously been realized, is the reduction of the variability of demand by publishing forecasts of demand and output; if believed these published data could reduce the degree of flexibility—the range of low-cost production rates—of plants, thereby promoting more efficient production at actual output levels. A third possibility is to provide estimates of output and demand or price for goods for which future markets do not exist; in this case the planners become a sort of surrogate for a nonexistent portion of the market mechanism.

Having cited these and some other possible functions of an indicative planning bureau, Wolfe then compares these prescriptions with the reality of planning in Western Europe. A considerable gap is noticed; for example, price forecasts are seldom produced by planners, and output forecasts are typically cast at so aggregative a level that they can hardly be classed as substitutes for a market. An especially serious and interesting gap concerns credibility. Planning agents have rarely devoted much effort to evaluating the performance of their forecasts and to developing more accurate and therefore more credible forecasts. In addition their close connection with other government agencies has at times raised questions as to whether their best forecasts are being published. This represents a rather substantial failure of adaptation to the norms of economic theory. However, as Wolfe points out, part of the problem may be the relative newness of indicative planning, part may be the inability of economic theory at present to give clear enough guidelines to even the purest of indicative planners, and part may be due to practical difficulties in implementing such guidelines as do exist.

As a final example of this approach we may take another study of the causes of inefficiency in market economies, Harvey Leibenstein's, "Allocative *vs*. X-efficiency." [12] The standard here is essentially the same as Bergson's efficiency rules, though emphasis is placed on the relative importance of deviations from the ideal due to market inefficiencies and

---

[11] In Hague, D. C., ed., *Price Formation in Various Economies*, New York, 1967.

[12] *American Economic Review*, LVI:3 (1966) 392–415.

to failures of incentive or ignorance. Studies of the social cost of monopoly and of tariff barriers indicate that the removal of these particular deviations from the ideal will have a trivial impact on efficiency. On the other hand scattered evidence on enterprise efficiency indicates that a great many firms in a variety of market environments operate for extended periods sufficiently off the efficient cost function to permit reduction of net cost by 10–20 per cent and even more, and that often the information necessary to effect these changes is readily at hand. Consequently economists might do well to pay rather more attention to the motivation of participants in the economy and less to problems associated with market failure.

The Leibenstein paper falls short of proving its case conclusively, but like the other studies surveyed so far it opens a plausible line of speculation, in this case one which suggests a rather substantial restructuring of economic research. One may also speculate as to the implications of the X-efficiency hypothesis for studies of the Soviet economy. Students of that economy have generally placed the problem of motivation at the center of discussion. The interesting question is whether the hypothesis applies even so; that is, are the inefficiencies in the Soviet system attributable to inadequacies in the price and targeting system less important than those attributable to a failure of motivation for participants to operate on the production function? As a point against the hypothesis one may note the strong pressure under which Soviet management operates, while much of the evidence cited in the Grossman and Bergson studies mentioned above do in fact refer to allocative inefficiencies.

Perhaps enough has been said to convince the doubting reader that this can be an effective approach to comparative economics. The danger that the writer—or, more likely, the reader—of such a study will confuse reality and ideal and conclude that the cited deviations from the ideal prove that the organization under consideration is less effective than other real organizations is certainly present. That it ties description of an organization to an already familiar framework of analysis is the chief merit of the approach. Like all such efforts at "domestication," some distortion results. The method provides a rather strong basis for comparison, provided it is coupled with a recognition that departure from ideal does not in and of itself constitute a measure of comparative effectiveness of organizations; and of course the standard need not be limited, as the studies cited were, to static efficiency comparisons.

4. Neoclassicism

The essence of the neoclassical approach is its emphasis on the decision as the unit of analysis. The approach has been applied to organizational comparisons for generations, including comparisons of capitalist and socialist allocation rules within the general-equilibrium framework. In the last twenty-five years, with the appearance of much more sophisticated techniques for dealing with bargaining, dynamics, and uncertainty, the approach has undergone a substantial development. Nevertheless we will apply within this box the same argument that has been applied between our classification boxes, namely that the peculiar problems of comparative economics make both the old-fashioned and the modern techniques useful for some purposes.

4.1. Marshallian Analysis

In Marshallian analysis a single organization, such as a representative firm, is the subject of investigation. Other organizations in the environment are treated essentially as a part of the environment rather than as entities possessing the power to bargain with the organization under analysis. The environment can then be specified as a set of independent alternatives any one of which may be chosen by the organization. The organization itself is characterized in terms of its criterion of choice. However, the form of organization may also expand or restrict the range of feasible alternatives. The analysis thus produces a choice of an alternative by an organization, and the ways in which that choice will be affected by changes in environment or criterion may be studied. Though Alfred Marshall did much more than this in his *Principles*, it is perhaps not an unfair characterization of his orientation toward economic analysis to call this approach "Marshallian."

Probably the most familiar organizational comparison in economics is the Marshallian analysis of competitive and monopolistic firms. In this analysis both firms have the same criterion, profit maximization over some time period; but they operate in different environments, because only the monopolistic firm has any effective control over market price. With appropriate assumptions the two forms of organization can be contrasted in a market environment which is consistent with the survival of both forms and in which technology and other prices are the same. In this way a rather strong theorem contrasting output policies and a weaker welfare proposition can be developed.

Another application of this approach has produced several models of enterprise decision-making under various forms of cooperative production régimes. For comparative purposes the range of feasible alternatives may be taken to be the same as, say, under the competitive capitalist firm, with organizational differences captured only by varying the criterion of choice. For example, in the Illyrian model,[13] an idealization of the forms of

[13] Ward, B., "The Firm in Illyria: Market Syndicalism," *American Economic Review*, XLVIII:4 (1958) 566–589.

enterprise established in the early 1950s in Yugoslavia, it is assumed that the criterion is maximization of profits per worker.

This kind of characterization was based on several aspects of actual Yugoslav conditions but referred, especially at the time of its publication a decade ago, rather more to legal formulas than to actual practice. Under these institutions, markets had been established for producer goods, direct allocations of inputs had formally ceased, and price controls had been abolished. A committee of workers, elected by their co-workers in the enterprise, were given essentially the powers of a capitalist board of directors. In some industries there were a fairly large number of enterprises, suggesting that a competitive environment might be approximated. The state encouraged enterprises to operate efficiently and at times has encouraged them to lay off surplus workers; the workers' council—eventually—was given full formal power to hire and fire workers.

Analysis of the idealized model showed that the Illyrian competitive firm would behave differently from its capitalist counterpart. The most significant difference was the smaller elasticity of supply for output by the former; under circumstances in which labor was an especially important input, the supply curve would have a negative slope, while the capitalist firm's supply curve would have conventional properties.

Clearly the model severely oversimplified Yugoslav reality or even reality in a real-world environment consciously structured to model Illyrian assumptions. On the environmental side no account was taken of the underdeveloped nature of Yugoslav markets or of dynamic conditions, such as the effect on short-run economic policy of the very rapid expansion of industrial capacity. With respect to the criterion, no account was taken of uncertainty, or of the existence of workers of different skill levels within the enterprise, or of the influence of outside organizations on the enterprise's decisions, or of the consequences of the nonintuitive nature of the behavior prescribed by the model for a council of workers of modest educational attainments.

Because of these and other distortions of reality, such a model can at best have only a very modest purpose. It can give a rather gross picture of the directions in which incentives—in this case materialistic incentives—will tend to push an enterprise in a broad but not exhaustive class of situations. Models of this kind can be more interesting if they can be related to norms of performance. In the present case, short-run behavior would seem to deviate, at times substantially, from efficient decision-making; the long-run market or enterprise equilibrium however need not be inconsistent with production efficiency, though a more substantial role must be allowed the state than is required under comparable capitalist conditions.

It seems that often behavior can be fairly sensitive to organizational change. Domar for example modified the above model by assuming that membership in the organization was fixed, but that the supply of effort by individual members might be varied by their own choice.[14] This change in the environment—the criterion of the enterprise remained unchanged[15]— captured some features of the possible environment in which *kolkhozy* might operate if they were freed of production controls, were allowed to market their own goods, were given control of *kolkhoz* decision-making, but remained constrained to continue with the existing size of *kolkhoz* membership. Emphasis on the supply of effort was appropriate in the sense that this has·been a crucial problem of actual *kolkhoz* operation in the Soviet Union. This change in assumptions produced a much more conventional comparative statics for the model, though substantial deviations from short-run efficient allocation could still occur.

In a rather different model, Amartya K. Sen has evaluated the consequences of using a rule of allocation according to needs as opposed to the conventional market rule of allocation according to work.[16] The analyzed organization contains a number of families which engage in joint production, using their own labor and other factors which are either internally owned or bought on a market, and distributes the entire net product among the family members. Assuming conventional technology, equilibria are analyzed under the two allocation rules and the principal result shows that the distribution-according-to-needs rule produces less labor offered than conventional Pareto-optimality, while the distribution-according-to-work rule produces more. The latter result occurs because, with sharing of the joint production, the offering of an additional unit of labor by a family increases the family's share in the total product as well as earning it a share of the marginal product of its additional labor.

The first two coop models offer varying analyses of organizations in which the profit criterion is modified as a consequence of the special treatment accorded one of the factors of production by the organizational form. Sen's model extends the range of forms analyzed to one in which mutual sympathy among members and nonmarket notions of equity are

[14] Domar, E. D., "The Soviet Collective Farm as a Producer Cooperative," *American Economic Review*, LVI:4 (1966) 734–757.

[15] The environment is actually changed more than indicated in the text, for alternative work opportunities emerge, and the criterion now ranges over this newly defined set of alternatives. The criterion is not fully specified, given the opportunity for social choice and variations in individual work opportunities, as indicated by A. Bergson in his "Market Socialism Revisited," *Journal of Political Economy*, LXXV:5 (1967) 655–673. The assumption must be made that each addition to supply is provided equally by the members, or their asymmetric attitude toward work and leisure will influence any social choice of an optimum.

[16] "Labour Allocation in a Cooperative Enterprise," *Review of Economic Studies*, XXXIII:4 (1966) 361–371.

built into the organization. It is possible to carry the approach even further from the conventional environment to the analysis of administrative sub-units of a hierarchy, as has been attempted in various models of the enterprise in the Soviet-type environment.[17] In such a case it must be recognized that a variety of conflicting organizational factors will impinge on enterprise decision-making, which means that the tendencies problem arises with special strength in evaluating the analyzed factors. Nevertheless it seems that persistent pressures in the direction of the results of the analysis may be effectively isolated by the approach.

4.2. Game Theory

This powerful and abstract method of analysis would seem to have strong relevance for comparative economics. It places the relation between the structure of a situation and the outcome in the central position for analysis and gives wide latitude for introducing various kinds of organizations into specific models. The environment of choice is specified for a number of decision-makers. Each is viewed as selecting from a list of alternatives according to a criterion. The alternatives can be specified in a variety of ways, some of them rather complex; and the value to one decision-maker of a particular choice is affected by the choices of the other participants. A variety of quite general theorems describe various properties of plausible choices with limited specification of the structure of alternatives and the criteria of participants.

We will consider two applications of game theory to comparative economics, both by Shapley and Shubik. The first attempts to provide a general formula for measuring the power of an individual decision-maker in a variety of organizations.[18] The formula was applied, for example, to an idealization of formal political decision-making under the United States Constitution. The decision-makers are members of the House and Senate, and the President, assuming alternatively that a simple majority or a two-thirds majority of each body is necessary to pass a proposal. The formula considers all possible coalitions of members of the organizations to be equally likely. Each of these coalitions is assigned a value, based on its ability to produce desirable outcomes, on the assumption that all members not in the coalition have themselves formed a single coalition. The power of a participant is then computed as the sum of the incremental additions by that participant to all coalitions containing the participant,

[17] For two rather different examples see R. D. Portes, "The Enterprise Under Central Planning," mimeo., June 1968, and B. Ward, *The Socialist Economy*, New York, 1967, Ch. 4.

[18] Shapley L. S., and M. Shubik, "A Method for Evaluating the Distribution of Power in a Committee System," *American Political Science Review*, XLVIII:3 (1954) 787–792; see also R. D. Luce and H. Raiffa, *Games and Decisions*, New York, 1957, Ch. 12.

each increment being weighted to take account of the number of ways an individual can appear in that coalition. For example, the power ratios for members of the House, Senate, and the President are respectively 2, 9, and 350.

The second study applies game theory to the analysis of allocation of the product under various agrarian regimes.[19] A neoclassical production function defines the alternative products associated with various inputs. A regime is defined in terms of the ability of participants to gain access to land, the *sine qua non* of agricultural production. Outcomes are defined using game-theoretic solution concepts. These outcomes can then be compared as the properties of the production function of the regime are varied. One example is a regime composed of a single large landowner and a number of landless peasants who have no alternative to working the land for the landlord. The competitive equilibrium solution for this situation with the assumed production function (which for example allows output to increase indefinitely with increases in labor inputs) allocates half the product to the landlord and divides the remainder equally among the peasants. Various game-theoretic solutions, which take some account of coalition-forming possibilities, produce similar results, though most solutions award a larger share to the landlord than the competitive equilibrium, and none awards less. A variety of alternative and more complex regimes are similarly analyzed.

It is perhaps a little surprising to see game theory applied as a description of reality rather than as a normative theory of how players might best play the game. Even the latter interpretation is subject to the criticism that the assumed notion of rationality is a rather conservative one with respect to risk. As a descriptive theory it implies that people do in fact tend to behave rationally, as that term is interpreted by the theory. For example, in the case of an allocation to the players which is in the core, it is assumed that members of the winning coalition can find no other coalition in which they can do better. And in the case of the computation of the value of a game, it is assumed that the players themselves expect that the strongest possible coalition will be formed against any coalition in which they participate. Both the core and the value were used in the agrarian regime analysis. The power measure is weakened by the assumption of additivity, that is, if a participant were involved in two such committee situations, his power would simply be the sum of his power in each individual situation.[20]

Clearly the models described represent a very high level of abstraction from, and distortion of, real world behavior. Among the major objections

[19] L. S. Shapley and M. Shubik, "Ownership and the Production Function," *Quarterly Journal of Economics*, LXXXI:1 (1967) 88–111.

[20] This and most of the criticisms to follow are taken from Luce and Raiffa, *op. cit., passim.*

to these uses of game-theoretic solutions as behavioral descriptions of decision-making are the following: 1) it is assumed that side payments are permitted by participants and that utility is transferable from one decision unit to another; 2) each participant is assumed to know the payoffs to all others; 3) dynamic threat is absent; that is, it is assumed that a participant will not refuse to leave a nonoptimal coalition out of fear that the improvement will be destroyed as the result of later moves by others; 4) the characteristic function, based on the notion that all participants who are not members of a coalition are in a single coalition of their own (thus converting the n-person game into a set of two-person games), produces an excessively conservative estimate of the value of a coalition to its members; 5) by assumption, no coalition is more likely to occur than others; thus the orientation of participants toward issues is irrelevant to the solution values; and game solutions are quite sensitive to modest changes in payoff functions;[21] consequently over a long run in which much organizational change is occurring any particular solution is likely to be wide of the mark.

Nevertheless, these applications are interesting and the approach seems quite promising for comparative economics. The basic notion which is to define differences in property relations in terms of differences in the threat potentials of coalitions, whose power in turn is defined by the value to them of the various feasible alternatives, is attractive. The complexity of bargaining situations makes even highly simplified models potentially very useful aids to understanding. And experience with a variety of such models may produce further insights into the working of bargaining situations. One such analytic insight has already made its appearance: "A general rule of thumb seems to persist: the more power there is in the hands of the middle-sized groups (coalitions), the more narrowly circumscribed is the range of outcomes of the . . . game."[22] The development of alternative measures of power and the application of other available solution concepts are among the areas where developments have occurred or look promising.

4.3. General Equilibrium and Stability

General equilibrium analysis has been used to compare socialism and capitalism since the days of Pareto and Barone. The early arguments dealt essentially only with equilibrium, arguing that either a socialist or a capitalist régime was capable of sustaining a Pareto-optimal pattern of production and distribution once it was achieved, though the distribution

[21] Shapley and Shubik, "Ownership," *op. cit.*, p. 103.
[22] Shapley and Shubik, "Concepts and Theories of Pure Competition," in M. Shubik, ed., *Essays in Mathematical Economics*, Princeton, N.J., 1967, p. 72.

of wealth under the two régimes would be quite different. Initial discussion of stability, of the process of multiple market response to disequilibrium, did not really distinguish between the two forms of organization. In both cases it was assumed that the adjustment would occur by a process of price change proportional to the amount of excess demand. Of course at least implicitly the interpretation was different: For capitalism this adjustment rule was a behavioral proposition about markets, while for socialism it was a description of the rules to be applied by the central planners in seeking the optimal plan. One might make the distinction explicit in the models by assuming that actual trading of goods occurs during adjustment on the markets but not during the planners' search for an optimum. However, the stability discussions under either assumption so far have failed to establish the stability of a broad range of economically interesting equilibria.[23]

More success has been achieved by a rather unexpected route. Certain algorithms by which one can compute solutions to linear programs can be interpreted as processes of decentralized search for an optimum by a set of decision units under the limited guidance of a central authority. For example, both the revised simplex method and the decomposition algorithm have been so interpreted by Clopper Almon.[24] In the former, a manager is assigned fixed targets for inputs and outputs and knows the input-output coefficients for each of the set of linear production activities among which he must select a set which will minimize total labor cost, the manager being obliged to pay a labor certificate to each employed worker for each hour worked. Each step in the solution process can be interpreted as the result of optimizing behavior on the part of both the manager and the workers. The manager sets prices determined by each trial solution for labor and materials and sells the latter to the workers at those prices. The prices are such that the workers are encouraged not to waste materials, and labor cost is minimized for the given set of activities. The laborers search out new activities which will yield excess wages to them, and the manager, seeking to forestall them, adopts the activity that provides the greatest excess wage and then recomputes his prices. This process continues to the optimum, at which point no excess-wage process exists, the plan is exactly fulfilled, and labor cost is minimized.

A somewhat similar process occurs under the more sophisticated technology assumed for the decomposition principle. Though the interpretation of the scheme is rather mechanical, it does make it possible to tie a market-like incentive scheme to the search for an optimum choice among

---

[23] T. Negishi, "The Stability of a Competitive Economy: A Survey Article," *Econometrica*, XXX:4 (1962) 635–669.

[24] In George Dantzig, *Linear Programming and Extensions*, Princeton, N.J. (1963) Chs. 12, 23.

existing production facilities. The schemes seem to be quite information-saving because at each step only a limited amount of information needs to be known and processed by each decision unit. The convergence of the process to the optimum is equivalent to the assertion of stability in the competitive model, though both the technology and the organization are simpler.

The argument is usually made that a price-guided search for an optimum, like the one described above, requires a great deal less information and information-processing than a command process, in which the center issues trial output and input targets and requires information about the decentralized units' production functions to be communicated to it. This view has recently been challenged by Stephen Marglin who has constructed corresponding command-type algorithms for price-guided search under various assumptions, including the Lange-Taylor adjustment rule.[25] Each command scheme requires amounts and processing of information comparable to that of its price counterpart. Also, though prices and profits have certain advantages from the point of view of incentives, especially in maintaining an already achieved optimum, even here mixing price and command at times is advantageous, especially when the number of decentralized units is relatively small.

The introduction of limited information and uncertainty into the adjustment problem is another area of currently active research.[26] The framework is that of team theory, which means in effect that the incentives of the various participants are ignored. The resource manager allocates a scarce input to a set of enterprises, and the supply of the resource and parameters of the production function are assumed to be random variables. In addition, some restrictions are imposed on communication. Also the allocation decision is made before equilibrium is reached. In this very different environment from those considered above the sending of price messages by enterprise managers appears to be optimal in the sense that it leads to a maximum expected output by the system.

As a final example of multiple economic interaction I would like to return to the theory of competitive equilibrium, this time with the introduction of uncertainty, limited information, and limited computational capacity, as it has recently been presented by Roy Radner.[27] Perhaps the most striking feature of Radner's model is the essential incompleteness

[25] Stephen Marglin, "Information in price and command systems of planning," mimeo., n.d.

[26] Roy Radner, "Teams" and "Allocation of a Scarce Resource Under Uncertainty: An Example of a Team," working papers nos. 255 and 248, Center for Research in Management Science, University of California, Berkeley, June and March, 1968.

[27] Roy Radner, "Competitive Equilibrium under Uncertainty," *Econometrica*, XXXVI:1 (1968) 31–58.

that follows from the introduction of these additional factors. The latter two factors do not simply convert certain outcomes into expected outcomes; instead they convert equilibrium into a situation in which the participants are continually revising their plans, and even their methods of computing their plans, and the very notion of a social optimum begins to lose its significance. Among the major problems hindering further extension of the competitive optimality theorems is the unavoidable element of externality built into the nature of information, which has the effect of greatly extending the need for information by the various participants. And the Pareto-optima that can be derived are conditional on the given information structures, which effectively destroys their relevance for the traditional sort of capitalism/socialism comparisons; however, the comparison of efficient systems possessing alternative information structures which are determined by their organizational differences opens up a new and most interesting range of research opportunities.

None of the studies referred to in this subsection makes any extended attempt to specify the organizations which lie behind the alternative adjustment schemes—or equilibria—under discussion. Nevertheless, they can be considered as important studies in comparative economics, because the modeled differences do have organizational interpretations. It is interesting that much of this work hinges around alternative schemes for running an economic system in accord with the wishes of some central authority; the specification is sufficiently abstract however, so that this system might be either a socialist economy or a large capitalist corporation. One might speculate that this orientation reflects a growing feeling that decentralized economic systems must be subject to a variety of centralized controls if they are to operate efficiently. Price does not lose its significance as an aid to efficient decision-making, but it cannot function effectively unaided by a rather visible hand. Similarly the uncertainty-based equilibrium models reveal difficulties both in searching for, and in sustaining, an optimum in an economy provided only with an invisible hand. It is perhaps ironic that neoclassical economics in this modern form should be pointing in such a direction. In addition some organizational observations of less broad import emerge; for example, that contracts based on actual outcomes are less efficient for some purposes than contracts based on conditional states of nature[28] (Radner, Borch, Arrow). But by and large these models would seem to have primarily normative rather than descriptive relevance, unless some social mechanism like that hypothesized in the next section is in fact operative.

[28] Karl Borch, "The Economics of Uncertainty," in M. Shubik, ed., *Essays op. cit.*, pp. 204–205; cf. also Radner, "Competitive Equilibrium" *op. cit.*, 33–34, 46–47.

5. Adaptation to Inefficiency

Three distinct trends in economics seem to fit neatly under this rubric. One is essentially normative and conceives of the state as the agency which concerns itself with externalities and—hopefully—leaves the competitive markets to perform the other economic tasks. A clear and sophisticated presentation can be found in William Baumol's work on welfare economics.[29]

A second line of thought is associated with grand, more or less deterministic trends in history. Branko Horvat has recently adapted the Marxian notion of inevitability to this approach by defining it to mean a state of affairs which is practicable and clearly superior in terms of efficiency to the existing state of affairs, with state capitalism playing the latter role and worker-managed socialism the former.[30] Implicitly, feasibility plus optimality tend to produce adoption.

A third line of thought has been succinctly stated by Kenneth Arrow:[31] "I propose here the view that, when the market fails to achieve an optimal state, society will, to some extent at least, recognize the gap, and non-market social institutions will arise attempting to bridge it. Certainly this process is not necessarily conscious; nor is it uniformly successful in approaching more closely to optimality when the entire range of consequences is considered." This view provides something of a link between the normative theory of the state and a theory with descriptive relevance. It implies that within limits man is rational in dealing socially with essentially social problems as well as in dealing individually with his individual problems. However, though it often is so linked, this view need not be linked with neoclassical prejudices, as the following discussion is designed to indicate.

Bela Balassa's recent paper, "Whither French planning?" represents a strong instance of analysis in terms of adaptation to inefficiency.[32] It argues that as the French economy has become more open, planning, and particularly investment planning, has become less effective. Enterprises faced with strong competition from foreign firms within the Common Market have become much less willing to accept the government's programs for expansion of their facilities. This in turn has had its impact on the nature of the plans, which tend to place much more emphasis today

[29] *Welfare Economics and the Theory of the State*, Cambridge, Mass., 1952, Part ii.

[30] Branko Horvat, *Towards a Theory of Planned Economy*, Yugoslav Institute of Economic Research, 1964.

[31] "Uncertainty and the Welfare Economics of Medical Care," *American Economic Review*, LIII:5 (1963) 947.

[32] *Quarterly Journal of Economics*, LXXIX:4 (1965) 537–554.

on financial balances and much less on physical expansion targets. The government's notion as to appropriate relative rates of growth of various sectors of the economy has tended to give way in the face of the producers' desires to respond directly to market pressures. The government in turn has become concerned with balance-of-payments problems and the control of inflation and orients its planning effort accordingly. The change represents an adaptation of the planning organization to a change in environment which rendered previous practices inefficient.

This argument is certainly plausible, and it may be useful to contrast it with some of the conclusions of Wolfe's paper on indicative planning. First it must be noted that the French have not engaged in toothless planning, particularly in the early plans. The French authorities had a variety of instruments by means of which they could apply pressure on businessmen, though the views of the latter also had considerable weight in constructing the plans. Nevertheless the shift away from detailed planning seems surprising within Wolfe's framework. For clearly the opening of the French economy to competitive pressures has not made it easier to predict future prices and outputs. On the contrary, the variance of demands surely has increased, partly as a consequence of the reduction in control of capacity expansion by the government. This situation is one in which, by Wolfe's standard, indicative planning in some detail of prices and outputs could be very desirable. The issue cannot be resolved here, but perhaps enough has been said to suggest that Arrow's distinction between attempted and successful adaptation to inefficiency is quite important in applying this approach.

Some years ago John R. Commons argued that, as market economies developed, the common law courts provided a mechanism for adaptation to inefficiency arising out of the social costs of ignorance and risk-bearing.[33] The combination of buyer ignorance and the doctrine of *caveat emptor* tended to produce "nasty and adulterated" goods. "Yet, without returning to the past, the courts began to adapt themselves to the uncertainties of the present." Along these same lines Guido Calabresi has offered an extended discussion of the recent development of legal doctrine in the case of torts.[34] In the nineteenth century the dominant criterion was fault liability, the idea that whoever committed the tort was liable for the damages. A notion that might have improved social efficiency was enterprise liability, which allocates liability to the activities creating the injuries, regardless of fault. Calabresi argues that this doctrine did not develop in the nineteenth century, because most industries faced decreasing average cost, so that allocation of damages by enterprise liability would have inhibited growth.

[33] *Legal Foundations of Capitalism*, New York (1924) pp. 204, 264.
[34] "Some Thoughts on Risk Distribution and the Law of Torts," *Yale Law Journal* LXX:4 (1961) 499–553.

However there has been a strong trend toward enterprise liability in the present century, while the notion that fault creates liability has been steadily weakened. The adaptation is far from complete, and the notion of spreading the burden of damages over those most able to pay has been giving the enterprise-liability doctrine some competition; but the trend toward adaptation to inefficiency in this area of strongly judge-made law is clearly asserted. Product liability, the notion that a manufacturer may be responsible for the quality of his product to third parties with whom he has had no dealings, exemplifies the attempt to adjust to the risks of using goods in a complex society by fixing liability for failure on parties able to correct the deficiency. It represents an almost spontaneous adjustment of legal notions to the changing structure of the social environment. This trend has occurred in a number of other legal systems, apparently reflecting a rather broad adjustment even of codified law to similarly changing demands of society.[35]

The convergence hypothesis seems to fall clearly in the adaptation-to-inefficiency box. The requirements of contemporary technology, urbanization, and affluence, it argues, create pressures toward the establishing of similar institutions for organizing economic and political decision-making. Presumably—writers are not always entirely clear on this point, however—these pressures occur, because there is in some rough-and-ready sense a "one best way" to make these decisions. No attempt can be made here to assess this argument, but the present framework offers the opportunity to pose the problem in a somewhat different way.

The substitution for capitalism of socialism with central planning in physical terms has been interpreted by many writers over the last century or more as an adaptation to the inefficiency of a market economy. Long lists of these inefficiencies have been presented, and of course long debates have been held over the appropriate social process for bringing about the adaptation. However, once central planning has been installed, a situation quite parallel to that of the market economy is created, so that "when central planning fails to achieve an optimal state, society will, to some extent at least, recognize the gap, and noncentralized social institutions will arise attempting to bridge it." A line of argument based on this hypothesis might be designed to test the idea that there are two locally stable institutional forms, each of which represents adaptation to the failures of an ideal; and then one could discover the extent of difference between the two equilibria.

The ideal states in question, complete central planning and perfect laissez-faire, have of course never existed. In both cases one must seek out the areas in which the ideal would clearly fail if actually attempted and see if one can find institutions that may be conceived as adaptations to those

[35] W. Friedmann, *Law in a Changing Society*, Berkeley, 1959, pp. 162–164.

failures. In the laissez-faire case the establishment of a law of contract to enforce promises is an example of an adaptation to inefficient levels of uncertainty, an adaptation requiring organization to administer it. Under central planning there are contracts between enterprises which are, to a limited extent, open-ended, reflecting the imperfect information in the hands of the planners and the consequent inefficiency of plan targets. When central planners operate under inefficiently high levels of uncertainty regarding the environment there is some tendency for decisions to be shifted to lower levels and for mechanisms to be installed which produce adjustment to changes in relatively aggregative instruments; for this reason a relatively stable price system (as compared with market economies) may support the manipulation of output targets couched in aggregative terms.[36] A laissez-faire counterpart to this is Wolfe's hypothesized use of indicative planning to reduce the variation of demands, that is, the uncertainty level of enterprises with respect to future levels of demand for their outputs. A thoroughgoing characterization of adaptations along these lines might provide insight into the extent of rational convergence to be expected of capitalist and socialist economic institutions.

6. The Behavioral Approach

Though an oversimplification, it is roughly true to say that behaviorism arises in economics to play *ex post* to neoclassical decision theory's *ex ante*. Behavioral analysis involves descriptions of actual behavior in terms of the principal determinants of that behavior. The consumption function is a leading example of a behavioral relation. It may be rationalized by a model depicting the consumers' criteria and the range of alternatives they face, but the behavioral interest is directed primarily toward the outcome of the decision and its consequences rather than toward the nature and process of decision-making.

An interesting comparative behavioral study of government economic policy has been carried out for developed market economies by Kirschen and Morissens, and applied to the Soviet Union by Frank and Waelbroeck.[37] The instruments of policy are classified into three broad groups: financial policies, direct controls, and control of the institutional framework, with sub-categories within each of the three. Using this system, every relevant, identifiable government measure is classified, and in effect a history of economic policy is written by identifying the aims of policy,

[36] The more stable price system can provide greater stability of planners' expectations as to the disaggregative effects of target changes. See B. Ward, *The Socialist Economy, op. cit.* (n. 17), 92–94.
[37] E. S. Kirschen *et al.*, *Economic Policy in our Time*, 3 vols. Amsterdam, 1964; Z. Frank and J. Waelbroeck, "Soviet Economic Policy Since 1953: A Study of its Structure and Changes," *Soviet Studies*, XVII:1 (1965) pp. 1–43.

also classified, and associating particular policy measures with those aims. Countries then may be compared in terms of the relative frequency with which they resort to particular types of policy measures to serve particular goals. Quite expectedly, for example, the Soviet Union makes relatively far greater use of direct controls in the service of nearly all goals than the Common Market countries, while the latter make relatively far greater use of financial controls. The most interesting aspect of the study, however, are not the differences it discloses among countries but the similarities. The classification of both policy measures and goals seems to fit with a minimum of distortion countries with quite varied institutions. No explicit causal framework is presented and no attempt is made to display the interrelationships among the policy variables and goal variables. However, policies are rather explicitly related to the institutions administering the policy variables, so that a surprisingly uniform framework emerges for comparative organizational analysis.

Much of organization theory, particularly that part of it associated with the approach of Herbert Simon,[38] belongs in our neoclassical box, for it is concerned with the rationalization of acts by analyzing the context in which decisions are made. Nevertheless within this general rubric a good deal of work emphasizes the description of behavior rather than the analysis of decisions. A good example can be found in the leading studies of the Soviet enterprise[39] where such phenomena as the tendency to accumulate relatively high inventories of goods in process, to pay less attention to financial than to physical targets (at least during the Stalin era), to establish a sort of informal coalition between enterprise managers, key subordinates, and local party officials, and so forth, are documented. This kind of behavioral study of an institution and of its interaction with other institutions is of intrinsic interest and is also a necessary prerequisite to the development of neoclassical models of decision-making in the institution or of models of behavioral interaction. Though the framework may not be explicitly comparative, comparison is never far from the surface, at least when a relatively exotic institution is under study.

7. Adaptation to Injustice

Several years ago Coase studied some aspects of the law of torts, and particularly the law of nuisance, from a neoclassical point of view.[40] He

---

[38] Herbert Simon, *Administrative Behavior*, New York, 1947; J. G. March and H. Simon, *Organizations*, New York, 1958.

[39] David Granick, *Management of the Industrial Firm in the USSR*, New York, 1954; Joseph Berliner, *Factory and Manager in the USSR*, Cambridge, 1957.

[40] R. H. Coase, "The Problem of Social Cost," *Journal of Law and Economics*, *III* (1960) pp. 1–44.

argued that over a wide range of cases involving externalities it makes no difference, as far as Pareto-optimality is concerned, which party must pay damages. What matters is that there be a decision as to who is responsible, so that a basis for voluntary agreement among the affected parties is established. Thus if a business next door begins to make disturbing noises, it does not matter whether it is legally allowed to continue without paying damages or whether it is liable, provided one or the other is in fact established at law. For in either case it will be in the interest of the parties to make a voluntary agreement to alter the legal outcome if and only if social welfare is improved thereby. For Coase social welfare *is* Pareto-optimality and the attempts, perhaps not always entirely happy ones, of judges to find equitable criteria are dismissed.[41]

One may contrast this with Commons' approach.[42] He argued, for example, that the legal notion of a going concern was developed on equity grounds, in particular to establish a just sharing of the burdens of government. Because property value is an important basis of taxation, it becomes necessary on grounds of justice that the state establish an equitable formula for measuring the value of property. In enterprise taxation, Commons' example, involved placing a value on such intangibles as good will.

This sort of adaptation to injustice does not seem to be a widely used criterion in economics and little analysis appears to exist of the implications of justice as a criterion for judging economic alternatives. Nevertheless the box has been inserted because it seems to have considerable promise for organizational economic comparisons. For example, commercial arbitration in the United States appears to be governed by the notion of equity with respect to the contending parties, but in the Soviet Union a basic criterion for commercial arbitration is contribution to the plan.[43] It might be interesting to explore the implications of these distinct criteria for the resulting arbitration decisions. Or to take a more fundamental and much vaguer problem, it might be interesting to develop comparative models of equity rather than efficiency as a means of analyzing alternative institutions.

8. Ideas and Organizations

Though this topic is treated in another paper in this volume, a few words are in order here if only to fill our set of boxes. Ideas and ideologies, if

[41] *Ibid.*, p. 15.
[42] *Legal Foundations, op. cit.* (n. 33), p. 180.
[43] M. Domke, *Commercial Arbitration*, Englewood Cliffs, N.J., 1965, passim; H. J. Berman, *Justice in the USSR*, New York, pp. 124–144.

effective, create predispositions toward certain kinds of behavior; therefore, as long as they are effective, differences in ideas and ideologies will produce predictable differences in organized behavior.

The early students of comparative systems were perhaps overly simplistic in dealing with this causal sequence. In studying both Nazism and socialism there seems to have been a tendency to take the leaders or expositors at their own word instead of analyzing actual behavior and attempting to relate this to ideology. However, correctives were introduced rather early. For example in 1937 Robert Brady, in a classic analysis of Nazism, pointed out the many similarities between political and economic behavior in Germany and behavior in other capitalist economies, and in particular the very limited practical application of notions of corporatism.[44] And Gregory Grossman, quite early in the postwar development of Soviet studies in the United States, pointed to the apparently rather limited impact of the Marxian theory of capital—which the Soviets were vehemently reaffirming—in actual Soviet investment decision-making.[45]

Zauberman's recent book on Soviet mathematical economics seems to lay to rest, at least for his area of study, another theory of the relation between organization and ideas.[46] This theory, which in its modern form seems to date back to the anthropologist and linguist Whorf, postulates that a particular culture and variety of experience will strongly condition the kind of theorizing that a population will develop. Thus one might expect that the drastically different form of economic organization existing in the Soviet Union would tend to produce a very distinctive body of theorizing about economic problems. Zauberman's book amply displays and analyzes the conventionality of Soviet mathematical economics down to the present.

Such a finding of course does not discount the possibility that the development of this new "school" of economics in the Soviet Union will have a fundamental long-run impact on the nature of the Soviet economy, for example, as an instrument for the adaptation to inefficiency. This remains an open question and a fascinating one.

9. Conclusion

The field, if that is an appropriate name for it, of comparative economic systems has developed as an attempt to come to grips with two main problems: the economic structure of the good society and the broad, long-run tendencies of economic change. Both these themes are central in Adam

[44] *The Spirit and Structure of German Fascism*, New York, 1937.

[45] "Scarce Capital and Soviet Doctrine," *Quarterly Journal of Economics*, LXVII:3 (1953) 311–43.

[46] Alfred Zauberman, *Aspects of Planometrics*, New Haven, 1967.

Smith; on the former there is the comparison of mercantilism with competition, and on the latter the natural history of the relative development of agriculture, manufactures, and commerce. They have not always been of central concern to mainstream economics since Smith's time and perhaps are not central today; even so, it would be rather hard to deny that they are interesting and important questions. And clearly organization has a good deal to do with both issues. In conclusion I shall look briefly at the ways in which the boxes, the types of studies described above, relate to these two themes.

The display of grand historical tendencies often meets the objection that the exhibitor is being deterministic. In evaluating such objections it is useful to treat determinism/indeterminism as a more-less rather than an either-or category. For example, consider the assertion that one of a given set of events is about to occur, each of the events being equiprobable. This may be considered a deterministic statement both with respect to the range of possible events which may occur and with respect to the probability of occurrence of each event. And this in turn implies that all operational theories contain some elements of determinism. The principal reason why a theory may be called overly deterministic is its insufficient richness in its description of alternative possible states of affairs.

Contemporary theorists of convergence have emphasized the "logic of modern technology" as the basic causal factor promoting similarities in modern cultures, including similarities in organization. Probably there is general agreement on the enormous cultural impact of industrialism. However, in such works as Galbraith's,[47] though there is some analysis of the ways in which technology assertedly imposes closely resembling organizational forms, there is little discussion of alternative forms even if only to dismiss them or of causation running the other way, i.e., of the shaping of technology to fit cultural "imperatives." I think it reasonable to say that the extent of uniformity imposed on society by modern technology remains essentially untested.

Adaptive failure is a kind of nonconvergence with respect to the standard of comparison. The described studies all deal with failure to move farther toward an efficient or Pareto-optimal state. This is not directly related to the convergence thesis, except to the extent that static efficiency is in a sense a kind of completed adaptation to the possibilities of current technology. The adaptation-to-inefficiency hypothesis is somewhat more closely related to convergence, for it assumes that society does make an attempt to respond to its opportunities. At least in the Arrow version this approach too raises the possibility of a failure to adapt appropriately, though in

[47] J. K. Galbraith, *The New Industrial State*, Boston, 1967. The vast literature on the modernization of nonwestern societies is quite explicitly devoted to studying the ways and means by which "they" can become more like "us."

cases of failure some kind of "pressuring" mechanism is assumed to continue to operate. As for groping, the approach carries no implications for convergence. As it happens, two of the studies dealt with the issue and pointed toward strong convergence as a possibility; but one theory was very old and the other of very limited relevance for most parts of the world.

I suspect that someone who believes that all, or even most, of the approaches under discussion are potentially useful could not be very deterministic about convergence. Looking at the problem from these various perspectives has a tendency to reveal a considerable variety of alternative timepaths for society which cannot be eliminated as realistic possibilities. And so the possibility is opened up that deliberate choice will play a fundamental role in determining which alternatives will actually occur. In fact choice seems to be slipping into the grand schemes in an ineradicable way. Most striking and symptomatic perhaps is Horvat's redefinition of inevitability in terms of choice: A new economic system is by definition inevitable if it is feasible and superior to the existing one.[48]

The first theme—the economics of the good society—may well be more fundamental than the second because of the openness of the situation we face. Of course this may be deceptive; the openness may be a product of our ignorance rather than a measure of our power to control the environment. But still, it seems to be a more natural way of interpreting the cited approaches than grand historical determinism, even in the weak form we have used.

As a consequence neoclassicism becomes the central approach. However, it must be admitted that recent developments have not produced any great breakthroughs in our understanding of the economics of the good society. This approach contains the most deterministic of models in the defined sense. The Marshallian analysis by and large ignores both interorganizational and intraorganizational interaction; general-equilibrium theory ignores most of the organizational factors listed in the introduction to this paper; stability analysis is typically very crudely mechanistic in its assumptions; and game theory is a kind of cloud cuckoo land all its own. Surely the neoclassical approach must be rejected as the one best way to understand an open economic environment. However, the alternatives have their difficulties as well, so that despite its inadequacies many insights may still be gained from its use.

There is no need to linger on the choice aspects of the other approaches. An area that has not been treated in this paper which emerges from this orientation, however, might be mentioned. Decision mechanisms, particularly those involving social choice, are at work in making the choices hypothesized by the adaptation approaches. Some understanding

[48] *Op. cit.*, pp. 80–81.

of the results of adaptation, or of the failure to adapt, may be gained by attempting to formulate models of these decision environments and studying the circumstances under which appropriate decisions are made. Economists as well as political scientists have recently been at work in this area, using the more traditional of the neoclassical frameworks,[49] so perhaps some integration of the boxes may be possible. It may also be appropriate to mention here the obvious fact that much comparative economics is unavoidably interdisciplinary, because organization tends to derive many of its properties from the social and political environment in which it is embedded.

Finally, the question of values requires some comment. In this area economics performs rather badly. Even in such a broad and quite interdisciplinary field, research seems to be heavily dominated by considerations of Pareto-optimality and of efficiency. Not only is this a rather limited social value, its exclusive analysis may actually hinder understanding how decisions are actually made. For example, general equilibrium theory displays as part of its output the set of Pareto-optimal points, which have the well-known property that moving from one of them to another provides gains to some at the expense of losses to others. This formulation, and particularly the implication that the function of the polity is to choose among Pareto points, tends to maximize the divisiveness inherent in political-economic choice. It bears very little resemblance, for example, to the process of political decision-making, and particularly to the technique of packaging sets of issues as a means of compromising conflict. Perhaps one must perceive the problem of distribution in a special way before much conflict can be resolved. Economists pretend that these matters are of no concern to them, thereby running the risk of seriously hindering the effort to understand how basic economic decisions are in fact made.

This survey has covered a small number of studies in a very broad area. It concludes, with appropriate tentativeness, that there is no methodological basis for confining research to one or a few of the boxes that contain present research, that the present state of research leaves us with little basis for very deterministic predictions, and that a choice-oriented framework is perhaps most appropriate for the problems of comparative economics, but that our understanding of criteria of choice, of values, is in a very unsatisfactory state.

[49] E.g., Anthony Downs, *An Economic Theory of Democracy*, New York, 1957; J. Buchanan and G. Tullock, *Calculus of Consent*, Ann Arbor, 1962.

PART II

Alternative Approaches to the Comparison of Economic System Performance

5

On Comparing Planned Economies*
(A Methodological Inquiry)

by HERBERT S. LEVINE

1. Introduction

Alexander Gerschenkron has recently written:

"If I were a political scientist or a sociologist of the modern brand of reckless quantifiers, I should find little difficulty in supplying a precise answer. Taking my leaf from people who can quantify anything, be it alienation, incestuous impulses, or entrepreneurial vigor, I should readily develop a quantitative measure for the stability conditions of modern dictatorships. I should call it 'stab,' and I should be able to show how many stabs are needed for the minimum stability of a dictatorship, and I could, by adding up the individual stability conditions, arrive at a precise statement regarding the present situation in Soviet Russia as compared with that of five years ago. Unfortunately, however, I come from a profession in which quantification is a serious business."[1]

The present paper offers some rather reckless thoughts of a serious, but unhappy, economist. The advantages of the comparative approach in the study of planned economies have not been well exploited; as yet the comparative method has not been very fruitful in increasing our understanding of economic planning as a system of economic management, of the factors which give rise to planning, and of its results.

The potential advantages of the comparative approach in the study of planned economies are substantial. Much work—very productive work—has been done on Soviet economic planning. Our understanding of how the Soviet economy operates has increased significantly in the past twenty years. Clearly, however, it is dangerous to generalize freely about *economic planning*, its characteristics and consequences, from this one observation. For what is observed in the Soviet experience is a consequence, of course,

* I wish to thank Peter Wiles, Alfred Zauberman, the members of the Seminar on Economic Problems of the Communist World at the London School of Economics, the members of the International Economic Studies seminar at the University of Glasgow, and the participants in the Michigan conference for their helpful comments and suggestions.
[1] *Continuity in History and Other Essays*, Cambridge, Mass., 1968, p. 4.

not only of the Soviet system of economic planning, but also of many distinctive features of its Russian environment: geography, resource availabilities, political structure, pressures on the economy exerted by political leaders, and so forth.[2] In order to study economic planning as a distinct phenomenon we need more than one observation. That is, in order to derive universal propositions about economic planning, and in order to reduce general statements to specific statements about different types or levels of economic planning, and to develop new specific statements, we need observations on many planned economic systems.[3] I imagine few will dispute this. But in addition, and what is of concern here, we need a methodology for handling these observations.

The work on comparing planned economies has usually employed one or more of several common approaches.[4] One approach has been to treat the national unit as the unit of observation and comparison. In this approach, the planning system in, say, the Soviet Union is compared with

[2] I have written, elsewhere, on the problem of disentangling the consequences of centralized planning from those of excessive pressure on economic resources in the Soviet experience with economic planning. See my article, "Pressure and Planning in the Soviet Union," in Henry Rosovsky ed., *Industrialization in Two Systems*, New York, 1966, pp. 266–285.

[3] Cf. Amitai Etzioni, *A Comparative Analysis of Complex Organizations*, Glencoe, New York, 1961, p. xiv.

[4] The literature is large. For examples of texts on the general question of comparative economic systems, see William Loucks and William Whitney, *Comparative Economic Systems*, 8th edition, New York, 1969; and Gregory Grossman, *Economic Systems*, Englewood Cliffs, N.J., 1967. See also Robert A. Dahl and Charles E. Lindblom, *Politics, Economics and Welfare*, New York, 1953; and Irma Adelman and Cynthia Taft Morris, *Society, Politics and Economic Development*, Baltimore, Md., 1967.

For a more direct focus on comparative economic planning, see Peter Wiles, *The Political Economy of Communism*, Cambridge, 1962; Jan Tinbergen, *Central Planning*, New Haven, 1964 (especially pp. 32–41 and the Appendix, "An International Comparison of Planning Processes"); Benjamin Ward, *The Socialist Economy*, New York, 1967; Economic Commission for Europe, *Economic Survey of Europe in 1962*, Part 2: *Economic Planning in Europe*, Geneva, 1965; E. S. Kirschen *et al.*, *Economic Policy in Our Time*, 3 Vols., Amsterdam, 1964; Bert G. Hickman, ed., *Quantitative Planning of Economic Policy*, Brookings Institution, Washington, D.C., 1965; Max F. Millikan, ed., *National Economic Planning*, New York, 1967; Alan Brown and Egon Neuberger, eds., *International Trade and Central Planning*, Berkeley, 1968; Frederic L. Pryor, *Public Expenditures in Communist and Capitalist Nations*, London, 1968.

For some relevant literature outside the field of economics, see A. Etzioni, *op. cit.*; Williams M. Evan, "Indices of the Hierarchical Structure of Industrial Organizations," *Management Science*, IX:3 (1963) 468–477; Thomas A. Marschak, "Economic Theories of Organization," in James G. March, ed., *Handbook of Organizations*, Chicago, 1965, pp. 423–450; Robert M. Marsh, *Comparative Sociology*, New York, 1967.

that in France or Yugoslavia and the similarities and differences noted. The exercise, if done well, can produce many insights into the workings of the individual economies concerned. But its ability to generate universal propositions of an economic nature about economic planning is limited, because the units of comparison are in the wrong dimension. They are not in the economic dimension but in the political dimension.

Another common approach has been to construct several pure models of planning systems with different types of decision and control mechanisms, and through the process of deduction to analyze their operation, and then to compare actual economies with these models. This approach has produced useful results but mostly in the realm of theory. For when it comes to matching actual economies with the pure models, the actual economies usually turn out to be varying mixtures of different models.

Perhaps the most common approach lies somewhere between the preceding two. An economy is identified as a prototype of a certain class of planned economies, e.g., the Soviet Union as a prototype of command and France as a prototype of indicative planning, and then the prototypes are compared. This approach is supposed to produce general propositions about economic planning, because the two economies are supposed to represent major classes of planned economies. Again, the results are often illuminating; but their significance is limited, because in actuality the classes are either ill-defined, or if defined with any precision, are found to be sparsely populated, in fact perhaps populated by the prototype alone.

Another approach is to focus on various key economic decisions (input combinations, capital investment, technological change), or economic institutions (the firm, the farm, money and banking system), or economic sectors (industry, agriculture, foreign trade), and to compare these different decisions, institutions, or sectors in different planned economies. This approach, too, increases our knowledge and understanding of the mechanisms of economic planning. But in its nature it is disjointed and at best provides only partial pictures of economic planning.

What is required, if substantial progress is to be made in our understanding of real, planned economic systems, is an approach which will focus on a systematic categorization of economic planning. The scientific method in the comparison of planned economies should consist of relating the different observations to different levels of the phenomenon under investigation, namely economic planning. The planned economy as a whole, or an important aspect of it, should be categorized in some systematic or ordered way and then, from the different observations derived through comparative analysis, the ordered levels of economic planning should be related to observed levels of other phenomena which can be either of a causal or a consequential nature. What I am suggesting, simply, is that the basic scientific method used generally in economic analysis be used in the comparative study of planned economies; that from the various observations which are made of different planned economies, relationships be drawn between different levels of the variable "economic planning" and different levels of other variables which are deemed to be of interest; and that in some of these relationships, economic planning can be viewed as a dependent variable, and in some as an independent variable.

In order to proceed along such an approach, we need to be able to differentiate in some ordered way various types, levels, or degrees of economic planning or "economic plannedness." It is, of course, exceedingly difficult to classify and order a complex organism like a planned economy or even a given aspect of it. But the possibilities and the problems that would be faced should at least be investigated. This is what is intended in the present paper. First, the main elements of a possible methodological approach will be set out. Second, the components which might go into a measurement of plannedness will be presented and examined. Third, the possible uses of the methodological approach will be described. And fourth, a number of problems and difficulties will be discussed.

2. The Approach

It would seem proper that a discussion of a methodology for comparing planned economies should begin with a definition of economic planning. I take economic planning roughly to mean social control over an economy through a process which includes the drawing up of a picture of a desired state of an economy at a future point in time and the utilization of some instrumentalities to bring about this desired state. It is not necessary, however, for the purposes of this paper, to decide which real economies should be included in the set of planned economies thus defined and which should be excluded. The methodological approach to be discussed, since it involves the ordering of economies according to degrees of economic plannedness, does not require that a precise boundary be drawn between the set of planned and nonplanned economies.[5]

The second element of the methodological scheme is more crucial. As has just been suggested, what we seek is a scale of economic plannedness to use for the ordering of observed economies. Unfortunately, the degree

[5] March and Simon begin their book on organizations: "But for present purposes we need not trouble ourselves about the precise boundaries to be drawn around an 'organization' and a 'non-organization'. We are dealing with empirical phenomena, and the world has an uncomfortable way of not permitting itself to be fitted into clean classifications," James G. March and Herbert A. Simon, *Organizations*, New York, 1958, p. 1.

of plannedness of an economy is not a simple matter. First of all, plannedness can be visualized in different ways, that is, in terms of different aspects of planning. For example, the focus may be on who controls the allocation of economic resources (center or periphery), or it may be on how resources are controlled (administrative versus economic methods, or the generation and use of information). Second, the different aspects are not mutually exclusive. They contain common elements. They overlap like different two-dimensional planes cut into a three-dimensional figure. Which aspect should be chosen as the basis for ordering economies according to plannedness? There is no unique answer to this question. To a great extent the choice of focus depends upon the conceptions of planning and interests of the particular researcher and on the type of questions to be asked about the process of economic planning and its consequences. Furthermore there need be no unique answer. More than one aspect could, and perhaps should, be treated. But for purposes of illustrating the methodological approach in this paper, we will focus on one aspect of plannedness: Who controls the allocation of economic resources.

The word "control," however, has certain ambiguities. If it is said that "the center exercises control," this might be understood on the one hand to mean the exercise of authority by the center or, on the other, the exercise of influence by the center. The former refers to the center's wielding of power and the latter to the center's ability to achieve the outcome of economic activity it desires. Moreover, under certain circumstances the two may move in opposite directions. If, say, the center has perfect knowledge of the behavioral patterns of peripheral units, then it could limit the exercise of its authority to the setting of certain parameters (prices) and could get the allocation results it wanted through the autonomous behavior of the periphery. Such an economy would exhibit a low degree of plannedness in terms of exercise of authority but a high degree in terms of exercise of influence.

It may therefore be wise to concentrate on one of the possible meanings of the word control. But again the answer to the question, which one, is not unique. Either could be chosen. For a number of reasons in this paper we will focus on the *exercise of authority* by the center.[6] First of all, it is

---

[6] By the term "center" we have in mind the ruling group and its central bureaucracy (including the central political party bureaucracy where appropriate), that is, more than a single ruler or executive board but less than the entire state bureaucracy. This is a general definition; an operational definition of "center" will have to be determined when an actual study is undertaken. As was suggested by Alec Nove at the conference, this will involve a number of problems. To mention just one, the center need not be a homogeneous group. Various parts of it (for example, those at the head of production branches) may have interests in protecting their subordinate bureaucracies from the exercise of authority by other parts of the center while at the same time exercising their own central authority over their subordinates.

already a common focus. Both those who observe and analyze planned economies and those who design and reform them frequently view planning systems in terms of their degrees of centralization and decentralization. And though the dichotomy, centralization-decentralization, has been given many meanings, the degree of centralization in the exercise of authority is one of its main ideas. Second, given this focus in planning practice, it could be thought that the degree of centralization of authority is a promising variable to help explain the variance in the experiences of different planned economies which, after all, is the objective of the approach being described. Third, it is perhaps somewhat more amenable to the methodological approach than other aspects of plannedness and thus is more appropriate for a preliminary illustration of the methodology.

On the other hand, some may argue that planning is a process wherein economic activity is organized so as to achieve certain goals, and therefore any measurement of plannedness must include the extent of goal achievement as its main, or one of its main, elements.[7] I do not agree.[8] But there is no need to make a major issue of the point. The methodology to be described in this paper concerns the measurement of the *centralization of authority* in a planning system, by which is meant the degree of formal and informal possession and exercise of authority by the center. I look upon it also as a measure of plannedness in the sense of the intensity of central social intervention in the economy. The reader, if he prefers, may look upon it solely as a measure of centralization of authority. The methodology itself will be little affected by the interpretation chosen. However, it should be kept in mind that in the approach we are taking the degree of goal achievement is not part of the scale to be used to order different planned economies but is to be treated as one of the dependent variables.

The operational parts of the approach consist of three key classes of planning instruments and activities, thirteen significant elements within these classes, and their respective descriptive scales. Planning instruments and activities are separated into the three classes: the plan, the construction of the plan, and the implementation of the plan. The elements of planning contained within each of these classes are sufficiently different from the elements of the other classes as to warrant separate attention, and each of these classes of planning elements is important in defining the centralization of authority, and the three comprise its main determinants.[9]

[7] At the conference, Oldrich Kyn and Branko Horvat put forward arguments of this nature.

[8] One problem is the generality of the definition as it stands. Under it, the classical perfectly competitive system might be said to possess a high degree of plannedness. (Perhaps it was not a coincidence that the above argument was made by a member of a seminar held in the Adam Smith Building at the University of Glasgow.)

[9] It is not true, as might be argued, that the ways in which the plan is implemented are sufficient to define the intensity of the centralization of authority.

Planning elements within each class were selected for the significance they bear in defining the degree of centralization of authority. To each element a descriptive scale is attached which is related to the characteristic centralization of authority. Each scale is to be divided into, say, five (or more) intervals identified by quantitative or intensity adjectives or by letter grades.[10] For example, in the first class, the plan, one element used is "the detail of the plan," and the descriptive scale runs from "highly aggregative" (low degree of centralization) to "very specific" (high degree). The number of such planning elements which might be included could be great. However, in this exploratory sketch an attempt has been made to keep it small and yet sufficient to suggest how centralization of authority in a planned economy might be delineated.

The idea then is that each planned economy to be observed is to be placed on each scale in relationship to the other planned systems in the interval deemed most appropriate. From the individual scales an overall scaling of the observed systems according to the characteristic centralization of authority is to be derived.

Each step of this procedure entails many troublesome problems. But before touching on some of them, let us first turn to a brief discussion of the three key classes, the planning elements and descriptive scales chosen for use.[11]

3. Classes and Descriptive Scales

3.1. The Plan

A. Periodicity of the Plan (Long Term——Short Term).[12]   The first aspect of the plan which bears on the centralization of authority in the system is the periodicity of the plan, i.e., the length of the period covered by the plan.

First of all the plan itself plays a role; for even if there is little overt implementation, the plan document may well affect the environment in which economic decisions are taken in a number of ways. It may provide information about certain governmental intentions which may influence economic decision-makers. It may also establish a set of temporary constraints which act as starting points for bargaining among economic decision-makers and between them and agents of government.

Second, the methods of plan construction play a role. There is a difference for the centralization of authority between a situation in which the plan is constructed in a very democratic way, with no imposition of the center's will, and its opposite, whatever the implementation system used.

[10] I am indebted to E. S. Kirschen for his advice on this point. Adelman and Morris, in their study, use letter grades with pluses and minuses. See Adelman and Morris, *Society, op. cit.* (n. 3).

[11] These are listed below in an appendix.

[12] The descriptive scales run consistently from low intensity of centralization of authority to high intensity.

The argument is that the shorter the period covered by the plan and thus the more frequent the issuance of new plans, the more intensive is the exercise of authority by the center.[13] The descriptive scale to be used runs from long-term to short-term, where long-term indicates plans of twenty years' duration or more, and short-term indicates plans of one year or perhaps less.

In those economies where more than one type of plan is constructed, the most important one or the operational one should be chosen. Thus, since in the Soviet Union the annual plan rather than the five-year plan is the operational one, the Soviet Union would be placed at, or approximately at, the short-term end of the scale.

In some economies, no document precisely termed a plan exists, but decisions are taken at governing levels about economic goals and policies. These could be treated as plans. If the periodicity of such a "plan" is vague, it might be wise to place the economy near the long-term end of the scale.

B. Scope of the Plan (Small Part of Economy——Entire Economy). A second aspect of a plan relevant to centralization of authority is its scope or the portion of the economy covered by the plan. The larger the part of the economy covered by the plan the greater the centralization of authority. The scale, running from "small part of the economy" to "entire economy," could be most directly calibrated in terms of percentage of gross social product (production of final and intermediate products). However, this would provide an insufficient reading on centralization of authority, because the prices used as weights in the measurement of social product do not always adequately reflect the relative importance, to the central authorities, of different types of economic activities.

C. Plan Coverage of Investment (None——Entire). One such activity is investment.[14] Therefore, a separate indicator of the planned coverage of investment should be added. As above, the larger the part of total investment covered by the plan the greater the centralization of authority.

D. Plan Coverage of Distribution of Materials (None——Entire). Another aspect of plan coverage concerns control of the distribution of materials

[13] The periodicity of plans, of course, bears some relationship to the matters being planned. Some things, in their nature, require long-period plans. The argument here, however, is that if the short-period aspects of the long-period plan are reflected in short-period plans, the degree of centralization of authority is greater than it would be if the center issued only one long-period plan and then let the implementation system and nature take its course.

[14] This special attention given to investment reflects a biased interest in industrialized and industrializing economies and a bias of the center within these economies for the control and fostering of dynamic growth and change. In an underdeveloped economy, as pointed out at the conference by Knud Erik Svendsen, the center might have more interest in, say, agricultural development.

(as distinguished from the planned setting of levels of wholesale trade, which is included under B above. The centralization of authority is increased to the extent that the economic plan covers not only levels of outputs but also the allocation of materials, i.e., states who is to receive which input materials. If this element were to be ignored, then for example much of the increase in centralization in the United States economy during World War II would be missed, not to mention the degree of centralization in the Soviet Union.

E. Level of Detail in the Plan (Highly Aggregative——Very Specific). The final aspect of the plan included here is its level of detail. The greater the level of detail in the plan the greater the centralization of authority. The scale used runs from highly aggregative, say, size of total output, toward increasing specificity of detail. As the level of detail increases, one would also expect to find a shift from the use of units in value terms to the use of physical units.

3.2. Construction of the Plan

The issues of interest for an investigation of the centralization of authority in this second class of planning elements concern the extent and type of participation in the construction of the plan by units at the periphery. The greater the extent to which the center does all calculations and makes all decisions by itself, the greater the centralization of authority.

A. Extent of Participation by the Periphery (High Participation——No Participation). The first aspect of plan construction that I use is the general one, the extent of participation by the periphery, with the scale running from "high participation," indicating low intensity of centralization, to "no participation," indicating high intensity. This scale involves a number of different dimensions, some of which I will discuss below. The term participation is meant here to include all forms of participation. The term periphery is meant to include all units away from the center (as defined in footnote 6, above). The distance of the peripheral unit from the center, that is, its place in the hierarchy, could be considered as a separate element. But that distinction may not be necessary, for it can be taken into account in this scale. Thus, if participation in plan construction is limited to units in the upper bureaucracy, the extent of peripheral participation should be considered to be smaller than if participation extends to units lower in the bureaucracy and to basic production units.

A similar question is raised by the difference in types of decisions made at different levels. For example, as argued in the previous section, since investment decisions are of such importance in determining the course that a planned economy will take, those at the center might concentrate their power and authority on them.

B. Extent of Participation by Periphery in the Construction of the Investment Plan (High Participation——No Participation). Therefore, we again should give investment added weight and treat it separately. By construction of the investment plan I mean the decisions concerning the levels of output and allocation of capital goods in the economic plan. The more these decisions emanate only from the center, the greater the centralization of authority; the lower down the hierarchy the participation runs and the greater this peripheral participation, the lower the centralization of authority.

C. Type of Participation by Periphery (Authority to Initiate Proposals——Information Only). A further dimension of participation by peripheral units in plan construction is of importance: the type of participation involved. If their participation is restricted to supplying information only, say, about input coefficients and levels of inventories, then to that extent the centralization of authority is high. Whereas to the extent that the peripheral units have the authority to initiate proposals of their own, the centralization of authority should be said to be low.

The meanings of the terms "information" and "initiate proposals" may not always be clear, but the underlying aim in this descriptive scale is to disclose the dispersion of authority in the construction of the plan. Thus, if an economy constructed its plan by means of a programming model employing the decomposition principle[15] or the Malinvaud model,[16] the peripheral unit could be said to have some power to initiate proposals. For the data it provides to the center, in response to the prices the center sends it, contain information not only about production technologies but also proposals about composition and levels of outputs.

The question of the dispersion of power in plan construction, however, does not end there. We must also be concerned with how the center treats the proposals offered by the periphery. To the extent that the periphery's proposals are dominant and the function of the center limited to coordination, clearing of markets as it were, to that extent the centralization of authority is low. But if the center has the power to overrule the periphery's proposals for reasons other than plan coordination, that is, for reasons of imposing its will and its preferences on the economy, to that extent the centralization of authority is high. This aspect might be handled separately, but it is probably better to combine the different dimensions of the type of participation in one reading, because they are so closely intertwined.

[15] See George Dantzig, *Linear Programming and Extensions*, Princeton, N.J., 1963, Ch. 23.
[16] See E. Malinvaud, "Decentralized Procedures for Planning," in E. Malinvaud and M. O. L. Bacharach, eds., *Activity Analysis in the Theory of Growth and Planning*, New York, 1967, pp. 170–208.

3.3. Implementation of the Plan

This class of planning elements is the most important in delineating the centralization of authority. It is here that the culmination of the exercise of authority by the center is to be seen. The aspects of plan implementation of concern include the extent to which an attempt is made to implement the plan and the various methods used for implementation and their meaning for the centralization of authority.

A. Attempt to Implement the Plan (No Attempt——Strong Attempt). The stronger the attempt to implement the plan, the greater the centralization of authority. "Attempt to implement the plan" may have two shades of meaning. The strength of the attempt to implement could be distinguished from the strictness of the implementation, that is, great efforts might be made to have the plan observed without insisting on strict compliance. In fact, there might be cases where the plan is meant mainly to orient the economy, and government action toward the economy is aimed primarily at achieving coordination or equilibrium in some acceptable but not predetermined relation to the plan. It should not be too difficult, however, to judge these two aspects—strength and strictness—taken jointly: the stronger the attempt to implement and the stricter the compliance with the plan insisted upon, the greater the centralization of authority.

B. Means of Implementation (Manipulation of Parameters——Issuing of Directives). If attempts are made to implement the plan, the centralization of authority will then further depend upon the means of implementation used. This relates to whether the center attempts to implement the plan through manipulation of parameters or, at the other extreme, through the issuing of directives. With the former, the decision-makers at the periphery are free to act as they like, pursuing their own behavioral patterns, maximizing, minimizing, satisficing what they wish. The center, operating on some knowledge or assumption about the behavioral patterns of peripheral units, limits its attempts to implement the plan to the setting of certain parameters like prices or taxes and subsidies so as to bring about the economic activity it desires. To the extent that only such means are used, the degree of centralization of authority is low. At the other end of the scale is the issuing of directives by the center as the means of implementing the plan (the command economy). Here the center simply commands the peripheral units to do certain things, produce certain levels of outputs, use certain levels of inputs, and so forth.[17] To the extent that such means are used the centralization of authority is high.

[17] Directness of command might be differentiated; that is, centralization of authority is greater if the commands are given directly from the center to the basic producing unit and less if commands are filtered through many levels of a bureaucracy. (I am indebted to Richard Portes for this suggestion.) This relation

Some intermediate points on this scale are worth noting. Moving from low intensity of centralization of authority to high, the center, first, might use manipulation of parameters but might also prescribe the behavioral function that peripheral units were to follow (as is done in the Lange model). This pattern would represent somewhat greater centralization of authority in regard to plan implementation than parameter manipulation without behavior prescription. Further along the scale is the limitation by the center of access to types of activities, to inputs or to means of acquiring inputs, like foreign exchange or financial credit, in order to bring about compliance with the plan. This type of restriction is quite common and is usually accomplished through various types of licensing and rationing.

So far we have remained within the segment of the means-of-implementation scale in which the peripheral units retain initiative, and the center uses various means to influence their actions. A key point on the scale is that at which the center switches to what Peter Wiles calls "positive controls": that type of control in which the center actually tells the periphery to take a certain action.[18] The use of government contracts raises some difficulties in this regard. To the extent that the peripheral unit enters into the contract willingly, we are still on the low-intensity-of-centralization side of this point. But to the extent that the peripheral unit is forced into the contract or to the extent that after beginning willingly it is subsequently locked in and forced to do things it might not otherwise do, we are on the high-intensity side of the point.

C. Number and Detail of Directives/Parameters (Low——High). The ability of peripheral units to exercise discretion and initiative is further affected by the number and the level of detail of the directives or parameters (whichever is being used to implement the plan). *Theoretically*, the greater the number of directives and the greater their detail, the less the discretion left to peripheral units and thus the greater the centralization of authority. Similarly, the more numerous and more detailed the parameters manipulated by the center (many individual prices and price ratios rather than just the aggregate price level or rate of interest), the greater the exercise of authority by the center. However, though this may theoretically be true (which assumes that the center is able to handle great numbers of directives/parameters), actual practice (Soviet and other) indicates that when the number of directives becomes very large, the center is not able to make

---

would, however, depend on the efficiency of the bureaucracy. It would not be true of a Weberian ideal-type bureaucracy. Undoubtedly, though, it is true of real-world bureaucracies. The suggestion has the further advantage of making it possible to take into account the power that lower entities might exercise at the implementation stage, through bureaucratic bargaining processes.

[18] Peter Wiles, *Political Economy, op. cit.* (n. 4 above), p. 78.

the total set consistent. In such a situation, it is impossible for a peripheral unit to obey all the directives given to it, and consequently it must use its own discretion in deciding which to follow and which to violate. Thus, in practice, after a certain point, the greater the number of directives, the *less* the actual centralization of authority. Wartime experience in the West showed certain similarities in regard to price-controls. To the extent, then, that this factor is at work, the numbers and detail scale, after such a point is reached, will not provide a correct reading of centralization of authority. This must be taken into account in any application of the methodology.

D. Center's Plan Adjustment Mechanisms (Weak——Strong). The ability of peripheral units to exercise discretion is increased whenever the real situation, for whatever reason, differs from that foreseen by the plan. Therefore, to the extent that the center has a strong, well worked out mechanism for readjusting the plan to reality, to the extent it is able to produce, say, appropriate new directives to replace existing inappropriate ones, to that extent the possible exercise of discretion by the peripheral units is reduced and the centralization of authority maintained.

This element is important, for there is always a gap between plan and reality. Moreover, Soviet experience shows that one of the high-intensity characteristics from the first class of planning elements, the use of short-period plans (in the Soviet case, the annual plan), may lead to the need for plan-adjustment mechanisms in the plan-implementation stage. Soviet plan-construction methodology is an iterative process, essentially with instructions flowing down the hierarchy and information flowing up. However, the period of a year is insufficient to allow for convergence to a consistent plan.[19] The iterative process thus continues during the implementation of the plan. To the extent that the center is able to change its directives effectively to meet reality, centralization of authority is maintained; but to the extent that peripheral units are free to use their own discretion in adjusting to reality, the centralization of authority is low.[20] Planning mechanisms concerning methods and institutions for changing plans during the course of their operation are of importance here; but so also are such things as the degree of centralization of control of the

[19] Primitiveness of balancing techniques is also a factor. See H. S. Levine, "The Centralized Planning of Supply in Soviet Industry," in Joint Economic Committee, *Comparisons of the United States and Soviet Economies*, U.S. Govt. Printing Office, Washington, D.C., 1959, pp. 151–175.

[20] In those economies where the operational plan is a longer-term plan, say 4–5 years, there may be time for iterative plan-construction procedures to converge to a consistent plan, but by the time the plan is completed, the assumptions about the real world made at the beginning of the plan-construction process may no longer be realistic, and so again the center's readjustment mechanism is important.

financial mechanism and of the materials distribution system, since they impinge directly on the degree of discretion that peripheral units could exercise in adjusting the plan to reality.

E. Implementation Incentive Mechanism (Low Pressure——High Pressure). The type of incentive or enforcement mechanism used for the implementation of the plan is a further important element which overlaps with the other elements in this class. To the extent that the methods for gaining compliance are low pressure, centralization of authority is said to be low; to the extent they are high pressure, centralization is high. At the low-pressure end of the scale might be the use solely of appeals to social responsibility (this, though, depends on the society's system of values). A higher degree of centralization of authority is reflected in systems: a) which give specific material rewards, such as bonuses for the implementation of specific plan tasks, b) those that link administrative status and social position, promotion and maintenance, to plan implementation and c) those that use noneconomic institutions such as the Communist Party to apply pressure for plan implementation;[21] and on toward the highest pressure means of plan implementation enforcement: making the plan legally binding, and enforcing it with the police power of the state.

A major problem in regard to this planning element arises from the use normally in actual planning practice of a combination of more than one enforcement mechanism. Judgments will have to be made as to their aggregate character.

4. Possible Uses

If, through the use of the methodology just outlined, planned economies could be scaled according to the attribute characterized here as centralization of authority, what are some of the questions we might explore?

4.1. Centralization of Authority as a Dependent Variable

First, we might look at centralization of authority as a dependent variable. One of the sets of questions commonly asked concerns the effects on planning of such environmental conditions as property relations, ideology, stage of economic and political development, and size and resource endowment.

The role of property relations in planning has perhaps been excessively denigrated in much of the analytical work on planning done in the West. Although it is true, that the type of property institutions which exist in a society do not determine the type of planning employed, they may well have

[21] The position of this on the scale depends on the position and power of the noneconomic institutions.

a significant influence on it. Property relations affect a society's power structure and thus the setting of economic goals and indeed social values. Those with power can influence the formulation of a plan and can strengthen or constrain the means used for its implementation.[22] It would be interesting, therefore, to see what sort of a relationship might prevail between types of property relations and centralization of authority.[23]

Ideology and stage of development as system determinants are the subjects of other papers in this volume. Let me therefore defer any comment here other than to say their importance has often been argued; it would be clearly worthwhile to explore their relationship to the question of the centralization of authority in a planned economy.

One of the important ways in which size and resource endowment are thought to influence the planning system is in relationship to the scope of the resource endowment. To the extent that a nation possesses all the resources it requires for the operation of its economy and thus is free from the *need* to engage in foreign trade, to that extent the center's power to exercise authority over the economy is said to be greater. This, of course, does not mean that it will use the power. Conversely, the more dependent a country is on foreign trade, the more restricted, it might be argued, is the center's ability to exercise authority over the economy. Presumably this restriction is due to the center's lack of authority over the foreign sources of supply. According to this contention, one would not expect a small nation which is dependent on foreign trade to have a high degree of centralization of authority. This reasoning, however, is not completely convincing. For supplies from abroad might be quite reliable (predictable), and potential foreign sources of supply amply available. In such a case, the center's ability to exercise authority would not be constrained (at least not for the reasons stated). Moreover, if a negative relationship between dependence on trade and centralization of authority does appear, as in many East European countries in the more recent period, it is partly owing to the conclusion reached by these countries that the more intensive centralization they practiced in the past led to low-quality output which hindered their ability to earn the foreign exchange required for their imports.

The situation is further complicated by another argument sometimes made, that the causal lines run the other way: that in those economies where the centralization of authority is high, foreign trade will be low,

[22] Property is of course not the only source of power in a society. See, e.g., discussion in G. Grossman, *Economic Systems, op. cit.* (n. 4), Ch. 2.

[23] A serious problem would be encountered in classifying systems of property relations. Similar problems exist with the other causal variables to be mentioned e.g., ideology. They are less prevalent when we look at centralization of authority as an independent variable, where, owing to the work of Kuznets, Bergson, and others, many of the potential dependent variables have been quantified.

because the center does not want its exercise of authority reduced and it therefore consciously limits foreign trade. On the other hand, again in the East European Communist economies, the predominance of the planning goal of rapid industrial growth has led in practice to large importation of industrial inputs and machinery which could not (easily or quickly) be produced domestically.[24]

The picture thus is a confused one. But there is reason to believe that it would help to see what sort of relationship between centralization of authority and trade share might be shown by the approach outlined. At least, it might indicate upon which set of cross-currents analysis should be concentrated.

Another group of questions commonly asked in studies of economic planning has to do with the effects of the goals of planning on the type of planning system adopted.[25] The identification of the goals of any planned economy involves problems. On a philosophical level, it is often difficult to distinguish goals from values, ultimate goals from instrumental goals, means from ends. Furthermore, economies normally have more than one goal, some conflicting with others.[26] Economists generally are concerned with instrumental goals, and our aim here should be the identification of those which are dominant: for example, rapid industrialization and catch-up with the capitalist West in the Soviet Union; modernization and international competitiveness in France. In addition, for the purpose of investigating the effect of goals on centralization of authority, it is necessary to inquire into those aspects of goals which might affect centralization of authority and to classify planned economies according to these aspects. The approach could parallel the one already described.

We might, for example, distinguish three aspects of planning goals, one concerning the scope or degree of support they enjoy in the society, and the other two concerning their content. The scale for the first aspect would run from wide support to narrow support. The hypothesis is that the narrower the support for the dominant planning goals, that is, the more they reflect only the preferences of a small group or of a dictator, the greater the centralization of authority will have to be in order to bring about their accomplishment. The second aspect would concern the degree of economic and social change from the existing situation implied by the

[24] See papers in Brown and Neuberger, *op. cit.* (n. 4). It seems apparent from the East European experience that the imposition of planning does not necessarily lead to a decrease in trade. However, if one were able to rank the East European countries in regard to centralization of authority, some other relationship to trade ratios might be observed.

[25] See, e.g., Tinbergen, *Central Planning, op. cit.* (n. 4), pp. 68–69. For valuable discussions of the goals of planning see items in footnote 4 by Dahl and Lindblom, Kirschen *et al.*, and Economic Commission for Europe.

[26] See discussions in Dahl and Lindblom, *Politics, op. cit.* (n. 4), pp. 25–54, and Kirschen *et al.*, *Economic Policy, op. cit.* (n. 4), pp. 3–27.

planning goals. The scale would go from little or no change to drastic change; and the hypothesis: the more drastic the change called for, the greater will be the required centralization of authority. The third aspect is closely related but should be treated separately. It concerns the speed of change, slow to rapid. The more rapid the change called for by the planning goals, it could be argued, the greater the centralization of authority needed.

Each relationship, between centralization of authority as the dependent variable and the environmental and goal elements mentioned as the independent variables, could be investigated separately. A more ambitious project would involve an attempt to make some judgment about the relative effects of the various independent variables on the level of centralization of authority.

4.2. Centralization of Authority as an Independent Variable

Much of the work to date on planned economies has involved the measurement of economic performance, often with the implicit or explicit aim of shedding light on the effect of economic planning on various performance characteristics.[27] However, as I have argued, the accomplishment of this aim has been limited by the ways in which the economies studied have been classified or grouped (again implicitly or explicitly). The methodological approach I have described could be used to relate these measures of performance to the degree of plannedness of an economy or to one aspect of it, the degree of centralization of authority.

Because the conceptual problems here are not as severe as in the previous section, the discussion need not be lengthy. But its brevity should not indicate a low potential of profitable use for the approach in regard to the consequences of planning. Quite the contrary, it would be here that we would expect the results to be more meaningful because of the available quantification of many of the dependent variables we would wish to examine and because of the interest in the effects of planning.

First of all, we would want to see what relationship exists between a scaling of economies according to centralization of authority and such major measures of economic performance as growth and efficiency (technical, static, and dynamic). It is commonly argued that although high centralization of authority may lead to rapid growth, it may also lead to low efficiency. This argument is based mainly on studies and assumed classifications of the Soviet and, to a lesser extent, East European

[27] The literature is large but see especially the pioneering work of Abram Bergson, *The Real National Income of Soviet Russia Since 1928*, Cambridge, 1961; and *The Economics of Soviet Planning*, New Haven, 1964, Ch. 14; and the papers in A. Bergson and S. Kuznets, eds., *Economic Trends in the Soviet Union*, Cambridge, 1963. See also Joint Economic Committee, *New Directions in the Soviet Economy*, U.S. Govt. Printing Office, Washington, D.C., 1966, especially the article by Stanley Cohn.

economies compared with the West. It would be interesting to see whether it stands up when a concerted attempt is made to rank economies, both east and west, according to the degree of centralization of authority in the economy.

Likewise, it would be interesting to investigate the relationship between centralization and such other performance characteristics as economic stability, level of unemployment, composition of national income, and so forth. For example, George Staller's findings may be thought to have cast doubt on the assumption that planning reduces instability.[28] But his groupings were essentially East European planned, and Western non-planned, economies. How would the results look if countries were scaled by the degree of plannedness, as represented by the degree of centralization of authority?

Finally, as indicated earlier, it would be of interest to investigate the relationship between centralization of authority and the precision with which plans are fulfilled or the degree of goal achievement in planned economies (the two are not necessarily the same). The latter relationship would be a measure of the effectiveness of centralization of authority as a planning instrument.

Before leaving this discussion, a word about causal inferences. One would not expect to find a perfect fit between the rankings of economies according to the degree of plannedness (centralization of authority) and any of the possible dependent variables mentioned. But even if such a development did occur, one should be careful about drawing causal conclusions. Causal inferences in nonexperimental research present many basic difficulties. I do not wish to make the "everything is related to everything else" argument, but in this case the difficulties are compounded by the presence of third variables (including those regarded as independent variables in the previous section) which may directly affect both the centralization of authority and one or more of the dependent variables just discussed. Before any causal inferences can be drawn, this problem must be analyzed and, furthermore, theoretical explanations for the relationships must be explored.

5. Problems

If this paper has done nothing else, it has at least illustrated how complex and multi-faceted economic planning is. Numerous problems and pitfalls lie in the path of the methodological approach described. Let me discuss briefly some of the most important difficulties.

[28] See George Staller, "Fluctuations in Economic Activity: Planned and Free Market Economies, 1950–60," *American Economic Review*, LIV:3 (1964) 385–395. See also Martin Bronfenbrenner, (ed.), "Is the Business Cycle Obsolete?" New York, 1969.

Substantial limitations afflict our ability to observe. Our information about economies comes from many sources. One of these sources (and one which is important in the case of many planned economies) is official governmental descriptions. These descriptions at times consciously try to portray a picture at variance with reality. And even when they do not, they frequently provide only the official prescriptions for how the system is meant to operate, which itself is usually different from reality. Other sources include the writings of those (when we are lucky) who are or have been engaged in planning, those who are not, but who observe the planning system from within the country, and those who observe it from without (in decreasing order of value?). However, because economic reality is complicated and planned economic reality no less so, and since most planning systems undergo frequent changes of one degree or another, descriptions and analyses of how planned economies operate, even with the best intentions, leave something to be desired. In addition, some of the elements of planning relevant to our methodological approach are often not discussed. For example, in plan construction: the extent to which the center overrules or merely coordinates the proposals submitted by the periphery; or in plan implementation: the ways in which plans are adjusted when plan and reality conflict.

To cope with these problems, research methods which include close study of the literature, but also go beyond it, need to be pursued. Tinbergen, for example, sent a questionnaire to planners in many countries with results, however, that proved not altogether satisfactory.[29] On-the-spot study with interviews of those involved in planning should help to fill some information gaps. In the last analysis, though, the success with which the planned economies are accurately observed will depend to a large extent on the insight and perception of the researcher. But is this not generally true?

Assuming for the moment that we were able to achieve tolerable accuracy of observation, how would we then go about placing the planned economies on the descriptive scales for the planning elements selected? Needless to say, it must be done carefully with much study and thought. But since few of these descriptive scales involve completely objective criteria, the rankings will in the end reflect subjective judgment. In many cases, the relative placing of economies will be clear. In those that require close decisions, the skill of the researcher will again be paramount. This dependence on subjective judgment is clearly a weakness of the approach but not necessarily a fatal one.[30]

[29] Tinbergen, *op. cit.*, pp. 32–33.
[30] I suspect that the fellowship committees of different graduate economics departments, after studying the applications, records, and letters of the various candidates, come up with rather similar rankings, at least of the top 10 or 15.

A third set of problems arises from certain irregularities which appear in various aspects of some planned systems. One instance is the substitution of functions from one class of planning elements to another. For example, in analyzing French planning practices, it might be argued that much, though not all, of the implementation effort is concentrated in the plan-construction phase. Representatives of business, government, and (supposedly) labor, come together in the modernization commissions, where they work up sectoral plans based not only on information that each provides, but also on a process of bargaining (including bargaining with government). In the end, if it works, each has reached a position with which he is willing to live.[31] Implementation tends then to be self-enforcing. The researcher must be careful to take account of such substitutions of functions.

Another type of problem in this set involves the handling of "plan-like" activities. For example, what should be done with government licensing activities which are unrelated to any economic plan? These would have to be treated case by case. For instance, in most situations, unless clearly related to a plan, the licensing of doctors should be ignored; but the licensing of imports when used to encourage the importation of producers' goods and discourage the importation of consumers' goods should be included and the desired import mix treated as a plan. As in any research project, many such decisions will have to be made.

Last, but obviously not least, there is the problem of measurement. We have thirteen individual scalings, grouped into three classes of planning elements. How should we proceed to derive an overall scaling of the planned economies?

To a certain extent, we face a dimensional problem. The thirteen planning-element scales are not in the same dimension as dollars' worth of apples and airplanes are and thus can not be aggregated in the same sense. However, in another sense, since the planning element scales represent different facets of the common characteristic, centralization of authority, their aggregation, in order to depict the degree of the characteristic present in a system, does not appear baseless. But how is it to be done?

It would, of course, simplify matters if all individual scalings were to come out the same. There is an equilibrium principle in sociology, called "status congruence," which concerns the striving of individuals to achieve equal status in the different social and economic roles they play.[32] To the

[31] See, e.g., Bernard Cazes, "French Planning," in Bert Hickman, ed., *Quantitative Planning, op. cit.* (n. 4), 179–211, and Vera Lutz, *Central Planning for the Market Economy*, London, 1969.

[32] See George C. Homans, *Sentiments and Activities*, Glencoe, New York, 1962, pp. 91–102.

extent that a similar principle operated in the process of structuring a planning system, that is a striving for the same degree of centralization of authority in all planning elements, it would generate a tendency toward equivalent orderings on all scales. But unfortunately we cannot rely on its existence.[33] And even if a similar principle did exist, as with all equilibrium principles, it only argues a tendency to move toward equivalence. And since planning systems are constantly in some state of structural flux, there would be no reason to expect equivalent orderings at any point in time.[34] Thus our problem will not vanish.

A large literature in the field of psychology and sociology on "scale analysis" concerns the construction of scales mainly for measuring people's attitudes and the interpretation of the measurements thus derived.[35] Though these measuring systems apply mostly to attitudinal data, they may prove relevant to our problem. "Guttman scaling," for example, is a possibility. If our data were Guttman-scalable, different group-types of planned economies (in relation to centralization of authority) would be delineated and the planning elements arranged in a consistent order as indicators of the degree of centralization of authority for the entire set of economies observed.[36]

The simplest procedure for deriving an overall scaling would be to average (or merely sum) each economy's ordinal rankings over the entire set of thirteen rankings. Even putting aside for the moment the question of differential weights for the different planning elements, this procedure would not always be acceptable. For the ordinal rankings on any individual scale give us information only about the planned economies' *ranks* relative to each other, not about their *position* on the scale relative to each other, that is their distance from each other. If it happened, for

[33] If we could and if "status congruence" were always a certainty, then our task would really be simplified. We would only have to investigate one planning element in order to scale our economies!

[34] It would be interesting to examine changes in orderings over time as a means of testing the existence of a congruence principle in the structuring of planning systems.

[35] See Samuel A. Stouffer *et al.*, *Measurement and Prediction*, Princeton, N.J., 1950; Paul F. Lazarsfeld, ed., *Mathematical Thinking in the Social Sciences*, Glencoe, New York, 1954, especially Ch. 5; C. H. Coombs, *A Theory of Data*, New York, 1964; Margaret J. Hagood and Daniel O. Price, *Statistics for Sociologists*, New York, 1952, 143–155; Harry S. Upshaw, "Attitude Measurement," in H. M. and A. B. Blalock, eds., *Methodology in Social Research*, New York, 1968, 98–106; W. S. Torgeson, *Theory and Methods of Scaling*, New York (1958); Torgeson, "Multidimensional Scaling of Similarity," *Psychometrika*, XXX (1965) 379–393; Paul E. Green, *et al.*, "Nonmetric Scaling Methods: An Exposition and Overview," *Wharton Quarterly*, Winter-Spring 1968, 27–41.

[36] See Hagood and Price, *op. cit.*; Upshaw, *op. cit.*; and the applications of Guttman scaling cited in Marsh, *Sociology, op. cit.*, (n. 4 above), p. 34.

example, that on every scale but one all the economies were grouped closely together, but on that one they were spread apart, or one economy stood far from the rest, a simple average of the ordinal rankings might not correctly delineate the overall ranking.

Another possibility, therefore, would be to assign cardinal numbers to the intervals, or grades, on each scale and then average these cardinal numbers. The trouble with this procedure is that it would give a spurious air of precision to the whole exercise.

Finally, the terrible problem of differential intra- and inter-class weights. I tend to feel that an attempt to construct differential intra-class weights is unwarranted. First of all, some thought has been given to the selection of elements within each class which were roughly of similar importance (note the separate treatment of investment). Second, given the relatively limited differences in importance that might exist among intra-class elements, the level of precision possible in a study of this sort does not call for the construction of differential intra-class weights.

Differential inter-class weights, however, are another matter. The three classes of planning elements are not of equal importance in defining the intensity of planning. Most people would agree, I imagine, that plan implementation is more important then either of the other two classes. But I do not see how we could be very precise in the choice of weights. It is not like the choice of weights in the aggregation of national product, where in theory at least prices are supposed to reflect relative importance. We have no objective criteria to fall back on. The choice must be based on a subjective appraisal of what is reasonable.

At a minimum, alternative (reasonable) weighting systems should be tried, to see what difference alternative weights might make. If they make a difference, then the practice followed in studies of the Soviet and other Communist economies might be employed and alternative scalings based on alternative weights presented. If the scalings are very different, then the reader would be duly warned of the tentativeness of any of the relationships between centralization of authority and the other variables. If, however, alternative weights do not lead to very different scalings, more confidence may be placed in the results.

6. Conclusions

I agree with the sentiments of Alexander Gerschenkron expressed in the passage placed at the beginning of this paper. Quantification should be treated as a serious business. I am convinced, however, that efforts to systematize our conceptualizations of planned economic systems are necessary if substantial progress is to be achieved in the use of the comparative approach in the study of planned economies. And it is only through the effective use of the comparative approach that we will be able to generate those universal and specific propositions about planned economies that we seek.

The aim of the approach described in this paper is to see how far one can go in explaining variations in the experiences of planned economies on the basis of the degree of plannedness or—more specifically—that characteristic of plannedness, the centralization of authority. Whether the approach will prove to be practicable and productive will depend, in large measure, on how complex the problems we have discussed (and others) turn out to be, on one's ability to cope with them, and on the sufficiency of the selected planning elements and their descriptive scales to define the centralization of authority in a planned economy.

The task appears formidable but perhaps not completely unpromising.

7. Appendix

LIST OF CLASSES AND DESCRIPTIVE SCALES

1. *The Plan*
   A. Periodicity of the Plan
      Long Term_____Short Term
   B. Scope of the Plan
      Small Part of Economy_____Entire Economy
   C. Plan Coverage of Investment
      None_____Entire
   D. Plan Coverage of Distribution of Materials
      None_____Entire
   E. Level of Detail in the Plan
      Highly Aggregative_____Very Specific

2. *Construction of the Plan*
   A. Extent of Participation by the Periphery
      High Participation_____No Participation
   B. Extent of Participation by Periphery in the Construction of the Investment Plan
      High Participation_____No Participation
   C. Type of Participation by Periphery
      Authority to Initiate Proposals_____Provision of Information Only

3. *Implementation of the Plan*
   A. Attempt to Implement the Plan
      No Attempt_____Strong Attempt
   B. Means of Implementation
      Manipulation of Parameters_____Issuing of Directives

C. Number and Detail of Directives/Parameters
   Low_____High
D. Center's Plan Adjustment Mechanisms
   Weak_____Strong
E. Implementation Incentive Mechanism
   Low Pressure_____High Pressure

6

Comparative Productivity and Efficiency in the Soviet Union and the United States*

by ABRAM BERGSON

1. Introduction

Over a half-century since the November Revolution, the economic efficiency of socialism is no longer quite the speculative theme that it once seemed, but it continues to be controversial. Perhaps the moral is that this is much too big and complex a matter ever to be dealt with very definitively, but further clarification still is properly sought. This essay represents the result of such an effort. Specifically, I present some comparative data on productivity in the USSR and the USA and inquire to what extent observed differences between the two countries in this respect may be due to a difference in efficiency between socialism as exemplified by the USSR and capitalism as exemplified by the USA.

I thus retrace some steps I have already taken in earlier studies[1] but now explore more fully than before diverse methodological issues and improve somewhat, and also elaborate much, on previous calculations. The data at hand on factor inputs and output may also permit more reliable computations of productivity than were possible in a previous study of a similar sort by Professor Joseph Berliner.[2] The present inquiry also diverges from his methodologically at some points.

As before, a comparison is made for a single year, 1960. For present purposes, this year does not seem to have been an especially unusual one in the USSR, though farm output was several per cent below the peak level of 1958. In the United States, in 1960 total output expanded to levels appreciably above the previous cyclical peak of 1957. Unemployment, however, was still a high 5.6 per cent. These facts should be kept in mind.

* This study was done with the aid of a grant (Contract G-1525) from the National Science Foundation.

[1] Abram Bergson, 1964, pp. 340 ff; Abram Bergson, 1968. [In the footnotes for this chapter, refer to the References for Chap. 6 (p. 215) for full bibliographic citations.]

[2] Joseph S. Berliner, 1964.

Some impression is also needed of the comparative stage of economic development of the two countries at the time considered. Stage of economic development is understood and measured variously, but for present purposes these indicators, computed from data compiled in this study, seem of special interest:

	Share of gross national product originating in nonfarm sector, per cent	*Share of employment in nonfarm sector, per cent*
USA	95.6	93.3
USSR	79.7	61.5

By any standard, then, the USSR was a fairly advanced country economically in 1960 but still lagged well behind the USA.

Socialism and capitalism are distinguished here, as they usually are, essentially in terms of ownership of the means of production, which under socialism is predominantly public and under capitalism predominantly private. On this understanding the two systems are, of course, exemplified by the USSR and the USA. But given ownership, whether public or private, a community's working arrangements for determining resource use may still be of diverse sorts. Moreover, under capitalism they have also come to vary widely in fact. That is a familiar feature which need not be labored. Under socialism, the famous system of centralist planning that originated in the USSR was in essentials still being widely employed at the time studied, but here too diversity has increasingly become the rule in the course of time. Indeed, working arrangements even in the USSR are now in flux, though changes thus far are not nearly as great as sometimes reported.

So far as the USSR and USA differ in efficiency, then, must we not consider that the difference characterizes not so much socialism and capitalism generally as the particular working arrangements employed in the two countries? What, too, of the possibility sometimes suggested that even similar working arrangements, whether socialist or capitalist, may perform differently depending on the specific cultural and social context, and on the stage of economic development? May not generalization about socialism and capitalism be the more difficult on such accounts?

Intriguing as these questions are, I limit myself here to a comparison of the USSR and USA. This comparison hopefully will illuminate the relative efficiency of socialism as found in the USSR and capitalism as found in the USA. To what extent the conclusions apply to socialism and capitalism more generally is largely left to separate inquiry. As already implied, however, we cannot ignore altogether the difference in stage of economic development in the two countries.[3]

2. Theoretic Considerations

The data to be considered relate to comparative levels of productivity at one time but are formally similar to data used in measurements of change in productivity over time which are by now familiar in Western quantitative economics. Thus, as with the latter measurements, output is related to a sum of major factor inputs, and both output and individual inputs are more or less aggregative in scope. In any but a formal sense, however, our data are of a rather novel kind, and that is also true of the use to which they are to be put. In any event, the available theory of productivity measurements which has been formulated primarily for data on change over time is not as readily applicable as might be supposed to data on comparative levels at one time. Suitably elaborated, however, some aspects of the analysis, including a recent contribution by Dr. Richard H. Moorsteen,[4] may serve as a point of departure.

Actually, the available theory seems to be applicable most readily to an ideal case which is unlikely to be realized even in the measurement of productivity change over time: The community considered is perfectly efficient statically in the sense that it fully realizes its production possibilities. These possibilities vary, however, owing to the advance of technological knowledge. Measurements of productivity change are supposed ordinarily to be indicative of such an increase in production capacity, together with any concomitant variation in static efficiency manifest in the degree of utilization of that capacity. For the ideal case in question, however, such utilization is always complete, so the measurements bear on the increase in production capacity alone.

For clarity, let us begin with measurements of change over time for such an ideal case. It does no harm, though, and will facilitate later discussion of the alternative kind of measurements of interest here, if we suppose that the two periods of time to be considered are separated by a revolution, so that there are in effect two communities, Smithiana and Marxiana. Exercising an author's prerogative, I assume that the revolution transforms Marxiana into Smithiana, rather than the reverse. All activities considered, therefore, are understood to be dated for Marxiana, as of one period, and for Smithiana, as of another and later one.

[3] In Bergson, *Planning and Productivity under Soviet Socialism* a limited inquiry is made into relative efficiency, as indicated by comparative productivity, not only for the USSR and USA, but for the USSR and a number of other Western capitalist countries.
[4] Moorsteen, 1961, Ch. 3.

The two communities are also assumed provisionally to produce a single consumers' good, X, in the amounts X_m and X_s respectively, and a single, perfectly durable capital good, I, in the amounts I_m and I_s respectively. This production takes place in each community by use of a stock of the capital good, amounting to K_m in Marxiana and K_s in Smithiana, and a single kind of labor, L, employment of which amounts to L_m in Marxiana and L_s in Smithiana. Production possibilities in Marxiana are given by the formula,

$$(1) \qquad F^m(X_m, I_m, L_m, K_m) = 0,$$

and in Smithiana, by the formula,

$$(2) \qquad F^s(X_s, I_s, L_s, K_s) = 0.$$

Thus, for any given volume of employment of the two factors, and any given output of one of the two goods, (1) indicates the maximum amount of the other that Marxiana can produce with available technological knowledge. Similarly for (2) and Smithiana. Since production possibilities supposedly are fully realized, the two production functions also represent mixes of inputs and outputs that might actually be experienced in the two communities. In each community, one such mix is realized in fact.

Because of the advance of technological knowledge, however, some mixes open to Smithiana may not be realizable in Marxiana. The variation in production capacity of interest here is usually understood in just these terms, but it is well to be explicit. Consider some mix of outputs and inputs, $\hat{X}, \hat{I}, \hat{L}, \hat{K}$. Let us call this a standard mix. For Marxiana, for any $\beta_m > 0$ there should be some $\alpha_m > 0$ such that

$$(3) \qquad F^m(\alpha_m \hat{X}, \alpha_m \hat{I}, \beta_m \hat{L}, \beta_m \hat{K}) = 0.$$

Similarly, for Smithiana, for any $\beta_s > 0$ there should be some $\alpha_s > 0$ such that

$$(4) \qquad F^s(\alpha_s \hat{X}, \alpha_s \hat{I}, \beta_s \hat{L}, \beta_s \hat{K}) = 0.$$

Consider the ratios

$$(5a, b) \qquad \pi_m = \alpha_m/\beta_m; \qquad \pi_s = \alpha_s/\beta_s.$$

The former indicates for Marxiana and the latter for Smithiana the volume of output per unit of inputs relative to that implied by the standard mix.

Consider now the further ratio.

$$(6) \qquad \pi_{ms} = \pi_m/\pi_s.$$

This indicates the comparative output per unit of inputs in the two communities, and hence is properly referred to as the coefficient of comparative factor productivity. The coefficient may also be written in another form of interest:

(7) $$\pi_{ms} = (\alpha_m/\alpha_s)/(\beta_m/\beta_s).$$

As (7) underlines, while the individual community ratios, π_m and π_s, depend on the levels of inputs and outputs in the standard mix, the coefficient of comparative factor productivity involves a comparison only of postulated inputs and of resultant outputs in the two communities. Only the structure of the standard mix matters, therefore, at this point. As is also inherent in the concept in question, one may take as standard one or the other of the mixes observed in the two countries, or some combination of the two. For obvious reasons, these are important features here.

While π_{ms} indicates comparative factor productivity, it evidently may also serve as a measure of the difference in production capacity due to differences between the two communities in technological knowledge. Thus, π_{ms} varies inversely with the degree to which production capacity in Smithiana owing to advances in technological knowledge, has come to surpass that in Marxiana. This relation however, assumes, an absence of economies or diseconomies of scale in production. This assures that the magnitudes of π_m, π_s, and π_{ms} are independent of the volume of inputs that is postulated for each country. In other words, π_m is independent of β_m, π_s of β_s, and π_{ms} of both β_m and β_s. With scale effects, π_{ms} may still indicate the change in productive capacity due to advance of technological knowledge, but strictly speaking this presupposes that $\beta_m = \beta_s$. So far as this condition is not met, π_{ms} depends not only on comparative technological knowledge but on the comparative scale of inputs of the two countries.[5]

Even without scale effects, reference is to inputs and outputs in each country that conform structurally to the standard mix. Conceivably, technological change might be of a neutral sort where the variation in production capacity does not depend on the structure of either outputs or inputs. If technological change should be neutral in this sense, π_{ms} would also be invariant of the structure of inputs and outputs, but so far as circumstances are otherwise π_{ms} is relative to that structure. As reflected in production capacity, in other words, the advance in Smithiana's

---

[5] With no scale effects, (1) and (2) are both homogeneous to the zero degree. It follows at once that π_m is unaffected by a change from β_m to $\lambda\beta_m$, for there is a corresponding change from α_m to $\lambda\alpha_m$. Similarly, for π_s, β_s and α_s. Note that if we take $\lambda = 1/\beta_m$ for Marxiana, and $\lambda = 1/\beta_s$ for Smithiana, we may introduce π_m and π_s explicitly into the production functions of the two countries:

(8a, b) $$F^m(\pi_m \hat{X}, \pi_m \hat{I}, \hat{L}, \hat{K}) = 0 \quad F^s(\pi_s \hat{X}, \pi_s \hat{I}, \hat{L}, \hat{K}) = 0.$$

technological knowledge over that of Marxiana would depend on the mix.[6]

We wish, then, to calculate π_{ms}. For this purpose, the following data are understood to be at hand: (i) Actual outputs and inputs in the two communities at the times considered: $\hat{X}_m$, $\hat{I}_m$, $\hat{L}_m$, $\hat{K}_m$, and $\hat{X}_s$, $\hat{I}_s$, $\hat{L}_s$, $\hat{K}_s$. (ii) Corresponding prices: p_m, q_m, w_m, $r_m q_m$ and p_s, q_s, w_s, $r_s q_s$. While q_m and q_s are the prices of the capital good in Marxiana and Smithiana, $r_m q_m$ and $r_s q_s$ are corresponding rental rates for a year's use of the good. In other words, the rate of interest is r_m in Marxiana and r_s in Smithiana. In each community, relative prices of goods supposedly correspond to their marginal rate of transformation. Similarly the ratio of the wage rate to the rental for the capital good corresponds to the marginal rate of substitution between the two factors. The rates of transformation and substitution are given, for Marxiana, by (1) and, for Smithiana, by (2). How may we gauge π_{ms} on this basis?

The production functions referred to are quite general. Let us begin with a special case: The production function for Marxiana is:

$$(9) \qquad X_m + AI_m = CL_m^\gamma K_m^{1-\gamma}$$

and for Smithiana:

$$(10) \qquad X_s + BI_s = DL_s^\rho K_s^{1-\rho}.$$

In each community, in other words, the marginal rate of transformation between the two goods is independent of the volume and structure of both inputs and outputs. This is also true of the elasticity of substitution (σ) between factors, which is everywhere unity. Thus, the two formulas, although rather novel, simply represent a variant of the Cobb-Douglas function familiar in productivity analysis, aggregation of products such as is assumed in the latter implicitly, being here represented explicitly.[7]

[6] While the concept of neutral technological change is familiar in growth theory, reference is usually made to a community where only a single commodity is produced. The usage adopted here, however, seems to represent a natural extension to the case where there is more than one such commodity.

[7] As may readily be shown, formulas such as (9) and (10) would in fact obtain if production in all industries conformed to one and the same Cobb-Douglas function, apart from the dimensional constant. Thus, suppose for one of the two communities production in the two industries in question conformed to these formulas:

$$(11a, b) \qquad X = RL_x^v K_x^{1-v}; \qquad I = SL_I^v K_I^{1-v}.$$

The corresponding marginal rates of substitution are given by the expressions: $(1-v)L_x/vK_x$ and $(1-v)L_I/vK_I$. Since the community is realizing its production possibilities, the two rates must be equal. Hence,

$$(12) \qquad L_x/K_x = L_I/K_I = L/K,$$

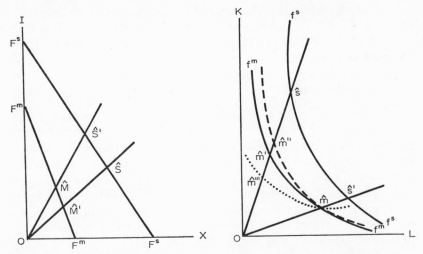

FIGURE 2: Output (2.1) and Input (2.2) Mixes in Marxiana and Smithiana.

The case is illustrated in Fig. 2. In 2.2 are shown the mixes of inputs observed in Marxiana and Smithiana, $\hat{m}$ and $\hat{s}$, and the corresponding isoquants, $f^m f^m$ and $f^s f^s$. Given by (9), the former schedule represents for Marxiana alternative mixes of inputs yielding the same aggregate output as $\hat{m}$. Similarly for $f^s f^s$, though reference here is to (10), Smithiana and $\hat{s}$. In 2.1 are shown the mixes of outputs observed in Marxiana and Smithiana, $\hat{M}$ and $\hat{S}$, and the corresponding transformation schedules, $F^m F^m$ and $F^s F^s$. The transformation schedule $F^m F^m$ indicates for Marxiana alternative mixes of outputs producible with the observed mix of inputs or its equivalent. Similarly for $F^s F^s$ and Smithiana. As given by (9) and (10), both schedules are linear.

Even in the special case considered, technological change is apt not to be neutral. Hence π_{ms} varies depending on the standard mix. Four such mixes are of particular interest:

where L is the total labor employed in the two industries and K is the total stock of capital. For some λ and $\bar{\lambda}$ summing to unity, therefore,

(13a, b, c, d) $L_x = \lambda L, \qquad K_x = \lambda K; \qquad L_I = \bar{\lambda} L; \qquad K_I = \bar{\lambda} K.$

From (11a, b) we also have:

(14) $$X + \frac{R}{S} I = R L_x^v K_x^{1-v} + R L_I^v K_I^{1-v}.$$

Substituting here from (13a, b, c, d) we obtain at once a production function of the form of (9) and (10).

(i) $\hat{X}_s$, $\hat{I}_s$, $\hat{L}_s$, $\hat{K}_s$, i.e., the outputs and inputs observed in Smithiana;

(ii) $\hat{X}_m$, $\hat{I}_m$, $\hat{L}_m$, $\hat{K}_m$, i.e., the outputs and inputs observed in Marxiana;

(iii) $\hat{X}_s$, $\hat{I}_s$, $\hat{L}_m$, $\hat{K}_m$, i.e., the outputs observed in Smithiana and the inputs observed in Marxiana;

(iv) $\hat{X}_m$, $\hat{I}_m$, $\hat{L}_s$, $\hat{K}_s$, i.e., the outputs observed in Marxiana and the inputs observed in Smithiana.

In Table 2, I show for each such standard mix the corresponding value of π_{ms} as indicated by (7). Thus, as (7) requires, π_{ms} is obtained for each standard mix by comparing for the two countries a relative of outputs of the standard structure with a relative of inputs of the standard structure. In the table, I also show index numbers calculated from observed prices and quantities that correspond to the relatives of outputs and inputs conforming to (7). In terms of observed prices and quantities, therefore, π_{ms} for each standard mix is supposed to be computed simply as the ratio of the indicated index numbers of outputs and inputs.

As shown, index numbers of outputs are calculated by arithmetic and index numbers of inputs by geometric aggregation. Also, with outputs or inputs observed in one country as standard, the aggregation entails use of weights that relate to the other country—prices in the case of outputs and income shares in the case of inputs. These features of the calculations follow from the nature of the production functions considered. Indeed, given these functions, the tabulated index number formulas turn out to be

Table 2

Calculation of π_{ms} for Alternative Standard Mixes

Standard mix (1)	π_{ms} (2)	Measurement in terms of observed prices and quantities	
		Index of outputs (3)	Index of inputs[a] (4)
(i) $\hat{X}_s$, $\hat{I}_s$, $\hat{L}_s$, $\hat{K}_s$	$\left(\dfrac{O\hat{M}'}{O\hat{S}}\right) \div \left(\dfrac{O\hat{m}'}{O\hat{s}}\right)$	$\dfrac{p_m\hat{X}_m + q_m\hat{I}_m}{p_m\hat{X}_s + q_m\hat{I}_s}$	$\dfrac{\hat{L}_m^{\gamma}\hat{K}_m^{1-\gamma}}{\hat{L}_s^{\gamma}\hat{K}_s^{1-\gamma}}$
(ii) $\hat{X}_m$, $\hat{I}_m$, $\hat{L}_m$, $\hat{K}_m$	$\left(\dfrac{O\hat{M}}{O\hat{S}'}\right) \div \left(\dfrac{O\hat{m}}{O\hat{s}'}\right)$	$\dfrac{p_s\hat{X}_m + q_s\hat{I}_m}{p_s\hat{X}_s + q_s\hat{I}_s}$	$\dfrac{\hat{L}_m^{\rho}\hat{K}_m^{1-\rho}}{\hat{L}_s^{\rho}\hat{K}_s^{1-\rho}}$
(iii) $\hat{X}_s$, $\hat{I}_s$, $\hat{L}_m$, $\hat{K}_m$	$\left(\dfrac{O\hat{M}'}{O\hat{S}}\right) \div \left(\dfrac{O\hat{m}}{O\hat{s}'}\right)$	$\dfrac{p_m\hat{X}_m + q_m\hat{I}_m}{p_m\hat{X}_s + q_m\hat{I}_s}$	$\dfrac{\hat{L}_m^{\rho}\hat{K}_m^{1-\rho}}{\hat{L}_s^{\rho}\hat{K}_s^{1-\rho}}$
(iv) $\hat{X}_m$, $\hat{I}_m$, $\hat{L}_s$, $\hat{K}_s$	$\left(\dfrac{O\hat{M}}{O\hat{S}'}\right) \div \left(\dfrac{O\hat{m}'}{O\hat{s}}\right)$	$\dfrac{p_s\hat{X}_m + q_s\hat{I}_m}{p_s\hat{X}_s + q_s\hat{I}_s}$	$\dfrac{\hat{L}_m^{\gamma}\hat{K}_m^{1-\gamma}}{\hat{L}_s^{\gamma}\hat{K}_s^{1-\gamma}}$

[a] $\gamma = w_m\hat{L}_m/(w_m\hat{L}_m + r_mq_m\hat{K}_m)$; $\quad \rho = w_s\hat{L}_s/(w_s\hat{L}_s + r_sq_s\hat{K}_s)$.

ideally appropriate in the sense that the resulting measures of π_{ms} correspond precisely to those indicated by (7). The proof is readily found and is left to the reader.[8]

To try to be more realistic, several departures from the special case are of interest:

i. A transformation locus is ordinarily thought to be curvilinear rather than linear. Without any knowledge of its precise shape, we may still fall back on arithmetic aggregation in compiling index numbers of comparative outputs, but the correspondence to the output relatives indicated by (7) is now approximate rather than exact. If the transformation locus is curvilinear, however, it is usually taken to be concave from below. Given this, the resulting error in the calculated π_{ms} is predictable; that is, as can be seen at once, π_{ms} is biased in favor of the community whose price weights are used in the aggregation of output. See Table 3, col. (2).

ii. While I have assumed unity elasticity of substitution between factors, it has been held that for an isoquant such as that considered σ tends to be less than unity.[9] If this is so and σ is known, the formulas for index numbers of inputs in Table 1 should be modified accordingly. If σ is not known, and these formulas are still applied, π_{ms} is subject to a further bias. Particularly, relative inputs tend to be overstated for the community whose inputs are taken as standard, and π_{ms} is biased accordingly. For example, with $\sigma < 1$ and $\hat{s}$ as standard for inputs, relative inputs according to (7) are indicated by $(O\hat{m}''/O\hat{s})$ in Figure 2.2. The corresponding index number formula in Table 2, however, still yields the smaller ratio $(Om'/O\hat{s})$.[10] It also follows that π_{ms} is biased favorably to Marxiana. More generally, the bias is as shown in Table 3, col. (3).

iii. It was also assumed that for any given output mix the marginal rate of transformation does not depend on the input mix and that for any given input mix the marginal rate of substitution between factors does not

[8] Hint: Given formulas (9) and (10), each transformation schedule and each isoquant in question is represented by a linear homogeneous function. Along any ray, the magnitude of such a function varies proportionately with its arguments. At the same time, with product and factor prices determined as assumed, alternative mixes of outputs which have the same total value arithmetically in terms of a community's own prices must be on one and the same transformation schedule for that community. Alternative mixes of inputs which have the same total value geometrically in terms of a community's own factor shares must be on one and the same isoquant for that community.

[9] See Arrow, *et al.* 1961; Sato, 1963; David and van de Klundert, 1965.

[10] With $\sigma < 1$, the marginal rate of factor substitutions is still supposed to correspond to relative factor prices at observed points. At other points, the isoquant for which $\sigma < 1$ necessarily is to the right of that for which $\sigma = 1$, as shown in Figure 2.2.

depend on the output mix. Such rates and mixes are likely rather to be interdependent. To the extent that they are, the index number formulas in Table 1 may still be used to calculate π_{ms}, but this procedure is now subject to a further error. Consider, for example, the computations where Smithiana's outputs and inputs, $\hat{X}_s$, $\hat{I}_s$, $\hat{L}_s$, $\hat{K}_s$, are standard. With interdependence, the output relative indicated by (7) is still approximated as it was before by the ratio $(O\hat{M}'/O\hat{S})$—reference is again to Figure 2—and by the corresponding index number formula for outputs in Table 2. The related index number formula for inputs, however, yields a relative for inputs equal to $(O\hat{m}'/O\hat{s})$. This, as we saw, diverges from the measure called for by (7) so far as $\sigma < 1$. But even if $\sigma = 1$, the formula in question still errs, since strictly speaking the isoquant $f^m f^m$ relates to Marxiana's outputs, $\hat{M}$. From this isoquant we determine $\hat{m}'$, the inputs of Smithiana's structure which for Marxiana are equivalent to its actual inputs $\hat{m}$. What we wish to determine rather is the inputs of Smithiana's structure which for Marxiana are equivalent to $\hat{m}$ in terms of another isoquant, particularly one in which Marxiana's outputs are not $\hat{M}$ but approximately $\hat{M}'$.

Table 3

Biases in π_{ms} Obtained from Alternative Index Number Formulas

Standard Mix (1)	Bias due to concavity of feasibility locus (2)	Bias due to less than unity elasticity of factor substitution (3)	Bias due to interdependence in production function (4)
(i) $\hat{X}_s$, $\hat{I}_s$, $\hat{L}_s$, $\hat{K}_s$	+	+	−
(ii) $\hat{X}_m$, $\hat{I}_m$, $\hat{L}_m$, $\hat{K}_m$	−	−	+
(iii) $\hat{X}_s$, $\hat{I}_s$, $\hat{L}_m$, $\hat{K}_m$	+	−	0
(iv) $\hat{X}_m$, $\hat{I}_m$, $\hat{L}_s$, $\hat{K}_s$	−	+	0

How do the inputs we wish to know, say, $\hat{m}'''$, compare with $\hat{m}'$? A partial answer is provided by an argument due essentially to Moorsteen and Yasushi Toda. Substitutions among factors which tend to make a country's factor endowment correspond structurally to that of another country should proceed more favorably to the increasing factor if the structure of output has already been modified to conform to that of the other country. This argument supposes that a country's output structure tends in some degree to reflect its factor endowment. A country that is relatively well endowed with capital, for example, is assumed to produce relatively more capital-intensive products.[11] While not unassailable, I find this reasoning impelling, and accordingly have recorded in Table 3, col. (4)

[11] Moorsteen, 1961; Toda, 1964.

the indicated bias in π_{ms}. This bias is negative, for $O\hat{m}'$ should exceed $O\hat{m}'''$. Hence, so far as our index-number formula for inputs yields an observation on $O\hat{m}'/O\hat{S}$, it tends to overstate the volume of inputs of the standard structure that Marxiana needs to produce a volume $O\hat{M}'/O\hat{S}$ of outputs of standard structure.

Thus far, Smithiana's outputs and inputs, $\hat{X}_s, \hat{I}_s, \hat{L}_s, \hat{K}_s$, have been taken as standard. By similar reasoning, one finds that, where $\hat{X}_m, \hat{I}_m, \hat{L}_m, \hat{K}_m$ are the standard, calculation of π_{ms} by use of the index number formulas in Table 2 tends at this point to overstate Marxiana's performance. Where the standard mix is a composite of outputs in one country and inputs in another, there curiously is no further bias in the calculations due to interdependence.[12]

In considering departures from (9) and (10), I have assumed that, with outputs or inputs of one community as standard, the corresponding index number price weights should, as before, relate to the other community.

[12] It may be useful to be more precise regarding the two sorts of calculations. Consider first that where outputs and inputs in one country, say, Smithiana, are standard. On other words, the standard mix is $\hat{X}_s, \hat{I}_s, \hat{L}_s, \hat{K}_s$. By implication in (7), α_s and β_s equal unity, while α_m and β_m are to be calculated. To refer first to α_m, this is implicitly given by the formula

$$(15) \qquad F^m(\alpha_m \hat{X}_s, \alpha_m \hat{I}_s, \hat{L}_m \hat{K}_m) = 0,$$

and is estimated from the relation,

$$(16) \qquad \alpha_m \sim O\hat{M}'/O\hat{S} = (p_m \hat{X}_m + q_m \hat{I}_m)/(p_m \hat{X}_s + q_m \hat{I}_s).$$

Taking outputs in Marxiana as given at the levels $\alpha_m \hat{X}_s, \alpha_m \hat{I}_s$, then, we wish also to determine β_m such that

$$(17) \qquad F^m(\alpha_m \hat{X}_s, \alpha_m \hat{I}_s, \beta_m \hat{L}_s, \beta_m \hat{K}_s) = 0.$$

This is estimated from the relation

$$(18) \qquad \beta_m \sim O\hat{m}'/O\hat{s} = (\hat{L}_m K_m^{1-\gamma})/(\hat{L}_s \hat{K}_s^{1-\gamma}).$$

The equation on the right presupposes that $\sigma = 1$, but even if it were so, β_m would only be approximated, for $\bar{\beta}_m = O\hat{m}'/O\hat{s}$ satisfies the relation

$$(19) \qquad F^m(\hat{X}_m, \hat{I}_m, \bar{\beta}_m \hat{L}_s, \bar{\beta}_m \hat{K}_s) = 0.$$

and hence differs from the desired β_m, which satisfies (17). For reasons stated, however, I assume that $\beta_m = O\hat{m} \cdots /O\hat{s}$ is less than $\bar{\beta}_m = O\hat{m}'/O\hat{s}$.

Suppose now one takes as standard outputs of one community and inputs of another, e.g., X_s, I_s, L_m, K_m. In (7), then, α_s and β_m equal unity, and α_m and β_s are to be ascertained. To begin with α_m, this is again implicitly given by (15) and estimated from (16). As for β_s, this is implicitly given by

$$(20) \qquad F^s(\hat{X}_s, \hat{I}_s, \beta_s \hat{L}_m, \beta_s \hat{K}_m) = 0,$$

and for $\sigma = 1$ precisely corresponds to $O\hat{m}/O\hat{s}'$. This is also measured exactly by the corresponding index number in Table 3, so there is no further error at this point.

When production diverges from (9) and (10), we can no longer be certain that this is in order, but if we proceed as though it were, the direction of bias in π_{ms} is predictable, and it may not be so otherwise. Moreover, the resultant observations, at least for output, probably will turn out more often than not to be the more accurate ones. According to the analysis of Moorsteen and myself already referred to, use of price weights relating to the other community yields the more reliable π_{ms} whenever the transformation locus is concave from below, or at least not very convex. Also, the "Gerschenkron effect" must hold, but that is usually so. Figure 2.1 illustrates a situation where that is true.[13]

I have referred so far to measurements of productivity change over time and for an ideal case, where static efficiency is perfect in the sense that production possibilities are always fully realized. Such possibilities vary over time, however, owing to the advance of technological knowledge. The measurements thus bear exclusively on the latter aspect. I turn to alternative measurements—of comparative levels of productivity in different communities at one time. Such data supposedly are to be used to appraise efficiency. If they do bear on that phenomenon, they evidently must relate to static efficiency as manifest in realization of production possibilities. Variations in technological knowledge, however, could again be a factor; but for the present I refer to another ideal case, though probably often a realistic one: Technological knowledge is the same in the two communities compared. Hence, while productivity could previously indicate variations in technological knowledge alone, as manifest in production possibilities, it must now bear instead only on realization of such possibilities.

But may not the analysis even so proceed essentially as before? Thus Marxiana and Smithiana are now seen as contemporaneous communities; but may we not still take (1) and (2) as indicating alternative mixes of inputs and outputs open to them, though now under their respective working arrangements, and so with due allowance for inefficiency?

---

[13] I refer to this kind of index number relativity: From the standpoint of situation I, comparison of aggregate output with that in situation II is favored if use is made of price weights relating to II. This strictly speaking is a somewhat more general phenomenon than the Gerschenkron effect; for the latter is usually construed as relating to measurements of changes in output over time in a single country experiencing industrialization, or by extension to measurements of comparative output in different countries at different stages of industrialization. A difference in degree of industrialization undoubtedly is a major reason why this kind of index number relativity should obtain for either sort of measurement. Especially in comparisons between countries. however, index number relativity might well obtain even if there were no difference in degree of industrialization. At any rate, what counts at this point is the relativity, whatever its causes.

And may we not then measure production capacity simply as before, but on the understanding that observed differences indicate variations in degree of realization rather than in extent of production possibilities?

The present inquiry, broadly speaking, has been organized methodologically in the manner suggested. As constrained by working arrangements, however, a production function is apt to be analytically somewhat elusive. After all, such constraints tend to be highly intricate. If only on that account, is not their import for production likely often to be something less than fully determinate, in any meaningful sense? Then, too, the analysis has presupposed that prices of products and factors correspond ideally to marginal rates of transformation and substitution. If production possibilities should be fully realized, the ideal would be attainable. For obvious reasons, prices actually prevailing should conform to it. What, however, if production possibilities should not be fully realized? If the working arrangements cause such inefficiency, are they not likely also to generate prices that depart from the ideal? And once prices do so, how can outputs and inputs be meaningfully aggregated?

Such questions are in order, and in organizing the inquiry, I necessarily had to grapple with them. Let me explain, then, that in calculating productivity here I take as a desideratum an "adjusted factor cost" valuation standard that I have applied elsewhere in a similar context.[14] This is adjusted factor cost: Prices correspond to average cost, where services of factors are charged for at uniform prices that are on the average proportional to factor productivities in different activities. Adjusted factor cost was formulated as a standard of output valuation, but the indicated charges for factor services are properly applied as well in the aggregation of inputs.

Adjusted factor cost is something of a practical expedient, but it has its theoretic rationale. I have elaborated on this elsewhere, but according to familiar theoretic reasoning, a community may fail to realize fully its production possibilities in three ways:

i. Owing to wasteful practices, a production unit may not obtain from the labor and capital at its disposal as large an output as available technological knowledge permits.

ii. Because of their misallocation within any industrial branch, labor and capital may yield varying marginal returns in different production units.

iii. Because of misallocations in the economy generally, the marginal rate of substitution between labor and capital may tend to vary as between branches.

In relation to these different types of waste, Adjusted Factor Cost may

[14] See Bergson, 1953, Ch. 3, and Bergson, 1961, Ch. 3, and pp. 118ff.

be construed in an interesting way that has not yet, I think, been made very clear. As can be shown, the Adjusted Factor Cost standard should be indicative of product transformation and factor substitution rates relating to a hypothetical production function. The hypothetical production function is such that, as inputs and outputs vary, waste of each of the foregoing kinds would be comparable to that experienced in the observed period. Unless production possibilities are fully realized and waste of any kind is nil, such a hypothetical production function must diverge from the one actually prevailing. It would seem, however, to be appealing surrogate for the latter.

The productivity measurements to be compiled are to be read in this light. Essentially for a mix actually experienced, they bear on the community's actual performance in the observed period. For an alternative, hypothetical mix, they bear on what the community's performance would be if waste of the three sorts distinguished were comparable to that associated with the mix actually experienced. This is still not all one might wish of measurements such as are compiled. But it may not be amiss to leave to separate inquiry the further question that arises as to the degree to which for the hypothetical mix waste would in fact correspond to that for the mix experienced.

To return to Adjusted Factor Cost, for a community such as is being considered, let the production functions of the *i*th production units in the X and I industries be denoted as

$$(21a, b) \qquad X_i = G^i(LI_{xi}, K_{xi}); \qquad I_i = H^i(L_{Ii}, K_{Ii}).$$

Reference is to the production functions that actually prevail and so reflect any waste experienced in the production units involved. Under the Adjusted Factor Cost valuation, labor is supposedly charged for at the same rate, w, everywhere. "Own rental rates" for capital goods in the *i*th production units, $r_{xi}q$ and $r_{Ii}q$, are understood to be such that

$$(22a, b) \qquad r_{xi}q/w = G_2^i/G_1^i; \qquad r_{Ii}q/w = H_2^i/H_1^i.$$

Here G_1^i and G_2^i are the partial derivatives of X_i with respect to L_{xi} and K_{xi}. Similarly for H_1^i and H_2^i, I_i and L_{Ii} and K_{Ii}. Average rental rates in the two industries, therefore, are:

$$(23a, b) \qquad r_x q = \sum r_{xi}q \frac{K_{xi}}{K_x}; \qquad r_I q = \sum r_{Ii}q \frac{K_{Ii}}{K_I}.$$

Summations here and below are taken over evident ranges. The average rental rate for the whole economy is

$$(24) \qquad rq = r_x q \cdot \frac{K_x}{K} + r_I q \cdot \frac{K_I}{K}.$$

I shall also refer to the "own price" of a production unit and the "own price" of an industry. For a production unit the own price corresponds to average cost, labor being charged for at w and capital goods at the production unit's own rental rate. For the own prices, p_i^0 and q_i^0, of the ith production units in the two industries, then, we have

$$(25a, b) \qquad p_i^0 = \frac{wL_{xi} + r_{xi}qK_{xi}}{X_i} \; ; \qquad q_i^0 = \frac{wL_{Ii} + r_{Ii}qK_{Ii}}{I_i} \; .$$

The own prices of the two industries are understood similarly, though here reference is in each industry to costs in terms of the average rental rate for that industry:

$$(26a, b) \qquad p^0 = \frac{wL_x + r_xqK_x}{X} \; ; \qquad q^0 = \frac{wL_I + r_IqK_I}{I}$$

and

$$(27a, b) \qquad p^0 = \sum p_i^0 \frac{X_i}{X} \; ; \qquad q^0 = \sum q_i^0 \frac{I_i}{I} \; .$$

The own price for each industry, thus, is an average of the own prices of the production units in it, the own price of each production unit being weighted by its share in industry output.

Finally, the adjusted factor-cost prices of the two products are:

$$(28a, b) \qquad p = \frac{wL_x + rqK_x}{X} \; ; \qquad q = \frac{wL_I + rqK_I}{I} \; .$$

In previous equations capital goods supposedly are valued at their adjusted factor-cost price as given in (28b).

We wish to evaluate the marginal rate of transformation between X and I. T_{xI}, corresponding to the surrogate production function, S, as defined above. We have

$$(29) \quad T_{xI} = \left(\frac{\Delta I}{\Delta X}\right)_{S,K,L} = \sum (H_1^i \, \Delta L_{Ii} + H_2^i \, \Delta K_{Ii}) / \sum (G_1^i \, \Delta L + G_2^i \, \Delta K_{xi})$$

This necessarily will diverge from p/q so far as there are scale effects, but passing by such effects (29), by use of (25) and Euler's theorem, may be reformulated as:

$$(30) \quad T_{xI} = \sum \frac{1}{q_i^0} (w \, \Delta L_{Ii} + r_{Ii}q \, \Delta K_{Ii}) / \sum \frac{1}{-P_i^0} (w \, \Delta L_{xi} + r_{xi}q \, \Delta K_{xi})$$

This still depends on the way in which different production units in an industry share increments or decrements of an input that industry generally is experiencing. For variations in conformity with the surrogate production function envisaged, I assume provisionally that a production unit must share in an increment of aggregate inputs accruing to the branch more or less in proportion to the aggregate inputs the production unit already employs, i.e.,

$$(31) \qquad \frac{w \, \Delta L_{xi} + r_{xi}q \, \Delta K_{xi}}{w \, \Delta L_x + r_xq \, \Delta K_x} = \frac{wL_{xi} + r_{xi}qK_{xi}}{wL_x + r_xqK_x} \, ,$$

and

$$(32) \qquad \frac{w \, \Delta L_{Ii} + r_{Ii} q \, \Delta K_{Ii}}{w \, \Delta L_I + r_I q \, \Delta K_I} = \frac{w \, L_{Ii} + r_{Ii} q K_{Ii}}{w L_I + r_I q K_I}$$

Given (25) and (26), it follows that

$$(33) \qquad T_{xI} = \frac{w \, \Delta L_I + r_I q \, \Delta K_I}{w \, \Delta L_x + r_x q \, \Delta K_x} \cdot \frac{p^0}{q^0} \, .$$

This generally will not correspond exactly to p/q, but note that $\Delta L_I = -\Delta L_x$ and $\Delta K_I = -\Delta K_x$. Given this, the correspondence is exact whenever $r = r_x = r_I$. This would be the case whenever the inefficiency is of type (i) only (above, p. 173), or if it is of type (ii) as well, but not of type (iii) so far as this causes average rental rates in the two industries to diverge. Where such rental rates do diverge, however, $T_{xI} \neq p/q$, but note too that in (33) p^0/q^0 differs from p/q only because in (33) different industries are charged with their own rental rates on capital goods rather than a single economy-wide one. Moreover, the term on the right in (33) other than p^0/q^0 tends in effect to deflate p^0/q^0 for the variation in rental rates. The deflation, however, will generally leave T_{xI} diverging to some extent from p/q.

I have been referring to the relation of adjusted factor-cost product prices to the marginal rate of transformation given by the surrogate production function. For the corresponding marginal rate of factor substitution we have

$$(34) \qquad S_{LK} = \left(\frac{\Delta L}{\Delta K} \right)_{S,X,I} = \frac{1}{\Delta K} \left[\sum \frac{G_2^i}{G_1^i} \cdot \Delta K_{xi} + \sum \frac{H_2^i}{H_1^i} \cdot \Delta K_{Ii} \right].$$

Hence

$$(35) \qquad S_{LK} = \frac{1}{w \, \Delta K} \left[\sum r_{xi} q \, \Delta K_{xi} + \sum r_{Ii} q \, \Delta K_{Ii} \right].$$

This reduces to the adjusted factor-cost rate, rq/w, if, much as before, variations along S are assumed provisionally to be such that the increment of capital goods, ΔK, experienced by the whole economy is shared by different production units in proportion to their initial stocks of such goods.

What of that assumption and the corresponding one made previously regarding the surrogate production function? As it turns out, both assumptions would be entirely valid in the following case: i) All production units in each industry, if fully efficient, would operate in accord with the same Cobb-Douglas production function; ii) The Cobb-Douglas function in question for either industry is the same as that for the other, apart from a dimensional constant. I shall leave the proof of this proposition to the interested reader. The case in question is not exactly realistic, but our assumptions regarding the surrogate production function should ordinarily not be far from the mark.

Among the four sets of formulas in Table 2, I shall give priority to those in the first two rows, that is, those where outputs and inputs are valued in terms of prices relating to the same community. I can apply adjusted factor cost only rather selectively here, but in employing the indicated formulas, it will still be of interest to experiment with a variant suggested by the preceding analysis. I refer to a computation where $\sigma < 1$. As will appear, the formula to be applied in this case is of a familiar sort.[15]

Theoretic principles such as have been formulated presuppose ideally a single market area. The calculations may be extended to many areas, however, if freight charges are determined in accord with the adjusted factor cost standard, and commodity prices vary regionally in accord with such charges. Charges for labor of any given kind should be such as to yield the same real wage in different areas but may vary monetarily to reflect the differential living costs. With this valuation, a country's real output will be found to be the larger the more of its workers are employed in high money-wage areas even though its economic performance as understood here is none the better. Output per unit of factor inputs is unaffected, however, if in the calculation of real inputs, labor inputs in different areas are evaluated correspondingly. These principles apply, among other things, in the valuation of farm relatively to nonfarm labor.[16]

[15] I shall favor formulas based on price weights of a single country, although priority is sometimes accorded to calculations based on mixed weights, such as those in the two remaining sets of formulas in Table 2, because in such cases there is no interdependence error. This aspect was first clarified, by Moorsteen, and his analysis accordingly has been taken as demonstrating the superiority of mixed weights. The absence of interdependence error is a virtue, but as shown this is only one of several biases to which the calculations are subject. Moreover, we must consider here the need to refer to a surrogate production function and the limitations of the valuation standard applied. One hesitates in the circumstances to commit himself to the esoteric computations required.

[16] With real wages the same in different market areas, money wages differ because of transport costs. If more workers are employed in high money wage areas, then, is not the higher real output that results simply a proper reflection of the greater volume of transport? Hence, in calculating factor inputs, does it not suffice to aggregate labor without the differential evaluation that is envisaged, though with the inclusion of labor engaged in transport? The answer to both questions is in the negative, for in the calculation of real output, as readily seen, transport volume is already allowed for in the aggregation of either value added or final products. Although regional differences in money wages affect real output, they cannot be considered as accounting for transport, at least not if real output is calculated correctly; but admittedly this is not generally the case regarding transport, particularly of final goods. I refer to the practice of valuing final goods at national average rather than, as is proper, at differentiated destination prices. With such valuation a country's real ouput tends to be the less, the larger the volume of its factor inputs it uses for transport as distinct from production of final goods. The differential evaluation of labor in different market areas in the calculation of inputs, therefore, may not be entirely appropriate after all. This should be kept in mind.

I have been referring to economies where capital goods are perfectly durable. So far as they are not, measurements of productivity, such as considered here, are often made on a "net" basis, with aggregate output and capital services calculated net of depreciation. It has been urged, however, that such measurements are more readily construed conceptually if reference is made instead to gross output and capital services. For my part, the latter view seems the more impelling, although I have made measurements of the net as well as gross sort.[17] I have also assumed thus far that Marxiana and Smithiana produce only a single consumers' good and a single capital good, and in production, in addition to the capital good, use only one other factor, a single kind of labor. This assumption, however, serves only for reasons of exposition. In principle the analysis applies equally if there are many consumers' goods, many capital goods, many kinds of labor and other factor inputs as well.[18]

3. The Calculations

The chief measures of output per unit of factor inputs for the USSR and USA in 1960 are set forth in Table 4. Also shown are the underlying data on output and on the two major factor inputs considered, labor and reproducible capital. The implied measures of output per worker and per unit of reproducible capital are also given. As indicated, I refer separately to the economy as a whole and to the nonfarm sector. For each sphere computations have been made in terms of alternative price weights. And depending on the sphere and the price weights, the measure of factor productivity varies, but in all cases the Soviet performance is far below

---

I have been assuming, perhaps not altogether rightly, that where there are different market areas a country's production possibilities are properly construed as representing its capacity not only to produce goods but to deliver them to different destinations. In effect, commodities delivered to different localities are treated as different commodities. For simplicity I have abstracted from differences in disutility of labor in different localities, and from differential distribution charges which affect comparative living costs in different localities, especially on and off the farm.

[17] Arguments for the gross approach seem to vary. In my opinion, the chief consideration is that in the production function capital inputs are more readily construed as gross than as net services. Compare Domar, 1961, pp. 761–717, 722–723; Jorgenson and Grilliches, 1967, p. 256.

[18] In respect of capital goods, however, the analysis abstracts from fixed coefficients and also from cases where a machine is specialized to one use only. This, needless to say, is an important limitation, but I must leave to separate inquiry the problem thus posed. Reference has been to "final" capital goods, but the analysis may, I think, be readily extended to capital goods of an "intermediate" sort, and for such goods fixed coefficients and specialized uses do not seem to pose any particular difficulty.

that of the USA. Thus, output per unit of factor inputs in the USSR is but 30.6 or 42.0 per cent of that in the USA, the particular figure depending on the price weights. The corresponding measures for the nonfarm sector are 39.1 and 58.7 per cent. For the present, attention is directed to figures outside parentheses and those where employment is in conventional units, as distinct from the alternative data which reflect employment adjusted for quality.

Our more ultimate concern is with comparative efficiency, but before exploring that matter we must consider the underlying calculations. I shall refer only to aspects of general interest. Further details on sources and methods are set forth in the Appendix. As explained there, some matters are to be treated further in separate inquiries.

In Table 4, gross product for all sectors corresponds to gross national product as usually understood in national income accounting. For the nonfarm sector gross product corresponds to its contribution to gross national product. For each sphere, data on inputs are intended to correspond in coverage to output. Provisionally, however, I exclude from the calculations certain final services: education, health care, defense, other government services of a more or less conventional sort, and housing. More precisely, for both the economy generally and the nonfarm sector, I omit from output the value added by the services in question (for housing, the contribution of material inputs had to be omitted as well); From inputs of labor and reproducible capital I omit the amounts of those factors employed in the provision of such services. These omissions apart, for countries at rather different stages, such as the USSR and USA in 1960, delimitation of my calculations in conformity with conventional national income accounting must pose some familiar questions as to comparability in a deeper sense. But what might be said on this matter is fairly evident and need not be labored.[19]

For both the economy generally and the non-farm sector, the alternative measurements of productivity in terms of different price weights result from the attempt to apply in turn the two sets of formulas in the upper rows of Table 2. Where ruble valuations are called for, I have sought to compile data in terms of ruble factor cost rather than prevailing ruble prices; for practical purposes this means valuation at prevailing ruble prices less the famous turnover tax plus subsidies. Where dollar valuations are in order, I have simply compiled data in prevailing dollar prices. In both cases, 1955 is taken as the valuation year.

I refer primarily to the valuation of output. In Table 4, the index

[19] To return to the services omitted, for the USSR, other government services include an allowance for internal security and Party administration. For both countries, highways are subject to special treatment. (See below, p. 188.) For further details on the scope of the different spheres studied, see also the Appendix.

Table 4

Output, Factor Inputs and Factor Productivity, USSR Compared with USA, 1960

Item	Nature of measurement	USSR as percentage of USA	
		All sectors[a]	Nonfarm[a]
Gross product	In 1955 ruble factor cost	31.5	26.8
	In 1955 dollars	49.7	47.4
Employment	Workers engaged	164.6	98.1
Employment, adjusted	Workers engaged, adjusted hypothetically to equivalent male, 8th grade graduate[b]	122.3	81.4
Reproducible capital[c]	In 1955 rubles	41.7	37.7
	In 1955 dollars	52.2	48.3
Major inputs (employment plus reproducible capital)	With ruble weights	$103.0\left(\begin{array}{c}95.6^{d}\\116.7\end{array}\right)$	$68.5\left(\begin{array}{c}65.0^{d}\\73.2\end{array}\right)$
	With dollar weights	118.2(107.2)[e]	80.7(77.9)[e]
Major inputs (employment adjusted, plus reproducible capital)	With ruble weights	$84.6\left(\begin{array}{c}79.9^{d}\\91.6\end{array}\right)$	$60.9\left(\begin{array}{c}58.4\\63.7\end{array}\right)$
	With dollar weights	95.7(90.8)[e]	70.5(69.2)[e]

Gross product per worker	With output in 1955 ruble factor cost	19.1	27.3
	With output in 1955 dollars	30.2	48.3
Gross product per worker, with employment adjusted	With output in 1955 ruble factor cost	25.8	32.9
	With output in 1955 dollars	40.6	58.2
Gross product per unit of reproducible capital	With 1955 ruble valuations	75.5	71.1
	With 1955 dollar valuations	95.2	98.1
Gross product per unit of major inputs	With 1955 ruble valuations	$30.6 \binom{32.9}{27.0}$[d]	$39.1 \binom{41.2}{36.6}$[d]
	With 1955 dollar valuations	$42.0(46.4)$[e]	$58.7(60.8)$[e]
Gross product per unit of major inputs, with employment adjusted	With 1955 ruble valuations	$37.2 \binom{39.4}{34.4}$[d]	$44.0 \binom{45.9}{42.1}$[d]
	With 1955 dollar valuations	$51.9(54.7)$[e]	$67.2(68.5)$[e]

[a] Here and elsewhere, unless otherwise indicated, selected services are omitted. See text.

[b] See text.

[c] Each index is an average of two indices, one for reproducible capital, including gross fixed assets, and the other for reproducible capital, including net fixed assets.

[d] Of paired figures in parentheses, upper ones refer to calculations where the rate of return imputed to Soviet capital is 16 per cent rather than 12 per cent as originally assumed, and lower ones to calculations where $\sigma = .6$ instead of unity, as originally assumed.

[e] Figures in parentheses refer to calculations where $\sigma = .6$ instead of unity, as originally assumed.

numbers of reproducible capital refer to stocks but are assumed also to indicate capital services. Each index number is obtained as an average of two relatives, one with fixed capital included gross, and the other with such capital included net, of depreciation. In compiling the latter relatives, depending on the required valuation, I have sought to aggregate capital goods in either prevailing ruble prices of 1955 or prevailing dollar prices of 1955. Finally, capital services are aggregated in turn with employment by use of weights representing, on the one hand, gross capital charges, including interest and depreciation, and, on the other, labor earnings.[20]

These are the essentials of the calculations, but some aspects require further consideration. To begin with, I compiled the output relatives in Table 4 especially for this study. In doing so, I drew on RAND studies by myself, Dr. Oleg Hoeffding and Nancy Nimitz on the Soviet national income in rubles, U.S. Department of Commerce data on national income in dollars, and a considerable volume of research, including unclassified CIA reports and a RAND study by Dr. Abraham Becker on ruble-dollar parities.[21]

On employment, I relied on the U.S. Department of Commerce data on persons engaged, which are intended to represent full-time equivalent man-years. In trying to compile comparable figures for the USSR I used the careful studies of Nancy Nimitz and Dr. Murray Feshbach, the latter's for the Joint Economic Committee. Average annual hours of employment appear to have been similar in the USSR and USA in 1960, and no translation was made from workers engaged to man hours.[22] For reproducible capital in the USA in dollar prices, I relied essentially on the work of Professor Raymond Goldsmith, and in compiling corresponding data for the USSR, I referred to the results of the Soviet capital inventory of 1959, as carefully analyzed by Professor Norman Kaplan, and to the major study by Dr. Richard Moorsteen and Professor Raymond P. Powell. Needed ruble-dollar parities were obtained by use of data and sources already mentioned.

In short, in compiling data on outputs and inputs, I could draw on a substantial volume of related research, but the calculations are unavoidably crude. For output, moreover, the results sometimes diverge

---

The national income accounting referred to is that practised in the West. According to the national income accounting applied in the USSR, services of the sort in question are usually excluded from national income to begin with.

[20] The aggregation unavoidably is linear rather than geometric, as the formulas in Table 4 would require.

[21] I am satisfied that the CIA reports are scholarly studies and have so used them. At important points the results would hardly have varied if reference had been made instead to alternative sources sometimes available.

[22] See Bergson, 1964, pp. 368–369.

significantly from similar figures derived in previous studies. It may be hoped, however, that it has been possible to improve on those studies here.[23]

[23] Any attempt to compare systematically data on output compiled here with similar data compiled by others must be left to the separate inquiries referred to above. But I should explain that I have been led to estimates of the 1955 gross national product of the USSR and USA rather different from the well-known ones of Morris Bornstein, which I myself have used previously. These are his results, together with mine, for Soviet output as a percentage of that of the USA:

	Bergson	*Bornstein*
In ruble factor cost of 1955	27.6	28.2
In US dollars of 1955	45.2	53.4

Reference is to the GNP including selected final services. For comparison with mine, I have translated Bornstein's data from prevailing rubles into ruble factor cost. See Bornstein, 1959, p. 385; Bergson, 1964, p. 363.

The divergence arises chiefly, I think, because Bornstein values farm income in kind essentially in urban retail prices, while I have felt it in order to value it more conventionally at average realized farm prices. I do so despite the possible resultant understatement in the value of farm labor services. See below, p. 190. Then, too, Bornstein includes admittedly speculative estimates of "concealed" Soviet defense expenditures, while I have felt that such outlays probably are sufficiently covered by estimates of other final uses. I may also have been able sometimes to improve on Bornstein's ruble-dollar parities.

My calculations for the nonfarm sector are rather novel, but the results may be compared with data compiled by others for industry alone. Soviet output is again shown as a percentage of that of the USA in 1955:

	Bergson, nonfarm	*Nutter, industry*	*Campbell and Tarn, industry*
In rubles	19.9	19.7	
In US dollars	32.8	23.4	43.2

In translating industrial value added from one currency to another, Professor Nutter attempts the very difficult task of compiling ruble-dollar parities which may be applied directly to value added. Campbell and Tarn attempt rather to aggregate physical output relatives with value added weights. Other methods, however, had to be applied in comparing output in engineering industries. See Nutter, 1962, p. 238; Tarn, 1964, p. 410.

In trying to compare nonfarm output in the two countries, I have felt it might be best to proceed by first converting the gross national product by final use from one currency to the other, for available ruble-dollar parities lend themselves at once to such use. I then determine nonfarm output in the two countries in comparable prices simply as a residual by deducting from the gross national product in terms of each currency: i) the value added by selected final services, which essentially is already determined in the calculations on the gross national product by final use; and ii) the value added by agriculture. The latter is calculated in comparable prices, as is appropriate, by separate deflation of gross output (including material inputs), and of material inputs alone.

I have referred to limitations on the data apart from the price weights applied and shall later consider the valuation of farm relatively to nonfarm labor. For the rest, ruble factor cost is not, of course, adjusted factor cost, but I have explored its limitations elsewhere[24] and need refer here only to three outstanding ones: the omission of a charge for agricultural rent as such (though some rent almost inevitably accrues to farmers on better land, and is treated here as labor earnings); the absence of any systematic charge also for interest on reproducible capital, and the inclusion of a more or less arbitrary charge for "profits." The import of these deficiencies may be judged to some extent from the following recomputation of output per unit of inputs in rubles. I revalue farm relatively to nonfarm output to allow, probably quite generously, for agricultural rent equal to 60 per cent of Soviet farm labor income. I also revalue such output to allow for interest on reproducible capital at 12 per cent (see below) and to exclude profits. With these adjustments, Soviet output per unit of factor inputs rises from 30.6 to 32.9 per cent of that of the United States. I refer to all sectors. Productivity in the nonfarm sector alone is, of course, unchanged.[25] How revaluations of output of a similar sort within the farm and nonfarm sectors would affect my results is conjectural.

Where capital goods are a factor input, valuation, to repeat, is in prevailing ruble prices. Such prices arguably might be preferable to ruble factor cost even if they diverged markedly from the latter. In fact they apparently tend not to do so. It follows, however, that they are subject to much the same deficiencies as affect ruble factor cost generally, though the omission of agricultural rent is no longer among them. Index numbers of reproducible capital in prevailing ruble prices must be read accordingly.

For the valuation of both output and reproducible capital as an input, dollar prices, of course, also have their limitations. These limitations, however, can hardly compare with those of prevailing rubles and ruble factor cost. For output, here too a factor-cost valuation might have been preferable to one in prevailing prices, but the results, I believe, would have been little changed by its use.[26]

In calculating factor inputs, as explained, I aggregated index numbers of

[24] Bergson, 1961, Ch. 8.

[25] The recomputation entails increasing ruble value added per unit of farm output by 55.6 per cent and reducing that per unit of nonfarm output by 2.6 per cent. I rely here on data in the Appendix on Soviet farm and nonfarm output in ruble factor cost in 1955, and the estimates (indicated by data in the Appendix and in sources cited there) of these relevant charges for the same year: for agricultural rent, 115.6 billion rubles; interest on farm and nonfarm capital, 30.3 and 120.2 billion rubles respectively; and profits and related charges, on farm products, 24.4 billion rubles, and on nonfarm products, 135.2 billion rubles.

[26] See Bornstein, 1959, p. 380.

capital services with corresponding measures for employment, using gross capital charges, including interest and depreciation as the weight for the former, and labor earnings as the weight for the latter. Under adjusted factor cost, such interest supposedly should be determined at a rate corresponding to an average of marginal internal returns on capital. Where calculations are in dollars, I take this desideratum to be sufficiently realized when I apply a rate of return indicated by i) total earnings imputable to US reproducible capital, as determined in a usual way from national income accounts, and ii) the corresponding US reproducible capital stock.

Where calculations are in rubles, for familiar reasons we must impute to reproducible capital an arbitrary return. The rate used, however, is 12 per cent. At least this does not appear to be a serious understatement when it is considered that the computed rate for the USA is but 9.5 per cent. Admittedly, a relatively high rate in the USSR may be indicated by that country's relatively low capital stock per worker (Table 4). Taken together with available data on comparative money wage rates and investment goods prices, the indicated rates of return imply a marginal rate of substitution of capital for labor in the USSR 3.2 to 4.2 times as high as that in the USA. This would seem to be a fairly generous margin.[27] It is also illuminating that the share of *net* capital income in the total of labor and *net* capital income taken together, for the economy generally, excluding selected final services, is for the USSR, 28.7 per cent and for the USA, 20.0 per cent. Related, though not comparable, figures compiled elsewhere are for the USSR, 25 per cent; the USA, 14 per cent; France, 18 per cent; and Italy, 20 per cent.[28]

It remains true, however, that the assumed rate of return is arbitrary. It should be observed, therefore, that if one imputes to Soviet reproducible capital a still higher rate, 16 per cent, Soviet productivity rises relatively to that of the USA to a very limited extent; see the upper of the paired figures in parentheses in Table 4, where calculations are in rubles. Only the calculations in rubles, of course, are affected.[29]

[27] Derived from the formula:

$$(36) \qquad MRS_s/MRS_u = r_{su} \cdot W_{us} \cdot P_{su}$$

where r_{su} is the ratio of the Soviet to the US rate of return, W_{us} is the ratio of the average money wage in the USA to that in the USSR, and P_{su} is the ruble-dollar parity for investment goods. The second term is found to be .45, from data in United States Department of Commerce, 1966, p. 108, and TSU, 1965, p. 555. Depending on whether weights used are Soviet or US, the ruble-dollar parity for investment goods is found to be 4.7 or 6.1 rubles to $1. See Appendix.

[28] The Soviet figure relates to 1955 factor inputs and 1960 earnings rates. Others relate to 1960–62. See Bergson, 1968, pp. 87ff, and Denison, 1967, p. 38.

[29] To return to Soviet pricing as it affects capital, as Moorsteen and Powell,

Calculations in accord with the formulas applied thus far assume that $\sigma = 1$, but empirical studies suggest that $\sigma < 1$, and perhaps appreciably so.[30] If productivity is recomputed with σ equal to, say, .6, however, our measures are again altered, but only very partially. As expected, measures in ruble values are somewhat reduced, while those in dollar values are somewhat increased. See Table 3 and the figures in parentheses in Table 4. For ruble measures, reference is to the lower of the parenthetically paired figures. So far as the ruble measures are reduced, the effect is evidently the opposite of that where a rate of return of 16 per cent is imputed to Soviet capital.

As is well known, given US factor shares and the magnitude of σ, one may compute the corresponding factor shares that would accrue to Soviet factor inputs if they were employed in conformity with the same isoquants as those in the USA. It should be observed, then, that, if $\sigma = .6$, the implied Soviet share of capital in the earnings of labor and capital together is 48 per cent for the economy generally and 44 per cent for the nonfarm sector. I refer to the share of capital including depreciation. The corresponding figures indicated by the assumed rates of return of 12 and 16 per cent on Soviet capital are 34 and 40 per cent for the whole economy and 38 and 43 per cent for the nonfarm sector. These calculations, therefore, seem to provide further support for the assumed rates of return.[31]

(1966) pp. 256–257, remind us, the Soviet failure to account properly for returns to capital means that capital goods tend to be undervalued relatively to labor. Unless allowance is made for this undervaluation, rates of return such as have been cited are not as high as they might seem. The assumed rates still seem generous, however, in the light of other evidence presented.

Although omitting a charge from prices for capital, the Soviet government has found it expedient to allow the publication and prescription of interest-like norms for use in investment-project appraisal. But such norms, which vary in different branches, do not seem very illuminating as to the rate of return on Soviet capital when it is considered that little is known about the extent of their application and still less about the actual returns generated under their use. See Bergson, 1964, Ch. 11.

I refer to Soviet pricing as it was prior to the reforms now in progress in Soviet planning. Under the reforms, principles of price formation are being changed along with planning arrangements generally. While implications as to the actual return on capital are still obscure, it should be observed that enterprises which previously received much of the capital they required in the form of interest-free budgetary grants are now to pay into the budget a charge, usually at 6 per cent, on their capital assets. Also industrial prices supposedly were reviewed in 1967 to allow a planned profit averaging about 15 per cent on the enterprise's capital. See Bergson, 1966, p. 48; Sitnin, 1966, p. 4.

[30] See the studies cited on p. 169, n. 9.

[31] In the alternative computations of productivity, output relatives are obtained by use of the same formulas as before, but relatives of total inputs entail use

To return to selected final services, the reasons for omitting these in the case of housing are chiefly two. First, when valuations are in rubles, the proverbially nominal rentals for housing in the USSR must be rejected along with prevailing ruble prices generally; but in view of the immense importance of capital inputs into housing, recourse to ruble factor cost rentals which omit any systematic charge for capital is hardly satisfactory either. Second, meaningful conversion from one currency to another is especially difficult for housing services because of the notable variation in their quality in each country.

As for selected final services other than housing, omission of these is, of course, dictated by the need, under the national income accounting procedure observed here, to measure their output by inputs and indeed essentially by inputs of labor alone. Given such a procedure, inclusion of

---

of a formula such as the following, which is implied by the CES production function:

(37)
$$\left[\left(\frac{\phi}{1-\phi}\hat{K}_m^{-\varepsilon}+\hat{L}_m^{-\varepsilon}\right)\Big/\left(\frac{\phi}{1-\phi}\hat{K}_s^{-\varepsilon}+\hat{L}_s^{-\varepsilon}\right)\right]^{-1/\varepsilon}$$

Where computations are in Marxiana's values, $K_m = 1.0$, and K_s is the corresponding index in such values, while

(38)
$$\frac{\phi}{1-\phi}=\frac{1-\gamma}{\gamma}$$

Where computations are in Smithiana's values, $K_s = 1.0$ and K_m is the corresponding index in such values, while

(39)
$$\frac{\phi}{1-\phi}=\frac{1-\rho}{\rho}.$$

On γ and ρ, see Table 2. For either computation

(40)
$$\varepsilon=\frac{1-\sigma}{\sigma}.$$

In calculating the ruble factor shares implied by US factor shares when $\sigma = .6$, I take the capital stock index to be a geometric mean of the indices for this item in dollars and rubles.

With the calculation just considered as a variant, computations have thus far been in terms of the formulas in the upper two rows of Table 2. Computations in terms of the alternative formulas in the lower two rows of Table 2 entail only a rematching of output and input indices (i.e., with output in rubles, inputs must be in dollars, and vice versa), and are left to the reader. But note that, while the effect here too is to widen the spread between computations in terms of alternative valuations, the extent of the widening is diminished when $\sigma < 1$. Indeed, with a single index for the capital stock, and with Soviet factor shares determined to conform to US factor shares and the assumed magnitude of σ, there would be no further widening at all; for formula (37) would yield the same relative for inputs, no matter whether calculations are in rubles or in dollars.

services such as are considered in calculations of comparative productivity is evidently rather pointless. Nevertheless, as Simon Kuznets reminded us long ago, these services are not only "final" but in some degree "intermediate," and so may favorably affect productivity in the economy as a whole. Although generally omitting these services from my calculations, therefore, I still include among the factor inputs covered the sizeable amount of capital invested in highways. Intermediate uses of highways are relatively tangible and important and should not be neglected. Highways, however, are incomparably more consequential in the USA than in the USSR, in terms of both capital invested and final uses that are here ignored, so the procedure followed is admittedly favorable to the USSR. Soviet output per unit of factor inputs would fall relatively to that of the USA by one or two percentage points if highway capital were omitted from inputs for both countries.[32]

On similar reasoning one might also wish to include with inputs covered in my calculations some of the factors employed in providing other services, for example, law and order. It is conceptually and statistically difficult, however, to delineate the relevant employment. Paradoxically, the share of the civilian labor force engaged in government in any conventional sense in the USSR appears to be smaller than in the USA, so any bias in my results at this point is probably favorable to the USA.[33] I have been considering the contribution of selected final services to productivity apart from their impact on labor quality. The latter aspect is examined later with reference to one outstanding service, education.

The data described must be given priority, but I have also calculated the comparative gross national product per unit of factor inputs with the inclusion of selected final services. The results are noted, together with some further data relating to net as distinct from gross product.[34]

[32] I use data here on US highway capital given in the Appendix and these figures on the corresponding Soviet stock as of July 1, 1960, in ruble prices of 1955: 95 billions gross of depreciation and 70 billions net of depreciation. These are rather arbitrary estimates inferred chiefly from data in Kaplan, 1963, pp. 104, 106. In this essay, where dollar factor shares are employed, I generally use those set forth in the Appendix, but these represent the results of a late revision. For purposes of judging the impact of minor illustrative variants. I continue to rely on computations using somewhat different dollar factor shares that had been compiled previously.

[33] On comparative employment in government in the USSR, see Gur Ofer, *The Service Sector in the Soviet Union*, Ph.D. thesis, Harvard University, 1968. In dealing with services in my calculations, I have benefited from discussions with Professor Simon Kuznets.

[34] With the inclusion of selected final services, gross product per unit of factor inputs for the whole economy in the USSR is 39.1 per cent of that in the USA when valuations are in rubles and 56.9 per cent of that in the USA when valuations are in dollars. The corresponding figures for net product per unit of

4. Sources of Productivity Differentials

To come to efficiency, we are concerned primarily with that of a static sort, particularly realization of production possibilities. Like the corresponding measures now familiar in growth studies our comparative data on output per unit of factor inputs are rather complex. As calculated, productivity must be affected by efficiency but also by other features. Some of these features are of the theoretic sort already explained, and some revolve about the statistical limitations of my calculations just discussed. Still other, however, remain to be considered.

· To begin with, though taken as homogeneous, labor is, of course, of diverse kinds and ideally should be treated as correspondingly many factors. That is not feasible, but it is illuminating that a recomputation reducing employment in a Denison-like way to its male, eight-grade equivalent raises Soviet output per unit of factor inputs relatively to the American but still leaves it far short of the latter (Table 4).

In following Dr. Denison, I also draw on him for the required coefficients evaluating workers of different educational attainment and sex. Denison compiled his coefficients to effect a reduction of employment to its male eighth-grade employment in the United States, and they supposedly represent corresponding productivity differentials in this country. Although in fact they hardly do so with any precision, they are properly applied here, as I apply them, in a comparison of Soviet and US productivity, where valuations are in dollars.

Where valuations are in rubles, however, use should have been made instead of corresponding Soviet coefficients, but the results perhaps would not be much more favorable to the USSR than those obtained. Thus, education is scarcer and no doubt more valuable economically in the USSR than in the USA. Hence, with application of Soviet coefficients, employment should be reduced and productivity correspondingly increased

---

factor inputs are 37.0 and 52.6 per cent. With selected final services omitted, the net product per unit of factor inputs for the whole economy falls to 28.6 per cent when valuations are in rubles and 38.9 per cent when valuations are in dollars. In computing net product per unit of factor inputs I use as weights factor shares in which capital charges are net of depreciation. In all these calculations labor is unadjusted.

In referring earlier to comparative data compiled by Berliner, 1964, on Soviet and US factor productivity, I indicated that in this essay I differ with Berliner methodologically and statistically. One of the metholological differences relates to the treatment of selected final services, for Berliner compiles data only for the whole economy and the nonfarm sector, inclusive of such services. For the rest. suffice it to mention that Berliner gives priority to mixed weight computations such as are referred to above, p. 177, n. 15. As for the statistical differences, I refer to the data on output and inputs. Among other things, Berliner relies on the output relatives of Bornstein, discussed above, p. 183, n.23.

in the USSR relatively to the USA.[35] According to Denison, however, a female worker is worth but .59 of a male one. One need not be a feminist to feel that this rating is unduly low, if not for the USA then for the USSR. Women do appear, as often claimed, to have had relatively great opportunities to enter the more remunerative professions in the USSR.[36] Women constituted some 43 per cent of all workers in the USSR (other than in selected final services) in 1960. For the USA the corresponding figure is but 29 per cent. If female labor is unduly discounted, therefore, the recomputation should, if anything, favor the USSR.

After allowing in these ways for educational attainment and sex, I find that in the USSR a farm worker is still equivalent to as much as .77 of a nonfarm worker. In the United States, the farm worker is found to be practically on a par qualitatively with a nonfarm worker. These calculations are especially crude, but if they are at all near the mark, they represent decidedly higher valuations of farm labor than are implied in the data compiled on output: .5 of an industrial worker in the USSR and .4 of an industrial worker in the USA.[37] In both the USSR and USA, the farm worker, of course, must have fared better in real terms than such implied money earnings might suggest. Still these further results, obtained when a farm worker in both countries is arbitrarily counted in labor inputs as but .6 of a nonfarm worker may be of interest:

	Gross product per unit of major inputs, USSR ÷ USA, per cent	
	With 1955 ruble valuations	*With 1955 dollar valuations*
With employment adjusted as in Table 4	37.2	51.9
With employment further adjusted	38.6	54.1

[35] To what extent, we may perhaps judge from a further recomputation: With educational attainment evaluated in accord with coefficients for that aspect that Denison has compiled for Italy, Soviet output per unit of factor inputs rises relatively to the USA by two percentage points. I refer to the calculation in rubles. Worker educational attainment in Italy is broadly similar to that in the USSR, so the Italian coefficients may serve as something of a surrogate for corresponding Soviet ones. See the Appendix, Bergson, 1964, pp. 371–372, Denison, 1967, pp. 80, 91.

[36] See Dodge, 1966, pp. 243ff.

[37] From data in the Appendix, in sources cited there, and in Denison, 1967, p. 37, I find that farm labor earnings, as represented in output, averaged 5244 rubles per man year in the USSR and $1762 per man year in the USA. Reference is to output in 1955, from which my figures for 1960 are extrapolated. As for the industrial worker, his services are evaluated in output at his average money wage. On the latter for the USA, see the Department of Commerce publication cited in the Appendix as the principal source of data on US output. For the USSR, see TSU, 1965, p. 555.

I refer to all sectors. The results for the nonfarm sector alone are unaffected.

What of possible differences between the USSR and USA in respect of labor effort? How labor effort compares in the two countries is obviously not to be settled here; but, according to a familiar socialist claim, under public ownership of the means of production, the worker might be expected to exert himself with notable diligence. By all accounts the Soviet worker has sometimes done so; but there are reasons to think that among workers, as among the population generally, ideological zeal has been on the wane for some time. We cannot rule out the possibility that effort is, if anything, greater in the USA than in the USSR, as a Soviet economist reportedly has affirmed to a foreign correspondent:[38]

> Really, there is no comparison between the working energy and efficiency of American workmen and Soviet workmen. The Americans are the best workingmen in the world. They possess the best traditions. After all, it was the energetic, able, skilled people who emigrated to America. They took with them the desire and ability to work hard and well.

In contrast, it appears, the Soviet worker is still affected by the "Tom Sawyer tradition," according to which "one man paints, the rest watch."

In whatever way effort differs in the two countries, productivity must differ correspondingly. My comparative data must be read accordingly. Effort may vary because of a difference in incentive arrangements. In this case, it is likely itself to indicate a difference in efficiency, though such efficiency admittedly lies somewhat beyond "realization of production possibilities" as usually understood. The difference in effort might also reflect a difference in the workers' preferences between work and earnings. If it does, it is rather difficult to construe it as indicative of a difference in efficiency of any sort.[39]

The stock of reproducible capital considered in this essay includes all such assets on hand, whether they are in use or idle. In the case of labor, however, reference has been only to workers actually employed. In appraising comparative performance in the two countries, therefore, unemployment itself must be considered a source of a shortfall from production possibilities. Despite continuing Soviet claims to the contrary, unemployment, of course, does prevail in the USSR. Though chiefly of a transient sort, it can hardly be negligible. In the United States, as indicated, 5.6 per cent of the labor force were reportedly unemployed in 1960. That year, however, was one of relatively low employment by more recent standards.[40] The effect on our results of extending our cal-

---

[38] *New York Times*, October 2, 1957, p. 18. See also Bergson, 1968, pp. 34ff.
[39] See *ibid.*, pp. 34–35.
[40] US Central Intelligence Agency, 1966; President's Committee to Appraise Employment and Unemployment Statistics, 1962, p. 220.

culations to allow for unemployment must be judged in the light of these facts.

As calculated, productivity represents output per unit of labor and reproducible capital and hence is affected, apart from efficiency, by differences between the USSR and USA in respect of two other productive factors, industrial resources and farm land. In view of well known facts about the abundance of industrial resources in both countries, a difference in this sphere is probably not important. Industrial resources, however, often appear less conveniently located in the USSR than in the USA. This may be a reason why, per unit of output, freight traffic in ton miles in the USSR is 1.5 to 2.4 times as great as in the USA. According to such indices, Soviet transport performance is not especially out of line with Soviet economic performance generally, as reflected in our productivity measures,[41] but a less favorable geographic distribution of industrial resources in the USSR may be a partial cause of the high freight costs there. So far as it is, it would tend, of course, to reduce Soviet productivity without efficiency necessarily being any the less.

I doubt, too, that differences in respect of farm land greatly affect productivity as measured, important though that factor is in the USSR. Thus, the Russians cultivated 1.53 times as much land as we did in 1960. In the light of careful analyses by Professor Gale Johnson, an acre of Soviet farm land is on the average qualitatively equivalent to perhaps but .5 of an acre of US farm land. In US equivalent, therefore, Soviet farm acreage comes to but .77 of ours. Inclusion of farm land, as so measured, as a factor input scarcely alters my results where valuations are in dollars. With ruble valuations, Soviet output per unit of factor inputs rises relatively to that of the USA by one percentage point. The increase is less than that if labor is in male eighth-grade equivalent. In the calculation in dollars, the weight for farm land is determined in a conventional way.[42] In that in rubles, I again impute to farm land income equal to 60 per cent of farm labor earnings.

As explained, efficiency is understood here to be distinct from economies of scale. Hence, differential opportunities to realize such economies must also be considered as a separate factor, which might affect productivity. These opportunities turn on market size which is not, of course, the same thing as size of the country. Transportation costs and freedom of access to foreign buyers also matter. For the USSR and USA this aspect, again, should not be among the more important factors affecting comparative productivity.

[41] On industrial resources in the two countries, Harris, 1953. On freight traffic, see Hunter, 1968, pp. 35ff, and Hunter, 1966, p. 576. In the text, I compare freight traffic with gross national product exclusive of selected final services.

[42] As in Bergson, 1964, 379ff.

Inferences from productivity to efficiency, as also explained, presuppose ideally that countries compared have access to the same body of technological knowledge. Although never completely true, among relatively advanced countries technological knowledge developed by one is not easily withheld from another. Moreover, if a country's stock of such knowledge should nevertheless lag because of its own ineptness in gaining access to foreign developments, that would in itself constitute a form of inefficiency. And if productivity should be impaired correspondingly, it would be of little moment that such inefficiency is perhaps to be viewed as dynamic rather than of the static sort of immediate concern.

Still technological borrowing takes time, and probably the more so for the USSR in view of well known US policies restricting economic relations with that country. The Russians for their part have not been exactly open about their own discoveries, and technological knowledge in the West generally must have suffered somewhat on this account. But the Soviet Union long relied primarily on borrowing rather than creation to increase its technological knowledge. It must still be more of a borrower and less of a creator of such knowledge than the United States. In brief, in respect of comparative productivity the USSR must even now be at a disadvantage at this point. The disadvantage, however, could not easily come to the productivity equivalent of more than several years of US technological progress, that is, a number of percentage points in terms of my productivity measures.

But if the USSR borrows rather than creates technological knowledge, is not this in itself indicative of inefficiency? Perhaps so, but for a country that was backward not so long ago the volume of research and engineering capacities to commit to innovation as distinct from borrowing, might be relatively limited. And here too any inefficiency must be of the dynamic variety, though my productivity measures embrace it.[43]

I refer to availability of technological knowledge. Productivity may suffer, of course, not only from a lack of such knowledge but from a failure to apply it. But a failure of this kind would still be indicative of inefficiency, and necessarily of the static sort.[44]

[43] The nature and functioning of Soviet working arrangements for creating and borrowing of technologies have yet to be studied systematically. Some aspects of interest here are discussed in Bergson, 1968, Ch. 3.

[44] Technological knowledge affects productivity so far as it limits the outputs producible with available inputs. Where it is of the "embodied" sort, however, such knowledge also affects the available inputs. To the extent that capital goods produced at different times, and hence embodying different technologies, vary in their productivity, their services in principle should be valued correspondingly in the computation of productivity measures.

Moreover, obsolescence supposedly has been allowed for in the data on capital inputs, but just how is not clear in the case of the data compiled for the USSR.

5. Conclusions

What may be concluded as to Soviet efficiency? Thanks to Western scholarship, we already know a good deal about efficiency under Soviet socialism. This must be inferred, however, primarily from qualitative information on the nature of economic working arrangements and the patterns of resource use that they generate. According to comparative data examined here, Soviet productivity falls notably short of that of the USA and seems to do so not much less after generous allowance for the differential impact of causal factors other than efficiency. As in the case of the comparable productivity residual found in studies of growth, the partial implication no doubt is that further research is needed.

But the data do seem to shed further light on Soviet efficiency. Thus, as was already evident from Western research, Soviet economic performance is often faulty, to say the least, but there is, I think, more of a presumption than before, that in terms of efficiency the Soviet economy must be markedly inferior to that of the USA. This is true both for the economy generally and for the nonfarm sector alone. Productivity in the USSR is especially low, however, for the economy generally. This may be due in part to misallocation of resources between the farm and nonfarm sectors, but not very surprisingly it probably also implies that efficiency is especially low in agriculture.

Both for the economy generally and for the nonfarm sector, productivity in the USSR is low whether valuations are in rubles or in dollars, but it is particularly low in the former case. My data are hardly comparable to those considered in theory, but on an analytic plane they imply that the

---

(See Kaplan, 1963, p. 100), and one wonders whether old assets may not be systematically overvalued there. This is probably true too, in the corresponding data for the USA (Goldsmith, *et al.*, 1956, p. 5). Also, because of its extraordinarily rapid expansion under the five-year plans, the Soviet capital stock was notably young in 1960, averaging in the case of fixed capital but 10.7 years (Moorsteen and Powell, 1966, p. 336). Although a corresponding figure is not at hand for the USA, it surely would be higher. If old assets are overvalued, therefore, my calculations should, if anything, understate capital services and hence overstate productivity for the USSR relative to the USA.

The degree of overvaluation of old assets, it is true, could easily be relatively greater for the USSR, whose embodied technologies often seem to be especially dated. Furthermore, this may to some extent reflect a Soviet disadvantage compared to the United States in availability of technological knowledge. Probably no less important, however, is the formerly influential Soviet view that obsolescence has no place under socialism and the related Soviet policy of producing notably long runs of machines of given design. How the inefficiency resulting from such a policy is to be classified is an interesting question which I leave to the reader. But here too it does not seem too bad that my measures of productivity may reflect it.

performance of the USSR is better where its own inputs and outputs, rather than those of the United States, are taken as standard. This again is a plausible result.

I have focused throughout on efficiency in the sense of realization of production possibilities. Closely related to this question, is the degree of optimality of the output structure. In conclusion, therefore, it should be observed that the data set forth bear on the latter as well as on the former aspect. Indeed, so far as the calculations in dollars are in prevailing prices rather than in factor cost, they are readily seen to be more relevant in principle to performance in the two spheres together than to realization of production possibilities alone.[45] Moreover, the calculations in rubles almost inevitably are only partly in factor cost as distinct from prevailing prices. Despite the deficiencies of prevailing ruble prices, with output valued in such prices again, productivity may be more or less indicative of optimality of output structure as well as of realization of production possibilities. Limitations of the data at this point probably are in any case not especially favorable to the USA. The Soviet performance does not seem to improve, therefore, as the inquiry is extended to embrace optimality of output structure along with realization of production possibilities. The former matter, however, is properly the subject for a separate study, and cannot be pursued further here.[46]

[45] I must leave to another occasion extension of the theoretic analysis of pp. 163–78ff to the problem posed, but so far as optimality of commodity structure is of concern, one is in effect seeking to appraise welfare. According to familiar reasoning, valuation in this case is more properly in prevailing prices than in factor cost. I refer to the valuation of output. As indicated, viewed as inputs, capital goods seem best valued at prevailing prices rather than factor cost even where attention is focused on realization of production possibilities.

[46] Where optimality of output structure is in question, not least among the limitations of my data, I think, is the overvaluation of the proverbially large volume of substandard or otherwise undesirable goods, which enterprise managers somehow tend to produce in the USSR (see Bergson, 1964, pp. 287ff). Such overvaluation appears unavoidable in view of the chronic seller's market there, though this was not so acute in 1960 as formerly. While only USSR data in rubles are affected in the first instance, as readily perceived, the comparative data must to some extent be distorted as well. Moreover, this should be so whether valuations finally are in rubles or in dollars. I refer primarily to the comparative data on output. Although those on capital inputs may also be affected, the result must, if anything, be a bias in my productivity measures favorable to the USSR.

At least for consumers' goods, optimality of commodity structure is usually seen in terms of consumers' preferences. As affected by the indicated aberration of enterprise managers, however, the Soviet performance in this sphere cannot be much improved by reference instead to any likely "planners' preferences." The Soviet government's own incessant complaints make this clear enough.

Appendix

Output and Factor Inputs, USSR and USA, 1960

This appendix explains briefly the sources and methods used in compiling the productivity data in Table 4 and in the text. These data tend to be crude, and data used in their derivation are often especially so. Although I feel that the data afford a basis for the calculation of factor productivity, the reader is cautioned that the figures to be set forth may be less reliable for other purposes.

In compiling the productivity data in Table 4 and in the text, I draw on results of research in progress, some aspects of which I expect to report on elsewhere. While the results include basic data on the national income of the USSR and USA, I hope I may have the reader's indulgence if, rather than trying to explain the underlying calculations in any detail now, I refer to the projected publications. These I shall designate collectively as *Soviet Inputs and Output.*

Gross and Net National Product by Sector.   To begin with output, the indices of comparative Soviet and US gross product in 1960 set forth in Table 4, and corresponding indices of net output used in compiling further measures referred to in the text, are all obtained from absolute figures on gross and net output for the two countries shown in Table 5. These absolute figures, in ruble factor cost and US dollars of 1955, are derived in turn from the data on gross output in the same terms for 1955 set forth in Table 6, for the USSR, and in Table 7, for the USA. As for the figures on gross product in 1955, these are to be explained in *Soviet Inputs and Output*, I should point out here, however, that, except as will appear, reference is to output gross of depreciation, but net of material inputs. The figures for all sectors, therefore, indicate the gross national product. Also, while a breakdown is shown by sector of origin, gross national product for each country has been calculated initially by final use.

For the USSR this is done first in terms of prevailing rubles as well as in terms of ruble factor cost of 1955. The calculations here represent a limited revision of previous computations by myself and associates for the RAND Corporation, and published in Hoeffding and Nimitz, April 6, 1959; Bergson, 1961, and Nimitz, June, 1962. The revision accounts chiefly for later information and for second thoughts on various methodo-

Table 5
Output and Factor Inputs, USSR and USA, 1960

Item	Nature of measurement	USSR				USA			
		All sectors	Farm	Nonfarm	Selected final services	All sectors	Farm	Nonfarm	Selected final services
Gross product	In 1955 ruble factor cost. bil.	1,278.6	260.1	884.4	134.1	3,768.2	331.9	3,300.1	136.2
	In 1955 dollars, bil.	247.2	17.5	163.0	66.7	444.8	19.4	343.7	81.7
Net product	In 1955 ruble factor cost, bil.	1,182.2	247.9	824.9	109.4[a]	3,406.1	310.8	3,079.4	15.9[a]
	In 1955 dollars, bil.	231.0	15.3	152.3	63.4[a]	391.4	16.3	311.1	64.0[a]
Employment	Workers engaged, mil.	102.1	39.3	47.3	15.5	65.8	4.4	48.2	13.2
Employment, adjusted	Workers engaged, adjusted hypothetically to equivalent male, eighth grade graduate, mil.	81.9[b]	25.8	40.6	15.5[b]	67.5[b]	4.4	49.9	13.2[b]
Reproducible capital, including gross fixed assets	In 1955 rubles, bil.	3,789.7	495.7	2,055.6	1,238.4[c]	12,580.9	715.4	6,031.8	5,833.7[c]
	In 1955 dollars, bil.	606.4	68.0	352.7	185.7[c]	1,785.8	81.6	820.3	883.9[c]
Reproducible capital, including net fixed assets	In 1955 rubles, bil.	3,030.1	397.2	1,658.9	974.0[c]	7,923.1	495.7	3,927.4	3,500.0[c]
	In 1955 dollars, bil.	474.7	51.0	278.4	145.3[c]	1,100.0	50.4	51.3	530.3
Cultivated arable land	Million acres	549	549			359	359		
Cultivated arable land, adjusted to U.S. equivalent	Million acres	275	275			359	359		

[a] Relatively limited magnitudes reflect depreciation accounting. See p. 201.
[b] Selected final services unadjusted. See text.
[c] Fixed assets only.

Table 6

Elements in Calculation of Gross and Net National Product of USSR by Sector, 1960, in Ruble Factor Cost and US Dollars of 1955

(Billions)

Sector	Gross product, 1955		Gross product, 1960		Depreciation, 1960		Net product, 1960	
	In 1955 ruble factor cost	In 1955 dollars	In 1955 ruble factor cost	In 1955 dollars	In 1955 ruble factor cost	In 1955 dollars	In 1955 ruble factor cost	In 1955 dollars
FARM	218.6	14.7	260.1	17.5	12.2	2.2	247.9	15.3
NONFARM	586.4	102.9	884.4	163.0	59.5	10.7	824.9	152.3
SELECTED FINAL SERVICES								
Health care, education	61.6	31.0	79.1 }	39.8 }	5.3 }	.4 }	117.5 }	57.6 }
Government administration, including internal security,								
Party	21.6	8.1	20.4	7.6				
Armed forces	38.8	17.7	23.3	10.6				
Housing	8.3	6.4	11.3	8.7	19.4	2.9	(−)8.1	5.8
All	130.3	63.2	134.1	66.7	24.7	3.3	109.4	63.4
ALL	935.3	180.8	1,278.6	247.2	96.4	16.2	1,182.2	231.0

logical matters. From the data in prevailing rubles of 1955, I obtain corresponding figures on the gross national product in 1955 US dollars by applying appropriate Soviet-weighted ruble-dollar parities to the different final outlays.

For the USA, data on the gross national product by final use are compiled in 1955 US dollar prices essentially by reference to United States Department of Commerce, 1966, though it was convenient to reclassify somewhat the final outlays listed in this source, and sometimes to supplement the Commerce Department data. Among other things, for the gross national product, I add to the Commerce Department figure of $397.96 billions a total of $1.6 billions to allow for omitted health-care expenditures of business organizations. The gross national product by final use as so determined is then converted to 1955 rubles by applying appropriate US-weighted ruble-dollar parities to the different final outlays. These calculations in the first instance yield data in prevailing rubles of 1955, but corresponding figures in 1955 ruble factor cost are derived by reference to coefficients of the relation of ruble factor cost to prevailing rubles that obtain for different final uses of the Soviet gross national product.

The ruble-dollar parities used in these calculations, both those with Soviet and those with US weights, are for the most part taken from, or adaptations of parities in, a variety of studies, including chiefly unclassified reports of the US Central Intelligence Agency and of Dr. Abraham Becker for the RAND Corporation (August 15, 1959). Some, however, were compiled especially for *Soviet Inputs and Output* from available ruble and dollar price quotations and related data.

As for the gross national product by sector, given the gross national product by final use, the contribution of the nonfarm sector can be calculated as a residual. Moreover, except for housing, the gross product of selected final services consists only of labor services, the amounts of which in both rubles and dollars were already determined for both countries in the calculations on the gross national product by final use. Housing here consists of aggregate household rental payments, actual and imputed, no deductions being feasible for material inputs. As so construed, the contribution of this sector too had already been determined in both rubles and dollars for both countries.

It remains, therefore, only to calculate the gross product of agriculture. In each country's own currency this can be computed from diverse information and converted to the currency of the other country by use of ruble-dollar parities derived from sources and methods such as were relied on in the corresponding calculations for final outlays. The conversion is performed, as is proper, through the separate translation of farm output inclusive of material inputs, on the one hand, and of material inputs alone, on the other. As before, the parities refer, in the case of the Soviet currency,

Table 7

Elements in Calculation of Gross and Net National Product of USA by Sector, 1960,
in US Dollars and Ruble Factor Cost of 1955
(Billions)

Sector	Gross product, 1955		Gross product, 1960		Depreciation, 1960		Net product, 1960	
	In 1955 dollars	*In 1955 ruble factor cost*	*In 1955 dollars*	*In 1955 ruble factor cost*	*In 1955 dollars*	*In 1955 ruble factor cost*	*In 1955 dollars*	*In 1955 ruble factor cost*
FARM	18.58	318.2	19.4	331.9	3.1	21.1	16.3	310.8
NONFARM	311.70	2,950.4	343.7	3,300.1	32.6	220.7	312.8	3,079.4
SELECTED FINAL SERVICES								
Health care, education, government purchases, n.e.c., armed forces	35.54	72.9	39.3	80.7	4.2	31.4	35.1	49.3
Housing	33.74	44.1	42.4	55.5	13.5	88.9	28.9	(−)33.4
All	69.28	117.0	81.7	136.2	17.7	120.3	64.0	15.9
ALL	399.56	3,385.6	444.8	3,768.2	53.4	362.1	391.4	3,406.1

to prevailing rubles; but equivalents in terms of ruble factor cost can be determined from available data on the sectoral incidence of the Soviet turnover tax and subsidies.

Data on gross product by sector in 1960 are obtained simply by extrapolation from corresponding figures for 1955. Net product for all sectors is net national product, or gross national product less depreciation. Hence net product by sector is obtained by deducting depreciation from gross product by sector. The extrapolated data on gross national product by sector in 1960, the depreciation charges deducted, and the resulting figures on net national product by sector in 1960 are all shown, together with the initial figures on gross national product by sector in 1955, in Appendix Table 6 and Appendix Table 7.

In extrapolating Soviet gross national product to 1960, I refer to index numbers of real gross national product such as appear in Cohn, 1962, p. 75, and Cohn, 1966, pp. 103ff, but as finally elaborated in a letter of Professor Cohn to me of January 26, 1967. For farm output, reference is made to index numbers of "net" agricultural output in Diamond, 1966, p. 346. For health care and education, I consider changes in total employment in "public health" and "educational institutions," together with one-half the employment in "science," as given in Feshbach, 1966, pp. 771–772. The extrapolation of government administration is rather arbitrary, though account is taken of the trend in employment in "administrative organs," as given *ibid.*, pp. 771–773. On the armed forces, see Bergson, 1961, p. 443, and Feshbach, 1966, p. 746. For housing, I refer to changes in public-housing equivalent space, as calculated from data in Bergson, 1961, pp. 315–316; Hoeffding and Nimitz, April 6 1959, pp. 98ff; Nimitz, June 1962, p. 57, Becker, Part I, June, 1965, pp. 105–107. Nonfarm output is obtained as a residual.

For the USA, I extrapolate gross national product to 1960 by reference to data in 1958 prices in United States Department of Commerce, 1966, pp. 4–5. For farm gross output and housing, reference is to similar data for these items, *ibid.*, pp. 28–29, 48–49. For selected final services other than housing, I consider the change in total employment in "medical and other health services," "educational services," "federal: general government," and "state and local: general government," as indicated, *ibid.*, pp. 112–113. Nonfarm output is again obtained as a residual.

Depreciation charges for all sectors for the USSR in 1960 amounted to 105.0 billion rubles in 1950 prices. See Moorsteen and Powell, 1966, p. 325. A corresponding figure of 96.0 billion rubles in 1955 prices is indicated by data on fixed capital investment in 1950 and 1955 rubles in Bergson, 1961, pp 381, 390. These figures are in prevailing rubles, but I assume that for fixed capital such rubles approximate ruble factor cost. As in Bergson, 1964, p. 365, I take depreciation charges in 1955 dollars for all sectors for the USA in 1960 to be 12 per cent of the 1955 dollar value of the US gross national product in that year. Ruble depreciation charges for the USSR are converted to dollars and dollar depreciation charges for the USA to rubles by reference to ruble-dollar parities indicated by the conversion of fixed capital investment from one currency to another.

In this way, I compute total charges for each country in both currencies. Corresponding sectoral data are obtained by reference to figures set forth below on 1960 gross fixed assets by sector in 1955 ruble and dollar values. Thus, for both housing and other selected final services, I take depreciation to be 2 per cent on such gross fixed assets. Depreciation on farm and nonfarm fixed assets is assumed proportional to the volume of gross fixed assets in the two sectors.

For selected final services other than housing, I deduct depreciation even though no such charge is included in gross output to begin with. Moreover, for housing I make a similar deduction from gross output in both ruble and dollar values even though in the case of the former, the rental rates in question are relatively nominal, and indeed, as my results indicate, even fail to cover depreciation alone, not to mention other factor charges. Although I think the deduction is in order in both cases, the results are obviously dubious. Among the output data used in this study to measure productivity, only those on net national product inclusive of selected final services are affected, but as noted in the text (p. 188, n. 34) extension of my productivity measures to include such services, which is dubious in any case, is the more so on this account.

Employment by Sector. Also shown in Table 5 are absolute figures on factor inputs that were used in compiling the factor input relatives and productivity measures in Table 7 and related data considered in the text. To refer first to the figures on employment, those for the USSR may be explained by reference to Appendix Table 8. For the present, I consider only the first numerical column of the latter table. For the most part, the figures cited are taken or inferred from data in Nimitz, November, 1965, p. 7, and Feshbach, 1966, pp. 746–747, 772–773, 788. Note that "Farm, other" corresponds to "Agricultural activities not specifically identified" in Feshbach, 1966, p. 788. "Employees, including artisans, nonfarm enterprises" is "Non-agricultural branches, workers and employees," plus "Independent Artisans" and "Forestry," as given in Feshbach, 1966, p. 788, less "Selected final services," other than the "Armed Forces." For "Nonfarm, other," I cite an arbitrary allowance for penal labor and certain other categories of workers who are otherwise omitted from the tabulation. Under "Education," I include all employment in "Educational institutions" and one-half the employment in "Science," as given in Feshbach, p. 772. Under "Government administration, etc.," I include .5

million of militarized internal-security personnel, or the same number of such persons as were assumed for 1955 in Bornstein (processed), 1961, p. 50, and 1.5 million civilians, or somewhat less than the total employment for 1955 implied by data on total and average earnings for these employees in *Soviet Inputs and Output*. A reduction in "Government administration, etc." from 1955 to 1960 seems indicated by data on employment in "Administrative organs" in Feshbach, 1966, pp. 772–773. For "Housing," I take one-half the employment in "Housing-communal economy," as given in Feshbach, 1966, pp. 772–773.

For the USA, data on employment by sector in Table 5 were compiled

Table 8
Employment by Sector and Sex, USSR, 1960
(millions)

	All	*Male*	*Female*
FARM			
Collective farmers, in 280 day man years	19.0	9.7	9.3
Collective farmers and others on household plots, in 280 day man years	16.1	3.2	12.9
Employees, state farms	6.3	3.6	2.7
Other	.5	.3	.2
All	41.9	16.8	25.1
Less:			
Collective farmers, nonfarm activities	2.1	1.1	1.0
Employees, state farm, nonfarm activities	.5	.3	.2
All, farm activities only	39.3	15.4	23.9
NONFARM			
Collective farmers, non-farm activities	2.1	1.1	1.0
Employees, state farm, nonfarm activities	.5	.3	.2
Employees, repair-technical stations	.3	.3	—[a]
Employees, including artisans, nonfarm enterprises	42.9	24.3	18.6
Other	1.5	1.0	.5
All	47.3	27.0	20.3
SELECTED FINAL SERVICES			
Health care	3.5	.5	3.0
Education	5.7	2.2	3.5
Government administration, etc.	2.0	1.2	.8
Armed forces	3.3	3.3	—[a]
Housing	1.0	.5	.5
All	15.5	7.7	7.8
ALL	102.1	50.1	52.0

[a] Negligible.

Table 9

Employment by Sector, USA, 1960
(millions)

	All
Farm	4.4
Nonfarm	48.2
Selected final services	
Health care, private	2.0
Education, private	.8
Federal, general government, civilian	1.7
State and local, general government	5.2
Military	2.5
Housing	1.0
All	13.2
ALL	65.8

from data on persons engaged by industry in United States Department of Commerce, 1966, pp. 112–113. The more pertinent figures in the latter source are repeated in Table 9, though with somewhat different captions. For "Housing," the cited figure is the total of employment in "Hotels and other lodging places" plus one-half the employment in "Real Estate," as given by the Commerce Department.

I have been referring to employment in terms of workers engaged, and turn now to such employment adjusted hypothetically to equivalent male, eight-grade graduate. The adjustment is made only for workers other than those in selected final services, and the resulting employment in the farm sector is calculated as a residual. In other words, the adjustment is made for all workers, other than those in selected final services, and for nonfarm workers.

The adjustment for these two categories of workers, as shown in Table 10, entails a reduction of workers engaged to their male equivalent and then a further reduction of the resultant to male, eight-grade graduate equivalent.

To consider first the reduction to male equivalent, I assume here for both countries that one female worker is equivalent to .59 of a male worker. This is the coefficient used in Denison, 1967, pp. 70ff, to adjust female workers of 20–64 years to their equivalent in terms of males of the same ages in the United States and Western Europe. It corresponds to the 1960 hourly earnings differentials between the two groups of workers in the United States.

For the USSR, therefore, reduction to male equivalent is achieved by applying this coefficient to female employment as given in Table 8 and

Table 10

Adjustment of Employment to Male
Eighth-Grade Equivalent, USSR and USA, 1960
(millions)

| | All sectors, excluding selected final services | | Nonfarm | |
	USSR	USA	USSR	USA
Workers engaged	86.6	52.6	47.3	48.2
Workers engaged, adjusted to male equivalent	68.5	46.4	39.0	42.3
Average male worker in male eighth-grade graduate equivalent	.97	1.17	1.04	1.18
Workers engaged, adjusted to male, eighth-grade graduate equivalent	66.4	54.3	40.6	49.9

aggregating the resulting totals with corresponding figures for male workers. The latter figures are derived as residuals. Those on female workers are computed primarily from percentage data on female employment in TSU, 1961 (C), pp. 124, 129. As in Bergson, 1964, p. 370, 80 per cent of the employment of collective farmers and others on household plots is estimated to be of females. For "Farm, others," I assume female employment to be 43 per cent of the total, the same as for state farm workers. For "Employees, including artisans, nonfarm enterprises," females are calculated as a residual from female employment in all sectors. The division of "nonfarm, other" between female and male workers is arbitrary. For "Government administration, etc.," the .5 million of militarized internal security forces are taken to be all male. Of the 1.5 million civilian employees in this sector, I assume 54 per cent to be female, the same as for employees in the "apparatus of organs of state and economic administration . . . ," in TSU, 1961 (C), p. 124. For housing, women are taken to constitute 47 per cent of all workers, as for all Soviet employees, in TSU, 1961 (C), p. 124.

Female workers in all sectors are calculated to total 52.0 millions including: i) 29.3 million employees, as given in TSU, 1961 (C), p. 120; ii) 9.3 million man–years of collective farm work; iii) 12.9 million man–years of work on household plots; and iv) .5 million of "Non-farm, other."

For the United States, according to Denison, 1967, p. 72, female workers worked 29 per cent of the man–hours worked by all civilian workers in 1960. I assume that this ratio also obtains for employment other than in selected final services. For nonfarm employment, the corresponding figure is raised to 30 per cent in the light of Bureau of Labor Statistics, October 1967, pp. 4, 9.

Further adjustment of male-equivalent employment as thus derived is made by application of the average coefficients shown in Table 10, above. In all cases the average coefficients are derived from corresponding coefficients indicating the earnings value of different levels of education for male workers in the United States in 1959, as given in Table F-2, col. (4), Denison, 1967, p. 374. For the USSR, average coefficients for all male workers other than in selected final services and for male nonfarm workers are computed by reference to the data in Table 11 on the distribution of employed workers generally and of employed nonfarm workers by educational attainment in January 1959. Employed workers of both sexes are considered in both cases. For such workers generally, I rely here on data compiled by Professor Nicholas De Witt. See Bergson, 1964, pp. 371–372. The corresponding figures for nonfarm workers were adapted from De Witt's data by reference to data on educational attainments of different occupational groups in TSU, 1961 (B), pp. 37ff, 50ff.

For the United States, for male workers other than those in selected final services, I compute an average coefficient by reference to data in Denison, 1967, p. 381, on the distribution of male civilians, 18 years and over in March 1959 by educational attainment. For male nonfarm workers I raise the average coefficient just derived by 1 per cent in the light of data in Bureau of the Census, February 4, 1960, p. 5, on the comparative educational attainments of workers in different occupations.

Table 11

Assumed Distribution of Employed Workers
by Schooling, USSR, January 1959
(per cent)

Schooling, Soviet	Schooling, U.S. equivalent	All	Nonfarm[a]
Literate, with 6 years or less	4 years	56.7	35.6
Partial secondary	9 years	25.0	37.2
Complete secondary	12 years	13.8	20.6
Partial higher education	2 years college	1.4	2.1
Complete higher education	college graduate	3.1	4.6
All		100.0	100.0

[a] Discrepancy between indicated total and sum of items due to rounding.

To repeat, in Table 10 the average coefficients for the USSR are computed from data on the educational attainments of employed workers of both sexes. Those for the USA are computed from data on educational attainments of employed male workers. For present purposes the latter procedure is probably preferable, but it should be observed that for the USA the average coefficient for employed workers generally would be 1.18, or only slightly different from that used if reference were made to workers of both sexes.

Reproducible Capital. The data on reproducible capital in Table 5 may be explained by reference to Table 12. To begin with the figures on reproducible capital in the USSR in 1955 rubles, those for fixed capital are derived from corresponding data for January 1, 1960, in rubles of July, 1965, in Bergson, 1964, p. 373. In that study, nonfarm includes selected final services other than housing, but fixed capital gross of depreciation in such services is also estimated to have totaled on January 1, 1960, 254.1 billion rubles in July 1, 1955 rubles. The corresponding figure net of depreciation is 199.8 billion rubles. See Bergson, 1964, p. 377.

I assume that for construction, the ruble prices of July 1, 1955 approximated the average level for the year. Thus, for basic industrial goods July 1, 1955 ruble prices were 102.6 per cent of the average 1955 level. See Turgeon and Bergson, June 12, 1957, p. 13. Construction wages on July 1, 1955, however, were probably somewhat below the average level for the year. For producers' durables, average 1955 ruble prices are assumed to be 113.3 per cent of those for July 1, 1955. For the farm sector alone, the corresponding figure is 107 per cent. See Moorsteen, 1962, pp. 386, 391, 392. For farm producers' durables, I average price indices obtained from Moorsteen for tractors, automotive vehicles and agricultural machines with weights of 2.3, 1.6, and 3.5. The weights are derived from diverse data on output, prices and supplies of these products to agriculture in Moorsteen, 1962, pp. 313, 382ff, and TSU, 1961 (A), pp. 291–292, 491.

Fixed capital on July 1, 1960, is extrapolated from that for January 1, 1960, by reference to these indices (July 1, 1960÷January 1, 1960, in per cent):

	Gross assets	Net assets
Nonfarm	105.4	105.4
Housing	103.2	105.4
Other selected final services	105	105
All	104.8	105.1

These indices are inferred from data in Moorsteen and Powell, 1966, pp. 323, 329, 335, and TSU, 1962, p. 68. Farm fixed capital on July 1, 1960, is obtained rather crudely as a residual.

For the United States gross and net stocks of fixed capital on July 1, 1960, in US 1955 dollars are taken from Bergson, 1964, p. 375. There too nonfarm assets include those in selected final services other than housing. On July 1, 1960, gross and net fixed assets in such services amounted

Table 12

Reproducible Capital, USSR and USA, July 1, 1960, in Rubles and US Dollars of 1955
(Billions)

	All sectors		Farm		Nonfarm		Selected final services	
	In 1955 rubles	In 1955 dollars	In 1955 rubles	In 1955 dollars	In 1955 rubles	In 1955 dollars	In 1955 rubles	In 1955 dollars
USSR								
Fixed capital, gross	3,045.0	510.4	308.4	53.4	1,498.2	271.3	1,238.4	185.7
Fixed capital, net	2,285.4	378.7	209.9	36.4	1,101.5	197.0	974.0	145.3
Inventories	604.6	88.3	47.2	6.9	557.4	81.4	—[b]	—[b]
Livestock	140.1	7.7	140.1	7.7	...[a]	...	...	...
All, including gross fixed capital	3,789.7	606.4	495.7	68.0	2,055.6	352.7	1,238.4	185.7
All, including net fixed capital	3,030.1	474.7	397.2	51.0	1,658.9	278.4	974.0	145.3
USA								
Fixed capital, gross	11,273.3	1,662.5	443.2	62.9	4,996.4	715.7	5,883.7	883.9
Fixed capital, net	6,615.5	976.7	223.5	31.7	2,892.0	414.7	3,500.0	530.3
Inventories	1,115.7	112.7	80.3	8.1	1,035.4	104.6	—[b]	—[b]
Livestock	191.9	10.6	191.9	10.6	...	...	...	...
All, including gross fixed capital	12,580.9	1,785.8	715.4	81.6	6,031.8	820.3	5,833.7	883.9
All, including net fixed capital	7,923.1	1,100.0	495.7	50.4	3,927.4	519.3	3,500	530.3

[a] ... = negligible.
[b] Included in nonfarm sector.

respectively to 297.4 and 187.5 billion dollars. See Bergson, 1964, pp. 377–378, where gross and net fixed assets in selected final services were estimated at 297.4 and 127.5 billion rubles respectively. These totals include highway capital, which for present purposes I classify with nonfarm assets (as was done inadvertently for the USSR in Bergson, 1964, p. 377). As for highway capital, I assume this to have totaled, in 1955 prices, 87 billion dollars gross of depreciation, and 60 billion dollars net of depreciation on July 1, 1960. These are rough estimates derived chiefly from data in Goldsmith, 1962, pp. 89, 209, 210, 218, 219, 367, and 385.

In Bergson, 1964, as implied, data are compiled on gross and net fixed capital not only by sector but by type, that is, according to whether the capital consists of producers' durables or structures. One currency is translated separately into another for these different kinds of assets by use of the following ruble dollar parities:

	Dollars per ruble with Soviet weights	*Rubles per dollar with US weights*
Structures		
Farm	.14	7.1
Nonfarm	.14	7.1
Housing	.15	6.6
Other selected final services	.15	6.6
Producers' durables		
Farm	.23	7.0
Nonfarm	.24	

The ratios for structures are from Central Intelligence Agency, August 1964, p. 1. The Soviet and US weighted parities given in this study for all structures are assumed here to apply to both farm and nonfarm structures. The CIA derives a parity for housing only with US weights. I take the corresponding parity with Soviet weights to be the same. This parity is also applied to selected final services other than housing. The parities for nonfarm producers' durables correspond to those used in *Soviet Inputs and Output* to deflate current investment in all producers' durables. Of the latter parities, that with Soviet weights is obtained essentially by aggregating ruble-dollar price ratios for producers' durables given in Becker, August 15, 1959, using Soviet weights derived from Moorsteen, 1962. The corresponding US weighted parity is adapted from one in Becker, August 15, 1959, p. 31. Thus I modify Becker's parity to make it cover metal-working machine tools and to relate to average 1955 ruble prices rather than to those of July 1, 1955. Soviet and US weighted parities for farm producers durables are derived from ruble-dollar ratios for pertinent products in Becker, corresponding Soviet output data in Moorsteen and in TSU, 1961 (A), pp. 291–292, 491 and rather arbitrary weights for the USA.

For present purposes, fixed capital in selected services other than housing is taken to consist only of structures.

Inventories in all sectors in the USSR amounted to 600.5 billion rubles on January 1, 1960 and to 637.8 billion rubles on January 1, 1961. See Moorsteen and Powell, 1966, pp. 341 and 606, and Becker, Moorsteen and Powell, 1968, p. 19. I take the corresponding figure for July 1, 1960 to be an average of these two figures, or 618.9 billion rubles. These data are in ruble factor cost of 1950. Deflation of the Soviet gross national product implies that ruble factor cost in 1955 was 97.7 per cent of that of 1950. See Bergson, 1961, p. 149, and Nimitz, June 1962, p. 153. If ruble factor cost for inventories varied similarly, inventories on July 1, 1960 amounted to 604.6 billion rubles in 1955 ruble factor cost. In the light of data in Moorsteen and Powell, 1966, p. 338. I take 7.8 per cent of the inventories to be in the farm sector and allot the balance to the nonfarm sector.

From data in Goldsmith, 1962, pp. 117, 119, and 206, I calculate that inventories in the United States on January 1, 1959 totalled $106.8 billions in prices of 1955. Considering data in United States Department of Commerce, 1966, pp. 5, 159, I take the corresponding figure for July 1, 1960 to be $112.7 billions. I assume farm inventories to be 7.2 per cent of the total, and allot the balance to the nonfarm sector. See Goldsmith, 1962, pp. 117, 206.

From data in Moorsteen and Powell, 1966, pp. 107, 337, I estimate that Soviet livestock herds on July 1, 1960 totaled 140.1 billion 1955 rubles in terms of average realized farm prices, a valuation which I accept here. By reference to Goldsmith, 1962, pp. 117, 119, I find that livestock herds in the United States on January 1, 1959 amounted to $10.6 billions in 1955 prices. Herds are assumed to have been at the same level on July 1, 1960. While they increased slightly in that interval, the increment is already allowed for in the estimate of inventories for July 1, 1960.

Conversion of inventories and livestock herds from one currency to another is made at these rates:

	Dollars per ruble, Soviet weights	Rubles per dollar, US weights
Inventories	.146	9.9
Livestock	.055	18.1

These parities are implied in the calculations in *Soviet Inputs and Output*. The parities for inventories represent average deflators obtained by conversion of the Soviet gross national product, exclusive of selected final services, from ruble factor cost to 1955 US dollars, and by conversion of the US gross national product, exclusive of selected final services, from US dollars to 1955 ruble factor cost. The livestock parities relate to livestock investment in kind and meat products.

Cultivated arable land. See Bergson, 1964, p. 379.

Input Weights. Reference thus far has been to the derivation of data on output and inputs used in compiling productivity measures in Table 4 and in the text. I turn to the weights used in aggregating inputs. Such weights had to be compiled for all sectors together, for all sectors excluding selected final services, and for the nonfarm sector. The weights applied are shown in Table 13. For each factor, the indicated weight is intended to represent actual or imputed income earned in 1960 with factor services valued at 1955 rates.

To refer first to Soviet weights, and particularly those for labor, Soviet households earned in 1955 some 691.7 billion rubles. See Nimitz, April 6, 1959, p. 4. I omit from my total imputed net rent and also an arbitrary allowance made by Nimitz for penal-labor subsistence. With the exclusion of these items, the earned income of households in 1955 in Nimitz, April 6, 1959, p. 4, comes to 694.0 billion rubles. I have reduced this total by 2.3 billion rubles in order to take account of revisions of Nimitz's calculations that I have made in *Soviet Inputs and Output*, and also to allow for turn-over taxes and subsidies on military subsistence, including that of the militarized internal security forces, as estimated there. The weight for labor for all sectors is obtained as the product of the total earned income of households in 1955, as thus computed, and the index of employment in the USSR in 1960 compared with 1955 which is 107.5 per cent. Employment in 1960 was 102.1 millions. See Table 8. The corresponding figure for 1955 was 95.0 millions. The latter figure is obtained by use of the same sources and methods as were employed in the derivation of employment for 1960, though for 1955 I raise to 2.0 millions the allowance for penal and other labor not covered in the cited sources.

Earned income of labor in all sectors other than in selected final services is obtained by deducting 131.4 billion rubles for labor earnings in selected final services, including:

	Billion rubles
Health care, education	79.1
Government administration, etc.	20.4
Armed forces	23.3
Housing	8.6

For health care, education, government administration, and so forth, and the armed forces, see Table 6. For housing, I cite the product of employment in 1960, 1.0 million (Table 8), and the average wage of all employed workers in 1960, 8,580 rubles, as given in TSU, 1966, p. 567.

Nonfarm earnings of Soviet households, other than in the armed forces, amounted in 1955 to 453.4 billion rubles. This is the sum of civilian

Table 13

Weights Used in Aggregating Factor Inputs[a]

Factor inputs	Soviet Billion rubles	Soviet Per cent (i)	(ii)	(iii)	US Billion dollars	US Per cent (i)	(ii)	(iii)
All Sectors								
Employment	743.6	61.8	67.2	56.3	258.4	67.2	78.1	66.7
Reproducible capital:								
Gross services	460.1	38.2		34.8	126.0	32.8		32.5
Net services	363.6		32.8		72.6		21.9	
Cultivated arable land	117.9			8.9	2.9			.7
All (i)	1,203.7	100.0			384.4	100.0		
(ii)	1,107.2		100.0		331.0		100.0	
(iii)	1,321.6			100.0	387.3			100.0
All Sectors, excluding selected final services								
Employment	612.2	65.8	71.3	58.4	216.3	71.2	80.0	70.5
Reproducible capital:								
Gross services	318.4	34.2		30.4	87.7	28.8		28.6
Net services	246.7		28.7		54.1		20.0	
Cultivated arable land	117.9			11.2	2.9			.9
All (i)	930.6	100.0			304.0	100.0		
(ii)	858.9		100.0		270.4		100.0	
(iii)	1,048.5			100.0	306.9			100.0
Nonfarm								
Employment	429.2	62.4	68.3		210.3	72.5	81.0	
Reproducible capital:								
Gross services	258.6	37.6			79.6	27.5		
Net services	199.1		31.7		49.3		19.0	
All (i)	687.8	100.0			289.9	100.0		
(ii)	628.3		100.0		259.6		100.0	

[a] Percentage data and totals designated (i) refer to weights where capital services are gross and land is omitted. Those designated (ii) refer to weights where capital services are net and land is omitted. Those designated (iii) refer to weights where capital services are gross and land is included. Differences between sums of figures and indicated total are due to rounding.

nonfarm wages and salaries, other than penal labor subsistence, earnings of cooperative artisans, and other money income currently earned, as given in Hoeffding and Nimitz, April 6, 1959, less an allowance of .5 of turnover taxes and subsidies on subsistence of militarized internal security forces. According to data in Feshbach, 1966, p. 785, civilian nonfarm employment rose from 48.2 millions in 1955 to 58.0 millions in 1960. Allowing for penal and other workers not covered, who are taken to total 2.0 millions in 1955 and 1.5 millions in 1960, employment in the sectors in question in 1960 amounted to 118.5 per cent of the 1955 level. By implication the earnings of these workers in 1960 amounted to 429.2 (i.e., 453.4 × 1.185) billion rubles at 1955 rates. In Table 13, the earned income of nonfarm workers in 1960, at 1955 rates, is this total less labor earnings in 1960 at 1955 rates of civilian workers in selected final services, amounting, according to data given above, to 108.1 billion rubles.

Soviet reproducible capital in Table 13, is assumed to earn 12 per cent. Hence, earned income of such capital, taken here to represent the value of net services of capital, is calculated by reference to the following data (see Table 12) on the total stock of reproducible capital, including net fixed capital, on July 1, 1960 at 1955 prices:

	Billion rubles
All sectors	3,030.1
All sectors, excluding selected final services	2,056.1
Nonfarm	1,658.9

Corresponding magnitudes for gross services of capital are obtained as the sum of interest income and depreciation as given in Table 6.

In Table 4, I refer to alternative calculations of aggregate inputs for which a rate of return of 16 per cent is imputed to Soviet capital. These weights, which are not shown in Table 13, are derived in the same way as those where the rate of return is 12 per cent.

Agricultural rent in the USSR is taken to have totaled 60 per cent of farm labor income. See Bergson, 1963, p. 20. Farm labor income in 1955 amounted to 192.7 billion rubles. I rely here on Hoeffding and Nimitz, April 6, 1959, p. 4, though again I make certain revisions referred to above. In calculating agricultural rent, I allow for an increase of 2.0 per cent in cultivated arable land from 1955 to 1960. See Bergson, 1964, p. 381.

The US weights for all sectors in Table 13 represent a very limited revision of calculations made in Bergson, 1964, pp. 379ff. In the revision, I take into account the revisions in US data on income and employment made in United States Department of Commerce, 1966. The rate of return imputed to reproducible capital remains as before at 6.6 per cent, but this is now applied to an estimated stock, including net fixed capital, as of

July 1, 1960, of $1,100.0 billions in 1955 prices, which differs somewhat from the corresponding figure considered previously.

For all sectors, excluding selected final services, I deduct from the $258.4 billions of labor income as thus calculated 1960 labor earnings, at 1955 wage rates, in selected final services, including $39.3 billions in selected final services other than housing (Table 7) and 2.8 billions of labor earnings in housing. This is the product of employment in housing in 1960, 1 million (Table 9), and the 1955 average wage of such workers, assumed to be $2,850 in the light of data in United States Department of Commerce, 1966, p. 108. Interest income of $54.1 billions is obtained by application of an imputed rate of 9.5 per cent to the July 1, 1960 US stock of reproducible capital, including net fixed capital, amounting to $569.7 billions in 1955 prices (Table 12). The imputed return of 9.5 per cent is that estimated to have been earned on private nonresidential capital in 1955. The estimate takes into account data in Denison, 1967, p. 38, and Goldsmith, 1962, pp. 117–118.

As for the nonfarm sector, employees other than those on farms earned $222.1 billions in 1955. See United States Department of Commerce, 1966, p. 93. By methods used in Bergson, 1964, p. 381, I estimate that the labor earnings of nonfarm proprietors amounted to $19.7 billions. Hence, nonfarm labor earnings totalled $241.8 billions in 1955. A corresponding figure of $252.4 billions for 1960 at 1955 wage rates is obtained by allowing for an increase in nonfarm employment by 1960 to 104.4 per cent of the 1955 level. See United States Department of Commerce, 1966, pp. 112–113. In Table 13, US nonfarm labor income is obtained by deducting from this total the 1960 earnings at 1955 rates of workers in selected final services, estimated above at $42.1 billions. Interest income is calculated at the imputed rate of 9.5 per cent for a July 1, 1960 stock of reproducible capital, including net fixed capital, amounting to $519.3 billions in 1955 prices (Table 12).

For capital, reference has been to net services. Gross services, not computed in Bergson, 1964, are obtained as the sum of interest income and depreciation as given in Table 7.

References

ABBREVIATIONS

JEC: Joint Economic Committee, Congress of the United States
RAND: The RAND Corporation
TSU: Tsentral'noe Statisticheskoe Upravlenie

LITERATURE CITED

Arrow, Kenneth, Hollis B. Chenery, Bagicha Minhas and Robert M. Solow,
  1961   "Capital-Labor Substitution and Economic Efficiency."
          The Review of Economics and Statistics, 43(3), 225–250.
Becker, Abraham S.
  1959   *Prices of Producers' Durables in the United States and the
          USSR in 1955*. RAND, RM-2432, Santa Monica, California.
  1965   *Soviet National Income and Product 1958–1962*. Part I,
          RAND RM-4394-PR. Santa Monica, California.
Bergson, Abram
  1953   *Soviet National Income and Product in 1937*. New York:
          Columbia University Press.
  1961   *The Real National Income of Soviet Russia Since 1928*.
          (Cambridge, Mass: Harvard University Press).
  1963   "National Income." *In* Abram Bergson and Simon Kuznets,
          eds., *Economic Trends in the Soviet Union*. (Cambridge,
          Mass.: Harvard University Press).
  1964   *The Economics of Soviet Planning*. (New Haven: Yale
          University Press).
  1967   "The Current Soviet Planning Reforms." *In* Alexander
          Balinky *et al.*, *Planning and the Market in the USSR*. (New
          Brunswick, N.J.: Rutgers University Press).
  1968   *Planning and Productivity under Soviet Socialism*. (New
          York: Columbia University Press).
Berliner, Joseph S.
  1964   "The Static Efficiency of the Soviet Economy." *American
          Economic Review*. 54(2):480–489.
Bornstein, Morris
  1959   "National Income and Product." *In* JEC, *Comparisons of
          the United States and Soviet Economics*. Part II, (Washing-
          ton: U.S. Government Printing Office).
Bornstein, Morris *et al.*,
  1961   *Soviet National Accounts for 1955*. (Processed). (Ann Arbor:
          University of Michigan Press).
Bureau of the Census
  1960   *Current Population Reports: Population Characteristics*.
          Series P-20, No. 99.
Bureau of Labor Statistics
  1967   *Labor Force, Employment and Unemployment Statistics,
          1947–61*.

Central Intelligence Agency
    1964   *1955 Ruble-Dollar Ratios for Construction in the USSR and the US.*
    1966   *Unemployment in the Soviet Union: Fact or Fiction.* (March).

Cohn, Stanley H.
    1962   "The Gross National Product of the Soviet Union." *In* JEC, *Dimensions of Soviet Economic Power.* (Washington D.C.: U.S. Government Printing Office.)
    1966   "Soviet Growth Retardation". *In* JEC, *New Directions in the Soviet Economy*, Part II-A, (Washington D.C.: U.S. Government Printing Office).

David, P. A. and Th. van de Klundert
    1965   "Biased Efficiency Growth in the U.S." *American Economic Review*, 55(3), 357–394.

Denison, E. F.
    1967   *Why Growth Rates Differ.* (Washington D.C.: Brookings Institution.)

Diamond, Douglas B.
    1966   "Trends in Output, Inputs and Factor Productivity in Soviet Agriculture." *In* JEC, *New Directions in the Soviet Economy*. Part II-B, (Washington, D.C.: U.S. Government Printing Office).

Dodge, Norton
    1966   *Women in the Soviet Economy.* (Baltimore, Maryland: Johns Hopkins Press).

Domar, Evsey D.
    1961   "On the Measurement of Technological Change." *Economic Journal*, 71(4) 702–729.

Feshback, Murray
    1966   "Manpower in the USSR." *In* JEC, *New Directions in the Soviet Economy*. Part III, (Washington D.C.: U.S. Government Printing Office).

Goldsmith, Raymond W. *et al.*,
    1956   *A Study of Saving in the United States.* Vol. III (Princeton, N.J.: Princeton University Press).

Goldsmith, Raymond W.
    1962   *The National Wealth of the United States in the Postwar Period.* (Princeton, N.J.: Princeton University Press).

Harris, Chauncey D.
    1953   "Industrial Resources." *In* Abram Bergson, ed., *Soviet Economic Growth.* (New York: Row, Peterson).

Hoeffding, O. and N. Nimitz
  1959   *Soviet National Income and Product, 1949–1955.* RAND,
          RM-2101, Santa Monica, California. April 6.
Hunter, Holland
  1966   "The Soviet Transport Sector." *In* JEC, *New Directions in
          the Soviet Economy.* Part II-B (Washington D.C.: U.S.
          Government Printing Office).
  1968   *Soviet Transport Experience.* (Washington D.C.: Brookings
          Institution).
Kaplan, Norman M.
  1963   "Capital Stock." *In* Abram Bergson and Simon Kuznets,
          eds., *Economic Trends in the Soviet Union.* (Cambridge,
          Mass.: Harvard University Press).
Kendrick, J. W. and Ryuzo Sato
  1963   "Factor Prices, Productivity and Growth." *American
          Economic Review.* 53(4) 974–1003.
Jorgenson, D. W. and Z. Grilliches
  1967   "The Explanation of Productivity Change," *The Review of
          Economic Studies.* 34(3) 249–285.
Moorsteen, Richard H.
  1961   "On Measuring Productive Potential and Relative
          Efficiency", *Quarterly Journal of Economics.* 75(3) 451–467.
  1962   *Prices and Production of Machinery in the Soviet Union,
          1928–1958,* (Cambridge, Mass.: Harvard University
          Press).
Moorsteen, Richard H. and Raymond P. Powell
  1966   *The Soviet Capital Stock, 1928–1962.* (New Haven, Conn.:
          Yale University Press).
New York Times
  1967   October 2.
Nimitz, Nancy
  1962   *Soviet National Income and Product, 1956–1958.* RAND,
          RM-3112-PR, Santa Monica, California.
  1965   *Farm Employment in the Soviet Union, 1928–1963.* RAND,
          RM-4623 PR, Santa Monica, California.
Nutter, G. Warren
  1962   *Growth of Industrial Production in the Soviet Union.*
          (Princton, N.J.: Princeton University Press).
Ofer, Gur
  1968   *The Service Sector in the Soviet Union.* Ph.D. thesis, Harvard
          University.

President's Committee to Appraise Employment and Unemployment Statistics.
  1962   *Measuring Employment and Unemployment.* (Washington D.C.: U.S. Government Printing Office.

Samuelson, Paul A.
  1950   "Evaluation of Real National Income." *Oxford Economic Papers,* (January) 1–29.

Tarn, Alexander
  1964   "Dollar Value of Soviet Industrial Production, 1955–1960." *The Review of Economics and Statistics.* 46(4) 406–412.

Toda, Yasushi
  1964   "On the Consistency of Dr. Moorsteen's Efficiency Index." (Typescript).

Sitnin, V.
  1966   "The Economic Reform and Revision of Wholesale Prices of Industrial Products." *Current Digest of the Soviet Press,* (November 2) 3–6.

TSU
  1961   *Narodnoe khoziaistvo SSSR v 1960 godu.* Moscow (A).
  1961   *SSSR v tsifrakh v 1960 godu.* Moscow (B).
  1961   *Zhenshchiny i deti v SSSR.* Moscow (C).
  1962   *Narodnoe khoziaistvo SSSR v 1961 godu.* Moscow.
  1965a   *Narodnoe khoziaistvo SSSR v 1964 g.* Moscow.
  1965b   *Narodnoe khoziaistvo SSSR v 1965 godu.* Moscow.

United States Department of Commerce
  1966   *The National Income and Product Accounts of the United States, 1929–1965,* (Washington D.C.: U.S. Government Printing Office).

Turgeon, Lynn and Abram Bergson
  1957   *Prices of Basic Industrial Goods in the USSR, 1950 to 1956.* RAND RM-1919, Santa Monica, California.

7

On The Measurement of Comparative Efficiency

by EVSEY D. DOMAR

This piece began as an ordinary comment on Professor Bergson's paper. If by now it has become rather long and involved and has strayed into other, let us hope not unrelated subjects, the fault is his and not mine: his paper was simply too interesting and too stimulating to be left in peace. On my first reading of Bergson's paper I jotted down even more comments than are reported here, only to find that Bergson, with his usual conscientiousness, had disposed of most of them in the next paragraph or on the next page. Obviously, it is impossible to comment on every aspect of his paper; utilizing my comparative advantage, I shall say very little about his statistical data (except at the very end) and shall concentrate instead on his general methods and on the meaning and significance of his results.

1. The Theory

The theoretical part of the paper continues the discussion of inter-temporal and interspatial comparisons of index numbers of inputs and of outputs began by Bergson and Moorsteen some years past.[1] There is no doubt that everyone who constructs index numbers transgresses against honesty, and that every user thereof is an accomplice in the act: It is impossible to reduce a vector of quantities or of prices to a single number in an honest way. But what Bergson and Moorsteen have done is to make clear and explicit the assumptions on which the construction of these index numbers rests, and the rationale involved in preferring one set of weights to another, even if no true set of weights exists. I have learned much from Chapter III of Bergson's *magnum opus* and so have my graduate students.

And yet, after all these illuminating explanations, we still have to construct index numbers of inputs and of outputs in a more or less traditional way. Having constructed them, we usually obtain the Index

[1] Abram Bergson, *The Real National Income of Soviet Russia since 1928*, Cambridge, Mass., 1961, particularly Ch. III; Richard H. Moorsteen, "On Measuring Productive Potential and Relative Efficiency," *The Quarterly Journal of Economics*, LXXV:3 (1961) 451–467.

of Total Factor Productivity (to use Kendrick's term), or what I have called elsewhere the Residual, and of their interspatial equivalents, either by fitting to them a simple production function like the Cobb-Douglas, or by assigning to the inputs and the outputs a certain set of weights, like income shares, the two methods yielding very similar results.[2] Because the results are so similar, I would suggest either the use of less restrictive and more interesting production functions, with constant elasticity of substitution, for instance, as Weitzman has recently done, or the use of unpretentious index numbers with assigned weights, as Bergson has done through most of his paper.[3] In the latter case, I think, the emphasis should be placed on logical consistency and on simplicity, so that the reader could see exactly what the investigator is doing.

In a sense, Bergson's comparative index is a hybrid: It has two outputs—consumer and investment goods—which are aggregated arithmetically, and two inputs—labor and capital (the latter including land) aggregated geometrically. (The Cobb-Douglas formula with assigned weights adding to one is merely a weighted geometric index.) Although I prefer the geometric index for comparisons of this kind (for reasons explained elsewhere), I must admit that a pure geometric index is too laborious to be constructed in practice, and that every geometric index hides arithmetic sub-aggregation.[4] The recognition of a large number of separate components makes each of them more homogeneous and minimizes the aggregation problem within each component, thus resulting in a purer geometric index, but neither I nor any other consumer of Bergson's products can fairly ask him to spend additional time and effort on a more refined aggregation. I doubt that Bergson's general results, which have so large a margin to spare, would be much affected if he used a pure geometric or a pure arithmetic index. For algebraic manipulations, however, his hybrid is rather clumsy and hard to handle. For this reason, I shall discuss here only the two pure varieties, the arithmetic and the geometric, without worrying about the practical difficulties of computing the latter kind.

---

[2] John W. Kendrick, *Productivity Trends in the United States*, N.B.E.R., Princeton, N.J., 1961; Evsey D. Domar, "On the Measurement of Technological Change," *The Economic Journal*, LXXI:4 (1961) 709–729, and Domar, "On Total Productivity and All That," *The Journal of Political Economy*, LXX:4 (1962) 597–608.

[3] Martin L. Weitzman, "Soviet Postwar Economic Growth and Capital Labor Substitution," Cowles Foundation Discussion Paper No. 256, Yale University, New Haven, Conn., October 30, 1968., since published in *The American Economic Review*, LX:4(1970), 676–692.

Bergson did consider the effects of different magnitudes of the elasticity of substitution between labor and capital on his results.

[4] See my two papers mentioned in Note 2.

A arithmetic index

E average factor productivity

G geometric index

L labor input

K capital input

T Residual or Index of Total Factor Productivity

Y real output of one or of several sectors

i rate of return on capital stock

p price of output

w wage rate

λ share of labor

$\mu = 1 - \lambda$—share of capital

$$\rho = \frac{1 - \sigma}{\sigma}$$

σ elasticity of substitution

Subscripts

A US

R USSR

L labor

K capital

In summation formulas the variables of summation have been omitted to avoid an excessive number of subscripts.

1.1. The Arithmetic Index

In Soviet prices, this index A_{R} is defined as

$$A_{\mathrm{R}} = \frac{\dfrac{\sum Y_{\mathrm{R}} p_{\mathrm{R}}}{\sum Y_{\mathrm{A}} p_{\mathrm{R}}}}{\dfrac{\sum L_{\mathrm{R}} w_{\mathrm{R}} + \sum K_{\mathrm{R}} i_{\mathrm{R}}}{\sum L_{\mathrm{A}} w_{\mathrm{R}} + \sum K_{\mathrm{A}} i_{\mathrm{R}}}} .$$

After a few simple manipulations A_{R}[5] can be expressed as

(2)
$$A_{\mathrm{R}} = \lambda_{\mathrm{R}} \frac{E_{\mathrm{LR}}}{E_{\mathrm{LA}}} + \mu_{\mathrm{R}} \frac{E_{\mathrm{KR}}}{E_{\mathrm{KA}}},$$

which is a weighted arithmetic mean of the ratios of the labor and capital productivities (Soviet divided by US), each weighted by its corresponding Soviet income share.

In US prices the index A_{A} is similarly defined, and after a few manipulations[6] it can be expressed as

(3)
$$A_{\mathrm{A}} = \frac{1}{\dfrac{\lambda_{\mathrm{A}}}{\dfrac{E_{\mathrm{LR}}}{E_{\mathrm{LA}}}} + \dfrac{\mu_{\mathrm{A}}}{\dfrac{E_{\mathrm{KR}}}{E_{\mathrm{KA}}}}}$$

Thus the A_{A} index is a weighted harmonic mean of the ratios of labor and capital productivities (Soviet divided by US), this time weighted by US income shares.

Since for any unequal positive numbers an arithmetic index is larger than a harmonic one, it follows that A_{R} should be larger than A_{A}, provided the two indexes are composed of the same productivity ratios and use the

(see footnotes overleaf)

[5] The expression (1) in the text can be rewritten as

$$A_R = \frac{\dfrac{\sum Y_R p_R}{\sum L_R w_R + \sum K_R i_R}}{\dfrac{\sum Y_A p_R}{\sum L_A w_R + \sum K_A i_R}}.$$

Its numerator is one by definition. Therefore

$$A_R = \frac{\sum L_A w_R}{\sum Y_A p_R} + \frac{\sum K_A i_R}{\sum Y_A p_R}.$$

Multiply each numerator and denominator by the same magnitude and reassemble the terms:

$$A_R = \frac{\sum L_A w_R}{\sum Y_A p_R \sum w_R} \cdot \frac{\sum Y_R p_R \sum w_R}{\sum L_R w_R} \cdot \frac{\sum L_R w_R}{\sum Y_R p_R}$$
$$+ \frac{\sum K_A i_R}{\sum Y_A p_R \sum i_R} \cdot \frac{\sum Y_R p_R \sum i_R}{\sum K_R i_R} \cdot \frac{\sum K_R i_R}{\sum Y_R p_R}.$$

Now the expression $\dfrac{\dfrac{\sum Y_A p_R}{\sum L_A w_R}}{\sum w_R}$ is the average productivity of US labor, with

Soviet prices and Soviet wages used as weights to be indicated by E_{LA}. The next term is the average productivity of Soviet labor also with Soviet prices and wages, while $\sum L_R w_R / \sum Y_R p_R$ is the share of Soviet labor in the value of the Soviet output. The same reasoning applies to the capital items. Thus we obtain

$$A_R = \lambda_R \frac{E_{LR}}{E_{LA}} + \mu_R \frac{E_{KR}}{E_{KA}}.$$

[6] A_A is defined as

$$A_A = \frac{\dfrac{\sum Y_R p_A}{\sum Y_A p_A}}{\dfrac{\sum L_R w_A + \sum K_R i_A}{\sum L_A w_A + \sum K_A i_A}} = \frac{\sum Y_R p_A}{\sum L_R w_A + \sum K_R i_A},$$

because American outputs and inputs cancel out by definition (as the Soviet ones did when Soviet prices were used). Performing the same manipulations as we did with A_R we'll have

$$A_A = \frac{1}{\dfrac{\sum L_R w_A}{\sum Y_R p_A \sum w_A} \cdot \dfrac{\sum Y_A p_A \sum w_A}{\sum L_A w_A} \cdot \dfrac{\sum L_A w_A}{\sum Y_A p_A} + \dfrac{\sum K_R i_A}{\sum Y_R p_A \sum i_A} \cdot \dfrac{\sum Y_A p_A \sum i_A}{\sum K_A i_A} \cdot \dfrac{\sum K_A i_A}{\sum Y_A p_A}}$$

$$A_A = \frac{1}{\lambda_A \dfrac{E_{LA}}{E_{LR}} + \mu_A \dfrac{E_{KA}}{E_{KR}}} = \frac{1}{\dfrac{\lambda_A}{\dfrac{E_{LR}}{E_{LA}}} + \dfrac{\mu_A}{\dfrac{E_{KR}}{E_{KA}}}}.$$

same weights. But the Soviet income shares (or the shares of other countries less developed than the United States) favor capital more than US shares do; a larger capital share should work to the Soviet advantage because capital productivities of the two countries are much closer to each other than their labor productivities are; finally, in the A_A index the ratio of capital productivities, being close to unity, plays a much smaller role than that of labor productivities (note that it is US to Soviet, and not the other way around in this case), which is a rather large number (about 3 in this case).[7] For all these reasons, if the ratios of respective productivities in Soviet and in US prices were the same, the A_R index should be larger than the A_A one. And yet in every international comparison that I have seen, each country does better in foreign prices than in its own.[8]

This contradiction between my theoretical expectations and empirical results is caused by the inequality of the ratios of factor productivities in Soviet and in US prices; the relative factor productivity of each country is favored by the use of the other country's prices. This phenomenon is well known and it is usually called the "Gerschenkron Effect."

While constructing indexes of Soviet machinery output, Professor Gerschenkron found that early-year weights impart an upward bias to an output index as compared with one based on later-year weights, because the rates of growth of specific outputs and of their prices are negatively correlated.[9] Evidently, the same situation holds true in international comparisons, that is, a negative correlation must exist between ratios of outputs and ratios of the corresponding prices. Thus Bergson found that the ratio of Soviet output to US is 49.7 per cent in US prices, and only 31.5 per cent in Soviet prices.[10]

The A_R and A_A indexes, however, are not merely ratios of outputs, but ratios of outputs divided by the corresponding ratios of inputs. Does the Gerschenkron Effect exist in input ratios as well? The Soviet capital stock is 52.2 per cent of the US in US prices, and 41.7 per cent in Soviet prices.[11]

[7] To see this point, express (3) as

$$A_A = \frac{1}{\lambda_A \dfrac{E_{LA}}{E_{LR}} + \mu_A \dfrac{E_{KA}}{E_{KR}}}.$$

[8] See Table 1 below, and Edward F. Denison, *Why Growth Rates Differ*, Brookings Institution, Washington, D.C., 1967.

[9] Alexander Gerschenkron, *A Dollar Index of Soviet Machinery Output, 1927–28 to 1937*, The RAND Corporation, Santa Monica, Calif., 1952. For a mathematical treatment of the Gerschenkron Effect see Edward Ames and John A. Carolson, "Production Index Bias as a Measure of Economic Development," *Oxford Economic Papers*, XX:1 (1968) 12–24.

[10] Table 4, pp. 180–181.

[11] *Ibid.*

So the Gerschenkron Effect is certainly present here, though in a weaker form than in the output comparisons above. I wonder why this is so. Perhaps the Soviet capital industry, presumably the most advanced sector of the Soviet economy, is closer to its US counterpart in the structure of its output and of its prices than the rest of the Soviet economy; or perhaps the Gerschenkron Effect is weaker in any particular sector, as compared with the economy as a whole, because of the given sector's greater homogeneity of output.

It would be interesting to discover whether the Gerschenkron Effect exists in the aggregation of labor as well, that is, whether US wage rates used as weights give a higher ratio of Soviet to US labor input than Soviet wage rates do. Is there a negative correlation between the ratios of labor inputs by occupation in the two countries and the ratios of the corresponding wage rates? Perhaps it does exist; both countries have many workers in poorly paid occupations: in Soviet agriculture and in US services (though services were excluded from Bergson's comparisons). Unfortunately, labor is usually aggregated by adding unweighted man-hours (or man-days, or man-years), or man-hours adjusted by sex and by educational level. This is not a satisfactory method because these characteristics need not correspond closely to wage rates by occupations and hence, hopefully, to the corresponding values of the marginal product of labor.[12] In the spirit of aggregation used for output and for capital input, each labor series should be weighted by its wage rate, first Soviet, then US. This task is laborious but also rewarding: If a substantial Gerschenkron Effect is found in the ratios of labor inputs as well, it will counteract this Effect in the output ratios and thus bring Bergson's two estimates (in Soviet and in US prices) closer together—a most welcome outcome.

1.2. The Geometric Index

Whether Soviet or US weights are used, the expressions are formally identical, because the geometric index is reversible. As mentioned above, I assume that both inputs and outputs were properly aggregated by summing up the weighted logarithms of the individual series and use the symbol Y as the total output in this sense. The geometric index is defined as

$$(4) \qquad G = \frac{\dfrac{Y_R}{Y_A}}{\left(\dfrac{L_R}{L_A}\right)^{\lambda} \cdot \left(\dfrac{K_R}{K_A}\right)^{\mu}}$$

[12] In one of his variants, Kendrick, *op. cit.*, (note 2), did weight the labor input in each industry by the corresponding wage rate.

and can be transformed into a more convenient expression

(5) $$G = \left(\frac{E_{\text{LR}}}{E_{\text{LA}}}\right)^{\lambda} \cdot \left(\frac{E_{\text{KR}}}{E_{\text{KA}}}\right)^{\mu}.$$

Thus, the G index is a geometric mean of the ratios of labor and capital productivities, each weighted by its income share (Soviet or US).[13]

The construction of the comparative geometric index is based on the assumption that it is one country's *income shares* (both in inputs and in outputs), and not prices, which exist in the other country as well. Since Soviet capital productivity is fairly close to that of the US, while the labor productivities are far apart, and since the Soviet capital share is usually assumed or found to be larger than that of the US (see below), the use of Soviet rather than of US weights should favor the USSR unless a strong Gerschenkron Effect is present in the geometric index as well. I do not know whether in a given country a negative correlation exists between the rates of growth of specific quantities (outputs or inputs) and of their income shares; or whether in international comparisons such a correlation is to be found between the respective ratios of quantities and of their shares. It is quite possible that this correlation does not exist, or even that it is positive. In the latter case, the Gerschenkron Effect would work in reverse, reinforcing the favorable impact of Soviet weights on Soviet performance.

Thus it does not necessarily follow that each country is favored by the other country's weights. The outcome depends on the particular index chosen and on the system of aggregation used. I think this subject deserves further study.

[13] From expression (4) in the text, we derive

$$G = \frac{Y_{\text{R}}L_{\text{A}}^{\lambda}K_{\text{A}}^{\mu}}{Y_{\text{A}}L_{\text{R}}^{\lambda}K_{\text{R}}^{\mu}} = \left(\frac{Y_{\text{R}}}{L_{\text{R}}}\right)^{\lambda} \cdot \left(\frac{Y_{\text{R}}}{K_{\text{R}}}\right)^{\mu} \cdot \left(\frac{L_{\text{A}}}{Y_{\text{A}}}\right)^{\lambda} \cdot \left(\frac{K_{\text{A}}}{Y_{\text{R}}}\right)^{\mu},$$

from which (5) readily follows.

It may be interesting to note that the Residual, or the Total Factor Productivity, obtained from the constant-elasticity-of-substitution function, indicated here by T, can also be expressed in terms of factor productivities. Let

$$Y = T(\lambda L^{-\rho} + \mu K^{-\rho})^{-1/\rho}, \quad \text{with} \quad \lambda + \mu = 1.$$

Then

$$T = \frac{Y}{(\lambda L^{-\rho} + \mu K^{-\rho})^{-1/\rho}} = \frac{1}{\left[\lambda\left(\frac{L}{Y}\right)^{-\rho} + \mu\left(\frac{K}{Y}\right)^{-\rho}\right]^{-1/\rho}};$$

$$T = \left[\lambda\left(\frac{Y}{L}\right)^{\rho} + \mu\left(\frac{Y}{K}\right)^{\rho}\right]^{1/\rho} = (\lambda E_{\text{L}}^{\rho} + \mu E_{\text{K}}^{\rho})^{1/\rho}$$

2. Several Small Points

Let me leave the main subject of my discussion for a moment and make several minor digressions.

2.1. Rates of Return on Capital

The Soviet rates of return on the capital stock—12 and 16 per cent—assumed by Bergson are much higher than his US rate of 9.5 per cent. I have often wondered why it is taken for granted that the Soviet rate of return—and by assumption the marginal productivity of capital—must be so high. No doubt, a good American or German capitalist, if given the opportunity, could make more than the 12 or 16 per cent on *his* investment in the Soviet Union, but do the Russians themselves use their capital so efficiently? Their own complaints on this score are well known; they have been investing a very high fraction of their national product; the average productivity of their capital has been falling, and in the sectors examined by Bergson it was below that of the US in 1960. And yet Weitzman has found that the income share of Soviet capital in that year was 59 per cent gross of depreciation.[14] Allowing some 6 percentage points for depreciation, yields the net income share of capital as 53 per cent. With an average net capital (and land) coefficient of 2.0–2.3[15] this implies a net rate of return on capital of 23–26 per cent, a figure even higher than Bergson's. It seems that my doubts should be put aside, at least for the time being. But if Weitzman's (and my) calculations are correct, the weight of Soviet capital assigned by Bergson should be increased; this adjustment would favor the USSR when their weights were used.

2.2. Depreciation

Quite correctly Bergson includes the depreciation charge in the share of capital: Depreciation, together with interest (or profit) is the true cost of capital, just as the wage, which also includes an element of depreciation, is that of labor.

---

[14] Weitzman, *op. cit.*, (note 3), p. 11. The capital share of 58.7 per cent was obtained from calculations based on Western sources; Soviet sources yielded an even higher share—69.9 per cent.

Weitzman has excluded not only services (like Bergson) but agriculture as well. It is hard to tell what effect this exclusion had on the share of capital because both agricultural prices in the Soviet Union and Western estimates of Soviet agricultural rent are rather arbitrary. Combining Weitzman's capital share with Bergson's estimates of depreciation and of capital-output ratio in the same economic sectors (that is, excluding farms) gives a rate of return, net of depreciation, of 27 per cent.

[15] From Bergson's Appendix, Table 6.

When it comes to the capital stock, he takes neither the gross stock nor the net but the mean of the two. Since an old piece of capital commands a lower rental than a new, the net stock of capital should be used in estimating the rental value rather than the gross. But Bergson may feel that existing methods of capital write-off, particularly in the US, though hardly in the USSR, may exaggerate actual depreciation; hence, the net-gross mean may be a better approximation to the true value of capital than either component alone. One cannot argue about this procedure without a thorough examination of depreciation methods in the two countries. Let me just mention in passing that in the US the net-gross mean is some 29 per cent larger than the net stock, while in the USSR it is 12 per cent above the net.[16] So Bergson may be giving the USSR the benefit of the doubt, which is not inappropriate in view of my comments on the Soviet capital share above and of his treatment of unemployment.

2.3. Exclusion of Unemployed Workers

Bergson's labor input in the US excludes the 5.6 per cent of unemployed workers in 1960. If he aims at the comparison of what each country does with its employed resources, his procedure is correct, though a similar adjustment should perhaps be made to the stock of capital as well. But if he tries to compare the relative efficiency of the two systems, then the elimination of what is probably the greatest single cause of US inefficiency is questionable. In his defense it can be said that Soviet discussions about the presence of labor reserves, particularly in smaller cities and towns, undoubtedly point to the existence of some unemployment. But no unemployment statistics are published in the Soviet Union, because officially unemployment does not exist. So if US unemployed were included in the labor input, the Soviet jobless would have to be treated likewise, a rather difficult statistical task.

2.4. Exclusion of Services

Bergson has good reasons for this decision, because productivity in many service sectors (education, public health, the military, and general government, for instance) is difficult to conceptualize, let along to measure. But because the US service sector is relatively larger than the USSR's, and because productivity (essentially of labor) in the services is thought to be lower than elsewhere, this exclusion may favor the United States.

2.5. Turnover, Sales and Excise Taxes

Bergson's exclusion of Soviet turnover taxes from output totals is accepted by most investigators, because these taxes fall almost exclusively on consumer goods, and their retention would distort relative output

[16] From Bergson's Appendix, Table 5.

shares. But why should the same procedure not be followed in respect to US sales and excise taxes: They also fall mostly on consumer goods and amount to some 7 per cent of consumer expenditures.

The total impact of these five points which act in different directions would be very small, even if all were accepted by Bergson. His general conclusion that both in US and in Soviet prices, Soviet inputs are much less productive in generating outputs, as they are usually defined and measured, would not be affected, even if his indexes were to advance or to fall by a few percentage points. The interesting question lies not in the exact magnitudes of his indexes but in their meaning and significance.

3. The Meaning of the Results

The word "efficiency" used in the title of Bergson's paper is one of the most difficult economic concepts to define, let alone to measure. In physics it usually means the fraction of the maximum potential which a given machine can produce. Perfectly efficient machines do not exist; the efficiency of existing ones could frequently be increased to some extent, but at a cost. Hence, of two machines the one with a higher physical efficiency may or may not be more efficient from an economic point of view.

The application of some efficiency criteria to a country's performance over time or to a comparison of a pair of countries raises even more difficult problems. For instance, the Soviet Union and the United States could each increase its own efficiency by reorganizing its agriculture; yet both refuse to do so for ideological (when the Russians are obstinate) or political (when we are) grounds. Obviously, the social welfare function of each country, as seen by its government, or by its "ruling circles," to use a Russian phrase, is not composed of economic variables alone. Since these noneconomic objectives—and even some economic ones, like income distribution—never become sufficiently explicit to be assigned proper weights, we usually find ourselves in an uncomfortable position between two extremes: on the one hand, justifying much foolishness by reference to noneconomic objectives, and on the other, denouncing any departure from narrow economic goals as inefficient. In other words, we do not know where the influence of noneconomic factors ends and true inefficiency begins. It seems that governments or ruling circles of all countries enjoy their own political systems well enough to be willing to pay high economic prices for maintaining them.

But even if we knew the proper social welfare function of each country, the pursuit of efficiency would result in the fulfillment of certain conditions *on the margin*. In general, it would not take the form of the maximization of the average productivity of some factor, such as labor, nor of that of some particular combination of factors. Thus the cultivation of marginal lands in the Soviet Union will depress the Bergson Index (this term referring to all comparative indexes in his and in my papers), unless the quality of land were very carefully measured, and yet that cultivation may be economically justified. If the Soviet authorities dismissed all but the best of their workers, or shipped to Africa (a few years ago I said "to China") all their obsolete capital, the Index would register an improvement (again unless the quality of labor and of capital were properly allowed for), even if the Soviet people had less to eat and less to wear.

But let me not overdo my criticism of the Bergson Index. A firm's profit need not necessarily be raised by an improvement in labor productivity, but frequently it will be. Similarly, a country's "true" relative efficiency need not be positively related to the Index, but usually such a relationship will exist. Hence, if the Index shows that the average factor productivity in one country is markedly inferior to another, greater efficiency of the latter is not an unreasonable hypothesis. But there may be other explanations as well.

Table 14 contains several such comparative indexes for a number of countries computed by Bergson himself. We find that the Soviet Union and Italy are very close to each other, with the former doing a bit better in Columns 3 and 4. It comes as a surprise that West Germany—our symbol of efficiency—is so close to the ailing United Kingdom, and that the latter is slightly superior to France in Columns 1 and 2. And all these countries are way behind the United States.

Table 14

Real National Income per Unit of Factor Inputs, Selected Countries, 1960
(USA = 100 per cent)

	With employment unadjusted		With employment adjusted for labor quality	
	Based on foreign national price weights	*Based on US price weights*	*Based on foreign national price weights*	*Based on US price weights*
	(1)	(2)	(3)	(4)
United States	100	100	100	100
Northwest Europe	50	63	53	67
France	49	62	53	66
Germany	52	63	56	69
United Kingdom	50	63	52	66
Italy	28	45	32	52
USSR	28	45	34	56

Source: Abram Bergson, *Planning and Productivity under Soviet Socialism*, New York, 1968, Tables 1 and 2, pp. 22 and 26.

It seems to me that Bergson's calculations testify not so much to Soviet inefficiency, however great it may indeed be, but to an earlier stage of economic development, as confirmed by the presence of 38.5 per cent of Soviet labor force in agriculture.[17] Historical studies of particular countries, such as the United States, that have been conducted in a manner very similar to Bergson's interspatial comparisons, suggest that around 1925, in terms of the Index of Total Factor Productivity this country was, roughly speaking, at the same stage as the Soviet Union in 1960.[18] Now, in what sense was the US economy inefficient in 1925? Of course, the US technology of 1960 was unavailable in 1925, but at that time this country need not have made any poorer use of its then available resources than it did in 1960. What these historical studies show is that the growth rate of a particular country's output cannot be completely explained in terms of growth of inputs of labor, capital, and land, as they are traditionally defined.[19] The same evidently holds true in international comparisons as well, although with one important qualification: If modern US technology was not available in this country in 1925, much of it was certainly available to the Soviet Union in 1960. Yet studies of economic development show that borrowing foreign technology is not an easy and simple process.

The two hypotheses suggested here to explain the relatively poor Soviet performance in terms of the Bergson Index—low efficiency of a socialist economy to which Bergson is inclined, and an early stage of development (as compared with the US) which I would favor—need not be mutually exclusive. Each can provide a part of the explanation. Usually problems of this type can be solved, or at least investigated, by means of a multiple regression, in this case of the Bergson Index for a number of countries regressed against the relative stage of each country's development and the presence or absence of socialism. Unfortunately, this procedure will not work here, because just about every index of economic development, such as per capita income, labor productivity, or the fraction of the labor force in nonfarm occupations, depends to a considerable extent on the efficiency of the economy; in addition, the large weight usually assigned to labor in the calculation of the Bergson Index assures a high correlation between labor productivity, or per capita income, and the Index.

[17] Bergson, p. 162 above.
[18] I assume that the US Residual was growing at some 2 per cent a year as found by Kendrick, *op. cit.*, and that in 1960 the Bergson Index amounted to 50 per cent. An annual rate of growth of 2 per cent implies doubling every 35 years.
[19] The growth of output can be almost completely explained if inputs and outputs are properly redefined. On this see D. W. Jorgenson and Z. Griliches, "The Explanation of Productivity Change," *The Review of Economic Studies*, XXXIV:3 (1967) 249–283.

But it may be possible to stabilize the data for the stage of development by taking pairs of countries which were at the same stage, more or less, before one of them went socialist, and compare their performance on the Bergson scale at a later date. Such pairs may consist of East and West Germany (probably the ideal pair), Czechoslovakia and Austria, Yugoslavia and Greece, or either of these Balkan countries may be compared with Bulgaria or Rumania (to judge the performance of the Yugoslav as compared with the Soviet-type socialism). It is too bad that two other good pairs—North and South Korea, and North and South Vietnam—have been devastated by wars, but perhaps Burma (if that country can be regarded as socialist) and Thailand may make a pair, as may Cuba and some other Latin-American country.

Even if the socialist member of such a pair has fallen from the original state of parity with its capitalist partner on the Bergson scale, this fact by itself is not sufficient to establish the inferiority of socialism as an economic system. Suppose, for instance, that the socialist partner invested a much larger fraction of its national product and thus grew more rapidly than the capitalist one, but because of diminishing returns to capital, or because of poorer allocation of resources in general, it performed worse on the Bergson scale. How are we to tell which path of development, the socialist or the capitalist, was better or more efficient? Is it more important to be efficient in the micro-sense and score well on the Bergson scale, or is macro-efficiency which is only partly registered on that scale more desirable? What about other economic criteria, such as income and wealth distribution or security of employment? All this brings us back to the homely truth that weighty questions, such as these, cannot be resolved on the basis of the behavior of one simple index.

So far (and rather wisely), I have not questioned the methods used by Bergson and by other western scholars in estimating Soviet output. Yet any reader of the *Economic Newspaper* (*Ekonomicheskaia Gazeta*), of the *Krokodil*, or of the delightful little book by Antonov[20] cannot help wondering about the methods by which Soviet production procedures, methods of pay, market organization, and the quality of products are recorded in statistics of output. In comparing Soviet performance over time, these troublesome questions are usually disregarded on the assumption that the defects of statistical recording, whatever they are, have persisted for some time and hence are not likely to affect the relative rate of growth of output and similar figures, even though the enlarged production of consumer

[20] O. N. Antonov, *Dlia Vsekh i Dlia Sebia*, (For Everyone and for Oneself) Moscow, 1965.
This is an excellent and an amusing description of defects of Soviet planning. It includes remedies, some of which are equally amusing: The author is an engineer.

durables may have intensified these problems in recent years. In international comparisons, on the other hand, these defects, if they are large, cannot be dismissed. I do not refer particularly to simple quality differences of supposedly identical products, such as the smaller number of threads per square inch of men's shirts counted by Nutter,[21] or the reportedly short longevity of Soviet tires. These can be duly taken into account by adjusting corresponding prices, however laborious this job would be.

Suppose for instance that workers in a Soviet truck plant stand idle for want of parts. If national product is measured as output (as it should be), the correct number of trucks produced will be properly recorded. On the income side, no problem arises if the workers are paid by the piece. If they are paid by the hour, their idleness should be reflected in lower profit of the enterprise; but Soviet profits are not a reliable statistic, and in our estimates of Soviet national income it is customary to replace profits by some more or less arbitrarily assigned rate of return on the capital stock. Now suppose that this production delay takes place on a construction site, a very common occurrence. If the workers are paid by the piece, no statistical harm is done, but hourly payments are likely to inflate the cost of construction; and construction expenditures are very difficult to deflate properly (in any country) because of the absence of a reliable unit of output. Hence, the output of the construction industry, and of the national product, may be exaggerated.

If a Soviet citizen buys a refrigerator, its production and sale are duly recorded. But if at a later date the refrigerator stands useless because of lack of repairmen or of parts, no method of social accounting known to me would record this fact. Nor would it be recorded that a portable ice box (to mention a report in the *Krokodil*), again duly included in the national product, turns out to be absolutely useless because its purchaser cannot buy any ice, or that airconditioning apparatus manufactured and installed, and thus again duly recorded, does not condition any air.

Let me not exaggerage this problem. Many deficiences of Soviet organization and of the type and quality of Soviet products are reflected in statistics of lower output, of lower labor productivity, and so forth, particularly when the production of intermediate products is involved. With capital goods the situation is more complex: at the time of its production a defective machine will be recorded in the output of capital goods without any allowance for its quality and usefulness, but these will be reflected at some later date in the lower output of the machine. To record the low quality of housing and of consumer goods in general, an extremely careful deflation of Soviet national product is required, and

[21] G. Warren Nutter, *The Growth of Industrial Production in the Soviet Union*, N.B.E.R., Princeton, N.J., 1962.

even such a deflation is not likely to catch the frustration and anger felt by buyers of poor consumer services and owners of useless consumer products.

Comment

by ABRAM BERGSON

I can refer to only a few of the many questions that Professor Domar has raised in his throughtful and provocative critique. In compiling compara- tive measurements of factor productivity in the USSR and USA, I apply different index-number formulas. Thus, the two major inputs, labor and reproducible capital, are usually aggregated geometrically. That, of course, is implied in my application there of a Cobb-Douglas formula with factor-share weights adding to unity. Within each major input, however, aggregation is arithmetic, and that is also true of the data compiled for total output. In all such calculations alike, Domar continues to hold (pp. 224–25), as he did before,[1] that in principle one should rely exclusively on the geometric mean formula. That formula should be used, in other words, for both inputs and outputs. Domar grants, however, that in practice, a "hybrid" calculation such as mine is apt to be unavoidable.

On this point, there evidently can be no very weighty difference between us. But Domar considers the choice of index-number formula essentially as a rather conventional matter. Thus, if one does aggregate inputs geometrically, "then common sense and consistency" call for a corre- sponding aggregation of outputs.[2] There apparently are similar, more or less pragmatic grounds for aggregating inputs geometrically to begin with. Perhaps I should explain, therefore, that in my essay I have sought to apply a quite different approach, which I for one find more illuminating. Essentially the choice of formula is seen as entailing certain assumptions. Thus, an assumption is made, in the case of inputs, as to the shape of the production isoquant, and in the case of outputs, as to the shape of the transformation locus. This follows at once from my conception of an index of outputs as translating one country's production into an equivalent volume of output of the other country's mix, and of an index of inputs as translating one country's inputs into an equivalent volume of inputs of the other country's mix.

[1] E. D. Domar, "On the Measurement of Technological Change", *Economic Journal*, LXXI:4 (1961) 709–729.

[2] *Ibid.*, p. 713.

The formula for inputs, then must turn on the assumed production isoquant and that for outputs on the transformation locus. Is the production isoquant seen as approximately one with a unity elasticity of substitution? If so, the geometric aggregation of inputs is indeed the appropriate one. This, however, ceases to be so if the elasticity of substitution is thought to be, say, much less than unity. For here the CES formula is to be applied, and with $\sigma < 1$, this entails an aggregation rather different from the geometric one. And, whatever the formula for aggregating inputs, one is still free to aggregate outputs otherwise. Indeed, one should do so, depending on the transformation locus. Among other things, a unity elasticity-of-substitution production isoquant, as shown in my essay (p. 169), might be associated with a linear transformation locus. In this case, a hybrid calculation, involving geometric aggregation of inputs and arithmetic aggregation of outputs, is in fact the analytically correct one.

The index-number formula or formulas, nevertheless, can hardly be chosen simply by reference to theoretic considerations such as these. At any rate, they could not be so chosen in my essay, for we obviously do not know the precise shape of either the production isoquant or the transformation locus in the two countries studied; and in choosing index-number formulas, it was necessary also to consider limitations of the data available, ease of computation, and the like. The calculations in other words, are to some extent admittedly conventional after all. But the theoretical analysis still seems of value so far as it provides a basis for provisional commitment to one or another formula for inputs and outputs, and also for inquiry into possible biases due to the divergence of the production isoquant and transformation locus from the loci that the formulas selected ideally assume. "Everyone who constructs index numbers," Domar tells us (p. 219), "transgresses against honesty." Perhaps he is right, but we may hope to ameliorate the transgression by elucidation of the biases involved, as I have sought to do. While I focus on the comparison of productivity in the USSR and USA, the theoretic analysis is entirely general. It may be hoped, therefore, that it will be found helpful in other contexts as well.

I refer to the analysis as it bears on the index-number formula. In my essay, I try also to grapple theoretically with another matter: the valuation standard to be applied when prevailing prices for one reason or another diverge from "scarcity values." Domar does not refer to this effort. Presumably here too he would incline to a more pragmatic approach. How properly so, I shall leave the reader to judge; but it should be observed that the problem of price distortions is inherent where, as in my essay, one seeks to measure inefficiency; that in the relevant literature it is nevertheless very often ignored in such a context; and that what is in question is not only the valuation standard to be applied but the degree to which inefficiency may in fact be measured by application of any particular standard. In my essay I try, I hope not too unsuccessfully, to clarify both aspects.

Domar is also somewhat skeptical, however, as to the precise import for comparative efficiency of comparative data on productivity such as mine. As I myself stress, comparative productivity is indeed apt to be affected by many factors other than differences in efficiency. I considered it an essential part of my inquiry, therefore, to explore the nature and possible role of such factors in the particular comparison made. One of the many factors examined is a difference in quality of land such as Domar cites (p. 229).

But Domar is not only concerned with the possible effect of factors such as these. He also points out (p. 228) that the very concept of efficiency is obscure. After all, what if a country should for political or ideological reasons prefer one sort of institution (the collective farm) to another (the independent peasant proprietor), and productivity is low on that account? Must we not then include such noneconomic objectives as desiderata in its "social-welfare function"? And if we do, is the country not efficient after all?

In normative theoretic analysis, it has long been customary to draw a distinction between material values attaching to goods and services produced and disposed of, and nonmaterial values that may be attached to working arrangements (institutions, policies, and procedures), quite apart from any impact they may have on the production and disposition of goods and services. Such nonmaterial values, in other words, are intrinsic to the working arrangements. The distinction is not always easy to make. (What, for example, if for some clients public medical practice is valued differently from private, simply because it is public, and even if there is no other difference between them?) But this distinction would seem to provide the basis for another one which Domar apparently neglects: between "social welfare," which includes, and "economic welfare," which abstracts from nonmaterial values. Efficiency, as usually understood, relates to performance from the standpoint of economic, not social welfare. And that convention, which is observed in my essay, is surely a useful one. After all, only through its adoption are we able to inquire meaningfully, as we wish to (and as Domar himself does), how economically costly dubious working arrangements may be. The calculation may be performed whether such working arrangements are valued for their own sake or not.

Although noting the limitations of my data as indicators of efficiency, Domar grants (p. 229) that "it is not an unreasonable hypothesis" that differences in factor productivity (such as I measure) signify, at least in some degree, corresponding differences in efficiency. In his opinion,

however, the differences in productivity may be more plausibly explained
otherwise: namely, by differences in the stage of economic development.
In proof, he cites additional comparative data on productivity in the USSR
and different capitalist countries from a recent study of mine.[3]

As I explained in my essay (p. 193), the low Soviet factor productivity,
compared with that of the USA, may be due partly to the late start of the
USSR towards industrialization and the associated inferiority of Soviet
relatively to US technological knowledge. So far as it is, the low Soviet
factor productivity is properly viewed as reflecting the less advanced stage
of Soviet economic development rather than inefficiency. Depending on
how factor productivity is calculated, Soviet performance by that yard-
stick might also be adversely affected in other ways by less advanced
development, and without efficiency being any the less. That must be so,
for example, where the calculation does not adjust labor for quality
differences. Considering all such factors, however, a large residual difference in productivity is difficult to explain otherwise than in terms of a
difference in efficiency. In my essay, I concluded, therefore, that efficiency
in the USSR probably is markedly below that in the USA. Domar, I feel,
provides no basis to abandon that conclusion.

But might not a difference in stage of economic development affect
factor productivity not only directly, but indirectly via efficiency itself?
And even if the direct effect is limited in the case considered, may not the
indirect one be consequential? Indeed, may not the low level of Soviet
efficiency, relatively to that of the USA, be due primarily to the less
advanced stage of Soviet development? May not the Soviet inefficiency, in
other words, reflect that rather than the socialist working arrangements of
the USSR? Although Domar does not raise these questions, they are in
order, and I commented on them briefly in the study just cited. But they are
large questions, and intriguing as they are, I felt it best to leave them for
separate inquiry.

As implied, however, I agree that differences in stage of economic
development must be an important cause of the differences in factor
productivity which have been observed among capitalist countries. So far
as such countries also differ in efficiency, the stage of development no
doubt is an important factor here too. But it can hardly be the only
factor of consequence. These, at any rate, would seem to be the implications of my comparative data on factor productivity in capitalist countries
(Domar's Table 14), when they are juxtaposed with corresponding data
quantifying diverse indicators of the stage of economic development.
Factor productivity must itself be considered one such indicator, and
others often cited (e.g., per capita GNP) are as a matter of logical necessity
closely related to factor productivity. For present purposes, however,

[3] *Planning and Productivity Under Soviet Socialism*, New York, 1968.

Table 15

Indicators of Stage of Economic Development, Selected Countries, 1960[a]

	Share of gross product originating in nonfarm sectors (per cent)	Share of employment in nonfarm sectors (per cent)	Reproducible capital per worker (USA = 100)[b]	
			With labor unadjusted	With labor adjusted for quality
	(1)	(2)	(3)	(4)
United States	96	92	100	100
France	90	78	48	51
Germany	94	86	42	46
United Kingdom	96	96	43	46
Italy	83	68	30	35
Soviet Union	71–80	58	37	48

a) See Abram Bergson, *Planning and Productivity under Soviet Socialism, op. cit.* pp. 65, 88, 89; and p. 162 of the present volume.

b) In comparisons of Western Europe and the USA, reference is to reproducible capital other than that in "general government," housing, and foreign assets. In the comparison of the USSR and USA, housing is again omitted. I also exclude government assets for the USA and broadly similar categories for the USSR. Reference throughout is to capital in US dollar prices. For the USSR, the index used, 58.1 per cent, differs from the index in dollar prices, 52.2, on p. 180, because highways are omitted along with government capital generally. For all countries data on workers employed include those in housing and government.

stage of economic development must somehow be gauged from indicators that are formally independent of factor productivity, at least to a substantial degree. I have assembled in Table 15 a few indicators that seem to be of this sort. Among the countries listed, factor productivity obviously varies broadly with these indicators, but only broadly. Note, for example, that in terms of the share of GNP produced by, and share of workers employed in, nonfarm sectors, the UK is fully as advanced as the USA, though in terms of factor productivity it still lags far behind the latter.

Reference has been to capitalist countries alone. To come to the comparison of the USSR with capitalist countries, Domar cites in his Table 14 data on factor productivity that I compiled previously for the USSR as well as for Western capitalist countries. Although the index numbers given there for the USSR have been somewhat revised in my Table 4, p. 180–181, they serve well enough to place the Soviet performance relatively to that of the capitalist countries considered.[4] Juxtaposing these data, then, with

[4] In Table 4, p. 180–181, I use revised estimates of comparative inventories in the USSR and USA, and also include highways in the US stock of reproducible capital. As I became aware only later, in the calculations for my Fairless lecture volume highways were included in Soviet but omitted from US reproducible capital. In contrast to the procedure in Table 4, in the Fairless lecture volume I

my compilation on the stage of economic development, which has also been extended to include the USSR, we see that factor productivity in the USSR, although lagging far behind that of the USA, is about the same as that of Italy. Moreover, the USSR appears to be at a stage of economic development broadly similar to that of Italy. What follows as to the role of the stage of economic development in the low level of Soviet efficiency, as indicated by comparative factor productivity relatively to that of the USA?

We do not have comparative data on factor productivity among socialist countries such as have been compiled for capitalist ones. Furthermore, in the previous study referred to I cautioned against the easy assumption that efficiency must vary with the stage of development under socialism in the same way as under capitalism.[5] Forces causing such variation under the two systems may be similar but they may also be different. Under both systems, for example, continuing transfers to industry of an initially large "surplus" population in agriculture should yield higher efficiency as development proceeds, but under socialism the transfers might well be less than commensurate with the industrial expansion. This lag would occur wherever, because of, say, defective capital costing, overly capital-intensive projects are favored in industry.[6]

Again, it is difficult to rate the complexity of the economy (the number of enterprises, the variety of products, and the like) as an important source of inefficiency under capitalism. Complexity is by all accounts, however, a cardinal source of inefficiency under socialism, at least if there is "centralist planning." Yet under either system complexity must tend to increase as development proceeds. It is easy to think of still other examples of the differential impact of economic development on efficiency under the two systems.

Perhaps the moral is, nevertheless, that efficiency depends predominantly on the stage of development, and so is in reality little affected by the social system. If so, the moral is certainly paradoxical. In effect, we should

use index numbers of reproducible capital in dollars to compute factor productivity in both dollars and rubles. Also employed workers there include those occupied in housing and in government services. It should be observed, however, that some of the foregoing revisions make the index numbers of factor productivity in the USSR in Table 4 less, rather than more, comparable to those for Western European countries, than those in the Fairless lecture volume.

[5] *Planning and Productivity Under Soviet Socialism*, pp. 63ff.

[6] This, of course, has been the experience in the USSR, and may be among the reasons for the apparent incongruity between different indicators of the stage of economic development for that country. Thus, in terms of share of gross product originating in nonfarm sectors and share of employment in nonfarm sectors the USSR turns out to be distinctly less developed than in terms of reproducible capital per worker (Table 15, p. 237).

have been led to a "materialistic" theory of efficiency that might have confounded Marx himself, and surely would confound many Marxians today. Perhaps, though, the moral is rather the one already implied, that more research is needed. But in the meantime we may at least conclude that socialism, as exemplified by the USSR, is markedly less efficient than capitalism, as exemplified by the USA, though perhaps about as efficient as capitalism as exemplified by Italy, a country at a broadly similar stage of development.

On the relation of factor productivity, efficiency, and the stage of development, one aspect of Domar's argument still remains to be considered: "Historical studies of particular countries such as the United States, conducted in a manner very similar to Bergson's interspatial comparisons," he points out (p. 230), "suggest that around 1925 in terms of the Index of Total Factor Productivity this country was, roughly speaking, at the same stage as the Soviet Union in 1960. Now, in what sense was the US economy inefficient in 1925?"

Throughout my essay efficiency is understood in a conventional analytic sense. Thus, reference is particularly to "static productive efficiency," which is construed in terms of realization of production possibilities. At any particular time, such possibilities are delimited in turn by available technological knowledge and resource supplies. Seen in this light, the answer to Domar's question must be simply that, as he recognizes, technological knowledge in the USA in 1960 must have been quite different from that in 1925. The presumption must be, therefore, that the increase in factor productivity in the USA from 1925 to 1960 was due in good part to the advance of technological knowledge. Very possibly, though, there has been some gain in efficiency as well. One need not probe deeply to be aware that forces making for such a gain have been operative.[7] It is not easy to see, however, what bearing all this has on my contemporaneous comparison of the USSR and USA. As indicated, even here there may be differences in technological knowledge, but these should be relatively limited compared to those between the USA in 1925 and in 1960.

The fact that I seek only to gauge static productive efficiency perhaps also needs to be stressed in view of Domar's further comments about the difficulty of judging from "one simple index . . . the inferiority of socialism as an economic system" (p. 231). I agree that that is difficult; and in fact I did not at all attempt that task. I hope, however, that, by illuminating static productive efficiency, my essay will contribute to the overall appraisal that is sought.

Domar rightly emphasizes finally (pp. 231–232) the problem posed for meaningful measurement of factor productivity in the USSR by the

[7] See Abram Bergson, "Market Socialism Revisited", *Journal of Political Economy*, LXXV:5 (1967) 672, n. 21.

pervasive production of inferior or low-quality goods. The problem, however, is especially acute where the concern is not merely with realization of production possibilities but with optimality of the product mix. I have already commented on Soviet performance from that standpoint (p. 195, n. 46) and shall not pursue it further here.[8]

[8] In conclusion Domar also refers to the problem posed for measurement of factor productivity by such possible aspects of ruble pricing as the overpayment of construction workers and the resultant overweighting of construction in the calculation of real national income. This is essentially the problem of the valuation standard that I mention above.

PART III

Some Environmental Variables and
System Characteristics

8

Notes on Stage of Economic Growth as a System Determinant

by SIMON KUZNETS

1. Elements in a Stage Theory

A stage theory of long-term economic change implies: 1) distinct time segments, characterized by different sources and patterns of economic change; 2) a specific succession of these segments, so that *b* cannot occur before *a*, or *c* before *b*; and 3) a common matrix, in that the successive segments are stages in one broad process—usually one of development and growth rather than of devolution and shrinkage.[1]

These three elements—differentiation, sequence, and community within a broad process—seem to constitute the minimum in a stage theory of historical change; or for that matter in a stage theory of many physical and biological growth processes.

How can such a simple design be a summary description or analytic classification of a vast and diverse field of historical change sufficiently plausible to warrant the formulation and persistence of many variants? The answer, at least for economic history, is suggested if we look at the past. We find that, first, the tools that raise economic productivity do not become available before a specific date, say, the late 18th century for the steam engine. If this and similar technological and social innovations are of major importance for long-term economic change, the period *before* the innovation is distinguished from the one *after*; and a minimum of two

---

[1] "*Development* is any change which has a continuous *direction* and which culminates in a phase that is qualitatively *new*. The term 'development' should be used to characterize any series of events in thought, action or institutional arrangements which exhibits a directional cumulative change that either terminates in an event marked off by recognized qualitative novelty or exhibits in its course a perceptible pattern of growth." (see *Social Science Research Council, Bulletin 54*, "Theory and Practice in Historical Study: A Report of the Committee on Historiography," Social Science Research Council, New York, 1946, p. 117). Devolution is development in reverse. Growth and shrinkage emphasize the quantitative rise or decline but also include greater or lesser diversification.

Stage theory is most closely associated with a uni-directional rather than cyclic view of history. In the cyclic view the stages are recurrent; in a uni-directional view, a stage materializes, runs its course, and never recurs. Even in the process of devolution and decline, the return to a level experienced previously is not viewed as a recurrence of the earlier stage.

stages, one closed (before) and the other still open (after), is indicated. Second, the technological (or social, or any other relevant) innovation that makes for differentiation (before and after) also introduces a specific, irreversible sequence. To use the same example, the period before the late 18th century cannot be classified as a stage *following* the steam engine, and the period after the late 18th century cannot be designated as a stage *preceding* the steam engine. The sequence is fixed and unchangeable. Finally, the steam engine is seen to add significantly to economic productivity; and its innovative application appears as part of a longer process in which similar innovations have added to productivity previously and others are expected to add to it in the future—not only to aggregate economic productivity, but, more specifically in this illustration, to the long-term growth of mechanical energy for production purposes. This view leads to the assumption that the period marked by the steam engine must *terminate* when another innovation replaces it as the major source of growth in mechanical energy for production purposes. Thus a single major innovation, viewed as part of a continuous process, sets up a sequence of three distinct stages—before, during, and after—a sequence that is irreversible, contains these differentiated stages, and is part, necessarily, of a longer process. Although two of these three phases, *before* and *after*, are defined negatively and need additional content to indicate the source of growth that dominates them, they still serve to specify that the major innovation defining a stage positively grows out of a matrix of the longer growth process, and is brought to an end by some factors within the latter. Clearly, this view of combined effects of major innovations and the cumulative process of relevant economic change is at the base of many past stage theories—whether the innovation be in the organizing means of exchange (barter, money, credit); or in the size of the market and hence the character of the organizing institutions (household, city, nation); or a combination of methods of production and control over production resources (slavery, feudalism and serfdom, class society, classless society).[2]

But a stage sequence is suggested not only by the "before," "during," and "after" periods of one innovation; or, what is the same, the "during" periods of several innovations viewed as parts of one larger process. It is also suggested by the spread of a *single* innovation within the "during" period; and in that sense there are several substages within one stage of a broader sequence. Thus the emergence of economical steam power in the late 18th century was only the beginning of a long process, which at the several levels at which it can be observed—spread to various applications

[2] For a recent review see Bert F. Hoselitz, "Theories of Stages of Economic Growth," in Bert F. Hoselitz, ed., *Theories of Economic Growth*, Glencoe, New York, 1960, pp. 193–238.

of the stationary engine, to internal water transport, land transport, and ocean transport; increasing efficiency within and among these applications; spread first to the more developed, then to the less developed countries—also reveals distinct patterns in a specified sequence largely determined by time distance from the initial breakthrough. The process was cumulative in character, with changes in the level and pattern of its growth parameters as in the course of time the easy opportunities of initial spread were exhausted and newly emerging competing innovations (e.g., electric power and internal combustion engines) exerted their constraining influence. Here we have the minimum framework of distinctive stages, in a specified sequence, and part of the same continuous process, provided by the changes in potential with increasing distance from the date of introduction; the requirement of earlier improvements to permit further increases in efficiency; and the limitation of the cumulative process to one innovation, assuring a common base for sequential stages. This intra-stage phase sequence is typical of many classifications of early, middle, and late capitalism; and of the Rostovian stages within modern economic growth, if we start the sequence with take-off and omit the pre-take-off segment (which is not actually a stage).

Indeed, such a sequence *within* each stage may be considered an indispensable part of a complete stage theory, because the latter covers several separate stages that emerge and then eventually disappear. Hence, it is difficult to conceive of a stage as static, as part of a process in which its emergence and eventual disappearance are the only relevant and major changes. Internal dynamics is implicit in a stage; and therefore it is likely, if not logically necessary, that a stage follows a sequence of its own from emergence to decline as a major source of growth. We call this sequence of changes integration, as contrasted with the sequence of different innovations marking off distinct stages. *Innovation* and *integration* are then the basic conceptual counters in the game of designing stages—and this is hardly surprising. By definition, innovation represents something *new* that differentiates one historical segment from another; and integration represents the movement of this new (so long as it is effectively new) in its interaction with the *old*. In combination, these two counters portray the continuous process of long-term growth as a succession of major innovations, each denoting a stage and each subject to its own phase pattern of spread (or inter-action with the old) that helps to fill the canvas between one major innovational breakthrough and the next.

2. The Scope of Stage-Setting Innovations

Innovations can differ widely in their economic magnitude and in the aspects relevant to economic growth. Large and complex innovations may contain sub-innovations that may contain sub-sub-innovations, and so on down to the narrowest significant innovation. Hence, what are inter-innovational stages at one level may become stages in intra-innovational integration at another. One can easily envisage a vast hierarchy of innovations, corresponding sets of stages, and relevant lines of economic growth within which these innovations, stages, and phases of spread loom large. Within such a hierarchy we must choose those innovations and corresponding stages that affect the systems in which economic societies are organized.

The choice should be governed by the desire to use the stage approach in classifying, with intellectual economy, the largest volume of historical data related to the economic growth processes in which we are interested, and which are eventually to be explained; and the intellectual economy means the least loss of detail on major factors that determine economic growth in return for the clearest view of them. The choice is therefore governed by hypotheses identifying the important factors that determine the economic growth process—the latter observed in its most significant manifestations in economic study. Although a stage sequence is not a theory, it is based on preliminary notions concerning the major growth factors and their changing succession, and it is used to organize the data in the light of these notions for the greatest insight into the relevant factors. It should thus clear the way for the next round of richer and more testable hypotheses.

The following discussion of stage of economic growth as system determinant is based upon one guiding notion, the economic epoch. Judging at least by the economic history of Western European peoples (and their offshoots overseas) and possibly by the economic history of other parts of the world, we can distinguish economic epochs—long historical periods, extending over several centuries, during which economic growth appears to have been dominated by a major source that can be identified as the epochal innovation.[3] Within broad historical limits, several successive economic epochs can be viewed as stages within one long uni-directional process of growth. For example, we can set up a succession from the "pure" (pre-city) feudal epoch of Western Europe of the 9th to 11th centuries; to the medieval city economy of the 11th through the 15th centuries; to the epoch of overseas expansion and merchant capitalism, extending from the 16th through the late 18th centuries; and finally to the modern economic epoch, which began in the late 18th century and is still going on. But this sequence of economic epochs which can be viewed as stages in a cumulative process of economic growth, cannot be assumed to extend over the full span of economic history, even if it is limited to part of

[3] For a brief discussion, see my *Modern Economic Growth*, New Haven, 1966, pp. 1–16.

the world community. That history cannot be usefully conceived as a single uni-directional trend, the basic assumption of grand-stage theories claiming universality and complete coverage of the historical canvas. Even if a wider view, which I am incompetent to present, were to reveal a broad upward trend in economic magnitudes over the millenia since the emergence of human societies, the major breakdowns in time and scope within the closer range of the historical past (as distinct from pre-history) could not be neglected in a simplifying assumption of a continuous upward sweep.

These economic epochs, easily distinguishable in the accepted surveys of economic history, which form stages in a continuous process of economic growth only over a limited part of the historical past, fail to satisfy another aspect of the criterion of universality. Although, during any historical period (say a century), a given epoch may characterize the economic growth of several human societies in the world, it does not follow that it characterizes *all* human societies. Although we have boldly referred to the economic history of Western Europe (and its offshoots overseas), we cannot precisely define the group of economic societies involved. Some Mediterranean countries, Spain and Portugal for example, participated vigorously in the overseas expansion that introduced the epoch of merchant capitalism but have only recently entered the modern economic epoch; and others, like those on the Italian peninsula, were never dominated by "pure" feudalism. But even if we disregard the difficulties involved in identifying the economic societies whose history from the 9th century to the present could be viewed as a succession of several economic epoch-stages, we have no basis for assuming that the economic epochs distinguished in European history were worldwide, especially since many human societies have been separate and relatively isolated until as late as a century ago. Many groups of societies lived for centuries with little contact with, and little effective knowledge of, each other—for example, the European societies and those in the Americas, which the former "discovered" only in late 15th century and continued to "discover" thereafter; or the African and Asiatic societies, whose contacts with the European societies were extremely limited. Each of these separate complexes of societies was responding to its own natural environment, was undergoing a historical process that had its own roots, and was removed from significant contact with the other groups of societies. Why should we expect them to experience economic epochs similar in content to, and roughly identical in timing with, those found, say, in the economic history of Western Europe? For all we know, for the 600 years from the mid-14th to the mid-20th century China, the one society that incidentally had through this long period a much larger population than all Europe combined, may have experienced only one economic epoch, with the economy dominated by ever-expanding intensive agriculture which constituted the major growth industry while, during the same period, Western Europe went through at least three successive epochs (although two of them were incomplete).[4]

Although economic epochs cannot be generally viewed as stages in a comprehensive and universal sequence, or perhaps because they are not advanced as such stages, the construct is useful in reformulating our topic. Some characteristics of the two concepts—the economic epoch and the epochal innovation—are relevant to this purpose; and in presenting them, we can restate the topic and raise the questions that will govern the discussion in the rest of this paper.

· a. The magnitude of an epochal innovation—its capacity to affect the growth of a number of societies over a relatively long period—implies that it also affects several aspects of society. If the major innovation originates in the sphere of material production, as it seems to in the modern economic epoch with the application of science to problems of economic production, the magnitude of the impact necessarily involves institutional and cultural adjustments—changes in the economic, political, and cultural framework essential for the proper use of the greatly expanded power of the production structure. Radically changed production forces could no more be organized under the old institutions than a large railroad or airline could be operated within the institutional framework of a personal or family firm. This is equally true of the more remote realm of ideology, for if an epochal innovation in material technology is, as it must be, a major addition to the stock of knowledge shared by at least a part of mankind, that addition must modify the earlier conceptions of man and nature shared by the societies in which the epochal innovation occurs. On the other hand, if the epochal innovation originates at the institutional level, e.g., in the formation of cities (or in the case of the Roman Empire, in the organization of a would-be universal state, with the major growth factor being the extension of sovereignty by which previously isolated and politically disturbed regions are joined and assured of stability), it does not become the base of an economic epoch until and unless it succeeds in radically affecting economic output and activity.

If economic epochs are complexes of major innovations in material technology, institutional organization, and ideology, the question implicit in our topic can be answered simply. Stages of growth, in so far as they are economic epochs and the latter, whether or not they are stages in the process of growth, are system determinants *by definition*.[5] For if "system"

---

[4] This observation follows from my reading of Dwight Perkins' monograph, *Agricultural Development in China, 1368–1968*, Chicago, 1969. Professor Perkins is not responsible for this broad interpretation of his findings.

[5] This applies even more clearly to sequences of stages in the grand theories of

refers to the long-term arrangements by which various units within an economic society are induced to cooperate in production, distribution, and use of the aggregate product—including means of control over productive factors, freedom or constraint on individual units in the existing factor or goods markets, and so forth—then clearly the vast differences in economic technology represented by the several economic epochs imply sufficiently marked differences in the size and character of the economic systems prevalent in the participating economic societies to constitute distinct systems. If this were a promising approach, our discussion would have to emphasize the different economic systems associated with different economic epochs whether or not they are stages in a continuous process of economic growth.

But such a direction for our discussion is not promising; nor would it contribute much, or be relevant, to the problems of comparability of economic systems as I infer them from the outline for this volume. Study of economic systems with vast differences in material technology, in the stock of useful knowledge, and in other major components of economic epochs, would not contribute to an understanding of the differences between economies in which the comparative analysis of systems per se is of primary importance. Is a comparison of the economic system of a tribe in the isolated wilderness of the Amazon with that of an advanced economy like Sweden, or for that matter, of the "oikos" economy of some early Greek settlement with that of a city-state in the Hanseatic League, of real interest for the theme of this volume?

The very definition of economic epochs, which implies radically different bases of economic life and growth, renders that inter-epochal sequence— whether or not it is a stage difference or sequence—inappropriate for our purposes. Perhaps a more appropriate comparison would be that of different economic systems *within* a single economic epoch—of systems in which, despite their differences, the dynamic source of the epoch is a common factor. The appropriate stages would then be those that develop with the integration of the epochal innovation, as a single economic epoch unfolds.

b. I shift now to phases of growth *within* an economic epoch and, more specifically, within the modern economic epoch, extending back to the late 18th century; and reformulate our topic to ask how the sequence of phases in the development and spread of the modern economic epoch determines the system that characterizes the world's economic societies. Several aspects of this reformulation ought to be noted.

---

the Historical School and some of its later followers, in which stages were almost completely identified with the different modes of organization of economic activity, i.e., with the different economic systems in the usual meaning of that term.

First, the modern economic epoch is best observed in terms of nation-states, i.e., societies in which political power sets the arrangements for internal mobility, interdependence, and cooperation of domestic economic resources, which permit the economy to operate as a relatively self-sufficient unit—granted that these nation-units can still interact in both peaceful international flow of resources and armed conflict. In the observation of modern economic growth this unit—rather than firms, industries, class groups, tribes, religious communities, and so forth—is chosen, because political power is basic for decisions that channel economic growth, given the transnational potential of the stock of useful knowledge, of material and social technology, available to all. And this choice of unit is all the more relevant here, since our topic is the relation to economic systems, whose concrete, observable applications are within the political units that comprise diverse resources and complex interrelations among them, or among the various branches of the production structure. But in observing the modern economic epoch, we combine the nation-state with the major transnational source of modern economic growth, the underlying epochal innovation; that is universal in its potential availability and, in many respects, in actual impact. It therefore follows that the sequence of changes within the modern economic epoch comprises phases not only of internal growth of any participating nation-state, but also of the spread of modern economic growth to other nation-states. The international spread then has further effects on the connections between modern economic growth and the elements of the system within the participating (or otherwise involved) nation-states.

Second, the modern economic epoch is the first in human history which has had worldwide impact—in the sense that the countries that shared in the epochal innovation developed the capacity, at least by the second half of the 19th century, to reach effectively and significantly any and all parts of the world. Previously, as already indicated, groups of communities could live apart from and even without any knowedge of, each other. But this breakthrough to a potentially universal economic epoch means the coexistence of, and significant contact among, nations and communities following a sequence of growth stages that in the long-term past may have been quite different from the sequence in which modern economic growth is the most recent stage.

Given these broad features of the modern economic epoch—the variety of phases internal to the participating nation-states and distinguishable in the sequential spread of modern economic growth to an increasing number of these units, as well as the significant universality of international interaction—the relations between these phases (or stages) of modern economic growth and economic systems can be numerous. The discussion that follows deals with four examples of such relations: i) the effect of major phases in the development of modern economic growth within the older developed countries; ii) the effect of coexistence on the economic structure and system of the less developed countries; iii) the possible connection between system-deviation and delayed entry into modern economic growth; iv) the possible convergence in system-organization in the catching up process after successful, if delayed, entry. What I take to be the main theme of this volume, the problem of comparability between the Communist-party-state system and the free-market-economy system of developed countries, is involved significantly only under points iii) and iv). But since our purpose is to outline more fully the problems of international comparability of economic organization, it seemed useful to extend the view beyond the confines of a Communist-non-Communist dichotomy.

3. The Older Developed Countries

The possible connection between phases in modern economic growth and an economic system can best be brought out by an imaginary but realistic illustration. Assume that 100 to 125 years ago country *A*, a developed and free-market economy, had an efficient small-scale agricultural sector which dominated its output and accounted for three-quarters of its labor force and, in addition, had some few handicrafts and manufacturing industries and a relatively adequate (for the time) infrastructure in the way of canals, roads, railroads, harbors, shipping, and so forth. Assume also that the state was important, but that its function was primarily to resolve the conflicts that usually arise in economic growth—treatment of public domain, control of currency and credit, freedom of labor markets; and that it was not directly involved in production or in the control of the material assets of the country. Assume that today this country is developed and industrialized, with the agricultural sector producing less than 10 per cent of total output and employing an even smaller share of the labor force, but that it is plentifully supplied with, and has a large export capacity in, agricultural products. Further, assume that in addition to agriculture, which is dominated by a few large farms, some twenty-five huge, billion-dollar corporations dominate about a dozen crucial sectors (manufacturing, transport, construction, electric light and power, and so forth), a variety of nonprofit nongovernmental organizations provide education, health, and similar services, and the government sector is directly engaged in a large volume of economic activity (e.g., high-energy atomic production), because of the danger of entrusting it to private hands or because of the security problems in the international turbulence of the mid-20th century. Finally, assume that during this long span, within which we could presumably distinguish phases or stages if we had the data, time, and patience, there were free markets, liberty for anyone to engage in all activities except those considered dangerous by the society, full rights of private property—in short practically all of the appurtenances of a free-market economy. Are the arrangements in this country at both terminal dates one and the same economic system?

The point of this question is whether, with its focus on the principle of internal organization, the definition of an economic system can be independent of the number and size of the parts that are organized into a system. The dictionary definition of the term, from the Greek *syn+ histanai*, to place together, is, in its broadest sense, "an aggregation or assemblage of objects (or ideas, or activities) united by some form of regular interaction or interdependence" (*Webster's New International Dictionary*, unabridged, 2nd edition); and it has two components—the principle of organization and the objects that are being organized. Both the principles and the particular objects can differ, but the former is not fully independent of the latter. Thus in an economic system, one type of organization can be based on thousands of small, individual producing units or on a score of giant, nonpersonal corporations, private, public, or a mixture of both. Unless the principle of organization is so specified that the free-market mechanism operates in the same way for all the producing units, an economy may retain the principle of organization, but may change markedly because different assemblages of basic producing units are organized at different times.

This issue can perhaps be seen more clearly if we view the economy of any country as so many groups of production units, each differing from the others with respect to economic behavior and hence with respect to the application of any of the several principles of organization of the economic system. Examples of such groups are general government, government-owned and operated enterprises, private nonprofit institutions, government-regulated private enterprises (such as public utilities), large private corporations which are in effect public because their actions affect the public interest, small corporations, and personal firms. No observable economy, particularly among the developed countries, consists exclusively of one such group. Hence no economy can be a pure example of a system if the latter is defined by one principle of organization. Even the Soviet economy has always had a small component of private enterprise—individual plots cultivated by peasants, and, I assume, some individual handicraft shops. In the non-Communist developed countries, however, the distribution of total output, labor force, and capital among such groups has changed significantly in the course of modern economic growth; and differences may still exist among various developed countries, all of them in the free-market category or system. If such changes over time or differences in space are classified as "variants" of one and the same economic system, any comparison of systems defined as abstractions may have limited analytical interest, unless it is supplemented by specific consideration of these major variants.

Four complexes of long-term changes in modern economic growth appear to have contributed markedly to the rapid shifts in the size and character of the several parts of the economic system of the older developed countries, and hence in the character of the system itself. First, shifts in the structure of production and in the underlying technology led to much larger optimum or minimum scales of plant and enterprise—with a tendency toward monopoly which led to regulation, or toward quasi-public status of the enterprise. This familiar aspect of industrialization has been discussed at length in an enormous literature. Second, the turbulence of the last half century—the increased international tension and greater tendency toward major conflicts associated with the spread of modern economic growth to more nation-states, particularly the larger ones—stands in sharp contrast to the century before World War I, with its Pax Britannica which is implicitly credited to the effective limitation of economic development to Great Britain and its natural allies (like the United States). Third, a complex of trends, not unconnected with the first two, stems from the increasing recognition of the responsibility of the modern state (and hence of the economy) not only for the juridical and political equality of all its citizens, but also for the equality of economic opportunity—and most recently also for a minimum economic base. These trends clearly lead to the provision of public facilities to implement this purpose when and if the free-market private sector fails to do so. Obviously, the extension of collective action to provide health and education services, to supplement income, and so forth, has marked effects on the distribution of production among different groups of producing units. Finally, a new set of trends has become evident recently, and it stems from the scientific field as an increasing source of economic growth in the most advanced countries. The effects of this source of economic growth on the fate of man are so far-reaching and potentially overpowering that society is reluctant to allow profit-oriented, private enterprise to develop it—at least in the early stages and even later only under specific conditions and limits. The development of atomic energy is one example; another is the current expansion of space exploration; and DNA is a potential third, if and when further research reaches the possibility of control over the hereditary structure and endowments of man.

These four sets of trends, leading to the new industrial state, the new military state, the new welfare state, and the new scientific state—to coin convenient terms—are clearly significant variants of the free-market, individual enterprise state. The mixture of these variants may differ among the presently developed countries—outside of the Communist system and to some extent also within the latter. It would be intriguing to investigate these different mixtures as exemplified by various developed countries, but this would take us too far afield. The discussion so far should suffice to illustrate the main point. Phases of growth in the older developed countries brought about major transformations of the economic system that characterized them originally; and these changes may have differed in the different countries or groups of countries even among the non-Communist developed countries. Comparative analysis of economic systems should perhaps take account of these variants; and discussions of the feasibility and development of planning, even within the older developed countries, should not ignore the possible cause-and-effect relationship with these successive and major transformations or variants of the underlying abstraction of a market economy.

4. The Underdeveloped Countries

Offhand, the less developed countries of today, particularly the non-Communist, might be viewed as societies at the same stage of growth, and characterized by the same economic system, as the presently developed countries at their point of entry into modern economic growth. If this were so, much of the preceding discussion of the stages of growth within the current economic epoch with reference to the older developed countries could be applied here. It could be assumed that the under-developed countries are at that early point of the initial phase in which the free-market, individual-enterprise system is beginning to be transformed by industrialization, increase in scale, and greatly widened role and responsibility of the state. Indeed, much of the current analysis of economic growth which relies on cross-section comparison among developed, intermediate, and underdeveloped countries, assumes this similarity—in a sense equating the less developed countries to the early stages of the presently developed countries. This assumption may be questioned; and we mention three major considerations that point up the lack of similarity between the economic system of the underdeveloped countries and the initial phases of the presently developed countries.

First, there is the marked difference at the aggregative level of economic activity. Output per capita is much lower in the underdeveloped countries today than it was in the presently developed countries at the date of entry—a period rather than a point of time—into modern economic growth, i.e., when growth of per-capita product (with an already high rate of population growth) began to accelerate, the shift toward nonagricultural sectors occurred, modern technology (modern by the times) was adopted, and so forth. However difficult the comparison of per-capita gross product at such distances of time and space, the weight of the evidence clearly suggests that, with the single and significant exception of Japan (the records for which are still to be fully tested), the pre-industrialization per-capita product in the presently developed countries, at least $200 in 1958 prices (and significantly more, in the offshoots overseas), was appreciably higher than per-capita product in underdeveloped countries in the late 1950s—certainly in most of Asia and Africa, and in a good part of Latin America.

Yet this statistical difference in aggregate output per capita is less important than what it represents. It implies that even today these underdeveloped countries still have such a low product per capita that they are not at the same stage as the presently developed countries were at their initial stage of modern economic growth. This seems to be the case despite access to modern technology and despite the existence of a modern sector within these countries (no matter how small). These underdeveloped countries are either at some earlier stage within the long-term trend of the presently developed countries—in terms of the Western European sequence perhaps at the period of city formation in the early Middle Ages; or, what is far more defensible, they are at some stage in a sequence of long-term growth separate and distinct from that of the Western European cradle of the modern economic epoch and are following a time and phase sequence that may be quite different.

Only a scholar familiar with the long history of the Asian, African, and Western Hemisphere native communities would be competent to spell out the sequence of which the presently underdeveloped countries are the terminal products. Even then, some allowance would have to be made for the effect on this sequence of adverse contact with the developed West in recent centuries (of which more below). China, for instance, built an empire on intensive agriculture, with central political controls through irrigation, canals, and a literate bureaucracy; and it relied upon a common system of quasi-religious mores and an extended family as the basic unit of social organization. It does seem to me, with only superficial knowledge, that the stage and the corresponding organizational structure represented by this agricultural empire has no close parallel in the sequence of growth stages in Western Europe, certainly not back to the early Middle Ages, and not even in the Roman Empire of Hellenistic times. Some tribal economies in Africa may have reached their present stage by types of growth and organization for which there are also no effective parallels within the historical past of Western European societies. In short, one major component in the structure and system of underdeveloped countries today is an inheritance from a past that developed along lines that were either quite different from those of the Western European societies in which modern economic growth originated; or, if similar, correspond to a stage of growth in the latter that long preceded the stage just before entry into modern industrialization.

The second relevant consideration is that the presently developed countries (again with the single exception of Japan) were, even before their industrialization, among the more developed, economically advanced parts of the world. This does not mean that even in the late 18th century those countries that eventually became the developed group were in advance of the rest of the world in all sectors of productive activity. But by and large any substantial economic inferiority was a matter of the longer past; and the pioneers or the early followers were the economic leaders of the world even before industrialization (with the possible exception of the Netherlands, which despite an apparently high per-capita product in the 18th century, was slow to take advantage of modern industrialization). It is a crucial characteristic of the presently under-developed countries that they *are* underdeveloped while others are much more developed—and this situation has lasted a long enough time to affect markedly the structure of the underdeveloped countries; and also to cover several phases in the changing impact of the developed upon the underdeveloped parts of the world.

This impact, in the broadest terms, is the introduction of a modern component into the structure of the otherwise traditional underdeveloped countries. The magnitude of this component, its specific economic content, and the way in which it was introduced, confined, or encouraged, could and did vary widely. In a territory with colonial status a substantial modern sector often emerged but was organized by Western entrepreneurs of the metropolitan country. In a politically independent underdeveloped country with an export sector oriented toward the developed countries' markets the economic organization was and is quite different from that in a country with domestically oriented agriculture or industry. And in some others, a few members of the native elite educated in some Western lore are participating in administration and attempting to introduce Western elements into what may still be a purely traditional economic society.

Obviously, in the countries that are still underdeveloped, this modern component, even if in existence for a long period, has not expanded sufficiently to shift the country to developed status, and in most cases has not even raised its per-capita product to an intermediate level. Given the long coexistence of developed and underdeveloped economies, it is no exaggeration to argue that a major result of such coexistence in the under-developed economies is their dual structure. There are two distinct components, the modern and the traditional; and in marked contrast with the past record of the presently developed countries, the two components continue to perform without the modern one, despite its greater produc-tivity, rapidly outpacing the other. It is the *persistence* of the dual structure and the confinement or limitation of the modern sector that are crucial, for the two have operated simultaneously but for a shorter period in the developed countries also.

Third, while the presently developed countries had begun to reach out to other parts of the world long before the modern economic epoch, this contact was still incomplete in the late 18th century. Since that time major changes have taken place in technology, in scope, and even in the leading views affecting the relations between the developed and underdeveloped countries.

Because of these sequential changes in technology, economics, and political philosophy, the scope and character of the impact of developed countries on the various underdeveloped regions of the world also differed. For example, some countries in Latin America, after a long period of colonial status, became politically independent early in the modern economic epoch—so that the dual structure that remained was the result of domestic forces rather than of persistent colonial status. Others, like many in sub-Saharan Africa, continued in relative isolation from the developed countries until fairly late in the 19th century (largely for technological reasons), but since the 1890's have been subjected to their impact and resulting colonial partition. Still others, mostly in South Asia, were already colonial at the beginning of the modern economic epoch, and were not fully freed until after World War II. Some, like those in East Asia (China, Thailand, and so forth) were politically independent, but their sovereignty was severely limited. In view of these differences in timing, character, and source of impact of the developed countries in combination with the marked differences in structural and system characteristics of historical heritage among the various groups of underdeveloped countries, the variety of mixtures and the resulting characteristics of economic systems represented by the underdeveloped countries in the world today must be wide indeed. It is probably much wider than among the developed countries, where the dominance of the modern component dictates considerable similarity, because it is drawn from one and the same current source of economic advance in the modern technology.

I do not feel competent to discuss the methods by which this variegated underdeveloped world can be effectively classified for the analysis of the structure of economic organization and thus for what might be called the economic system elements.[6] It may well be that if these countries were carefully examined, some types of organization and system would emerge

[6] For an interesting attempt at such a classification which groups underdeveloped countries by the major obstacle to their economic modernization and growth, see John K. Galbraith, "Underdevelopment: An Approach to Classification," in David Krivine, ed., *Fiscal and Monetary Problems in Developing Countries*, Proceedings of the 3rd Rehovoth Conference, New York, 1967, pp. 19–38 and discussion, pp. 38–45.

as common to several units reflecting their long-term past (e.g., the intensive agriculture empire; the tribal extensive agriculture complex, largely self-sufficient and with little exchange except for administrative or ritualistic purposes; the almost feudal structure of some of the more developed units). These different types of economic system could then be combined with the various types of modern sectors reflecting the impact of developed countries. Such a classification would probably involve the application of several economic systems with different weights to the several groups of underdeveloped countries. But again, I can only suggest; I cannot provide specific indications of the relation between stages of growth—in this case in different sequences among the underdeveloped countries, as well as changes in the technology and history of the impact of the developed societies—and the economic system prevailing in these underdeveloped societies.

The suggestion that the economic structure of underdeveloped countries may represent combinations of economic systems—some of which belong to a past different from that of the presently developed countries—with a modern component representing the impact of the present, may apply to Communist underdeveloped countries also. Unless the Communist system is taken in the literal meaning of its official theory, permitting no significant variants and claiming to exhaust the full economic meaning of the life of the country in which it is supposedly operating, its major components cannot be conceived in isolation from their embodiment, first in the historical experience of the pioneer, viz., the Soviet Union. As a result, the modifications of the system in other Communist countries can be quite marked; and in the underdeveloped countries, like China, may be associated with their distinctive historical heritages—as well as with their emergence as Communist *follower* countries. It may therefore help in comparative analysis to recognize that significant variants exist not only for the free-market economy but also for the Communist system; and that these variants in the underdeveloped Communist countries, like those in the underdeveloped non-Communist countries, may reflect elements of the historical past—although not necessarily the same elements or with the same weight.

5. System Deviation and Delayed Entry

The main issue in this section is whether the formation of a new variant of an economic system, or better, of a new type of economic system, may not be a link in the process of *spread* of modern economic growth in a world of competing political entities like nation-states. If we view the primary source of modern economic growth as a transnational stock of technological and social knowledge available for exploitation by any society that gears itself for this purpose, and if in the course of historical change in the structure of the various nation-states, the preparation for exploitation of the growth potential involves a change not only from a country's own past arrangements but also from those followed by heretofore developed countries, then a *new* system may be generated. In a sense, the new system is a response, sufficiently successful to merit recognition and attention, to opportunities of economic growth, a function of the latter, a new installment in the spread of modern economic growth. More specifically, if the new economic system emerges fairly late in the spread of modern economic growth, and the carrier is therefore a relative late-comer, it can be viewed as a deviation from the prevalent organizational pattern and a function of delayed entry, of the pressures that the backwardness implicit in such delayed entry exercises (in addition to the opportunities that it may provide).[7]

It would be tempting to set up a model in which prolonged delay in entry into modern economic growth produces greater pressure of increasing backwardness—so that those units that make a belated entry, rely increasingly upon the power of the state in response to this greater pressure to catch up. The increasing exercise of this power may eventually lead to an economic system sufficiently different to be recognized as new, and to a pattern of industrialization that also differs markedly in its sequence from that followed by the pioneer and early follower countries. This model could be expanded by adding the proposition that the delayed entry, with the consequences just suggested, was in turn due to a greater "lack of preparedness," i.e., a greater difference between the social and economic institutions of the country under review and those of the pioneer and early follower developed countries at the early stages of their modernization. It would follow that radical changes would have to be made in these institutions; and indeed radical political and institutional changes often precede the successful entry into modern economic growth by the late-comers. Given such radical political changes, the new state would presumably feel a greater responsibility for catching up and participate more actively in the economic growth process. Thus the connection between delayed entry and the emergence of a new economic system is *via* the greater role of the state for two reasons: the greater

[7] The similarity of such an approach which links deviant forms of the economic system to delayed entry in the process of modern economic growth to Alexander Gerschenkron's hypothesis is obvious (see his paper, "Economic Backwardness in Historical Perspective," published in 1952 and reprinted a decade later in his collection of essays under the same title, Cambridge, Mass., 1962, pp. 5–30; and the supplementary discussion in the same volume, "The Approach to European Industrialization: A Postscript," pp. 353–64). However, we do not claim that our approach is a logical extension of Professor Gerschenkron's hypothesis.

pressure (as well as opportunity) of backwardness, and the greater need to eradicate the old and inappropriate economic and social institutions.

The model explains the greater reliance on the powers of the state, and hence some of the development policies and patterns of the late-comers in the period of transition from underdevelopment to development. However, it fails to yield a new economic system as a necessary, or even as a likely, result—assuming that our definition of an economic system is not so narrow that a limited variant would have to be viewed as new (in which case a different system would be generated by practically every country that enters modern economic growth).

This inadequacy of the model is illustrated by the cases of Japan and Russia, both late-comers in the historical spread of the modern economic system. Japan was under much greater pressure to exploit the potential of modern economic growth than the earlier entrants in Europe and the United States, for its national independence was in danger, and the repetition of India's and China's experience threatened as a grave possibility. Furthermore, since its economic and social institutions were so far removed from those of the pioneer and early follower European countries and of their offshoots overseas, and radical, indeed revolutionary, changes were essential, Japan was a most conspicuous case—far more so than Russia. As is well known, the state did play a crucial role in Japan in the early periods of the Meiji Era, introducing a series of major changes in the political, legal, social, and economic institutions and itself engaging in several modern productive activities. Yet all this was done to facilitate the formation of a market economy, a system that despite some interesting differences is not so unlike those characterizing the other developed countries as to be recognized as a new economic system. In contrast, Russia, where backwardness was far less of a danger, where social institutions were far more akin to those of the developed West, and where an earlier attempt at modernization and entry had followed rather customary and nonrevolutionary patterns, ended with a violent overthrow of the existing social and institutional framework and a radically different and *new* economic system. In achieving modern economic growth, it became sufficiently successful to merit attention and raise problems of comparative analysis.

The link between the spread of modern economic growth and the emergence of a new economic system, which we have not yet specified in the model, can be suggested, even if the suggestion bears all the earmarks of hindsight wisdom. Let us assume that in the course of its development and spread, modern economic growth generated an ideology that combines a great admiration for the technological attainments of the epoch with an equally great abhorrence of the social institutions, the system within which these attainments had been channelled previously;

an ideology that considers the existing social system not only a dispensable part of the modern economic epoch but one that actually limits the full use of its technological potential; and an ideology that entertains this dogma with a fervor that justifies the use of an authoritarian minority party to pursue any policies, no matter how violent, in order to overthrow rather than gradually modify the existing system, i.e., one that is aimed at a new system (however ill-defined) rather than at some variant. The real question is whether such a specifically formulated ideology is a necessary consequence of the spread of modern economic growth—as distinct from a generally critical ideology that does not contain radically violent, authoritarian elements. Let me assume that such an ideological twist is a *possible* result of the institutional and human upheavals created by dynamic modern economic growth.

Given this specific ideological product of the evolution and spread of modern economic growth (i.e., of the epoch), the new economic system *may* emerge if the party-carrier of such ideology attains control; and having attained it, experiments with the new economic system sufficiently to demonstrate significant success—in the sense that it can raise the country's aggregate product rapidly and appreciably through the adoption of modern material technology at an adequately rapid and cumulative rate. The shift of power can be achieved in a country only if previous efforts to exploit the potential modern economic growth under the old system were not successful enough to build up group interests within that system which could effectively resist violent change in the political and social structure; and only if the country has had enough of an awareness of modern economic growth so that a significant minority group has been imbued with the specific ideology suggested. Success, after coming to power, depends in turn upon various special conditions if it is to be sufficiently marked, and the new system sufficiently different, to warrant recognition and become the concern in comparative analysis of the type emphasized in this volume. This violent change and attempt at a new system must occur in a *large* country—for only a large country can reap the benefits of economic growth in terms of world power and influence; and only a large country can effect the necessary revolutionary departures without being forced to compromise by the larger and less deviant developed nation-states. Furthermore, this violent change must occur in a large country that remains large despite the strains imposed upon it by the violent upheaval; and this means a country where past history has created a community of culture and feelings that have provided a sufficient substratum of unity. Whether we would be as much concerned with the Soviet economy as a new economic system if the results had been similar to those for the Austro-Hungarian Empire after World War I, is a moot question; and it is a serious question, because such an outcome would imply that this type of entry, this attempt to exploit the potentials of modern economic growth, is too destructive of national viability to be practicable. Finally, the violent overthrow in a large country with an established history and unity that can stand the strain without decomposition into separate parts, must also occur at a high enough level of development of modern technology, so that an authoritarian minority party can dominate the country by exercising repressive force long enough to mobilize the economic resources for a rapid transformation. Even more important, the effective application of this technology, which can be borrowed, must be achieved without reliance upon the skill of the labor force (which is very low to begin with) and upon the loyalty of the majority of the labor force (which, particularly if we include the agricultural classes, is questionable). Only with the tractors, the heavy producers' goods, and the capital-intensive infrastructure was the minority party in Russia able forcefully and rapidly to transform the technological base of the country. It could do so, furthermore, under a new system that initially and for a considerable period ran counter to the immediate economic and other interests of the majority of the population—however much these interests may have been transformed later by attachment to the new bases of the economic and social system once these were created.

All these speculative notions may not stand up under scrutiny in the light of greater knowledge of the relevant stretch of economic, political, and intellectual history. But they are advanced as a preliminary attempt to illustrate the possible interplay of stages in the spread of the modern economic epoch with some specific singular elements, in giving rise to a new economic system.[8]

I would like to emphasize again that our recognition of a different economic system as new is a reflection not merely of its difference from the prevalent system but also of its *weight* in the world—and this means its success in a society large enough to affect the balance of power in this competitive world. If this is true, it is not only the economic system of socialism that interests us: Such a system, in the sense of state ownership of means of production and control over economic activity, including whatever planning may be fancied, can theoretically also permit political freedom, many political parties, democratic decisions on the choice of plans, and so forth. In realistic terms, our interest concerns the new

[8] The elements—size and national viability of the country; failure in adopting modern economic growth and yet sufficient participation to have an effective Communist party; a level of technology that permits the transformation despite the disloyalty and resistance of much of the population—are singular in that each is the result of a vast complex of antecedent causes not likely to recur or occur at more than one place in the world. They are not chance, in that they are not the product of a vast variety of uncorrelated unbiased elements, each of which is too small to warrant identification and study.

economic system operated by a Communist authoritarian party, with complete repression of political activity, and fairly tight restraints on the choice not only of economic plans but of all other issues of society. And it is because of this distinctive combination of political authoritarianism, an ideology that stresses economic growth as measured by material output, with the tight control of the relations among men in the social sphere and in cultural creativity, that the Communist system interests us. This role of the Communist system affects the economic fate not only of the countries that adopt it—and these are important because of their very size—but also of others, since the relations among them are more affected by the political ideology than by the purely economic aspects of the system. It is in order to try to explain the emergence of the new economic system, as exemplified by the USSR, not to formulate a socialist or Communist economic system abstractly defined, that the discussion above suggested the relevant inter-play among the stages in the spread of modern economic growth, the delayed entry on the part of some nation-states, and the possible break-through to a new system based partly on the specific ideology generated by past economic growth, and partly on a combination of the singular elements that permit such a successful breakthrough.

6. Change in Later Growth

Implied in the discussion just presented is a view of the breakthrough to a new economic system as a contingency that might not have occurred if some of the required singular components had not been present at the appropriate stage of spread of the modern economic epoch; and a view in which the chances of such concurrence are slight, not too favorable, and clearly not inevitable. This conclusion is hardly surprising if, as has been argued with respect to the USSR, a new system, differentiating itself from the old by hostility, can be successful only in a large country that possesses the national unity to withstand a great deal of pounding. The distribution of nation-states in the world is skewed: A few (not more than a dozen) are very large (say with a population well over 50 million, to use the current scale), and many (over a hundred) are quite small (say with a population appreciably less than 20 million). Hence the number of units within which a successful breakthrough to a new economic system can occur is limited; and in view of the variety of further singular requirements, the chances that even one would be successful cannot, in the nature of the case, be high.

But whatever the probability of the contingency, once the breakthrough to a new system occurs and is successful enough to be recognized as an effective response to the potentials of modern economic growth, the new system begins its own process of internal modification and external spread. We shall not deal here with the spread of the new system beyond the country of origin—except in its possible bearing upon internal evolution within the pioneer country.

This new economic system, which originated in a belated response to the unexploited potentials of modern technology and modern economic growth, applied an essentially negative ideology to experiment with alternative ways of allocating resources under a different set of political and social institutions, and successfully made a rapid transition to a much higher level of aggregate economic performance and technology. Will it not then have served its purpose and be subject to substantial modification, particularly if the system fails to induce the still higher level of economic performance already attained in the other developed countries? In other words, is the new economic system, as exemplified in the Soviet Union so far, compatible with attainment of a higher level of economic performance, of another stage of economic growth? We should not overlook, of course, the possibility that the modifications required for further economic growth need not be made (although there presumably would be pressure in that direction).

This issue of compatibility between the Soviet Communist system and further economic growth and attainment is a question of *what* change, *how much* of that change, and how much in economic growth. Here we face the difficulty implied in our earlier discussion, viz., of identifying the nature, and gauging the magnitude, of any change that we would recognize as a variant in any economic system, to be related to an identified stage of economic growth. This difficulty led us to a rather sketchy and illustrative discussion of variants in the market-economy system of non-Communist developed countries (Section 3); and of the various types of combination of modern sector and traditional components in the systems represented by underdeveloped countries (Section 4). We had no such difficulty in associating different types of economic system with different stages of growth, when the latter represented sequences of major economic epochs and epochal innovations (Section 2); or when we discussed the emergence of a sharply contrasting new economic system, as exemplified by Soviet Communism (Section 5). But here, when we ask what changes in this new economic system would be required for a further advance in economic growth, we face the problem of identifying the organizational and system aspects necessary for some specific stage of growth. Whether or not we can resolve the difficulty, it should at least be recognized as a central problem in the comparative analysis of economic systems, if the latter are to be conceived as more than extreme abstractions (free-market economy, centralized command economy, and so forth) unaffected by realistic variants.

We can only illustrate the difficulty by reference to both parts of the compatibility issue, the system and the stage of growth. Every functioning economic system undergoes *some* changes as the components that it organizes change in the course of growth, and hence the very principle of organization is necessarily modified in its application. Changes have already occurred in Soviet Communism over the four decades since its crystallization in the first five-year plan. However one would weigh the element of historical accident in the brutality of Stalinist dictatorship, one could reasonably argue that the internal policies followed during the period of forceful wrecking of older institutions and of older economic and social groups had to change. Some of the organizational features had to be modified, once the new economic bases made it possible for new group and class interests to emerge, and the latter could pursue a policy unconcerned with the pressure for removal of internal resistance or for external catching-up. In the sense that the functions of the new economic system in the later decades would differ somewhat from those in the earlier decades, there would be a change. But how should we evaluate this change, how much weight should we assign to the observable changes? The question calls for criteria in identifying and measuring changes in an economic system; and one wonders how far comparative analysis can proceed without such criteria for identifying the components of the system and measuring their magnitude. Was the shift from Stalinism to post-Stalinism—with the broadening of the decision base in planning from a small party faction to a wider group which may be more responsive to the interests and desires of a larger fraction of the population—a change in the new system? And how significant was this widening of the decision base in terms of allowing greater play of various interests and conceptions of the needs of economy and society? Would we consider some of the recent reforms, or even the Yugoslav type of organization, significant new variants, assuming the continued monopolization by the Communist party of political and cultural life? Obviously we need some testable typology of variants of the new economic system (as we do for the non-Communist economies) before we can trace the relation of these variants to stages of economic growth.

If it is difficult to define a change in the economic system, in this case the Communist, it is also difficult to define levels of economic performance and stages of growth (within the complex of modern economic growth). Assume that the Soviet Union allows for a moderate rise in per capita supply of consumer goods, but increases total and per capita output by concentrating on the production of military goods, producers' equipment, space exploration, output for foreign power diplomacy—while still controlling the country's political life, press, arts, education, man's choice of career, and at intervals tightening the Iron Curtain. Obviously, marked increases and higher levels of aggregate economic product can be attained in this way with practically no change in the Soviet Communist system, unless one argues that devotion of the greater share of input to increasing output along the lines suggested would arouse such a reaction in the population that further economic growth would necessarily be reoriented to the desires of the people.

The issue of compatibility can thus be rephrased. What change in the Soviet Communist system should be recognized as a major modification rather than a minor variant, and does the next stage or even simply further economic growth require this major modification? Such a requirement may be claimed by saying that the members of the Communist society will not cooperate in *further* economic growth unless the modification is forthcoming, e.g., unless they are given a more important role in decisions about consumption and production plans. The validity of this basis for the requirement, and hence incompatibility with further growth, can be determined, if at all, only by close students of the Soviet society and economy. Or it may be argued that greater freedom of economic, social, and cultural life is indispensable if the higher stage of economic growth is to generate further innovations and thus sustain itself. However, this is a condition of growth of the most advanced pioneer country and not a general requirement for all participants in an advanced stage of growth. The USSR may attain a higher level of per capita growth, and even of consumption, while retaining its authoritarian structure, by continuing to adopt the innovations generated in the freer and more creative economies of the West. Finally, it may be claimed that further economic growth involves, *by definition*, much greater freedom of members of society to participate in decisions on economic plans, and in choices between economic and other aspects of social life. In that sense the kind of economic growth illustrated in the preceding paragraph, is no growth at all. But this only means that *if* we *define* more advanced stages of economic growth as those in which pluralistic and decentralized decisions can be given adequate weight, then it follows that the Soviet Communist system is incompatible with further economic growth. But this is a value judgment and belongs to a different level of discourse.

Little in this discussion of the compatibility issue bears on the *likelihood* of significant changes in Soviet Communism. Exploring the latter would mean taking into account pressures for change generated within the Soviet Union—partly by its economic growth, partly by its continued co-existence with the non-Communist developed countries and the demonstration effect of the latter at least on some groups within Soviet society, partly by the evolution of the Communist system elsewhere (whether in demonstration of the advantages of modification, or of such disadvantages of accentuation as have occurred in Mainland China). But exploration of recent trends, viewed as sources of pressure for change, while possibly relevant as illustrations of linkages between changes in economic system and stages in spread of an economic epoch, would take us too far afield; and is, in any case, beyond my competence.

7. Postscript

The rather disjointed discussion in this paper dealt with selected topics in the broad field of the relation between phases of economic growth and economic system. The field was broad because of a decision to view an economic system not merely as a clear-cut, extreme formulation of some single principle of organization regardless of the parts being organized and hence of the variant ways in which one and the same principle would be applied; but as a concept permitting significant variants. With these variants viewed as important elements in comparative analysis, their association with stages of economic growth would reveal a variety of links. These could be covered here only illustratively and with emphasis on definitional and conceptual aspects.

The discussion was perforce illustrative, because I had neither an established typology of these significant variants of economic systems nor the empirical data by which they would be linked with equally well identified and measured phases of economic growth—although for modern economic growth, the supply of well-organized data and ad hoc hypotheses on phases of growth is richer than that bearing upon economic systems in their significant variants.

That our discussion was so largely in the nature of semantic clarification was perhaps inevitable—for in a field as broad as that outlined in the topic, clarification of meanings is the first indispensable step. It is only to the extent that some agreement is secured in this first step that further analysis and empirical testing become possible.

How much further analysis in the field can proceed, only the future will show. But the main import of this paper is to suggest that the broad social and ideological implications of the measures of economic performance and growth must be carefully noted in any empirical references to phases of growth (particularly within a given economic epoch); and that the typology of the significant variants of economic systems must be a major concern before the relation between phases of growth and economic system can be fruitfully studied.

9

Ideology as a
System Determinant

by ALEXANDER GERSCHENKRON

It was with a feeling of considerable envy that I looked over the titles of
the papers assigned to the other participants of this symposium. They all
appeared so perfectly comprehensible. By contrast, the title of my own
paper was extremely puzzling: "Ideology as a System Determinant." It
seemed that every word in the title called for some clarification. What is
"ideology," and what is "system" and above all what is "determinant?"
These notions, vague enough when taken separately, become three times
as nebulous when joined together. The natural thing for me to do would
have been to confess that I did not understand the title and accordingly
could not write a paper about it. But this, I realized, would have been a
flagrant violation of our rules of togetherness, a brazen attempt to shake at
the very foundations of our intellectual order. I might as well have tried to
occupy the office of the President of my University and to steal his
personal correspondence. But I am not rebellious. I know that the rules of
social behavior, cruel as they are, must be obeyed. The paper had to be
written. Yet in these circumstances it could be nothing else but a series of
groping speculations about the meaning of the intriguing and mysterious
title.

1. Theoretical Systems and the Meaning of Ideology

First of all, what is a system? Is it to be understood as a consistent
theoretical construct, or is the term system meant to cover in a vague way,
which does violence to the term, the historically given economies, or
rather a number of not necessarily consistent features of such economies?

The Walrasian concept of general equilibrium yields indeed a consistent
system. What about the ideology of such a system? Since it is actuated by
men and since men's actions are motivated by their brain processes, in
other words, by their ideas, and since the Walrasian systems functions,
and the general equilibrium is established by men trying to maximize
utility, the idea of utility maximization may be regarded as the ideology of
the system. It would seem a matter of choice whether one says that this
ideology is a determinant of the system or is merely implied in the system.
At any rate, in this case the relationship between the system and its

ideology is simple and unambiguous. The relationship is only a little bit more complex in the case of Oscar Lange's system of the socialist economy. For the system to work in the desired fashion, the Central Planning Board in setting the rate of net investment must be guided primarily by the welfare of the consumers and is supposed to operate with reasonable time horizons; and similarly the managers of the enterprises must be willing to observe in the process of production Lange's two fundamental rules, even though they might find it profitable for their enterprises (and possibly for themselves) to disregard them. Lange failed to provide a mechanism, be it economic or juridical, to compel a manager to push production to the point at which marginal cost and price are equalized. It must be assumed that he felt that a socialist economic system of this type—an incarnation of goodness and justice—would generate a social environment within which compliance with rules that are socially so desirable will be forthcoming readily and spontaneously. The working of a system based entirely on free market decisions with the heterogeneity of purposes—*Heterogenie der Zwecke*—built into the system, requires a simpler set of motivations, that is to say, a simpler ideology. The pure economic man has simpler ideas than the pure socialistic man who must be an economic man up to a point (the consumer following his preferences, the worker choosing his employment) and something else in addition. Within the theoretical construct of the socialist system there may be a conflict particularly between the entrepreneur as the economic man and the socialistic man. Yet, what so far has been called ideology or ideologies is an integral part of the respective constructs. Without such a set of ideas the systems would become unworkable and, in fact, unthinkable. In either case, theoretical reasons may cast doubt on the workability of the system, but they have no bearing on the problem. What matters is that in the light of the foregoing it is indeed meaningful to speak of ideology as a system determinant, but the relationship between ideology and system, so conceived, is rather unproblematic and by the same token, bereft of interest.[1]

When one descends from the abstract heights of theoretical constructs into the plains of historical reality, the scenery and with it the nature of both concepts changes drastically. We no longer operate with a consistent economic system but with a heterogeneous phenomenon called economy. We may indeed try to pare out the body economic from the total body social, but it is no longer possible to relate it to a unique and unambiguous set of ideas called ideology. Ideology then is no longer a set of definite ideas tailored to fit a clearly defined system, or rather implied in it.

---

[1] It is probably superfluous to add that, in obedience to my title, I am concerned here with the ideology of systems and not with that of theoretical system makers. Whatever ideology may have motivated Walras or Lange and influenced their scientific processes is of no relevance here.

Ideology then becomes a very complex matter, raising a host of difficult conceptual and historical problems. And what determines what (and in what sense) in such connections as do exist between ideology and economy becomes a very uncertain proposition. To say this does not mean that some generalizations on these connections are impossible, but the chances are that they will be far removed from the simplicity implied in my assigned title.

As should be clear from the foregoing, I want to use the term ideology simply as a complex of ideas, which are somehow—be it positively or negatively—related to economic action. Later on, I may refer to ideologies in the narrower and more specific sense. This may be Marx's or rather Engel's "false consciousness," meaning either inability of individuals to understand the real motives of their actions or "falsely" understood interest; falsely, that is, in terms of some objective analysis, or else in terms of another specific ideology. A specific ideology may cover Bacon's *idola fori* and *idola teatri*, or the sham reasoning of Pareto's "derivations," or Sorel's "mythos," or Nietzsche's "false judgments" (*vulgo* lies, which he considered to be a rather wonderful "life-affirming" thing), or finally, Mannheim's "particular ideology." But for the purposes of this discussion, let us assume—as I believe did the inventors of my title—that intuitively we know what ideology means. In conformity with present common usage, let us, therefore, employ the term in the previously mentioned broadest connotation and start with a historical example.

2. German Agriculture, Industry, and Ideology

At the turn of the century, a debate raged in Germany, described by the contemporaries as a controversy between the industrial and the agrarian state. Men, such as Oldenberg and Wagner, Voigt and Pohle, depicted in moving terms the dangers of Germany's continuing on the road of industrialization. Industry—the upstart—was in the process of destroying the old and venerable agriculture.[2] Marxian terms were borrowed, or purloined, in order to describe the threatening "immiseration" of German agriculture. The Malthusian ghosts were invoked to demonstrate the threat of starvation in Germany, once its agricultural base had been reduced. A nation could live without industry, but not without agriculture.[3] An industrial state would be defenseless in case of war against a hostile blockade of its shores; and without a strong agricultural population, it was said, the manpower of the German army would be sapped. For urban life was degenerating. But, war apart, it was highly dangerous to surrender the food supply of the nation to the hazards of international crop failures.[4]

[2] Karl Oldenberg, *Deutschland als Industriestaat*, Goettingen 1897, p. 3.
[3] *Ibid.*, p. 4.
[4] *Ibid.*, p. 29.

At the same time, economic development in grain-producing lands beyond the seas was bound to lead to a sudden cessation of grain exports within a relatively short time and result in mass unemployment and starvation in Germany. Because of stagnation in export industries, some 30–40 million people would almost overnight find themselves deprived of all means of subsistence. Thus, increasing misery in agriculture would be followed by catastrophic misery of the proletariat, although for other than Marxian reasons. Capital (meaning the capitalists) which directed the growth of the economy was unable to look beyond the profitabilities of the moment. Its time horizon was low. When the crisis came, the only alternative left would be to compel the United States by force of arms to continue its grain exports, but the outcome of such a warlike conflict was dubious, although not necessarily for military reasons.[5] An industrial state was an obnoxious phenomenon anyhow. It meant domination by Jewish speculators and Jewish bankers, whose activities were economically unsound and sooner or later were bound to end in a general catastrophe. As Adolph Wagner (who described himself as only "a relative enemy of the industrial state") put it, "large-scale industrialism together with the stock exchange are the most disturbing and the most disgusting forms of private capitalism."[6] By contrast, large-scale estates in East Elbia were neither disturbing nor disgusting, and their owners—the Junkers—were described as "important, nay, indispensable members of the whole organism of the economy"[7] who had been suffering "increasing misery." An industrial state, it was argued, did not correspond to "total national interest"; autarky was a blessing from the point of view of that interest, even though it was bound to place burdens on the consumers; but then, it was added, every good thing, be it army or courts, was bound to cost something, and so did the agrarian state.[8] But the cost would be relatively low, and economic arguments (e.g., the assertion that the influx of workers into industry from rural areas was pressing on wages of industrial labor)[9] and statistical demonstrations were used to make this assertion possible. At any rate, undue concern with the economic interests of the urban masses was criticized as "Byzantinism downward," that is to say, as incongrous grovelling not before the superiors but before the inferiors on the rungs of the social ladder.[10]

The thoughts sketched out in the foregoing entered the intellectual arsenal of a powerful movement in favor of tariffs on grain as advocated

[5] *Ibid.*, pp. 31–32.
[6] Adolph Wagner, *Agrar- und Industriestaat*, Jena, 1901, p. 14.
[7] *Ibid.*, p. 58.
[8] *Ibid.*, p. 24.
[9] Oldenberg, *op. cit.*, p. 45.
[10] Wagner, *op. cit.*, p. 4.

by the *Bund der Landwirte*—the Union of Agriculturists—which was created and dominated by the Prussian Junkers. In the process of propagandizing, their views were amplified—for instance by adding aversion from "mechanistic" parliamentarism and praise of the "organic corporate state"; they were also rendered more violent by stressing the virtues of the peasants' *Bodenstaendigkeit*—rootedness in the soil—as against the immorality of the uprooted urban masses and particularly against that of the nomadic and dishonest Jew. It is obvious that several decades later many, if not all, of these ideas became fully accepted by National Socialism. The latter no doubt proved a more powerful and also much more successful movement; but the importance of the Junker-led campaigns was very considerable in contemporaneous terms, quite independently of the sinister legacy which they left for the future. Now, what kind of enlightenment can be drawn from that historical case for the problem at hand?

I take it that there will be no hesitation to characterize this body of thought as anti-industrial ideology. But what features of ideology can be deduced from this example? And what is the system it may have "determined"?

First of all, there is the mixture of explanatory or analytical with normative elements. The connection is not simple. To some extent, analysis is presented as leading to certain normative conclusions. But to some extent analysis is used to support a value-determined course of action that has been accepted independently of any analysis. For the decline in the position of agriculture in the economy would have been bemoaned even if the allegedly ineluctable collapse of the industrial state had not been threatening. On the other hand, analysis, while it may contain correct elements, is likely to abound in propositions that cannot stand up under a dispassionate investigation. Oldenberg, a professor of economics, did not hesitate to conjure up the danger of "international crop failures," even though clearly world trade in cereals insured against disastrous harvests on a national scale. But as Theodore Geiger has pointed out, an ideology is likely to be doubly false.[11] For untenable factual and interpretative statements are conjoined with references to values which were not the true value judgments of the defenders of an ideology, but were designed to disguise, and to deflect attention from, those true values.

Also here, a mixture prevailed. Many statements may have glorified the Junkers as a most valuable group within the German society, but this was not where the weight of emphasis lay. Protection of grain growing was justified with reference to "total national interest," the military power of Germany, the future standard of living of the low-income consumers in the cities, and, last but not least, the interests of the German peasantry.

[11] Theodore Geiger, *Ideologie und Wahrheit, Eine soziologische Kritik des Denkens*, Stuttgart-Vienna, 1953, p. 34.

It is with regard to the last vindication that the specific double falsity of the ideology appeared with particular force. For, as was shown time and again, the prosperity of the German peasantry did not depend on protection of grain output; the contrary was true. Low prices of cereals were essential for the profitable readjustment of the peasant economy to the output of converted products. By contrast, the Junker economy was inextricably bound up with the continued growing of rye. Nor was there anything in the past history of the East Elbian gentry to suggest any concern for the welfare of the peasantry. False arguments were married to false, that is to say, pretended values. Since the vote of the peasants in the parliament (*Reichstag*) was needed to assure adoption of a tariff protecting rye, it was necessary to convince the peasants that such protection was also in their interest. It would not have done to admit that protection was needed in order to maintain the traditional standard of living of the gentry and to preserve the economic basis of its social position. The leaders of the Junker-led Union of Agriculturists as well as the average Junker may indeed have believed that the continued existence of the group was in some sense in the national interest of Germany, or at least of Prussia; there is little doubt that they were opposed to capitalism, the stock exchange, the banks, and the Jews. But there is also no doubt that all those readily salable values were offered in joint supply with, and designed to make more acceptable, the truly crucial point: The peasantry was made to believe that its economic interest was identical with that of the Junkers. This was deception—conscious deception—and the operative factor connecting ideology and action.

Thus, ideology appears as an immensely complex thing in which analytical and normative propositions, the former both correct and incorrect, the latter both honest and deceptive, are commingled to constitute a hybrid whole. And the question is what system was determined by this concoction brewed of cognition and error, truth and lie.

Werner Sombart once tried to produce a definition of the concept "social class." After rejecting a number of definitions based on wealth, occupation, and other characteristics, he decided to define class as the group whose ideas (*"der Idee nach"*) represent a certain economic system. He then listed four classes: 1) The Junkers representing the feudal estate economy; 2) the Bourgeoisie representing capitalism; 3) the Petty Bourgeoisie representing the handicraft economic system; and finally, the Proletariat representing the future socialist economy.[12] Something more will be said later about socialist labor, the problems of its ideology, and its relation to economic systems. What matters at this point is the extreme ambiguity of relating the Junkers to the feudal system. If feudal system

[12] Werner Sombart, *Die deutsche Volkswirtschaft im neunzehnten Jahrhundert und im Anfang des Zwanzigsten Jahrhunderts*, Berlin, 1927, pp. 440–441.

means what it normally means, that is, a hierarchical order based on homage and service with enserfed peasantry standing at the bottom of the system, its economy enmeshed through labor services or payments in kind or money and capital supply with the seignioral economy, then it is fairly obvious that at the turn of the century such a system no longer existed in Germany. The peasant and the Junker economies were separated. The latter were serviced not by peasants, but by landless laborers. To be sure, many features in the position and in the behavior of the members of the Junker class were usually described as "feudal." Loose as the connotations of the term were, in some sense those features represented traits that survived from pre-industrial times. But the Junker economies, taking the size of the estates and the natural conditions of soil and climate as given, were efficiently operated, following as they did, a rational calculus rather than a traditionally set custom of the manor. The inefficiency resulted from exogenous processes that had occurred in the world, far away from the borders of Germany. To describe the Junker estates as a feudal or seignioral economic system would strain both the noun and the adjectives beyond reasonable meaning. And, system or not, what motivated the actions of the Junker group was a specific power ideology—their *libido dominandi*—together with sheer economic interest.

Both were "true" ideologies, even though more implied than explicitly avowed. They could have been deduced from actions, even if no word had ever been uttered to betray their existence. It is those "true" ideologies that, among other things, created the ideology described in the previous pages. The latter, however, with which alone we are concerned here, was not implied in the "system," nor did it in any way determine it. Its purpose was to influence foreign commercial policy and, more specifically, the rates of the German tariff on grains. Since peasant votes in the *Reichstag* were insufficient to assure the adoption of the tariffs, the agricultural block agreed to support the tariffs on iron and steel as a quid-pro-quo for nonagrarian votes for the grain tariffs. The so-called "solidarity block" whose vote determined the structure of the German tariff was at variance with significant elements of the agrarian ideology, that is to say, its anti-capitalistic features. To some extent, the ideological difficulty was overcome by the distinction between "good" productive capitalism and "bad" rapacious capitalism, thus adumbrating the national-socialist distinction between *schaffendes* and *raffendes* capital. Still, some ideological cost had to be paid. For the agrarian ideology in its attacks upon the industrial state usually stressed that German capitalism, concentrating, as German industry did, on output of investment goods contributed little to increases in the supply of consumers' goods.[15] To increase the profitability of the iron and steel industry at the expense of

[15] Oldenberg, *op. cit.*, p. 9.

finished goods should have been abhorrent to the representatives of the agrarian ideology. We must conclude that in historical reality the relation between ideology and action differs radically from that of theoretical constructs. A considerable discrepancy between the two can exist, and this still leaves open the question to what extent the result of the action— the level and the structure of the German tariff can be meaningfully regarded as a system. This alone would seem to render the question of ideology as a system determinant quite uncertain.

But the situation is even more complex. The iron-and-steel industry was the leading branch of German industrialism, or, if one wishes to use the word, of German capitalism. If we grant that the agrarian ideology contributed importantly to the adoption of the "solidarity" tariff, we must admit that an anti-capitalistic anti-industrial ideology was instrumental in strengthening a pillar of the German industrial complex. Was it then a system determinant? And if the German economy of the time is regarded as a capitalist system, it becomes rather difficult to say by which ideology, if at all, it was determined. The only thing that can be said with some confidence is that a curious "idea-mix" was composed of references to real and merely alleged facts, of analytical and para-analytical interpretations, and above all, of value judgments inextricably commingled with facts and interpretations thereof; and that this tangled skein was helpful in producing certain actions, and accordingly, was instrumental in shaping certain aspects of the German economy in a way that was partly consonant and partly at variance with the "idea mix."

As said before, the term "system" should imply internal consistency.[14] Let us return for a moment to the previously quoted statement of Werner Sombart's. He sought to define class in terms of the economic system,

[14] At the Conference which formed the basis for this symposium volume it was fascinating to watch how a number of participants would use the term "system" with complete *désinvolture*, assuming that the meaning of the term was entirely unambiguous. Then someone would object to the glaring lack of a rigorous definition and try to offer one, usually with indifferent success. One suggestion was that system should always be defined in terms of the given analytical purpose. This may make good sense, but from the point of view of my contribution, it would clearly follow from this position that an indefinitely large number of systems can be discernible in any historically given economy and that those constructed systems naturally cannot all be expected to be commensurate with any uniquely given ideology. That the term system remained shrouded in uncertainty was perhaps best shown by an attempt to elucidate its meaning by reference to its Greek etymology. It is perfectly natural to mention the etymology of an artificially formed neologism such as monopsony or oligopoly. But when one turns to the etymology of a well established word, this is a give away, that is to say, an unmistakable indication that its meaning is nebulous. No one would try to explain the meaning of such terms as profit, or interest, or capital, or pecuniary economies by looking up the respective etymologies.

defining the latter in turn in terms of its "idea." So stated, the idea does indeed determine the system. Formally, this is precisely what was said before about theoretical constructs. Substantively, the justification of speaking of a system depends on the internal consistency of what is covered by the term idea. Elsewhere Sombart speaks of spirit, form (i.e., regulation), and nature of technology as system determinants. Capitalism as a system appears to him as determined by individualism, profit motive, rational calculus, scientific (rather than empirical) technology, and absence of regulations. Assuming that all those things—and not just "spirit"—constitute the "idea" of the system, they may be said to add up to a noncontradictory, that is, a consistent whole. It may also be granted that such a concept has its usefulness in distinguishing in a generalizing way certain features of modern economies from their predecessors. At any rate, there is definitional identity between idea and system, and hence there is no problem. The difficulty begins when we realize that there is a long way from this "idea" of the capitalist system to the "ideology" of the actually existing capitalistic economies. Let us illustrate, again by an example from German history.

Professor Hans Rosenberg in his recent book supplied a quotation from a statement by the Trade and Industry Association for Rhineland and Westfalia, that was published as early as 1859 in behalf of the German iron industry. In that statement it was urged that the German iron industry be protected and furthered "as a precious treasure" so as to make sure "that German soil is tilled by German iron, that German land is defended by German iron, and that German iron rails carry the great idea of German power and unity through all the *Gaue* of the far-flung Fatherland."[15] Thenceforth "protection of national labor" was firmly incorporated in the phraseology of the German iron and steel industry. It became an integral part of its ideology. Was this appeal to national interest deducible from the idea of a capitalist system? And was the device of protective tariffs deducible from that idea? Was recourse to the State consistent with economic individualism which is said to have been a constituent element of the idea of the system?

The average German entrepreneur, and particularly the German iron master, was no doubt a rugged individualist as "a master in his own house." As such he was opposed to the intervention of the State in labor relations and praised the virtues of free competition in the labor market. At the same time, his rugged individualism also displayed a special pre-capitalistic hue because in his relations with labor he had increasingly adopted "patriarchal" ideas which were at variance with the concept of an impersonal labor market and constituted assimilation of mental attitudes

[15] Hans Rosenberg, *Grosse Depression und Bismarckzeit*, Berlin, 1967, p. 156.

inherited from the "feudal" past. The rugged individualist did not object to a legal arrangement which gave him the right effectively to prosecute a worker for breach of contract, invoking the sanctions of the penal code, whereas he himself could only be sued ineffectively for reneging on the contract. He was not only ready to claim protection by the State against foreign competition, he was also willing to enter into monopolistic compacts in order to eliminate what was called "unhealthy competitive struggles" which, it was said, endangered the stability of the national economy. The concern with national labor and the national economy did not comprise concern with the national consumer when it came to discriminating against him by dumping German products abroad, and the theoretical possibility that dumping may serve to reduce domestic prices remained theoretical precisely because of the existence of cartels and trusts. But then, it was said, that conquest of export markets rebounded to the major glory of Germany, thus preserving the saving reference to national interest. Surely, an ideology composed of such contradictory elements cannot be a determinant of anything that deserves to be called a system. To be sure, behind the very inconsistent ideology may have stood—and in all likelihood did stand—a vested interest which may have been pure economic interest or power interest, or a certain mixture of both. The inconsistent ideology may be regarded as a consistent reflection of that interest. But then it is that specific interest—appearing as group interest— that determined the ideology and not the other way round.

To arrive at this conclusion, however, does not begin to do justice to the complexity of the phenomenon of ideology. First of all, there is the problem of the truth content of such an ideology in both senses of the word truth. The ideological references to national interest are relevant in this respect. Let us assume for the sake of argument that national interest can be defined in some simple and unambiguous way; let us say, for instance, that it is generally agreed that national interest is best satisfied by the greatest possible rate of growth of output compatible with constant per capita consumption of the population. There are neither competing nor higher goals, so that national interest so defined represents an ultimate value. Then it is quite conceivable that references to national interest by entrepreneurs seeking to obtain a protective tariff on their products, are indeed dictated by their specific interest, but that highly private interest happens to coincide with national interest. Again this may not be the case. The claim then is untrue in the sense that it can be refuted by an objective investigation. Then it may or may not be also untrue in the sense of being a deliberate deception. It may be based on an error resulting in self-decep- tion and the private interest may prove a powerful stimulus in increasing the propensity to err and to deceive oneself. Moreover, since, after all, national interest is a less-than-perfectly certain proposition, it can be unconsciously falsified so long until it coincides with private interest.

Barring believable confessions, a lie can be ascertained only by circumstantial evidence with a varying degree of probability. There may be clear cases on the part of men who profess devotion to national interest of behavior that is clearly inconsistent with it, such as, for instance, delivery of arms produced by a domestic manufacturer to a foreign country that is very likely to use them in a military conflict against the manufacturer's own nation. Most cases will be less flagrant. Still few would deny that ideologies very often abound in both errors on the one hand and deception on the other. Unfortunately, in things human both propositions hold: *errare humanum est* and *mentiri humanum est*. And ideology in general is an area least remarkable for the worship of truth in either sense. Again, error and lie are ill-suited to determine a system, that is, a consistent entity.

3. Ideologies of Industrialization

Still another and much more positive aspect to the problem of ideology forces itself upon our attention when we view the process of industrialization in 19th century Europe in its historical reality. I have discussed this aspect of ideology elsewhere, and, therefore, may be allowed to be brief.

It is true, of course, that those European industrializations exhibited traits commonly described as capitalistic. But let us forget for a moment about systems and determinants and the question whether those traits did or did not constitute a system. All that is necessary in this connection is to emphasize that those traits, and in fact the whole process of industrialization had to overcome considerable and manifold resistances. These resistances came from all parts of the social structure: They came from groups whose previously unchallenged dominant position in society was challenged and jeopardized by the industrial entrepreneurs, taking the concept in its broadest connotations, so as to include all those concerned directly or indirectly with the management of financing of industrial enterprises; they came from artisans whose small shops were being ruined by the competition of the factory; they came from intellectuals whose sense of both compassion and beauty was outraged by the conditions of factory labor, the misery that suddenly had become conspicuous, and by the ugliness of the workers' suburbs; they came from the restless, uprooted, and suffering labor force; and, finally, from all those whose preference for security, stability, and aversion from change were offended by the uncertainties and hazards of the new dynamic economy in the making.

No country in which industrialization took place was free of such resistances. But their intensity varied considerably and directly with the degree of backwardness of the country concerned on the eve and in the early stages of its industrialization. It is not surprising, therefore, that in backward countries an attempt was made to justify the process of industrialization and to make palatable the indubitable ills it implied by associating it with values that could be expected to find approval in large segments of society and to overcome, or at least to mitigate, those resistances. The result was the creation of specific industrialization ideologies, the intensity of which, again not surprisingly, varied, too, with the backwardness of the milieu in which the industrialization proceeded. The curious aspect of those ideologies consisted in their relative remoteness from what was actually happening in the realm of the economy. This is not true of England, the most advanced country. Ideologically, it may be said, England carried out its industrial revolution on a shoestring of laissez-faire tenets with the idea of rational allocation of resources and beyond it the assertion that any interference with the economy was either superfluous, or harmful, or—and this above all—ineffective. Whatever ills were brought about by the industrialization, nothing could be done about them, and, in the long run, it was the landed interests anyway who were to be the ultimate beneficiaries of the great transformation. Quite unlike it was the situation on the Continent where St. Simonism in France, nationalism in Germany, and Marxism in Imperial Russia can be justly regarded as the dominant industrialization ideologies. In each of these cases, there is little doubt that to some not inconsiderable extent those ideologies fulfilled their function not only in reducing external resistances to industrialization, but also in calming uneasy consciences of the industrializers themselves and providing them with a strong spiritual incentive in addition to the more "materialistic" and, at any rate, less respectable profit motive.

Thus, ideologies of this type were undoubtedly helpful in the creation of industrial economies. But their justifying function does not necessarily exhaust their effects. Modern ideologies, being more than a mere assertion of a normative principle, contained, as previously said, some theoretical or paratheoretical elements. As such they were more complex than, say, a mere reference to the will of the Lord, which incidentally was also used in justifying both preindustrial as well as industrial economies. If St. Augustin justified slavery, a false etymology apart, by the just punishment of God, meted out for the sins committed by the slaves, this was indeed a vindicating ideology, but it did not influence the operation of an economy based on slave labor. By contrast, the laissez-faire ideology provided effective arguments not only against pre-modern regulations, but also against governmental interventions in the field of social legislation and tended, among other things, to obstruct and delay adoption of factory acts.[16] St. Simonian ideology while greasing the wheels of the French

[16] During the discussion of this paper at the Conference, it was intimated that I had not devoted enough space to the laissez-faire ideology. I must refer the reader to my essay on "History of Economic Doctrines and Economic History"

industrialization of the 1850s contributed the seeds from which the powerful innovation of the industrial investment bank was to blossom forth. At the same time, however, it may be argued that the more backward an industrializing area, the less important were the operative substantive elements of the ideology under whose auspices industrialization was being carried out. Russian Marxism of the 1890s accomplished much to overcome the deeply ingrained populist values and to reconcile the intelligentsia and even segments of the imperial bureaucracy to modern industrialism. But it would be difficult to argue that Russian Marxism in any way affected the actual course of the process of industrialization.

Thus, to return to the unhappy topic of this paper, it seems very reasonable to say that such ideologies helped to clear the road for the advent of industrialization. It is also reasonable to say that in some way they affected some features of the industrialization. But it is not reasonable at all to say that St. Simonian socialism or Marxian socialism were the determinants of what was called French or Russian capitalism. It only

---

which I presented as a Richard T. Ely Lecture at the Meetings of the American Economic Association in December, 1968. The lecture, which to some extent overlaps this paper, deals more explicitly, although within a different context, with the subject of laissez-faire ideology. Here only two points should be added. As should be clear from the text, I have had no intention of minimizing the significance of laissez-faire and of its impact on minds and actions. The close relation between the ideology and an economy in which the free market had come to play a central role is obvious. But even in this case the role of the ideology as determinant of actions is problematic, to say the least. The materialistic conception of history has been debased in Soviet Russia to the level of a preposterous dogma, designed to provide answers even before proper questions have been asked. It is applied to periods and conditions to which it is patently inapplicable. But this does not mean that there are not other periods where a good deal of enlightenment can be derived from at least one of its elements, and the 19th century in Western Europe is probably the optimal case in point; all the more so, as in this respect, as in several others, Marxism just continued the intellectual tradition of classical economics, What this means from the point of view of this paper is that behind ideology stood well-conceived group interests. When it comes to determinants of action, therefore, one must ask whether it is not more natural and reasonable to take the short cut from interest to economic reality. This view receives powerful support if one considers the ease with which on the continent of Europe laissez-faire ideology in the area of commercial policies was abandoned and the protectionist measures taken under the pressure of changed interests. And even in England, free trade ideals were foresworn by heavy industry, once imperial preference held out more favorable prospects, and it was the exporting interests of Lancashire and the international position of the City of London that caused them to remain faithful to free trade and to defeat Birmingham's defection from the true doctrine. Whether an automobile will move forward or backward depends on the position of the gear shift. But it is the will—the interest—of the driver that determines and explains the direction of locomotion.

remains to add that the role of both St. Simonism and Marxism in its relation to industrialization was confined to brief initial periods of rapid spurts. St. Simonism was dead and buried in France of the 1860s. And after the Russian revolution of 1905 in the remaining years until the outbreak of World War I, it would be very difficult still to attribute any promoting or justifying effect to Marxism. By that time industrialization had been well launched and could proceed without the aid of an ideology that, after all, was quite alien to the industrial development as it continued to unfold.

St. Simonism presented itself as an ideology of social protest, conceived in the interest of the "most numerous and most suffering class." Marxism presented itself as a proletarian ideology concerned with the overthrow of the economic order that was created in the process of industrialization. As we saw before, Sombart defined proletariat, even though it was an integral part of the existing economy, as representing a future economic system, i.e., that of socialism. It accords ill with this view that a proletarian ideology could be instrumental or co-instrumental in removing the obstacles to the spread of what Sombart described as a capitalist system. Nor does the fact fit too well with a well-known Marxian pronouncement: "The ruling ideas of a time have always been the ideas of the ruling classes."[17] In saying this, one has to have in mind not just the special and rather peculiar case of Russian Marxism, but also the general case of Marxism; for it became a firm postulate within Marxian labor movements that technological progress must be accepted as hastening the economy toward the ultimate victory of socialism. This attitude was regarded within the Marxian labor movement as its peculiar feature, distinguishing it clearly from what was regarded as "petty-bourgeois" movements which were concerned with the evils of technological unemployment and were said to be unable to understand "the laws of capitalist development."

All this is worth noting in wondering about Sombart's view of classes and systems, which indeed seems to come very close to whatever thoughts have inspired the title of my present paper. And yet, the historical situation was a good deal more complex than can appear from the preceding remarks. To make this clear, something more must be said about the role of Marxian ideology in the labor movements in Central Europe, and more specifically in Germany and Austria.

There is a certain, at least superficial, resemblance between Calvinism, which Max Weber presented as the ideology of the rising bourgeoisie, and Marxism as it was accepted as the ideology of the rising proletariat. The latter was seen in the Marxian system as having been unconditionally

---

[17] *Das Kommunistische Manifest*, Karl Marx and Friedrich Engels, Gesamtausgabe, VI, Berlin: Marx-Engels Verlag, 1932, 543–544.

elected by the predestined course of history. Consonant with the difference between an individualist and a collectivist ideology, both predestination and unconditional election were converted from "micro-concepts" into "macro-concepts." Not the individual, but the class appeared as the elect. And both ideologies had to cope with the same paradoxical justification of vigorous action by reference to a pre-ordained course of events, to destinies which would seem to obviate the need for action.

4. Marxian Labor Movement in Central Europe

The main features of the Marxian ideology are well-known: Capital deepening, concentration and centralization, in conjunction with the immiseration of the growing working classes and the relative shrinking of markets was to produce a fatal conflict between the rapidly developing productive forces and the rigid framework of "production relations." The economy was propelled, or rather propelled itself, toward an impasse, from which at a given historical moment it was to be liberated and transformed by the revolutionary action of the proletariat. This view of the ineluctable process constituted the glad tidings that were incorporated in the programs of the Social Democratic parties in Germany and Austria (Erfurt, 1891; Hainfeld, 1889 and Vienna, 1901). The task of the labor movement was clear: The working class was being created as a "class in itself" (*Klasse an sich*) by the natural force of the economic development; it was to be transformed into a "class for itself" (*Klasse fuer sich*) by accepting Marxian ideology, as laid down in the programs. For the rest, until the dialectical turning point of the revolution, it was to concentrate on organization, while scrupulously avoiding any participation in the "ruling system."

Even in this form of total, or at least very far-reaching abstinence from interfering with the system, the labor movement contributed to its undisturbed evolution, not only by the previously mentioned aversion to Luddite attitudes but also by the proscription of terroristic activities, which had been favored by anarchist labor groups, and of wild outbreaks of violence which were pointless, as long as the capitalistic system had not become "ripe" for the great upheaval of the proletarian revolution. Thus revolutionary ideology, somewhat surprisingly, was in effect an instrument of political stability and a positive influence upon the economy the movement was to destroy.

The Revisionist attack upon orthodox Marxism was directed against the very foundations of that ideology. None of its basic elements escaped Bernstein's critical probing. What should have been destroyed was the belief in the inevitability of the collapse of capitalism and with it the belief in the dialectical discontinuity which was to reveal itself in the cynosure of the revolution. In actual fact, the vicissitudes of ideological evolution were more complex. The Revisionist strictures were effectively rejected by the labor movement. To all appearances, its ideology remained unchanged. What changed first were the actual policies. The rapid numerical growth of the movement, its striking electoral successes, the mechanics of opportunities which presented themselves in parliaments, diets and municipalities, the increased power of the labor unions, the more moderate, but still considerable and rather spontaneous expansion of consumers' cooperatives—all these made it difficult, if not impossible, to continue the attitude of patient preparation for the great day. A small movement, helplessly, though not hopelessly, weak had no choice but to wait. A large mass movement composed of men burdened with innumerable grievances —economic, social, juridical—could not and did not wait. For many of those grievances became remediable precisely as the size and strength of the movement had grown. In fact, in the very process of its organization, legal discrimination against labor in the form of disenfranchisement, censorship, limitations on the right of assembly, and unfair judicial practice had to be combatted; and the grievance of inequality before the law was attenuated, if not removed. In Austria, the process was more gradual than in Germany, where the abolition of the Anti-Socialist Act (1890) provided a rather discontinuous change. The struggle for higher wages and better working and living conditions, on the enterprise level and through social legislation, helped to maintain and to increase the share of labor in national product. And above all, the very development of the movement, to say nothing of its manifold educational activities, tended to imbue the membership with a sense of independence and human dignity. The sum total of these activities could not fail to have its impact upon the "capitalistic system." In particular, they tended to liberate the "system" from its patriarchal features. In this sense, it was the actions of the labor movement that cleansed capitalism of its feudal assimilations and let the system appear in a purer form.

There is no doubt that behind all this activity was a simple set of ideas, an ideology supporting and justifying it. Higher wages, better working and housing conditions, educational improvements, including reforms of the public school system—they all were given the stamp of ideological approval and were used in literature and daily propaganda as measures of success of the labor movement. To say this, however, leads to two conclusions:

1. Since the traditional ideology was not abandoned, after it had fulfilled its function of rallying the masses of urban labor, but came to exist side by side with new ideas, the aggregate ideological complex lost its pristine consistency. Attempts were made indeed to reconcile the two parts by arguing that a working class that was better paid, had more

leisure, and a higher standard of living all around was better prepared for the great task of carrying out the proletarian revolution and the subsequent socialist transformation. But the argument obviously could not hold beyond a certain point, and not a very high one at that. Once that point was passed, the proposition that the proletarians had nothing to lose but their chains was found to lose such validity as it may have possessed. It was precisely the conquests of the labor movement that might be lost in the storms of a revolution. At the same time, the actual willingness to engage in violent struggles was diminishing *pari passu* with the gradual improvement in labor's position. That the original ideology of orthodox Marxism was not abandoned was perhaps not surprising. To do so would have broken intellectually and morally the unity of life of men whose formative years passed under the aegis of the traditional ideology. To do so would have led to bitter internal strife, perhaps to a split of the movement before the First World War, and after the war would have made the Social Democratic Party and its unions even more vulnerable to Communist attacks. Moreover, the concept of inevitability of the Revolution was subtly altered to connote the inevitability of gaining ultimately decisive electoral victories as a basis for lasting labor governments. Furthermore, while the position of the oppressed group carried in itself its own moral justification and the labor movement, therefore, unlike other groups, did not find it difficult to admit that it was defending its own class interest, it was still desirable to sublimate that interest by connecting it with the vision of a good and just society of the future. And finally, and of particular importance in our context, was the fact that men do not find ideological inconsistency unduly intolerable. As Morley so rightly said: "It is only too notorious a fact in the history of belief that not merely individuals, but whole societies are capable of holding at one and the same time contradictory opinions and mutually destructive principles."[18]

It may be taken for granted that a certain measure of both deception and self-deception was involved in this process of ideological transformation. This is noteworthy, because minds trained in Marxian thought should have been quick to relate changes in ideology to changes in underlying

[18] John Morley, "On the Possible Utility of Error," in *On Compromise*, Chapman and Hall (1888) p. 68. Under certain conditions, ideological inconsistencies may indeed cause a certain malaise, as Gunnar Myrdal claims has been true in the post-bellum South where what Myrdal calls the "American Creed" and the attitudes toward the Negro were glaringly inconsistent. But the South managed to live with its malaise for a long time. As Percy Bridgman said: "There is no compelling reason why values should be consistent." P. W. Bridgman, *The Way Things Are*, Cambridge, Mass., 1959, p. 265. We may leave it open whether or not such inconsistency is compatible with Wundt's once so famous principle of unity of *Gemuetslage*, cf. Wilhelm Wundt, *Grundzuege der physiologischen Psychologie*, Leipzig, 1902, II, 342.

economic conditions. But Marxians seldom applied Marxism to Marxism. And so it was as late as 1924 when Rudolf Hilferding in a brilliant article gave an analytical description of the process in the course of which, as he put it, a "philosophy" became an "ideology." This is the use of the term in the previously mentioned narrower sense. This usage was natural for a Marxian scholar, as indeed, it has been for most of the relevant literature on the subject, even though it would not have fitted the title of this paper. But Hilferding made perfectly clear what he meant: "The idea," he said, "becomes ideology as soon as action is directly determined by other goals, which are only indirectly and ultimately related to the implementation of the idea, whether this relation is real or whether it exists only in the faithful fancy of the actors."[19] This candid statement from a most authoritative source is remarkable not only because it came so late, but also because it took still another quarter of a century before the German Socialist Party finally decided openly to forswear the creed outworn; a decision which the Austrian Socialists subsequently tried to imitate, but failed. This inertia of ideologies, that is to say, the survival strength of nonoperative elements in an ideology naturally should be noted by those who expect ideologies to act as system determinants.

2. The other conclusion can be stated much more briefly, but it is no less relevant. Such improvements in the conditions of labor as were brought about by the policies of the labor movement were achieved in the course of sharp conflicts which were particularly intense in the interwar period. Those were conflicts of interests and ideologies. From a historical point of view, however, what matters is that as labor accepted an active role in the economy, its actions, guided by the operative part of its ideology, were effecting considerable changes in that economy. If the latter is regarded as a "system," it must be concluded that a proletarian ideology had become an integral part of the "ruling ideas of the time" and was "determining" or "codetermining" the capitalist system in a much more far-reaching and more sustained way than the rather fleeting episodes of St. Simonism and Russian Marxism referred to before.

5. Soviet Russia

What has been discussed so far, dealt with what has commonly been called the capitalist system and what now has developed into a "mixed system," an expression that should give pause to those who realize that the adjective in the phrase tends to destroy the noun, resulting, that is, in a contradiction in terms. Let us turn now to what goes under the name of the "socialist system," where again both the adjective and the noun are

[19] Rudolf Hilferding, "Probleme der Zeit," *Die Gesellschaft*, Berlin, April 1924, 5.

equally dubious. Nearly seventy years ago, Pareto felt that admission of no more than a minimum of private ownership characterizes "the socialist systems."[20] In the interval, however, the concept of ownership has lost much of the significance that used to be attributed to it, and it is more than doubtful that it can be regarded as "system-forming." At any rate, our problem is "ideology as a system determinant" in Soviet Russia. Since I have expressed myself rather fully on the subject elsewhere, I can confine myself here to a brief restatement of my views.

Everything that happens in an economy is the work of men, however much this may be obscured by what appears to the individual as impersonal forces, that is, by what Marx called the fetishism of the commodity world. Still, it could be said that the Soviet economy, which has not grown organically, is man-made, that is to say, government-made, in a different and meaningful sense. One could expect, therefore, that the course of economic history of Soviet Russia and the nature of the resulting economy have been shaped by a consistent set of ideas, that is to say, by a definable and consistent ideology. And this is in fact correct, or nearly correct, once one is ready to distinguish between the official ideology and the real purposes that can reasonably be said to stand behind the actions of the Soviet government in the economic field.

The Soviet government does boast an ideology which was originally described as Marxism, then as Marxism-Leninism-Stalinism, and now goes under the truncated name of Marxism-Leninism. What has not been regarded as "Marxian" over the history of the Soviet state? Giving the land to the peasants and taking it away from them; the shameless adulation of Stalin and the present veneration of Lenin, and that in the name of a theory which vigorously rejected the role of great men in history; the establishment of the strongest tyrannical rule on modern record in the face of a theory that envisaged the dying away of the state and despite the vigorous stress on the anarchist elements in the Marxian theory of state. The latter, incidentally, must be regarded as Lenin's most significant contribution to Marxism, in as much as his book on imperialism was cribbed from Hobson and Hilferding, and his clumsy excursion into epistemology hardly deserves serious mention. The excesses of Russian chauvinism were said to be Marxian, as was, first, radical egalitarianism in income policy and, then, the tremendous differentials in wages and salaries. The policy of preferential growth of heavy industry was declared to be Marxian with irrelevant references to Marx' theory of markets. Marxian was the strict centralization of the economy, and Marxian were attempts at economic decentralization. Marxian was the contempt for the concept of diminishing returns, and Marxian were the attacks upon gigantomania.

[20] Vilfredo Pareto, *Les systèmes socialistes*, Paris, 1902, p. 108.

288 · *Comparative Economic Systems*

Just as men were becoming un-persons, ideas were becoming un-ideas at the pleasure of the government and corresponding to the needs of the time. The official Soviet ideology has been a curious bundle of propositions, inconsistent over time and at any given moment and either flagrantly at variance with the basic elements of Marxian thought or quite irrelevant to it. The function of that ideology was—and still is—to spread a cover of intellectual and moral respectability over whatever action was undertaken and for whatever reason by the Soviet government. As such, it is indeed an "ideology" in the narrow use of the term. It is essentially deceptive, a product of falsehood rather than of "false consciousness"; for in this case to surmise self-deception would certainly constitute an unwarranted insult to the intelligence of Soviet rulers; as it would be to our own, in view of the shameless prevarications that pervade the official pronouncements and the allegedly scholarly writings in Soviet Russia. The official ideology is indeed an ideology in Hilferding's sense. It may have influenced this or that detail in the Soviet economy, such as, for instance, the covert rather than overt use of interest rates. In this way, it may have been a source of economic inefficiencies. But taking the large view, I believe, it is correct to say that neither the great landmarks in Soviet economic history nor the institutional arrangements and the distribution of priorities in the policies pursued were deducible from a pre-existing ideological framework. The official ideology cannot be considered its "determinant."

In the introductory remarks in this contribution, I mentioned the difficulty of paring the economy from the body social of which it is a part. This difficulty is general. But it becomes absolute when dealing with Soviet Russia. For the crucial characteristic of Soviet experience, in my view, has been the primacy of the political factor, that is to say, the interest of the dictatorship in preserving and perpetuating its power. The economy of the country was made subservient to that goal; in other words, it was placed in the service of a power ideology. If Marxian ideas had been taken seriously in Russia, Soviet scholars should have been quick to point out the obvious similarity: The relations between the true ideology of class interest and the attempts to disguise it by false ideologies strictly paralleled the relations between the true power ideology and the false official ideology whose purpose it was to conceal the former. Unfortunately, no one in Soviet Russia is in the position publicly to discourse on the inoperative character of the official ideology; that is, to perform on the so-called Soviet Marxism the job which Hilferding had performed on the orthodox Marxism of the German labor movement. Just as no one in Soviet Russia could point to the obvious analogy between Marx's concept of "fetishism of commodity production" and the hypostatization or reification of the State in Soviet ideology.

The similarity, however, should not obscure an essential difference.

I am not referring to the obvious moral difference between a movement actuated by the desire to improve the economic and social position of an underprivileged group and an oppressive, tyrannical regime. I have something else in mind. The Soviet power ideology, precisely because its carrier has been an all powerful dictatorship, has indeed been a determinant of the Soviet economic system in a way that has no counterpart in the economic history of the West. And the official ideology, protected as it is by the dictatorial monopoly of the printed and spoken word and the servility of thousands and thousands of pens and tongues constitutes the most drastic example on modern record for the dictum of Karl Marx. The ruling ideas in Soviet Russia have been indeed the ideas of the ruling—no, not class—*group*. For the Marxian theory of state always had great difficulty in dealing with dictatorial governments whose power is independent of classes. But this is another matter.

Summing up and using the term "system" with all the hesitation it deserves, I should say that it is only in Soviet Russia where ideology—the concealed power ideology—can be meaningfully and clearly regarded as the determinant of the economic system. By contrast, in capitalism where interests of different classes produced a variety of "true" and "false" ideologies it is impossible to regard any single ideology, be it true or false, as a determinant of the system. The course of economic development there was fashioned by a rich multiplicity of ideologies: laissez-faire and state help, nationalism, various forms of socialist beliefs, feudal interests and ideas, ideas of social protest on the part of labor—they all combined to influence the nature of the complex and not very consistent entity that has been called the capitalist system. And thus the main and altogether unsatisfactory conclusion of this paper is a rather strong disapproval of the title that has been foisted upon its supine author.

Comment

Ideology: Mask, or Nessus Shirt?

by ALBERT O. HIRSCHMAN

Professor Gerschenkron has written in a contrary mood. His contribution might be subtitled "The Author in Search of Six Arguments Against His Title." It occurred to me that the organizers of the symposium should have asked him to expound on "The Irrelevance of Ideology to Economic Systems." In that case, perhaps, he might have adduced a number of richly textured historical illustrations to show that ideologies are indeed largely responsible for moulding economic systems and are the decisive factor for distinguishing one system from another!

Fortunately, however, his destructive stance turns out to be more apparent than real. In the process of pouring his ridicule on the notion that ideology could possibly "determine" any system whatever, Gerschenkron provides us in fact with quite a few generalizations or hypotheses relating ideologies to systems. Instead of commenting on them one by one, I shall make a brief attempt of my own to delineate a possible structure of these relations; an attempt that, as will become evident, ties in with most, if not all, of Gerschenkron's observations.

First a terminological remark. I shall use ideology in the sense of a moderately consistent set of ideas and beliefs arising from within a society and accounting for its socio-economic phenomena and containing also some guidance to action. The question whether these ideas and beliefs are propounded and held sincerely, or whether they are propounded insincerely by intelligent people to be believed sincerely by unintelligent people need not concern us: As Gerschenkron rightly says, it is not ordinarily subject to objective determination. But I do believe that the use of the term ideology should be reserved for beliefs and analyses that are actually articulated by groups *in and of* that society, be they majority or minority, dominant or deviant, ruling or insurgent.

These are wide limits, but when Gerschenkron says, toward the end of his paper, that the Soviet system is "placed in the service of the power ideology," he steps outside them. For what he says is that *he* can account for the economic institutions and policies of the Soviet Union by the unifying hypothesis that the Soviet leadership wishes to maintain its power; but since no one in the Soviet Union has proposed—or has been allowed to propose—this interpretation of Soviet economic reality, it does not qualify as a Soviet ideology at all. It might qualify as "Gerschenkron's ideology" if and only if our friend's analysis were one day to inspire a Russian movement for the reform of the Soviet system.

1. Dominant Versus Insurgent Ideologies

This terminological squabble brings me to a first distinction: that between *official dominant or pro-status-quo* ideologies (Mannheim's Ideology), on the one hand, and *insurgent* or *advocate* ideologies (roughly Mannheim's Utopia), on the other. In the earlier uses of the concept by Marx and his followers, only the former type of ideology was analyzed. The game consisted, as Gerschenkron has indicated, in "unmasking" the ruling ideas as the narrow and self-serving ideas of the ruling class.

Since then, Marxism *has* been applied to Marxism and other revolutionary movements and, in the process, it has become evident that recourse to ideological constructions is even more typical of the "outs" than of the "ins." An explanation is found in the following observations of Clifford Geertz:

> In politics previously embedded in Edmund Burke's golden assemblage of 'ancient opinions and rules of life', the role of ideology . . . is marginal. . . . It is . . . at the point at which a political system begins to free itself from the immediate governance of received tradition, from the direct and detailed guidance of religious and philosophical courses on the one hand and from the unreflective precept of conventional moralism on the other, that formal ideologies tend first to emerge and take hold.[1]

Clearly the "freeing from traditional governance" will be spearheaded by groups that are dissatisfied with the existing order, and therefore ideology is most desperately needed by these groups; it is only in reaction to these insurgent ideologies that attempts will be made by the previously care- and ideology-free rulers to construct conservative ideologies of their own. Or, sometimes, the insurgent ideologue will take it upon himself to put together the previously lacking ruling ideology—this is what Adam Smith did for the Mercantile System[2]—so that he, with his newly baked insurgent ideology, may have a worthwhile adversary (or a strawman) to fight against.

If we look at Gerschenkron's paper in the light of the distinction that has just been made we find that the author chose to deal primarily not with official or pro-status-quo ideologies, but with either insurgent or advocate ideologies, such as the French and Russian industrialization ideologies, the revolutionary phantasies of the German and Austrian Social Democrats, or the constructs of various agricultural or industrial interest groups clamoring for tariff protection in Germany. All these ideologies were fashioned for the purpose of either overthrowing or of substantially altering the existing order. Hence during the period of the ideological assault there is no reason to expect the economic system to reflect the ideology at all. The question is what happens when the movement that is animated by the insurgent ideology achieves partial or total victory. Gerschenkron shows how in some cases victory for the movement leads to the prompt "dismissal" of the very ideology which had given the movement much of its forward momentum. It would be of great interest to specify the circumstances under which ideology is liable to be treated so shabbily. It certainly is not always so. Especially, though by no means exclusively, when the movement that the ideology has helped propel

[1] "Ideology as a Cultural System", in David E. Apter, ed., *Ideology and Discontent*, Glencoe, New York, 1964, pp. 63–64.
[2] Cf. the interpretation of D. C. Coleman in "Eli Heckscher and the Idea of Mercantilism," *Scandinavian Economic History Review*, V: 1 (1957) 4.

achieves a total revolutionary victory, an attempt will be made to recast the world according to the canons of the ideology, so that some overlap between the ensuing system and the ideology is likely. Similarly, ideologies defending the status quo will usually exhibit such an overlap. The problem raised by the title "Ideology as a System Determinant" thus applies properly only to dominant ideologies or to insurgent ideologies that have become partly or wholly dominant.

The relation between dominant ideologies and economic systems is less tenuous and perhaps less capricious, so it seems to me, than a reader of the Gerschenkron paper is led to think, although I do agree that it is highly complex. Of course, an ideology does not define the system in any clear-cut, once-and-for-all fashion, but it does establish taboos, constraints, and biases which have important influences on the nature and the evolutionary path of the economy. Second, the inevitable gap between ideology and reality introduces a tension which itself reacts on both ideology and reality in various distinctive ways which have implications for our problem. I shall make some brief remarks on both matters.

2. Convergence of Systems With Distant Dominant Ideologies?

The most conspicuous, though perhaps not the most important, effect of a dominant ideology is that, as long as it is dominant, it precludes certain choices, such as, say, establishing a social-security system or letting foreigners own the country's basic industries. The extent to which such rules and taboos define a system is subject to doubt, but they certainly define a field beyond which a system is not supposed to move and moves in fact only with great difficulty. At one point in his contribution, Gerschenkron asserts that "the concept of ownership has lost much of the significance that used to be attributed to it." This belittling remark rather invites the classic retort "Vive la petite différence!" Theoretically it is conceivable for the difference between two economies, one with and the other without private property of the means of production (to use the Marxian phrase), to be as small as that between two democratic polities, one with a king and the other with an elected president as head of state; in fact, the differences have remained so important precisely because the taboos on expropriation and on private property, respectively, are strongly grounded in ideology (rather than, as in the case of the king, in respect for tradition). Not only are the taboo measures left out of one's field of vision when it comes to select the most appropriate instruments dealing with the country's problems; the very decision to define a certain situation as a problem that must be tackled and solved often depends on whether the beginning of a solution is already at hand.

Thus, when certain means are taboo the society will hesitate to pursue those ends that have a considerable affinity to the taboo means. In this fashion, ideological taboos can deepen the initial divergence between systems and counteract the tendency toward convergence which might be expected to result from a common—and rapidly evolving—technological environment.

Perhaps more important and pervasive than the absolute taboos imposed by ideology are ideology-motivated preferences for certain ways of handling emerging problems. The search for the solution of these problems will normally start with the most congenial policies or instruments and will then proceed to progressively less congenial ones. Gurley and Shaw have analyzed in just these terms the provision of finance in the course of economic development.[3] They see this course marked by "iterative probing for the optimal combination of saving-investment technologies" but recognize that "the search is guided in part by principle and prejudice," that is by ideology. A centralized planning system has an innate preference for what they call self—or internal—finance which draws mostly on the manipulation of prices charged by state enterprise as well as on taxation, whereas decentralized systems rely as much as possible on external finance, that is, finance external to the investing entity, which is secured through various intermediaries from voluntary savers. They even suggest a "Law of Financial Development" which they formulate as follows: ". . . each economy begins its development by intensive exploitation of a saving-investment technology that is chosen for historical, political, social, or perhaps economic reasons, and then, as this technology produces a diminishing net yield, experiments with alternative technologies that are marginally superior . . ."[4]

Here we have an explanation of the way in which ideology results initially in quite different economic-policy responses, if not totally different systems.

In a similar vein, Andrew Shonfield has noted that ideological differences regarding the appropriate role of the state in the economy have led to widely divergent approaches to economic planning in France, on the one hand, and in the United States and Britain, on the other. Owing to its Colbertian and Napoleonic etatist tradition, so he argues, France has never fully accepted the notion of the strictly limited economic functions of the state, and it therefore embraced the idea of some central guidance of economic decisions not only more readily, but also more pertinently, than the Anglo-Saxon world where laissez-faire, in spite of its French

[3] John G. Gurley and E. S. Shaw, "Financial Structures and Economic Development," *Economic Development and Cultural Change*, XV:3 (1967) 257–268.
[4] *Ibid.*, p. 268.

294 · *Comparative Economic Systems*

sound, has become far more entrenched as ideological dogma.[6] From this point of view, differences in ideology can account for comparative success of different systems in tackling emerging tasks: It is conceivable, for example, that the policies and institutions required to promote the tinkering-intensive stage of technological development are peculiarly congenial to the ideology of one country, while those of another are better suited to the research-and-development-intensive phase. Patterns of uneven or seesaw advance of different countries and systems may be in part explained in this fashion.

At the same time, this sort of reasoning provides of course a rationale for *eventual* convergence of systems with very distant ideologies. It is conceivable that two initially divergent systems increasingly come to resemble each other, as common environmental problems force similar solutions on them. When the move required by the problem happens to be in tune with the ideology, the "immortal principles" will be proudly invoked, while a system moving in the same direction but into a territory uncharted by its ideology will proclaim the need for a pragmatic response to new problems—this is exactly what the United States did during the New Deal.

In practice, however, such convergence of systems with highly distinct ideologies is not very likely, for the logic of the Gurley-Shaw argument makes one suspect that convergence in one area will be paralleled by renewed divergence in another: New problems continually arise and they will presumably again result in initially quite different probing and search patterns on the part of countries owing allegiance to different ideologies. In other words, unless the two antithetical or distinct ideologies themselves converge or are watered down or "dismissed," any lasting convergence of the respective economic systems themselves is not to be expected.

3. The Tension Between Ideology and System and Various Ways of Relieving It

The final topic on which I shall comment briefly is that of the gap between a dominant ideology and the economic reality which the ideology is supposed to shape. Gerschenkron delights in calling attention to these gaps as well as to the internal contradictions of the ideological "superstructures" themselves. His general position appears to be that men are extremely good at taking such inconsistencies in stride. But the matter seems to me too important to be laid to rest by disparaging remarks about human nature. Actually Gerschenkron himself shows that when the disparity between ideology and reality is too embarrassing, the ideology

[5] Andrew Shonfield, *Modern Capitalism*, Oxford, 1965.

may be abandoned outright—as in the case of the Saint-Simonian and Marxian industrialization ideologies in 19th-century France and Russia.

Hence we must distinguish between a number of developments that are possible in the wake of a gap between ideology and reality. In the first place, it is possible that the gap is closed as a result of the abandonment or withering away of the ideology. In this case reality overpowers ideology, even though the ideology may have been partly responsible for the reality, as in the French and Russian cases just mentioned. Occasionally, the ideology agonizes for an extraordinarily long time, at least from the point of view of an outside observer, as in the case of the long-delayed renunciation of orthodox Marxism by the German Social Democrats. But in all these cases, the incongruent ideology finally succumbs.

Are there any counter-examples—situations, that is, in which an economic system which initially bears only a faint resemblance to the ideology which it is supposed to embody, manages eventually to live up to that ideology? In one of his incisive philosophical essays, Kolakowski uses a compelling rhetorical device to convince us of the possibility of such an outcome. He first speaks of ideology in typical Marxian terms as a façade, a mask, or a garment of disguise, but then turns the relationship around while retaining the image of the garment: For he reminds us that in the Greek myth about the death of Hercules, the garment is not torn off or discarded; to the contrary, it clings to him who puts it on and burns him. In Kolakowski's words:

> The façade sometimes begins to live a life of its own, and when it contradicts a system, it produces and nourishes the seeds of the destruction of the system. When an excessive attachment to tradition prevents the system from throwing off this deceptive attire, it may become a Nessus shirt . . . Every social system that assumes a false front cannot help but enter into a pact with the devil who someday will claim his due.[6]

Kolakowski has in mind principally democratic and libertarian values that are first mere façade and eventually take on reality and vitality. But the same could happen with ideological props pertaining to the socio-economic realm such as "equality of economic opportunity" or "the end of exploitation of man by man." In fact, *reform* movements typically request that a country's long professed, but so far woefully unrealized, ideology be finally taken seriously, whereas *revolutionary* movements tend to be animated by a wholly new ideology. One might thus say that a system frequently finds itself in a position in which it faces the choice between either living up to the promises of its own ideology or being destroyed by an insurgent ideology.

[6] Leszek Kolakowski, *Toward a Marxist Humanism*, New York, 1968, pp. 152–153.

Whether a dominant ideology that is at odds with "its" system is finally discarded or whether it eventually makes the system conform more closely to its image, there will obviously be long periods during which the disparity between the ideology and the system will be painfully or ridiculously wide. Certain system-ideology pairs may be particularly disparity-prone in this way. This is for example most likely to be the case for imported or borrowed ideologies which have been so characteristic of politically and economically dependent countries. There is some danger, then, that when the fit between the ideology and "its" system is so poor the ideology will lose much of its function as gadfly. As Octavio Paz, the Mexican poet and essayist, has said in talking about post-Independence politics in Latin American the "lie installed itself almost constitutionally in our countries" so that lies have become "something we move in with ease."[7] Recently I put forward another reason why too great a disparity between ideology and reality may be undesirable as well as self-perpetuating: The urge to adapt the ideology to *changes* in the reality is hardly felt when the fit between the two is very poor to start with.[8] Ideology can here once again be compared to a garment, this time to one that is so ample that it fits the owner equally well or, rather, equally poorly no matter how his shape alters.

Nevertheless, we are often too impatient and eager to denounce and ridicule situations in which a dominant ideology and its system have little in common. Countries have different exigencies of consistency, as a result of differences in history, culture, and, I am tempted to say, ideology. In Latin America a long tradition permits and even requires that the community's unrealized *aspirations* be inscribed in the country's constitution and laws. It is recognized that it will take generations to translate these ideological laws into reality. But when, in the course of these generations, a situation arises in which a step in the ideology's direction can be made, the discovery that it is already the law of the land can be of considerable help.

One often quoted example—there are many others—is the transfer of Brazil's new capital to the interior of the country, a move which had been ordered by an article of the Constitution of 1890. It took more than 60 years for this article to be taken seriously, but it is doubtful that President Kubitschek would have been able to take the decision to build Brasilia without the moral authority derived from that article.

Just as a tolerance for prolonged inconsistency has its uses, so a national passion for consistency may be quite dangerous. For the compulsive need

[7] Octavio Paz, *El laberinto de la soledad*, Cuadernos Americanos, Mexico City, 1959, p. 102.
[8] See my article "Underdevelopment, Obstacles to the Perception of Change, and Leadership" *Daedalus*, XCVII:3 (1968) 931–932.

to conform reality to ideology can proceed along a number of very different lines. For example, when the creed that all men are created equal cohabits with oppression of a minority group the resulting conflict can be resolved either by lifting the oppression or by regarding the members of the minority group as subhuman—and by treating them accordingly. A country not committed to an egalitarian ideology or one that is so committed but is lax about consistency is perhaps less likely to emancipate its minorities; but it is also more likely to treat them humanely pending emancipation.[9]

In sum, ideologies do exert influences and pressures on systems. I have put forward some reasons why dominant ideologies which differ widely from one another may be expected to result in divergent, rather than convergent, systems and have later insisted on situations in which an ideology influences a system even when there appears to be a ridiculously wide gap between the two. This does not mean that the relationship is a simple one. Perhaps the major difficulty of our topic derives from the fact that, as I have said at the outset, the primary function of ideology is to attack, change, or destroy existing systems. Like most of us, it is far better in this role than in that of a builder of a new order.

Reply

by ALEXANDER GERSHENKRON

In replying to Professor Hirschman's Comments, let me first advert to what he chooses to call a "terminological squabble." This refers to his refusal to consider as relevant the concern with the degree of sincerity inherent in ideologies; and, furthermore, to his assertion that it is illegitimate to speak of the Soviet dictatorship as operating in the service of a power ideology. The problem, of course, is not at all a terminological but a methodological one and, in fact, one of the crucial problems of social sciences.

It is a peculiarity of social sciences that the objects of our study (unlike the rock that remains mute to the geologist or mineralogist) continually make statements about themselves. This is a blessing and a curse, a source of both enlightenment and confusion. The task of the social scientist is to separate the meal of truth from the bran of deception. To a very considerable extent, the literature on ideology has been concerned

[9] I am indebted to Professor Davis Potter for raising this point.

precisely with this problem. At the same time, a social scientist cannot confine himself to "unmasking" an ideology as an instrument of deception. He must probe more deeply. Since human action is directed by the brain, that is to say, by ideas, the scholar desirous of understanding social action must try to understand the ideas or the set of ideas, in other words, the ideologies that guide the actions: the true ideologies that are operative but remain hidden behind the façade of the deceptive ones.

It is in the very nature of such ideologies (which fully fit Professor Hirschman's definition) that they are not publicized, but this does not relieve the scholar of the obligation to study them. And the only way to do so, barring believable confessions and revelation of secret documents, is to construct from actual behavior a set of ideas, an ideology, that fits the behavior and explains it in a fashion that satisfies our sense of reasoned adequacy. What I have said about the "true" Soviet ideology may be ᵥdisproved (i.e., demonstrated to be implausible) either by showing that I am wrong in believing that it fits the actual behavior of the Soviet dictatorship, or by showing that such behavior can be equally well or better explained by reference to an alternative ideology. But it cannot be dismissed as a terminological inconsistency, unless one wants to obscure rather than clarify the issue.

It is only because Professor Hirschman fails to understand the methodology and turns away from the substance of the problem that he can, in speaking of "insurgent ideologies," assert that a dismissal of such an ideology after it has achieved "total revolutionary victory" is unlikely to occur. I am not competent to judge historical examples beyond those I have studied, and Professor Hirschman does not offer many such examples to support his generalizations.[1] But the whole history of Soviet Russia— and this surely is the most important case on record—is a story of actual abandonment of Marxian ideology, as I have tried to show in my paper. Professor Hirschman speaks rightly of the "long-delayed renunciation of orthodox Marxism by the German Social-Democratic Party," but he should have added that such a renunciation of Marxism (orthodox or unorthodox) is still missing and long overdue in the case of Soviet Bolshevism.

I have no desire to quarrel here with his distinction between ideologies that support and ideologies that oppose the status-quo. But he is quite wrong in saying that I have dealt in my paper only with the second type of

---

[1] I may refer, however, to one of his historical references: He speaks of Colbertian and Napoleonic traditions as having created an etatist ideology in France and influenced policies there in contrast to the laissez-faire ideology in England; he should have, however, looked at the history of factory legislation in the two countries before drawing his fallacious conclusion.

ideologies. I have devoted several pages in my paper to the Junker-inspired protectionist anti-industrial ideology. Its purpose was to perpetuate the economic and social position of the Prussian Junkers. When Professor Hirschman expressly includes that ideology among those "fashioned for the purpose of either overthrowing or of substantially altering the existing order," he must forgive me for saying that I do not know what he means and doubt that he does.

For the rest, I am happy to see him say in the concluding two sentences of his Comments: "Perhaps the major difficulty of our topic derives from the fact that, as I have said from the outset, the primary function of ideology is to attack, change, or destroy existing systems. Like most of us, it is far better in this role than in that of a builder of a new order," or, in other words, *than as a determinant of an economic system.* This is one way of stating what I have argued in my paper, and I naturally welcome this crucial admission of my critic.

10

"Eastern" Approaches to a Comparative Evaluation of Economic Systems

by ALEXANDER ERLICH

1. Introduction

This is a survey of changes in the comparative evaluation of capitalism and socialism by the "Eastern" school of Marxism over the half-century of its existence. The presentation begins with a brief summary of Marx' and Engels' views on the subject as the starting point. It moves on to modifications introduced by Lenin and to further departures made by Stalin, and ends with the discussion of the post-1953 developments in Soviet and East European economic thought.

A few words of added explanation may be in order. The term "Eastern" is used as synonymous with "Leninist": This eliminates such a towering figure of East European Marxism as Rosa Luxemburg, and precludes a systematic treatment of the ideas of Michal Kalecki and Oskar Lange; the latter two, however, are mentioned in the discussion of the post-Stalinist period when some of the most distinguished theoretical work in the East European area bore the mark of their influence. The lack of extensive references (and sometimes even of fleeting ones) to important intramural discussions such as, e.g., the industrialization debate of the 1920s or the Varga controversy of the late 1940s is harder to justify within the self-imposed limits of the paper; it is due simply to the limitations of space. The same reason accounts for the absence of a separate section on Eastern views of underdeveloped countries and for the exceedingly compressed discussion of the post-Stalin period. The author regrets these omissions and overcondensations; he hopes that nevertheless the overall picture that emerges is not seriously distorted.

2. The "Classical" Position: A Thumbnail Sketch

Socialism, as understood by Marx and Engels, is defined by predominantly public ownership of means of production and centrally planned allocation of resources. The major economic objectives of the system organized along these lines are, baldly stated, high and rising levels of economic abundance based on a rapid growth of the "productive forces," macroeconomic stability, smooth adjustment between the composition of output and the pattern of social wants, an end of economic inequality through abolition of class division, and a gradual loosening of ties between reward and work performance.

The above institutional data and the diverse goals are viewed as interlinked in several ways. Public ownership is a *sine qua non* for planning because it makes the whole economy one large decision unit. On the other hand, a comparatively high level of development of productive forces is taken to be a precondition for both. Central planning cannot function effectively unless the bulk of the output of various industries comes from a relatively small number of big plants operating on the basis of a fairly standardized and "calculable" modern technology. (The last point was not, to my knowledge, stated by Marx and Engels in so many words, but it is implicit in many pronouncements of their followers and seems definitely consistent with the spirit of the original doctrine.) At the same time only large-scale plants are assumed to be suited for public ownership because their productive activities are already "socialized" insofar as they constitute component parts of a large interdependent whole and are being carried out by teams of workers rather than by individuals. The case for a take-over is assumed to be stronger still whenever not merely labor but also management has been effectively separated from ownership, and is regarded as compelling whenever "means of production and distribution have actually outgrown the forms of management by joint-stock companies"; in such situations "the official representative of capitalist society—the state—will ultimately have to undertake direction of production" by converting to state property the respective areas of the economy.[1] Furthermore, a high level of economic development is an indispensable precondition for social equality; otherwise the abolition of classes would result in retrogression.[2] An even higher degree of affluence must be attained in order to sever the

[1] F. Engels, "Socialism: Utopian and Scientific," in K. Marx and F. Engels, *Selected Works in Two Volumes*, Moscow, 1962, II, 147.

[2] Cf. F. Engels, "On Social Relations in Russia," *ibid.*, pp. 48–49. The underlying reasoning is made explicit elsewhere: "So long as the total social labor only yields a product which but slightly exceeds that barely necessary for the existence of all; so long, therefore, as labor engages all or almost all the time of the great majority of the members of society—so long, of necessity, this society is divided into classes." (F. Engels, "Socialism," *op. cit.*, p. 151.)

A different and less urbanely worded interpretation of the link between the development level and class differentiation can be found in early Marx: "This development of productive forces ... is absolutely necessary as a practical precondition [for communism] for the reason that without it only want is made general, and with penury the struggle for necessities and all the old crap would necessarily reappear." (*The German Ideology*, New York, 1939, p. 24.)

connection between the worker's share in total net product and his labor input; the standard reference here is *Critique of the Gotha Programme.*

Thus far we have spoken about the level of economic development that must obtain in order to make the socialist economic system work. Actually, of course, Marx was putting forward a much stronger claim: Given the "right" level of development, socialism would be not merely feasible but decisively superior to capitalism which would prove increasingly incapable of mastering the stupendous productive forces it had generated, "like the sorcerer who is no longer able to control the powers of the nether world whom he had called up by his spells."[3] At this turn, feedback relationships between the key variables of the system become apparent. Central planning could eliminate massive waste of resources in recurrent depressions and the partial imbalance insofar as both kinds of disturbances are a product of the "anarchy of production" in an uncontrolled market economy: As a result, growth would be powerfully accelerated. At the same time, the more deep-seated causes of the macroeconomic instability could be successfully attacked. Public ownership will make the economy impervious to the downward trends in the rate of profit (or rather in that of its noncapitalist counterpart), and the egalitarian redistribution of income, coming in the wake of socialization, will do away with the "poverty and restricted consumption of the masses" which is "the last cause of all real crises."[4] Moreover, public ownership will be able to open up untapped sources of productivity by changing the prevalent attitudes toward work and by "guaranteeing to all the free development and exercise of their physical and mental faculties."[5]

The reasoning behind these general propositions is familiar, and so are the difficulties involved in it. Let us recall Professor Joan Robinson's critique of the "law of the falling rate of profit" and her demonstration that as long as capitalists, in conformity with Marx' assumptions, are fully reinvesting their savings, the "restricted consumption of the masses" need not pose a threat to the economic stability of the system; indeed, it should be viewed as a corollary of sustained and high-powered growth. If these relics of Say's law were eliminated by infusion of Keynesian analysis, and if a more defensible explanation of diminishing returns to investment were brought in, the argument would be strengthened. But it would still remain true that the Marxian notion of capitalism's becoming a fetter on further development of productive forces should not be interpreted as a prophesy of inevitable breakdown or of continual contraction. The dialectics of capitalist development cuts both ways.

[3] "Manifesto of the Communist Party," *Selected Works,* I, 39.
[4] *Capital,* Chicago, 1909, III, 568.
[5] F. Engels, "Socialism," *op. cit.,* p. 153.

"There are no permanent crises":[6] A slump begets an upswing just as an upswing begets a slump, and while the fluctuations of the business cycle are expected to increase in severity, the long-run trend of development is assumed to point upward, largely because of the system's ability to create powerful inducements for technological progress in times of triumph as well as in times of adversity.[7] Also the prediction of progressive impoverishment of the workers is (except for the early writings) less unqualified than one might gather from the tenor of the usually cited passages; the possibility of an increase in real wages is explicitly acknowledged,[8] and, on a more general plane, the "absolute general law of capitalist accumulation" according to which the "industrial reserve army" steadily grows as a share of the total labor force, is said to be "like all other laws, modified in its working by many circumstances, the analysis of which does not concern us here."[9] Lastly, the position with regard to micro-economic problems is likewise double-edged. Marx had no doubt that "wastes of social labor" as a result of the production of particular commodities in excess of demand would be avoided in a planned economy.[10] He was at the same time at pains to stress that the market mechanism *is* a vehicle, even though a highly imperfect one, for the eventual equilibration; and although he had serious reservations about what present-day economists would call the "static efficiency" of capitalism, he was emphatic about its "dynamic efficiency"—witness the much quoted passage from Volume III of *Capital* about "the general competitive struggle and the necessity of improving the product and expanding the scale of production for the sake of self-preservation and under the penalty of failure"[11] as powerful promoters of growth.

Two points of a rather different nature must be mentioned in order to round out our overview:

1. Marx saw the economy as operating within a definite structure of

[6] K. Marx, *Theories of Surplus Value*, New York, 1952 p. 373.

[7] "The present stagnation of production would have prepared an expansion of production later on, within capitalist limits . . . The same vicious circle would be described once more under expanded conditions of production, in an expanded market, and with increased productive forces." (*Capital*, III, 299.)

"If the rate of profit falls, there follows . . . an exertion of capital, in order that the capitalist may be enabled [through the use of better methods] to depress the individual value of his commodities below the social average level and thereby realize an extra profit at the prevailing market prices." (*Ibid.*, pp. 303–304; the half-sentence in square brackets was omitted in the English translation.) In periods of prosperity it is the increasing scarcity of labor that produces the strongest single inducement for innovation. Cf. *Capital*, I, Ch. XXV, *passim*.

[8] Cf. *Capital*, I, 662.

[9] *Ibid.*, p. 707.

[10] *Ibid.*, III, 221.

[11] *Ibid.*, p. 287.

class relationships which produce ideological and institutional defenses on both sides of the battle lines. It has been often assumed that the existence of these "superstructures" which tend to acquire a staying power of their own introduces added rigidity into the situation and makes the process of socio-economic change more explosive than it might have been otherwise. This interpretation, although containing a large element of truth, does less than justice to the full range of Marxian perception. Suffice it to mention Engels' remark that when antagonistic classes are stalemated, the state can temporarily acquire a measure of independence and assume the role of a quasi-impartial arbitrator.[12] But even the much-quoted and seemingly dogmatic statement of the *Manifesto* ("the modern state power is but a committee for managing the common affairs of the whole bourgeoisie")[13] implicitly points to the state's function as an integrator of, and mediator between, diverse interests of various groups or individual members of the capitalist class—a point spelled out very clearly in Marx' earlier writings. As a result, the bourgeois state can every now and then put across policies which go against the grain of its individual constituents although they are in keeping with their long-term collective interests. As Professor Joan Robinson pointed out, this was the way in which Marx interpreted the contemporaneous factory legislation.[14]

2. We have been concerned in our presentation with economic goals only. Obviously enough, Marx had a major non-economic goal—end of human alienation defined as the state of affairs in which "man's own deed becomes an alien power opposed to him, which enslaves him instead of being controlled by him."[15]

All considerations set forth until now were subordinated to this over-arching objective. It was not merely a figure of speech when Marx described the communist society of the future as a "community of free individuals (*Verein freier Menschen*) carrying on their work with the means of production in common" or "an association in which a free development of each is the condition for the free development of all."[16] Although freedom ranked highest in Marx' system of values, its realization was clearly dependent on attainment of certain economic preconditions.[17] Here, too, a modicum of interaction was assumed to exist—note

[12] F. Engels, "Origin of Family, Private Property and State," *Selected Works,* II, 320–321.

[13] *Op. cit.,* p. 36.

[14] J. Robinson, "Marx, Marshall and Keynes," in her *Collected Economic Papers,* Oxford, 1960, II, 8.

[15] *German Ideology, op. cit.,* p. 22.

[16] *Capital,* I, 90; *Manifesto, op. cit.,* p. 54.

[17] "In fact, the real of freedom begins . . . where labor under compulsion of necessity and of external purposiveness ends. In the very nature of things it lies

306 · *Comparative Economic Systems*

Marx' reference to the "all-around development of the individual" as one of the mainsprings of economic growth in the communist society.[18] It was this attitude of Marx which made some of his orthodox and unorthodox followers unwilling to see in public ownership and central planning a sufficient condition for considering an economy socialist—a disinclination fully shared by this writer.

3. Lenin: the Old and the New

It is generally known that interpretation of Marxian fundamentals by Lenin underwent major changes over the 30-odd years of his political life and resulted in substantial departures from the original. However, it is not always realized that the incidence of innovations was quite uneven; and also in the areas in which amendments were most pronounced, there was an evident determination to link the new and the old as closely as possible.

The analysis of the economic performance of capitalism showed least novelty in its basic orientation; it reflected faithfully the flaws as well as the strengths of the inherited doctrine. In his early discussion of the "problem of markets," for example, Lenin reproduced the familiar Marxian ambiguity; if anything, he compounded it by some backing and filling of his own. He repeatedly characterized capitalism as "a contradiction between the drive towards unlimited expansion of production and limited consumption." But he roundly denied that Marx ever explained crises as due to under-consumption, although Marx did this quite explicitly, even if not very convincingly and consistently.[19] He cast further doubt on the operational significance of the whole problem by observing that "this disparity [between production and consumption] is expressed (as Marx has demonstrated in his schemes) by the fact that the production of the means of production can and must outstrip the production of the articles of

---

beyond the sphere of material production in the strict meaning of the term . . . . The freedom in this field cannot consist of anything else but of the fact that socialized man, the associated producers, regulate their interchange with nature rationally, bring it under their common control, instead of being ruled by it as by some blind power; that they accomplish their task with the least expenditure of energy and under conditions most adequate of their human nature and most worthy of it. But it always remains a realm of necessity. Beyond it begins that development of human faculties which is an end in itself, the true realm of freedom, which however can flourish only upon that realm of necessity as its basis. The shortening of the working day is the fundamental premise." (*Capital*, III, 954–955.)

[18] "Critique of Gotha Programme," *Selected Works*, II, 24.

[19] "The Development of Capitalism in Russia," *Collected Works* (4th ed., Moscow, 1960), III, 58.

consumption;[20] and he emphatically denied that the capitalist drive to conquer foreign markets had anything to do with the lack of outlets at home.[21] Moreover (to mention a different but not unrelated matter), Lenin insisted that Marx did not propound a theory of absolute immiseration: "he spoke of the growth of poverty, degradation, etc., [while] indicating at the same time the counteracting tendency, and the social forces that could give rise to this tendency."[22] True, the wartime pamphlet on imperialism shows a perceptible shift in position. "Semi-starvation level of existence of the masses" is now flatly declared to be one of the main factors that restrict the investment opportunities in developed capitalist countries and thereby help to generate the expansionist outward push.[23] In spite of this bow to the underconsumptionist view, the old double-edged approach persists and reaches its climax in the statement that although imperialism should be viewed as a parasitic or decaying capitalism, "it would be a mistake to believe that this tendency to decay precludes the rapid growth of capitalism." Indeed, we are told that "on the whole, capitalism is growing far more rapidly than before";[24] this is likely to happen, *inter alia* because "the export of capital influences and greatly accelerates the development of capitalism in those countries to which [capital] is exported"; (on the other hand, this capital export "may tend to a certain extent to arrest development in capital-exporting countries.")[25] The whole argument which gives foreign investment a high

[20] "Reply to Mr. Nezhdanov," *ibid.*, IV, 162.

[21] "The need for a capitalist country to have a foreign market is not determined at all by the laws of the realization of the social product (and of surplus value in particular) . . . ." *Op. cit.*, p. 65.

[22] "Review of Karl Kautsky, *Bernstein und das sozialdemokratische Programm: eine Antikritik,*" *ibid.*, IV, 201.

[23] "Imperialism, the Highest Stage of Capitalism," *ibid.*, XXII, p. 241. The motives behind Lenin's permutations were presumably self-serving. He was undoubtedly disturbed by some specific uses to which the underconsumption thesis could be, or actually was, put by his ideological adversaries at one time or another—proving the impossibility of capitalist development in Russia (Populists); arguing in favor of a "high-wage economy" as benefiting workers and capitalists alike (Bernsteinian "revisionists"); expecting capitalism to collapse quasi-automatically on purely economic grounds which would tend to downgrade the importance of a highly maneuverable vanguard party as a leader by putting a higher premium on "spontaneity" at the expense of "consciousness" (Rosa Luxemburg). In his capacity of a *homo politicus* playing for keeps, Lenin must have felt more secure by removing the potentially dangerous mine once and for all rather than by trying to defuse it in a more subtle manner. By the same token, he had no compunction about shifting gears when the need to make a strong case for the "inevitability" of imperialism became a paramount consideration. All this, to be sure, is highly speculative.

[24] *Ibid.*, p. 300.

[25] *Ibid.*, p. 241.

rating for its impact on economic development of the backward areas while forcefully stressing its exploitative aspects is fully in line with Marx' treatment of the problem.[26]

It was likewise in keeping with the spirit of the received tradition when Lenin claimed that as a result of the transition from competition to monopoly "the motive force of technical and consequently of all other progress disappears to a certain extent," but was quick to add that "the possibility of reducing the cost of production and increasing profits by introducing technical improvements operates in the direction of change," and that the "process of technical invention and improvement becomes socialized," which clearly implied that it can develop on a much larger scale and hence be more effective than ever.[27]

No doubt, the main thrust of the analysis pointed to powerful centrifugal forces generated by capitalist imperialism which would push it through the sequence of wars and revolutions to the ultimate demise. But genuine respect for the economic dynamism of the system is very much in evidence; and the assertion that monopoly capitalism is able "to bribe certain sections of the workers, and for a time a fairly considerable minority of them"[28] is an added tribute to its resourcefulness. Lastly, Lenin's views on the nature of a capitalist state were more simplistic than those of Marx and Engels and made no allowance for situations in which such a state could be something other than a servant of the ruling class; this did not prevent him from giving some of these "servants" high marks for their ability to mobilize and control the productive resources of their societies in times of war and to use for that purpose the organizational machinery of the monopolies. Suffice it to mention his evaluation of the German war economy to which we shall be referring again before long.

The major breakthrough occurred in a different problem area. The essentials of the story are familiar and on the face of it, straightforward. As the leader and chief ideologist of the victorious anticapitalist revolution in a backward country Lenin decisively departed, and had to depart, from the notion that a highly developed economy is a necessary precondition

[26] Cf. his "British Rule in India" and "Failure Results of the British Rule in India," *Selected Works*, vol. I, and, more particularly, the following passage: "All the English bourgeoisie may be forced to do [in India] will neither emancipate nor materially mend the social condition of the mass of the people, depending not only on the development of the productive powers, but on their appropriation by the people. But what they will not fail to do is to lay down the material premises for both. Has the bourgeoisie ever done more? Has it ever effected a progress without dragging individuals and peoples through blood and dirt, through misery and degradation?" (p. 356).

[27] *Op. cit.*, pp. 276, 205.
[28] *Ibid.*, p. 301.

for planning and public ownership—a proposition which, it will be recalled, constituted one of the first principles of classical Marxism and which had, prior to 1917, no defenders more unflinching and dedicated than Lenin himself. The most succinct statement of the changed position is contained in the following paragraph of one of his last articles: "If a definite level of culture is required for the building of socialism (although nobody can say just what this level of culture is, for it differs in every West European country), why cannot we begin by first achieving the prerequisites for that definite level of culture in a revolutionary way, and *then*, with the aid of the workers' and peasants' government and the Soviet system, proceed to catch up with other nations?"[29] Yet an examination of the underlying argument would reveal that even here elements of continuity were by no means absent; and the uneasy co-existence of the old and the new was reflected in Lenin's attitude toward issues of our immediate concern.

To begin with, there is no doubt that antecedents of the post-1917 Lenin could be found in Marx. We have in mind the *Communist Manifesto's* assumption that the proletariat could come to power in a relatively un-developed country and that one of its major tasks would then be "to centralize all instruments of production in the hands of the State . . . and to increase the total of the productive forces as rapidly as possible."[30] Furthermore, Marx repeatedly stressed the active role of the "super-structure" in breaking the logjams at the "base"; one might quote his remark about force as economic power,[31] and the telling passage about "crutches" which rising capitalism borrows from its predecessors and then throws away after having grown stronger.[32] It is likewise evident, how-ever, that after the last echoes of 1848 had died down, Marx and Engels no longer anticipated "premature" proletarian seizures of power and were quite forthright about it.[33]

[29] "Our Revolution (Apropos of N. Sukhanov's *Notes*)," *ibid.*, XXXIII, 478–479.
[30] "Manifesto," *op. cit.*, p. 53. The quoted passage contains no reference to any particular stage of development. However, several pages later we are told that "the Communists turn their attention chiefly to Germany, because that country is on the eve of a bourgeois revolution . . . , and because the bourgeois revolution in Germany will be but the prelude to an immediately following proletarian revolution." Yet, as Marx and Engels stressed time and time again, the Germany of 1848 was not the most advanced country of Europe.
[31] *Capital*, I, 824.
[32] Cf. his *Grundrisse der Kritik der Politischen Oekonomie* Berlin, 1953, p. 544.
[33] "History has proved us, and all those who thought like us, wrong. It has made it clear that the state of economic development on the Continent at that time was not, by a long way, ripe for elimination of capitalist production." (Engels' introduction to Marx' "The Class Struggles in France 1848 to 1850," *Selected Works*, I, 125.)

Yet the author of the new strategy was by no means overconfident about his "agonizing reappraisal". In the remarks immediately preceding the quoted passage, Lenin put the case squarely in terms of the uniqueness of the political situation in Russia in 1917: A "combination of a 'peasant war' and working-class movement" in conditions of stunning military defeats created an exceptional set of opportunities which a revolutionary party worthy of its salt could not afford to pass up.[34] But although he berated his Social Democratic opponents for their unwillingness to recognize the 1917 scenario as an exception confirming the rule, he did not deny that some of the fundamental facets of the standard case were disturbingly present in the Russian situation as well: "The heroes of the Second International" did state an "incontrovertible proposition" when they insisted that "the development of productive forces of Russia has not attained the level that makes socialism possible."[35] To be sure, there was one obvious way out of the dilemma: A revolution in the industrially developed countries of the West could help to bridge the gap between the advanced socio-political "super-structure" of the Bolshevik Russian economy and its wretched "base." As Lenin repeatedly stressed, this had been his fervent hope on the eve of November 1917 and immediately thereafter.[36] Even then it was no more than a hope. In order to be able to hold out in expectation of rescue over a time period which could prove to be quite long, a realistic strategy was needed, and a host of fateful questions had to be resolved. Is there a level of economic development that could be regarded as a minimum prerequisite for a move toward socialism? What extent of socialization, scope of planning, and speed of economic growth are called for in order to bring the economy closer to the desired conformity between the relations of production and the character of productive forces? Presenting Lenin's answers in their full complexity would take us too far afield. But the broad contours of his position must be outlined nevertheless:

a) Lenin clearly replied in the affirmative to the first question when he observed (in a comment jotted down on the margins of Bukharin's *Economy of the Period of Transition*) that "without a certain level of capitalist development we would not have gotten anywhere."[37] More

[34] Cf. *op. cit.*, p. 478.

[35] *Ibid.*

[36] "It was clear to us that without the support of the international world revolution the victory of the proletarian revolution was impossible. Before the revolution, and even after it, we thought: Either revolution breaks out in the other countries, in the capitalistically more developed countries, immediately, or at least very quickly, or we must perish." ("Report on the Tactics of the R.C.P. to the Third Congress of the Communist International," *ibid.*, XXXII, 480.)

[37] "Zamechaniia na knigu N. I. Bukharina: 'Ekonomika perekhodnogo perioda,'" in *Leninskii sbornik* (N. I. Bukharin, V. M. Molotov, M. A. Savel'ev, eds.), Moscow, 1929, XI, 397.

concretely, "without large-scale mechanized production, without a more or less developed network of railroads, communications, educational establishments, it is quite certain that none of these two tasks [accounting and control over production, and rise in labor productivity] could be solved systematically and on a nationwide scale. Russia is in a situation when quite a few basic prerequisites of such a transition [to socialism] are present."[38]

b) Regarding the pace of the socialization in conditions of relative underdevelopment it was Marx and Engels of the *Manifesto* who first flashed the "go-slow" signal: In the very paragraph that urged the prospective revolutionary government to develop the productive forces "as rapidly as possible," they advised it "to wrest, by degrees, all capital from the bourgeoisie," and put forward a tentative ten-point program which faithfully reflected this spirit of gradualism. Lenin was, if anything, even more circumspect. On the eve of November 1917 he intended to nationalize only the banks and industrial cartels; moreover, it seems reasonable to assume that he had in mind tight controls rather than seizure of privately owned savings deposits and productive assets; the latter was to be used only as the ultimate measure of retribution for acts of economic disobedience.[39] But also after the logic of escalating social conflict had pushed the Soviet regime toward outright and wide-ranging expropriation of capitalist property, Lenin was outspoken in urging restraint. To his left-wing critics who called for "a most determined socialization policy . . . to put down the sabotage completely," he retorted that "today only a blind man could fail to see that we have nationalized, confiscated, beaten down and put down more than we have had time to count."[40] He derided his opponents for their reluctance to recognize that in a predominantly small-peasant country, "state capitalism" (an umbrella term covering all kinds of state-controlled activities of private entrepreneurs and cooperatives in the modern sector of the economy) would be a potent force for progress;[41] and he restated the argument with added

[38] *Polnoe sobraniie sochinenii* (5th edition), Moscow, 1967, XXXVI, 131.

[39] ". . . Whoever had fifteen million rubles [in a saving account] would continue after the nationalization of the banks to have fifteen million rubles . . . War must be declared on the oil barons and shareholders, the confiscation of their property and punishment by imprisonment must be decreed for delaying the nationalization of the oil business, for concealing incomes or accounts, for sabotaging production, and for failing to take steps to increase production." ("The Impending Catastrophe and How to Combat It," *op. cit.*, XXV, 330, 337.)

[40] "The Left-Wing Childishness and the Petty-Bourgeois Mentality," *ibid.*, XXVII, 334.

[41] "Is it not clear that the specific nature of the present situation creates the need for a specific type of 'buying out' which the workers must offer to the most cultured, the most skilled, the most capable organizers among the capitalists who are ready to enter the service of Soviet power and to help honestly in organizing 'state' production on the largest possible scale?" (*Ibid.*, p. 345.)

emphasis in the last years of his life while explaining the transition from "War Communism" to the "New Economic Policy" (NEP) which involved, among others, a measure of denationalization and a strong bid for foreign investment. Indeed, in that period Lenin was clearly prepared to loosen the reins of state control over the private sector and to put up with capitalism pure and simple both as a short run device for reversing the process of economic disintegration and as a valuable, if expensive, training program in modern economic management.[42]

c) Although Lenin favored gradualism in matters of nationalization, he was categoric in stressing the need for an extensive system of direct controls as one of the first orders of business. There can be no doubt that in the fateful years 1917–1921 Lenin viewed economic planning first and foremost as a huge emergency operation aimed at arresting the process of shrinkage and dislocation generated by World War I and later by the civil war: " . . . control, supervision, and accounting" were to him "the prime requisites for combating catastrophe and famine" because they would make possible "husbanding of people's forces, the elimination of all wasteful effort, the economy of effort" by "introduction of a proper distribution of labor power in the production and distribution of goods."[43] It was economics of besieged fortress writ large, with the wartime Imperial Germany as an organizational model to be emulated and with the Russian backwardness as well as the unparalleled intensity of Russian internal conflict powerfully adding to the urgency of the task; this was the meaning of the much-quoted words—"to perish or to forge full speed ahead."[44] Yet here too, some of the fundamental constraints, articulated in the classical Marxian notion of the interrelation between the productive forces and the forms of economic organization, asserted themselves with a

[42] "All . . . must be set going in order to stimulate exchange between industry and agriculture at all costs. Those who achieve the best results in this sphere, even by means of private capitalism, even without cooperatives, or without directly transforming this capitalism into state capitalism, will do more for the cause of socialist construction in Russia than those who 'ponder over' the purity of communism, draw up rules and instructions for state capitalism and the cooperatives, but do nothing practical to stimulate trade." ("The Tax in Kind," *ibid.*, XXXII, 354.)

"You will have capitalists beside you, including foreign capitalists, concessionaires and leaseholders. They will squeeze profits out of you amounting to hundreds per cent; they will enrich themselves, operating alongside of you. Let them. Meanwhile you will learn from them the business of running the economy, and only when you do that will you be able to build up a communist republic . . . And we must undergo this training, this severe, stern and sometimes even cruel training, because we have no other way out." ("The New Economic Tasks and the Tasks of the Political Education Departments," *ibid.*, XXXIII, 71–72.)

[43] "The Impending Catastrophe," *ibid.*, XXV, 324.

[44] *Ibid.*, p. 364.

vengeance and brought the breath-taking escalation of the "War Communist" methods to a grinding halt. Lenin conceded this with utmost candor: "Borne along on the crest of the wave of enthusiasm . . . we expected—or perhaps it would be truer to say that we presumed without having given it adequate consideration—to be able to organize the state production and the state distribution of products on communist lines in a small-peasant country directly as ordered by the proletarian state. Experience has proved that we were wrong."[45] He went beyond this admission, and broke distinctly new ground when he continued: "Not directly relying on enthusiasm, but aided by the enthusiasm engendered by the great revolution, and on the basis of personal interest, personal incentive and business principles, we must first set to work in this small-peasant country to build solid gangways to socialism by way of state capitalism. Otherwise we shall never get to communism." In a later pronouncement he made it crystal-clear that these "business principles" would not merely govern the exchange between industry and the millions of independent peasant producers but would strongly affect the economic operation within the public sector as well.[46] Although the implied acceptance of co-existence between central planning and the market constituted a momentous departure from the orthodoxy, it reflected a painful compromise imposed by backwardness and crushing poverty but not a change of heart. "State production and state distribution of products on communist lines" clearly remained a goal for the future.

d) Concerning the rate of economic growth under the Soviet system, Lenin was reticent. He firmly upheld the fundamental Marxian proposition that the "expropriation [of capitalists] will make it possible for the productive forces to develop to a tremendous extent."[47] And in one of his last articles he expressed the belief that if the civil war had not interfered, the Soviet economy would have been able right from the start "to develop the productive forces with enormous speed [and] to develop all the potentialities which, taken together, would have produced socialism."[48] But whenever he went beyond generalities and discussed the Soviet situation as it actually was and not as it might have been, he struck a different note. In the fall of 1917, as we have seen, he was primarily concerned about averting collapse. During the brief interval between the conclusion of peace with Germany and the beginning of the full-scale civil war repairing the damage appeared as the chief economic task.[49] In 1921,

[45] "Fourth Anniversary of the October Revolution" *ibid.*, XXXIII, 58.
[46] Cf. "The Role and Functions of the Trade Unions Under the New Economic Policy," *ibid.*, p. 185.
[47] "State and Revolution," *ibid.*, XXV, 468.
[48] "Better Fewer but Better," *ibid.*, XXXIII, 498.
[49] "Variant statii," p. 131.

finally, with the civil war won and the process of recovery under way, he kept insisting that the progress was bound to be slow unless and until a major change should occur in the international environment,[50] and that "owing to the present circumstances, the whole world is developing faster than we are."[51] True, Lenin repeatedly pointed to the opportunities for technological and organizational borrowing from advanced countries. Yet he strongly implied (in the paragraph from which the last-quoted sentence was lifted) that such a borrowing was possible only at a high cost; and while he stressed that this cost could be greatly reduced by generous help from outside coming in the wake of the victory of socialism in the West, he clearly viewed it as an increasingly remote prospect. Hence when Lenin outlined in bold strokes his vision of the modernized and industrialized Russia of the future, he remained silent about the pace at which he expected to advance toward this goal; but the few remarks he did make about the preconditions of such advance (retaining the confidence of the peasants, removing "all traces of extravagance" from the state apparatus) clearly pointed toward moderation.[52]

One might summarize Lenin's overall appraisal of Soviet economic performance by recalling Marx' often-quoted observation that the communist society would be, in its initial stage, "stamped in every respect, economically, morally and intellectually, with the birthmarks of the old society from whose womb it emerges."[53] The Soviet system, as Lenin saw it, was stamped, in addition, with marks of its economically premature birth. The classical Marxian package in which the appropriately high level of technology would firmly sustain the socialist economic structure and make for a smooth interaction of the component parts of the latter as well as for their wholesome feedback effects on the base had to be untied in the Soviet case. As the performer of the operation candidly admitted, its economic cost was high. The product that emerged was not only inferior to the Marxian "ideal type" of socialism; it lagged in efficiency behind its capitalist predecessor and could survive only at a price of uneasy accommodation with its remnants. Besides, the chances within the foreseeable future of breaking out of this position of relative weakness and thereby

[50] "The growth of the productive forces can and must be achieved . . . Here we cannot achieve our aims as quickly as we were able to in the political and military fields. Here we cannot proceed by leaps and bounds, and the periods involved are different —they are reckoned in decades. These are the periods in which we shall have to achieve successes in the economic war, in conditions of hostility instead of assistance from our neighbors." (*Ibid.*, XXXIII, 161.)

[51] "The New Economic Policy and the Tasks of the Political Education Departments," *ibid.*, p. 72.

[52] Cf. "Better Fewer but Better," *ibid.*, p. 501.

[53] "Critique of Gotha Programme," *Selected Works*, I, 23.

overcoming the instability inherent in the "in-between" situation were dim.

Yet this was clearly not the whole story. On the one hand, Lenin succeeded in turning calamity into a source of strength. He pointed out that the "bourgeois" material incentives could, within an appropriate institutional framework, be utilized for worthy social ends; he demonstrated that a recovery in the traditional sector of the economy could spill over into the modern sector; more generally, he showed how putting up with a plurality of socioeconomic settings could, if skillfully handled, achieve greater results in advancing toward socialism than a simpler method of frontal attack. But at the same time he could respond with exultant hope to real or alleged opportunities for dramatic breakthroughs such as self-sacrificing efforts of the small groups of "Communist subbotniks,"[54] or ambitious schemes of electrification.[55] Last but not least, for all his flexibility and his readiness to learn by doing, there was behind every turn and twist of the policy the same emphasis on the "absolute and strict unity of will,"[56] to be ensured by "thousands subordinating their will to the will of one," and the unbending resolve "to fight barbarism with barbarous means."[57] It is therefore not surprising that Lenin could, and did, mean different things to different people at different times although some of these interpretations have been definitely less justified than others as we will see presently.

4. Stalin

Contrary to the claims of the pre-1956 Soviet hagiography, Stalin did not simply take over where Lenin left off. He was definitely not one of the leading figures in the great debate of the mid-1920s in which basic issues of Soviet economic policy were submitted to searching scrutiny, and whenever he did speak up, he showed little originality. His distinctive position emerged around 1928 and was stated most fully in his *Economic Problems of Socialism in the U.S.S.R.* a quarter of a century later. In observations that follow we will primarily draw on this source as well as on the official Soviet textbook of political economy which appeared after Stalin's death but was impeccably Stalinist in spirit.

With regard to capitalism, the pronouncements by Stalin and his

[54] Cf. "A Great Beginning," *ibid.*, XXIX, 409–434.
[55] Cf. "Report on the Work of the All-Russia Central Executive Committee," *ibid.*, XXX, 334–336, and repeatedly afterward.
[56] "The Immediate Tasks of the Soviet Government," *ibid.*, XXVII, 268.
[57] "Left-wing Childishness," *ibid.*, p. 340.

.......wers contain several unmistakable departures from received views, all ritualistic genuflections notwithstanding:

a) The underconsumptionist component is definitely stronger than in Lenin's early writings and more articulated than in *Imperialism*. The causes of economic crises are seen in the "contradiction between the colossal growth in the productive potentialities of capitalism . . . and the relative decline in the effective demand on the part of the millions of the working people."[58] If anything, the reference to a *relative* decline in effective demand seems like an understatement in view of the unreserved acceptance of the "immiseration" thesis: "securing the maximum capitalist profit through the exploitation, ruin, and impoverishment of the majority of the population of the given country, through the enslavement and systematic robbery of the peoples of other countries, especially backward countries" is elevated to the rank of the "basic economic law of modern capitalism."[59]

b) The role of capitalism as promoter of technological progress is distinctly downgraded. ("Capitalism is in favor of new techniques when they promise it the highest profit. Capitalism is against the new techniques, and for resort to hand labor when the new techniques do not promise the highest profit.")[60] Moreover, while Lenin's remarks about slowdown of technological change under monopoly-capitalism are echoed, the counter-acting tendencies noted by him are obliquely hinted at rather than explicitly mentioned and relegated largely to the past.[61]

c) The treatment of the impact of Western capitalism on underdeveloped countries shows a similar departure from the original version. The notion that capital exports contribute to growth of capitalism in dependent areas is not abandoned, but toned down and rendered virtually meaningless by the insistence that "imperialist operations in the colonies retard the growth of productive forces and deprive these countries of necessary pre-conditions for an independent economic development."[62] At the same time the characterization of developed capitalist countries as increasingly parasitic and rentier-like is fully upheld.

d) If Lenin's rendition of Marxian analysis of the bourgeois state was oversimplified, Stalin's version is coarseness compounded. The notion of

[58] I. V. Stalin, Political Report of the Central Committee to the 16th Congress of the C.P.S.U., quoted in *Politicheskaia ekonomiia*, Moscow, 1954, p. 215.

[59] J. Stalin, *Economic Problems of Socialism in the USSR*, New York, 1952, p. 32.

[60] *Ibid.*

[61] "Hence the monopolies have a tendency toward stagnation and decay, and in certain circumstances this tendency prevails. This circumstance, however, did not rule out at all a relatively rapid growth of capitalism prior to the Second World War." *Op. cit.*, p. 254.

[62] *Ibid.*, p. 243.

"coalescence of monopolies with the state machine" was, in his view, too lame; "subjugation of the state machine to the monopolies" would be a more appropriate description of the prevailing situation.[63] Moreover, although the capitalist state was considered a near-perfect vehicle for the despoiling of the vast majority of the population, its ability to influence the stability and growth of the economy was rated virtually nil: " . . . all attempts at state 'regulation' of the economy under capitalism are powerless with regard to the elemental laws of economic life."[64]

It is therefore hardly surprising that the overall evaluation of the economic prospects of capitalism was more bleak than in the inherited doctrine. Stalin made this plain when he openly repudiated Lenin's statement that capitalism in its imperialist stage would be expected "on the whole" to grow more rapidly than ever before. Instead, he now predicted an actual contraction, with the alleged "disintegration of the single world market after the Second World War," as the most important single cause, and angrily insisted that within the capitalist segment of the world market, tensions were also mounting. (At this point he injected a note of unintended humor by describing Western Germany and Japan of the early 1950s as countries "languishing in misery under the jackboot of American imperialism.")[65] At the same time as capitalism is thus scaled down several notches, the evaluation of the Soviet system is revised dramatically upward, with its superior rate of growth viewed as the decisive criterion. Diverse sources of this superiority are cited:

a) The ability of the Soviet economy to sustain a comparatively high rate of investment and to raise it steadily is emphasized. This is the meaning of the renowned "law of the preponderant growth of the output of means of production" viewed as a necessary precondition of continuous economic growth[66] and traced to the two-sector model in the second volume of *Capital*. The mode of operation of this "law" is alleged to vary as between different social systems, with capitalism giving priority to the production of less capital-using and more profitable consumers goods in the early stages of industrialization, and socialism favoring the capital goods right from the start.[67] Such a difference in the way of allocating resources, moreover, is only one of the applications of the general rule that long-run social benefits rather than short-run private profits must guide

[63] Stalin, *op. cit.*, p. 35.

[64] *Politicheskaia ekonomiia*, pp. 259–260.

[65] Stalin, *op. cit.*, pp. 26–28.

[66] "The relatively higher rate of expansion of means of production is necessary . . . because reproduction on an extended scale becomes altogether impossible without it." (*ibid.*, p. 51.)

[67] Cf. "Rech' na predvybornom sobranii izbiratelei Stalinskogo izbiratel'nogo okruga goroda Moskvy 9 fevralia 1946g.," in his *Sochineniia*, Stanford, 1967, 3 (XVI), 14–15.

the investment decisions: "profitableness . . . not from the standpoint of individual plants or industries, and not over a period of one year, but from the standpoint of the entire national economy and over a period of, say, ten or fifteen years . . . is the only correct approach to the question."[68] On the institutional side, the whole operation is presumed to be greatly helped by nationalization of industry and banking "which made it possible to quickly get together resources and to transfer them to heavy industry" and by the collectivization which permitted, "within several years," to re-equip agriculture along the lines of modern technology and to increase its marketable share.[69]

b) "Superior technology" must be promoted also when capitalist criteria would have dictated different factor choices. This sounds like an echo of Marx' statement that "in a communist society there would be a very different scope for the employment of machinery than there can be in a bourgeois society," because "the limit [to capitalists'] using a machine is fixed by the difference between the value of the machine and the value of labor power replaced by it" rather than by the difference between the value of the same machine and the total quantity of labor made expendable by its application.[70] To Stalin, however, this proposition repeated by several Soviet economists in the early 1950s did not go far enough: "Machines in the U.S.S.R. always save labor; we do not know of instances when they wouldn't be saving labor in the conditions of the U.S.S.R."[71] On an earlier occasion, he tried to bolster his case by claiming for the Soviet economy the advantages of a latecomer not "weighted down" with obsolete plant and being therefore freer to borrow and to absorb up-to-date technology.[72]

c) The "learning by doing" on the part of the new entrants into the rapidly growing industrial labor force was viewed as a potent factor of Soviet growth, in spite of the heavy toll which it exacted (and which a capitalist economy presumably could not take upon itself). "Costs and over-expenditures, breaking up of machinery and other losses, paid off handsomely. This is the basis of rapid industrialization of our country."[73]

d) The last characteristic is more difficult to pin down and to put in precise terms, yet second to none in importance. It is grim determination to attain the objectives listed above and to wring from them further growth, at a rate of speed set in flagrant defiance of the limits of human endurance, organizational skills, and capacity of physical plant, with

[68] *Economic Problems, op. cit.,* (n. 59), p. 22.
[69] "Rech'," *op. cit.,* p. 15.
[70] *Capital,* I, 429.
[71] *Economic Problems,* p. 35.
[72] "Otchetnyi doklad na XVIII s'ezde partii o rabote Ts. K. VKP(b)," in *Sochineniia,* 1 (XIV), 346.
[73] "Vystuplenie na prieme metallurgov," *ibid.,* p. 48.

ultimate disaster asserted to be the only possible alternative. "Perish or forge full speed ahead"; "there are no fortresses which the Bolsheviks couldn't take"—these slogans of the late 1920s and the early 1930s epitomize the spirit of the man and of his creation.

No doubt, it seems difficult if not impossible to compare the views cited in preceding paragraphs with those of Lenin: The two men, it appears, addressed themselves to totally different problems. To a large extent, this was indeed the case. Lenin's thoughts about Soviet economic policies were formed against the background of catastrophic economic decline during the Civil War and faltering first steps on the road to recovery. With the living standards of the population abysmally low, output flows of the basic industrial material reduced to a few percentage points of the pre-1914 level, and trade with the outside world practically nonexistent, economic expansion in the sense of steady addition to the capacity of the economy was ruled out as a realistic immediate prospect. At the same time, a sharp reduction in the military drain on resources and reestablishment of halfway orderly conditions over vast areas of the country did create the possibility of tangible progress toward restoring the economy to full-capacity operation. This was particularly the case given sufficient determination, a scheme of reconstruction priorities based on clear identification of major bottlenecks and willingness to avoid the massive blunders of the past that had contributed to the calamity.

However, while the misfortunes of the early post-revolutionary years set the stage for the impressive recovery, the successes of the latter led to what looked like a formidable impasse. The resources on hand in the mid-1920s were substantially larger than in 1921; but the claims against them were mounting even faster. It was no longer possible to put off the resumption of the "big push" for modernization: The urgency of the task was starkly dramatized by the precariousness of Russia's international position, debilitation of her productive plant, sharp increase in propensity to consume as a result of the equalitarian redistribution of income, and, last but not least, by incongruity between incipient elements of collectivist socio-economic organization and laggard "productive forces." With capacity limits within sight, every major advance toward these objectives called for sizable net investment rather than for more intensive utilization of the already existing capital stock. Yet the same circumstances which demanded a steep increase in investment, made such an increase dangerous for economic stability; and the possibility of peasant supply strikes compounded the risks.

Lenin did not have to face this dilemma, but his successors definitely did; this was, in essence, what the industrialization debate was about. What eventually emerged as a dominant point of view toward the end of 1927 did represent, as it were, a sort of neo-Leninist synthesis. The new development strategy was dualistic in more than one sense. It implied a workable coexistence of mechanized and labor-intensive technology, public and private ownership, central planning and market, compulsory and voluntary saving, on the assumption that such a policy would reduce the dilemmas of industrialization to manageable proportions, raise the efficiency of the economy, and produce a rate of growth which would be high but not to the point of dangerously overstraining the capacity of plant and the endurance of living men; in short, a "better-fewer-but-better" approach projected into the future.

It was this strategy which Stalin decisively rejected in 1928 when he broke with his allies of the moderate wing of the Bolshevik party and moved farther than his leftist opponents had ever stood. By doing so, he clearly deviated from the letter and spirit of Lenin's heritage as well as from his own earlier views. However, to borrow Trotsky's felicitous expression, he carried out this switch with extinguished lights. The departure from the "old books" was never admitted. Indeed, a determined attempt was made to paper over the gap between the post-1928 "general line" and Lenin's position by a long string of carefully doctored quotations culled from the master's writings and purporting to prove 1) that Lenin believed in the possibility of successful socialist transformation of Russia without assistance from revolutions in the industrialized West as early as in 1915; 2) that in September 1917 Lenin regarded the "overtaking" of the capitalist countries as the most urgent task; 3) that in one of his last pronouncements he insisted on high priority for heavy industry, and 4) that his "cooperative plan" of 1923 was nothing but a blueprint for collectivization. Not a single one of these assertions was true.[74] The distortions were by no means confined to the realm of quotationsmanship; closely intertwined with them were eloquent silences. Stalin never admitted that the beating-the-clock type of industrialization pursued by him involved trade-offs between rapidity of growth and other ostensibly accepted policy objectives on a scale which was totally inconceivable from the viewpoint of the classical Marxian scheme of things and which would have

[74] More specifically, i) Lenin's 1915 statement cited in support of the first proposition clearly referred to developed capitalist countries and not to Russia— a point that was effectively made by L. Kamenev in 1926; ii) the "overtaking" Lenin had in mind in September 1917 was to consist, it will be recalled, in adopting (and improving on) the most advanced organizational forms of Western "war economy" in order to stave off the impending collapse and not in exceeding the Western level of economic development within a short span of time iii) Lenin's remarks about heavy industry made in 1922 dealt with the necessity to "save and restore" the heavy industry which had taken a much worse beating than light industry during the civil war and was very much slower in getting back on its feet; they contained no hint as to what priorities should be adhered to in the longer run; iv) the celebrated article "On Co-operation" is very explicit in urging support for marketing co-operatives but contains no reference whatsoever to producers' cooperatives.

been rejected as excessive during the pre-1928 Soviet debate by all its participants, including himself. The staggering sacrifices in living standards were glossed over; massive inefficiencies were played down or blamed on avoidable mistakes in the lower echelons if not on outright treason; sharply rising wage differentials were presented not as an enforced temporary retreat from socialist principles (as Lenin had done in early 1918 while defending the raise in managerial salaries), but as their supreme affirmation.[75] Another problem-dodging device consisted in promoting controversial policy decisions to the rank of a "law" which is an emphatic, if awkward, way of saying that harsh as these decisions may have been, they were inevitable. This approach comes through already in the often-quoted article which appeared in the Soviet Union during World War II and which described both the Stalin-style industrialization and the collectivization of agriculture as "laws of development."[76] But *Economic Problems of Socialism in the U.S.S.R.* are its *locus classicus.*

In letting the planners' acts of choice appear as economic laws, the Stalinist apologetic has reached its peak. Although it would be exaggerated to say in Engels' famous phrase, that "at its peak it toppled over," it did undoubtedly show a visible crack. Bringing in the notion of law served not merely the purpose of legitimizing the unpalatable; it also meant to serve notice that the sky was not the limit and that arbitrariness in economic decision-making on all levels must be somehow restrained. This was clearly the meaning of the acceptance of the validity of the "law of value" under socialism in spite of all qualifications and equivocations attached to it. A Czechoslovak economist writing in 1968 was entirely correct in observing that "paradoxically enough, new disputes and new developments started with the publication of Stalin's *Economic Problems of Socialism in the U.S.S.R.*"[77] To these "new disputes and new developments" we shall now turn.

5. After 1953: Back to Lenin and then Beyond

We are coming to what is perhaps the most exciting and definitely the most complex chapter of our story. The dead weight of Stalinist ideology

[75] One might argue, moreover, that Stalin never revealed, except in an oblique and inferential way, what were the underlying political motives behind his final option—fear of gradual erosion of one-party dictatorship under stresses and strains of a pluralist society undergoing rapid modernization, and resolve to counter the dangers by making the society less pluralist and the modernization even more rapid. Yet this particular interpretation of Stalin's motives is obviously speculative and controversial—although not more so than alternative hypotheses.

[76] "Teaching of Economics in the Soviet Union," *American Economic Review*, XXXIV:3 (1944), 516–517.

[77] J. Rybačkova, "The Price Mechanism in the Development of Economic Theory of Socialism," *Czechoslovak Economic Papers*, X, 113.

was lifted not at once but gradually and none-too-consistently, advances were followed by stops or partial retreats. Moreover, the process has varied in intensity from one Eastern country to another—indeed, one might almost say, from one economist to another; and it continues to be in flux as these lines are being written. A summary account cannot conceivably do justice to the variety in points of view and in the quality of theorizing; it can hardly do more than indicate the general thrust of the new ideas.

1. There has been an unmistakable tendency to recover Marx' and Lenin's sense of realism in identifying elements both of weakness and strength in capitalist economies and to come to grips with developments which the "classics" had not anticipated:

a) The most arrant nonsense of late-vintage Stalinism has been cleared away. The doctrine of "absolute impoverishment" which had its staunch defenders still in the late 1950s and early 1960s has been abandoned by now.[78] Its modified version, postulating a decline in the workers' *relative* share in national income, still enjoys general acceptance or at least has not thus far been openly challenged. This did not prevent a team of Soviet economists from observing that "expansion of the internal markets of leading capitalist countries is connected, to a considerable extent, with the rise in real wages of the working class" as well as with "active industrialization of agriculture." The same statement, by the way, delivers a *coup de grâce* to the forecast of a "shrinking world market" by explicitly noting the increase in the volume of international trade and by emphasizing the role of "integration of the economies of several leading capitalist countries" in promoting coordination and specialization in the field of production.[79]

b) The underconsumptionist strand has been affected in two ways. On the one hand, it developed into a much more coherent line of thought in writings of those Eastern European economists who were willing to strengthen the received doctrine by generous transfusions from Keynes or Kalecki and by paying more attention to Rosa Luxemburg. At the same time the argument is no longer taken to point toward the ultimate downfall of capitalism with the same certainty as before—and this is true also with regard to a vast bulk of more conservative members of the profession, for reasons already noted or still to be mentioned.

c) The technological dynamism of modern capitalism is no longer put in doubt: " . . . we live in the period of a veritable scientific technological revolution when the sphere of application of technological progress has tremendously increased and its rate of diffusion has accelerated

---

[78] Cf. E. Varga, "Vopros ob absoliutnom obnishchanii," in his *Ocherki po problemam politekonomii kapitalizma*, Moscow, 1965, pp. 117–131.

[79] "Uchenie V. I. Lenina ob imperializme i sovremenost'," *Mirovaia ekonomika i mezhdunarodnye otnosheniia* (hereafter abbreviated as *MEMO*), 1967, no. 5, p. 5.

manifold."[80] Statements of this kind are frequently coupled with side-swipes at unidentified "dogmatists" who "misinterpreted Lenin's references to imperialism as decaying and moribund capitalism, and argued that monopoly capitalism is incompatible with revolutions in technology."[81] Indeed, it is suggested that, in view of the accelerated pace of the inventive process and the large-scale research and development activities carried on by big corporations, "it is, as a rule, more profitable for monopolies to make use of inventions and improvements than to keep them under lock and key."[82]

d) A rapid pace of technological change is regarded neither as a purely coincidental factor nor as a mere by-product of the fierce rivalry among monopolist giants. A quasi-official explanation most frequently offered consists in pointing to the impact of the "competition between the two systems." Others while not rejecting this view seem to consider it a bit question-begging; there is no law that a strong challenge must always be met by a vigorous response. An eminent Czechoslovak economist articulated these doubts when he observed that "it is impossible to explain the scientific technological revolution merely by the fact that the world is split into two social systems . . . Capitalism was able to open the path for the scientific-technological revolution because it had adapted in advance its internal economic mechanism for that purpose."[83] But although most of his Eastern colleagues would not have phrased this quite as bluntly, there is an implicit agreement that an adaptation did take place. As a Soviet participant of the same discussion put it, "we have been long under-estimating the active role of the state."[84] Let us try to spell this out:

i) The partial planning done by individual monopolies is no longer brushed off as irrelevant or worse, particularly when it is intertwined with the economic activities of the state: "It is imperative to bear in mind Lenin's proposition that work in response to state orders for the treasury is not a work for an unknown market but for a known or at least largely known market."[85] (In a similar context Stalin is criticized for having practically abandoned Lenin's concept of the "state monopoly capitalism" as distinct from monopoly capitalism plain and simple; on the other hand,

[80] N. Inozemtsev, "Zhivaia dusha marksizma—tochnost' analiza, sila pre-dvideniia—imperializm nashikh dnei," *MEMO* 1968, no. 6, p. 9.

[81] I Tamarin, "Nauchno-tekhnicheskaia revolutsiia i obostrenie protivorechii kapitalizma," *MEMO*, 1967, no. 4, p. 42.

[82] "Uchenie," *op. cit.*, p. 6.

[83] L. Urban, "Izmeneniia v ekonomicheskom mekhanizme sovremennogo kapitalizma," *MEMO*, 1967, no. 6, p. 84.

[84] A. Mileikovskii, "O zakonomernostiakh mirovogo razvitiia," *ibid.*, p. 72.

[85] S. Men'shikov in A. A. Arzumanian and A.M. Rumiantsev, eds., *Problemy sovremennogo kapitalizma i rabochii klass*, Prague, 1963, p. 177.

conservative economists although recognizing the distinction, feel never-theless that state monopoly capitalism should not be classed as a separate stage of economic development while the "liberals" argue the opposite.)[86] The steadying influence of such an interaction on the economy is generally assumed to be stronger in present-day capitalism both because of the larger share of state expenditures in the gross national product, and owing to the rapid spread of the programming methods described a\ "an attempt to bring together different instruments of economic policy for the sake of attaining long-term objectives of the monopoly capitalism" and utilized "with varying degrees of effectiveness."[87]

ii) Partial nationalization in the Western countries is no longer dis-missed merely as "a bourgeois measure which did not change the economic nature of nationalized enterprises as capitalist enterprises" and was applied "in interests of the financial oligarchy."[88] The role of the nationalized industries in promoting technological change, accelerating concentration of production in most efficient plants and facilitating coordination of investments in closely interrelated areas of the economy is strongly emphasized.[89] Moreover, while the notion that Western nationalization ultimately serves to prop up the capitalist system is accepted, this is not seen as the end of the story. "The dialectics of development causes the expansion of the economic functions of the state and the statization of the economy to clash with the very principle of private ownership that is sacred to capitalism. Measures undertaken for the purpose of strengthen-ing the rule of monopolies are, in final analysis, undermining this rule."[90] (Another Soviet author is undoubtedly correct in pointing out that this position is very much in keeping with Engels' analysis in *Anti-Dühring*.) Professor Horvat of Yugoslavia goes very much further when he envisages a possibility that "various countries will be able to preserve the precarious equilibrium between two antagonistic social forces travelling slowly along the road of gradual nationalization one way or another . . . Every new 'labor' government will have to make another step in the direction of extending public ownership, and so private capitalism will be gradually replaced by state capitalism."[91]

iii) The notion that Keynesian policies could have a positive influence on stability and growth of Western economies has been bitterly resisted in the Soviet Union until quite recently: The line laid down by the textbook of

[86] Cf. Arzumanian's concluding remarks, *ibid.*, pp. 468–469 and Urban's speech cited above.

[87] "Uchenie," *op. cit.*, p. 9.

[88] *Politcheskaia ekonomiia, op. cit.* (n. 58), p. 310.

[89] A. Mileikovskii, "Burzhuaznaia politcheskaia ekonomiia i politika in-vestitsii," *MEMO*, 1967, no. 4, pp. 22–23.

[90] "Uchenie," *op. cit.* (n. 79) p. 4.

[91] B. Horvat, *Toward a Theory of Planned Economy* (Belgrade 1964), p. 82.

Political Economy remained in force for more than a decade and was reflected, among others, in an astonishingly blistering and obscurantist attack on "Keynesianism" by Eugen Varga who, with regard to many other issues, had been clearly on the side of sanity.[92] Yet, here too, things are changing. In the authoritative article cited above it is alleged that the Great Depression, on the one hand, and achievements of Soviet planning, on the other, "have pushed capitalism to the extensive utilization of Keynesian devices,"[93] with the clear implication that the operation was at least partly successful; besides, in the already noted semi-official statement, budget expenditures and, more particularly, deficit financing are quite explicitly mentioned as potent devices for stepping up the rate of economic growth.[94] It may be worth noting, moreover, that Eastern European economists (in the first place the post-1956 Poles and Hungarians, and the post-1965 Czechoslovaks) were, by and large, much quicker and less inhibited in reaching such conclusions than their Soviet opposite numbers.

All this, obviously enough, adds up to a very different overall view of the situation. Incontrovertible facts are no longer denied—it is openly acknowledged that the rate of industrial growth in the West during the postwar period has been higher than during the preceding six decades;[95] and there is general agreement that another downturn on the scale of the Great Depression is unlikely. (Indeed, some of the Eastern European economists argue that although occasional slumps may still occur, a discernible cyclical pattern of development no longer exists owing to the sustained state intervention; but this is presumably a minority view.)[96]

The conclusions drawn from all the foregoing with regard to the long-term prospects are more difficult to summarize. Many economists continue to talk in broad generalities about the inevitable downfall of capitalism under the pressure of its internal contradictions without indicating the operational content of such statements under the changed circumstance. Others are more specific and also more sober. Their general attitude seems to be that although capitalism has performed more creditably than the "dogmatists" had expected, things could be a great deal better under socialism, and that the stabilizing devices outlined above are beset with limitations which reduce their effectiveness. The last point, it may be noted, is often presented in terms strongly resembling the argument of the heterodox economists in the West. (Once again, this is more true of

---

[92] E. Varga, "O prichinakh populiarnosti keinsianstva," *op. cit.*, pp. 329–357.

[93] N. Inozemtsev, *op. cit.* (n. 80), p. 11.

[94] Cf. "Uchenie," *op. cit.* (n. 79), pp. 9–10.

[95] Cf. N. Inozemtsev, *op. cit.*, p. 10.

[96] F. Molnar, "Contemporary Capitalist Reproduction; Cyclical or Not," *Acta oeconomica Academiae Scientiarum Hungarica*, II (1967), no. 4, pp. 363–379.

Poland, Hungary, and Czechoslovakia than of the Soviet Union.) The prevailing scope of planning and nationalization is claimed to be less than adequate to ensure the fullest utilization of potentialities for technological progress because this requires a tighter coordination of investment decisions, a longer time horizon to work with, and greater determination to put social benefits ahead of private gains in speeding such matters as diffusion of inventions and the retraining of the labour force than is possible under capitalism;[97] the restiveness of the business community about the "overfull employment" is noted and occasionally put forward in terms of Kalecki's theory of the "political cycle"; the role of armament drives in sustaining high employment levels in some of the leading Western countries is emphasized; the built-in bias in favor of salable output and against nonmilitary public goods is brought out. In addition, two traditional Marxist arguments are advanced, albeit in a characteristically restrained manner. The labor-displacing effects of automation are viewed as serious but (in the short-run, at any rate) not explosive because the process of change is assumed to unfold gradually rather than abruptly.[98] The notion that Western imperialism tends to retard the development of the dependent areas and hence to increase their relative backwardness is upheld; in this respect the post-1953 writers seem to be closer to Stalin than to Lenin with his nineteenth-century faith in foreign investment as an unfailing "engine of growth." Here, too, are some novelties in approach. The prosperity of the advanced "North" is now to a much lesser extent imputed to its economic domination over the backward "South"; the widening disparity in productive potentials of the two is not infrequently presented as due more to cumulative advantages of economic superiority than to deliberate attempts of the rich to block the development of the poor;[99] lastly, the tendencies toward retardation arising from the co-existence of unequals are now formulated in a more circumspect way than in earlier writings.[100]

[97] Cf. W. Brus, "Bodźce ekonomiczne postepu technicznego a kierunki zmian w systemie planowania i zarzadzania," *Zycie Gospodarcze*, 1966 no. 15 (quoted by J. G. Zielinski in M. Pohorille, eds., *Ekonomia polityczna socjalizmu* (Warsaw 1968), p. 714–715.

[98] Cf. I. Tamarin, *op. cit.*, pp. 50–52, and Z. Chrupek, "Postep techniczny a wzrost gospodarczy (w rozwinietej gospodarce kapitalistycznej)" in J. Zawadzki and A. Lukaszewicz eds. *Teorie wzrostu ekonomicznego a wspólczesny kapitalizm*, Warsaw, 1962, pp. 365–378. For a concise and rigorous statement, see M. Kalecki and A. Szeworski, "Ekonomiczne problemy automatyzacj i produkcji w krajach kapitalistycznych," *Ekonomista*, 1957, no. 3, pp. 105–115.

[99] Cf. Z. Dobrska, "Nie zgadzam sie z Prof. Langem," *Zycie Gospodarcze*, 1957, no. 33.

[100] E.g., the cited document speaks of the capitalism's "complete inability to *liquidate* the huge economic backwardness of the overwhelming part of the capitalist countries" while Inozemtsev refers to the Western imperialism as "the

Taking all in all, the already quoted Czechoslovak economist did not seem to be very far out when he concluded: "We must reject the notion that capitalism will disappear as a result of an economic breakdown or of a revolutionary war of some kind . . . Only in process of (internal) development (of capitalism) can the requisite structural shifts and changes in relation of class forces conceivably occur; and only as a result of such development will the transition to full socialist take-over be presumably completed at long last."[101] This is, no doubt, the most far-reaching re-evaluation of socialist perspectives in the West that has ever occurred within the Leninist tradition. And yet it is overshadowed by the intensity and depth of the soul-searching that has gone on among the Eastern economists with regard to their own system after Stalin's departure from the scene.

2. Views concerning the goals of socialist planning have undergone a dramatic change; their ranking has been reordered, and they have become much more explicit. It has been widely recognized that in the Soviet Union and in East European countries the maximization of growth had been relentlessly pressed forward as a paramount objective at the expense of all others; and there has been considerable agreement i) that this policy has been, up to a point, inevitable in the early stages of the industrialization drive; but ii) that the trade-offs were even then pushed much too far from the viewpoint of even their declared purpose; and iii) that by now this policy has lost most of its justification. No doubt, different writers in different countries have argued each of these points in a different way with significant variation in levels of analytical refinement and in relative emphasis on alleged inevitability and on outright error in the appraisal of past performance. But the overall trend was unmistakably clear. Concretely:

a) The overwhelming emphasis on the achievement of most ambitious output targets has been critized as "voluntarist" and largely counter-productive. It has been pointed out repeatedly that this policy implied an invitation to all kinds of "corner-cutting," such as sacrificing quality, skimping on exploratory work, reluctance to engage in time-consuming experimentation with new methods and new products; a situation which evoked the melancholy comment that an "accelerated rate of growth involving obsolescent, non-effective, low-quality products disguises an actual slowdown in the rate of economic progress."[102] But the "beating-the

---

basic obstacle against the *fastest* liquidation of the economic lag of developing countries." (Italics supplied in both cases.)

[101] L. Urban, "Izmeniia," *op. cit.* (n. 83), pp. 85–86.

[102] A. I. Anchishkin, Iu. V. Iaremenko, *Tempy i proportsii ekonomicheskogo razvitiia*, Moscow, 1967, p. 21.

clock" approach was found wanting also in terms of its most literally interpreted objectives. A Soviet economist of a distinctly mainstream persuasion, after calling Stalin's demand for a 45 per-cent increase in industrial output within a single year, and Khrushchev's ill-fated plans for overtaking the United States in the output of livestock products, concluded that "infatuation with super-high tempos . . . leads to a dislocation in economic life."[103] A more generalized and rigorous criticism advanced by a prominent Czechoslovak economist drew attention to the quasi-cyclical fluctuations in the rate of industrial growth of Czechoslovakia, Poland, Hungary, and Eastern Germany resulting from disproportions due to lower-than-average supply elasticities in the highly capital-using basic material industries.[104] A noted Soviet economist seemed uncomfortable about the alleged all-pervasiveness of this phenomenon within the Soviet orbit; but he did not deny its existence and admitted that "unevenness in development . . . can be caused by *excessively* high tempos of growth of social production, *excessive* step-ups in the rate of productive accumulation and a *sharp* decline in its efficiency."[105]

b) The "law of the preponderant growth of the output of the means of production" came in for a good deal of questioning. To begin with, the internal consistency of the proposition was challenged; it was demonstrated that the "law" is valid, strictly speaking, only when the capital-output ratio is increasing and/or when economic growth is accelerating rather than merely "continuous" as Stalin had it, and that changes in the composition of imports can help to bring about the desired upward adjustment in either of the two without a corresponding intersectoral shift—a point which was explicitly recognized by Marx.[106] Following this line of reasoning, the notion that there was something inherently superior and peculiarly socialist about preponderant growth of the capital goods' sector in all places and at all times was severely qualified. The correct decision in this respect was shown to depend on such specifics as the country's endowment with suitable natural resources and basic social overheads, its opportunities to trade with, and to import capital from, the rest of the world, as well as its place in the historical sequence of the worldwide industrialization process. It was agreed the latecomers can

[103] S. P. Pervushin, "Proizvodstvo i protreblenie na novom etape" in V. G. Venzher *et al.*, *Proizvodstvo, nakoplenie, potreblenie*, Moscow, 1965, p. 20.

[104] J. Goldmann, "Short- and Long-run Variations in the Growth Rate and the Model of Functioning of a Socialist Economy," *Czechoslovak Economic Papers*, V (1965), 35–46.

[105] A. Notkin, "Tempy razvitiia sotsialisticheskogo proizvodstva i pod'em narodnogo potrebleniia," in *Proizvodstvo, op. cit.*, p. 57.

[106] Cf. M. Kalecki, "Dynamika inwestycji i dochodu narodnowego w gospodarce socjalistycznej," *Ekonomista*, 1956, no. 5, pp. 61–70, and K. Laski, *Zarys teorii reprodukcji socjalistycznej*, Warsaw, 1965, pp. 336–337.

borrow up-to-date technology from the older members of the club and hence start some of the most modern branches of the capital-goods sector at a much earlier stage of development. (In this context, the crucial importance of the fact that the Soviet Union in 1928 was not a typical underdeveloped country and did not have to start "from scratch" was made very explicit.)[107]

The necessity for a pronounced increase in the rate of investment during the early period of Soviet and East European industrialization was not questioned. As everyone agreed, such an increase was made imperative by the decision to step up the rate of economic growth, by the expected rise in the capital-output ratio during the early stages of the "big push," by the limited foreign trade, and lack of capital imports, as well as by the high levels of international tension. At the same time, the existence of sizable labor reserves in the Soviet Union and in Eastern Europe at the beginning of their first long-range plans obviated the risk that a high and rising rate of investment would in the foreseeable future lead to labor shortages that would force underutilization of plant capacity and thus require a slow-down in the expansion of the capital stock.[108] Completion of the formative stages of industrialization, it was recognized, would change this situation.

Moreover, it was felt that the Stalin formula with its characteristic combination of dogmatic rigidity and fuzzy open-endedness contained a considerable potential for trouble particularly when used in the "damn-the-torpedoes, full-steam-ahead" spirit that dominated the whole attitude toward growth in the past and was far from extinct at present. The dangers consisted in overcompression of consumption and its deleterious effects on the quality of the work force, on the one hand, and on the other in driving the economy into a host of bottlenecks and distortions by attempts to override the capacity constraints. (As will be seen presently, in at least one case the two kinds of resistances are bracketed together.)

The notions about the nature of constraints of the last-mentioned type show a good deal of variety. They comprise i) Branko Horvat's broad-gauged "absorption capacity for investment" encompassing health and consumption standards, the level of know-how and the institutional set-up of the economy;[109] ii) Michael Kalecki's "ceilings" which appear jointly or severally, and are due to limitations in natural resources and managerial skills, long construction periods and time needed for assimilating new

[107] Cf. speeches by V. Tiagunenko, B. Solov'ev, and V. Loginova at the research conference on problems of industrialization of developing countries, *MEMO*, 1967, no. 4, pp. 108–109; no. 5, pp. 99 and 103.

[108] Cf. W. Brus, ed., *Ekonomia polityczna socjalizmu*, Warsaw, 1965, p. 96, and K. Laski, *op. cit.*, p. 412.

[109] B. Horvat, *op. cit.* (n. 91), pp. 181–184.

technologies; whenever the rate of investment is raised in disregard of these barriers, further lengthening of the construction period and hence "freezing of capital rather than expansion of the industry in question"[110] is the inevitable result; and iii) frequent references to the fact that the absolute and relative size of the capital-goods sector at the time when the large-scale industrialization effort is launched will necessarily limit the rate of investment as well as the speed at which it can be increased. There was a general consensus that all these dangers did in fact materialize, to a degree varying over time as well as from country to country, in the course of economic development of the post-1928 Soviet Union and post-1948 Eastern Europe. Beyond this point, however, opinions varied. Many East European economists, with the Poles in the lead, rejected the "law" as an illegitimate and potentially harmful generalization of a special case, but the bulk of Soviet economists held on to an attenuated version of the Stalinist proposition, their argument based on an alleged necessity to maintain "at least a minimum edge" in development of the capital-goods sector for the sake of continued technological progress.[111]

c) There has been a major reorientation with regard to the criteria of technological choice. No one seems to dissent from the proposition that relatively backward countries are, by definition, facing wide gaps between the best-knowledge technology and the one that actually prevails. Consequently, "the transition from hand labor to advanced technology could secure a great increase in labor productivity even in case of non-optimal planning decisions."[112] But at the same time awareness has increased that such discontinuous jumps toward mechanization could not conceivably occur all the way down the line, because the investment potential even of the richest present-day economies would not be large enough for that. Hence, in order to avoid a massive under-employment of the existing labor force or a general overstrain, and to maximize the returns from the given addition to the productive plant, the application of the capital-intensive technology must be confined to uses where its advantages more than compensate for its low labor-absorbing capacity the sacrifices in growth potential due to the tying up of investible resources over long periods of time.[113] As was noted repeatedly, this was what the Stalinist planners had failed to do when they had tried to follow the quest for

[110] M. Kalecki, *Zarys teorii wzrostu gospodarki socjalistycznej* Warsaw, 1963, p. 53.

[111] S. P. Pervushin, *op. cit.* (n. 103), p. 32.

[112] V. V. Novozhilov, *Problemy izmereniia zatrat i rezul'tatov pri optimal'nom planirovanii*, Moscow, 1967, p. 32.

[113] For an unusually lucid statement (in particular reference to the problems of developing countries) see V. V. Kollontai's speech at the above-mentioned conference, *MEMO*, 1967, no. 4, p. 112.

"superior" technology all around, and had spurned the use of rationing devices—approximating the rate of interest—which some Soviet economists had suggested already in the late 1920s.[114]

A closely related problem area likewise caused apprehension. As indicated above, the Eastern economists of the post-Stalin era held firmly to the view that socialism had strong potential advantages over capitalism not only in its ability to chose the best kind of technology among existing alternatives, but also in its capacity to promote technological progress; and they strongly emphasized the importance of technological borrowing. But they argued that these potentialities had been used in a less-than-satisfactory way: "The Soviet scientists have many outstanding inventions to their credit . . . But capitalist countries are ahead of us in putting these inventions into effect and applying them on a wide scale in the national economy."[115] The difficulties were regarded in part, as side-effects of the attempts to expand the economy at a rate heavily overtaxing its physical and organizational capacity; the sellers' market, the rush after quick production increases at the expense of the expansion of research facilities as well as time consuming changes in processes or products; and substandard quality of the "above-planned" increment in labor force were cast in the role of major villains.[116] Yet this was not the whole story, as will be seen presently.

d) Perhaps the most momentous change occurred in the attitude toward problems of economic organization. The new ideas in this particular area have been extensively reported and discussed in the West; yet it might be worthwhile to refresh the readers' minds on several points. The reconsideration proceeded along several routes. The old system was accused of lacking meaningful criteria for optimal allocation of resources—a recognition which inspired the attempts to reformulate Marxian theory of value in terms compatible with marginal analysis, and brought about a phenomenal upsurge of Eastern mathematical economics. The centralized apparatus of economic administration was depicted as unable to cope adequately with the stupendous multitude and complexity of the decisions to be made and with the staggering volume of information to be collected,

[114] "Had the coefficient of efficiency of investment been introduced in our economic practice not in 1959 but about 30 years earlier (when its use was already advocated in the Soviet press), the investments which were made during the last three decades would be giving a much higher effect than they actually do." (V. V. Novozhilov, "Matematicheskii analiz sotsialisticheskoi ekonomiki kak vazhneishii faktor rosta proizvoditel'nykh sil" in *Planirovanie i ekonomiko-matematicheskie metody*, Moscow, 1964, p. 319.

[115] S. P. Pervushin, *op. cit.*, p. 35.

[116] Cf. W. Sadowski, "Optimum techniczno-renowacyjne," *Ekonomista*, 1967, no. 3, pp. 551, 578, and K. Ryć, "Problemy wzrostu dochodu narodowego i spozycia w warunkach napiecia inwestycyjneg *ibid.*, p. 658.

sorted out, and processed for that purpose. It was pointed out that the incentives of the lower-echelon men were not infrequently operating at cross-purposes with the intentions of central planners compounding some of the difficulties arising from the imposition of the excessively taut output targets on the economy. Attention was drawn to the managers' propensity to press for excessively large capital allocations to hoard materials and, last but not least, to be sluggish in introducing innovations that brought few tangible rewards to the enterprise while not infrequently involving a loss of bonus due to temporary slowdowns and disarrays coming in their wake. As a result, many Eastern economists are now leaning to the view that a Western market mechanism, for all its imperfections, is superior to the overcentralized planning in terms of static as well as dynamic efficiency; and some of them feel no compunction about stating that Marx did not anticipate such a situation, and that he may have tended to exaggerate the shortsightedness and the "expost" nature of market-oriented decisions.[117] The solution is generally sought in combining, in a variety of ways, firm central control of macroeconomic decisions and wide latitude for market-oriented behavior on the microeconomic level—an attitude strongly reminiscent of the position held by Lenin in the last years of his life, and defended by Bukharin and Bazarov during the Soviet debate of the 1920s. (The enthusiastic rediscovery of this debate, incidentally, has been one of the remarkable features of the Polish and Czechoslovak discussions of the last years.)

An important difference must not be overlooked. To Lenin and to most of his followers (as well as to quite a few early non-Communist Marxists) it seemed axiomatic that centralized planning would become more comprehensive and all-embracing, as socialist society moved to higher levels of economic development. The leading Eastern economists of the late 1950s and the 1960s hold an opposite view. To them overcentralization is a relic of the backward past, not unlike the "crutches" Marx was referring to when he spoke of state intervention in the early stages of capitalist development.

This was what Oskar Lange had in mind when he described Stalinist planning as a war economy *sui generis* in which a powerful central authority by its commands is able to revamp, much more rapidly than an ordinary market mechanism possibly could, the whole productive pattern

---

[117] Cf. O. Kyn, "Marx and the Mechanism of Functioning of a Socialist Economy," *Oeconomica*, III:1 (1968), p. 41. Dr. Kyn emphasizes that "the quality of coordination provided by the market mechanism is not the same under various circumstances," and that it is less than adequate in case of long gestation periods and under conditions of discontinuous change; but this can, in his view, be remedied by improvement in channels of information.

of the country in line with drastically changed priorities.[118] Speed would be of overriding importance in view of the issues at stake, so that the inevitable inefficiencies accompanying it would have to be accepted. The presence of cushioning factors rendered the inefficiencies less critical and, hence, more tolerable: untapped reserves of labor, high-quality natural resources, and (in the earliest stages of the process at any rate) under-utilized plants nobly performed this role. The tasks of centralized adminis-tration were not unmanageable owing to the low level of development of the economies involved; at the same time, benefits would acrue from the "advantages of backwardness." This view clearly implied that after the economy had been fundamentally restructured and made more complex, and after opportunities for extensive growth had largely disappeared, the old system would become, to borrow a Marxian term, a fetter on further development—a point made very forcefully by Professor Šik and stated most succinctly by Novozhilov.[119] Others saw in the lessening of inter-national tension another important factor. As an East German economist summed it up, while commenting on Professor Wiles' well-known 1956 article, the appropriate *motto* for the new planning system as distinct from the old, would be "Choices for Growth" rather than "Growth versus Choice."[120]

Interestingly enough, this position at present evokes not only the displeasure of conservative centralizers but also criticism from the opposite quarters. To cite an example, in a remarkable article on problems of developing countries, an eminent Soviet economist reproaches Lange for downgrading efficiency considerations in the early stages of planned development: " . . . in the socio-economic nature of the planned economy there is nothing that would contradict, on principle, making use of the positive properties of the market mechanism right from the start, provided that the centralized planning system . . . will play the leading role in determining the basic macro-economic proportions . . . juxtaposing market and planning as mutually exclusive 'either-or' alternatives is not

---

[118] O. Lange, *Political Economy of Socialism* (Warsaw, 1957), pp. 15–16. A Czechoslovak writer put it very succinctly several years later: "The directive model for the operation of the economy . . . is suited to abnormal conditions of economic development, brought about by technical and economic backwardness, by the need to accelerate structural transformations or by a war economy and the priority of national defense considerations." (Karel Kouba, "The Plan and Economic Growth," *Czechoslovak Economic Papers*, VI, (1966), 11.

[119] Cf. O. Šik, *Plan and Market under Socialism* (Prague, 1967), pp. 55–56, and V. V. Novozhilov, *op. cit.*, p. 33.

[120] G. Kohlmey, "From Extensive to Intensive Economic Growth," *Czechos-lovak Economic Papers*, VI (1966), 30.

conducive to the fullest mobilization of all resources and motive forces of society entering the path of economic progress."[121]

Our *tour d'horizon* would be seriously incomplete if we were to stop at this point. As indicated at the beginning of this section, the ranking of the planning objectives has changed radically; but in many cases (although surely not in all) these changes reflected a much more basic reorientation. When two Czechoslovak economists writing on the eve of the Soviet invasion declared that "economic growth serves no purpose unless it is reflected in living standards of people," this did sound novel, but less so than the passage that immediately followed: "At this stage, in connection with the renaissance of Marxist ideas, a belief is beginning to assert itself, that the true sense of development of society cannot be seen only in further increase of consumption. The principal aim must be liquidation of alienation, abolition of exploitation of man by man, and true democratization and humanization of society ... Because the focal point of democratization and humanization of society rests in this phase, only such methods of pursuing economic growth (i.e., such forms of economic management and planning) should be chosen, which would not conflict with these aims."[122] The already cited East German economist moved in the same direction when he stated that a "socialist economy can only become more rational if socialist democracy is widened."[123] The Poles, led by Oskar Lange, made a similar point ten years earlier when they raised the possibility of a re-emerging alienation in a socialist society whenever the bureaucracy puts itself in full control, and noted the negative effects of such a situation on economic and moral incentives.[124] The Soviet *avant-garde* economists did not put it quite so strongly; but they, too, insisted with varying degrees of emphasis that the impending economic reforms meant a step toward democratization.[125] The Yugoslavs pulled far away from the rest when they extended Engels' concept of state capitalism to any economy in which the means of production are owned by the state

[121] F. Shmelev, "Razvivaiushchiesia strany: formirovanie khoziaistvennogo mechanizma," *MEMO*, August 1968, no. 8, p. 54–55. Also every single item of more specific advice contained in the article (outright subsidies rather than tinkering with relative prices, warnings against "seller's market" and premature liquidation of the private sector) constitutes an implicit repudiation of Stalinist policies as a pattern to emulate. Instead, the planners in the developing country are urged to study the experience of Lenin's *NEP* and to bear in mind that "development of socialist countries moved along an uncleared path, and many things became evident only in process of practical experience of the socialist construction." (*Ibid.*, p. 61.)

[122] L. Rychetnik and O. Kỹn, "Optimal Central Planning in 'Competitive Solution'," *Czechoslovak Economic Papers*, X (1968), p. 31.

[123] Kohlmey, *op. cit.*, p. 30.

[124] O. Lange, *Pisma ekonomiczne i spoleczne Warsaw*, 1961, p. 135.

[125] V. V. Novozhilov, *op. cit.* (n. 112), pp. 33 and 39.

rather than by workers actually operating them, and drew from this the obvious conclusion that the Soviet-type economies were not socialist.[126] But for all these and similar varieties there can be no mistake about the overall direction of the trend. It is indeed a renaissance of Marxist ideas about the ultimate interdependence between economic dynamism, consumers' welfare, efficiency, and freedom—a harmony which has been conspicuously absent in the past but is believed to be attainable at present.[127]

The wheel seems to have gone full circle. However, the comparison might be extended in a less cheerful direction. Classical Marxism which proclaimed this harmony as the hallmark of the socialist society of the future produced a movement which helped to civilize a wasteful and inequitable economic system without changing its fundamentals. Will the re-emergence of these ideas in the Eastern post-Stalinist environment accomplish more—or much less? The question is a fateful one, and an attempt at answering it at the end of an over-long paper would be rash. So let us conclude by leaving it open.

[126] B. Horvat, *op. cit.* (n. 91), pp. 78–80.

[127] The proposition can be stated somewhat more formally. Particular components of the social preference function are both complementary and mutually substitutable within a certain range. The substitutional relationship clearly receded into the background whenever mature capitalism and socialism were evaluated, as it were, in terms of comparative statics on the grandest scale, with the level of productive forces taken to be high and equal in both cases. Socialism could then be shown to score better on all counts; indeed, the possibility to maintain proper balance in attending to particular objectives would be an important part of such superiority. Yet whenever the requisite minimum level of development is not attained, something would have to give way—let us recall tough statements by Marx and Engels regarding class inequality. Similarly, if the system has to move from one development level to another, and to do it rapidly, trade-offs are inevitable. But planners can overdo it by pushing the trade-offs well beyond the range of feasible substitutions and thus defeating their purpose to a greater or lesser degree. Marx was not concerned with such a possibility; his Eastern followers most certainly were.

PART IV

The Comparison of Economic Systems

11

An Integration

by MORRIS BORNSTEIN

The task of this paper is to integrate various approaches to the comparison of economic systems, including, but not limited to, those presented in other contributions to this volume. The first section briefly considers the concept of an economic system. The second examines various ways of comparing economic systems. The third reviews some of the current issues in the field. The final section presents some conclusions. Throughout, the discussion focuses on an examination of the scope and method of the field, rather than a review of the principal literature on the many subjects composing it. Thus, although specific works are cited for illustrative purposes at various points, the paper is a methodological, rather than a bibliographic, essay.

1. Concept of an Economic System

One may begin with the concept of a *system*, of which an economic system is a type. A general definition, advanced in Kuznets' chapter, is that a system refers to a collection of "objects, ideas, or activities united by some regular form of interaction or interdependence." Thus, two dimensions are involved: what is being organized, and how the components are related to each other.

A more sophisticated and complex definition is offered by Koopmans and Montias: The *participants* in a system may be individuals or different groupings of individuals. Through the *interactions* of participants, the actions of one participant simultaneously or sequentially affect other participants. Orders and rules govern these interactions. *Orders* are dated messages calling for a specific response from the participant(s) to whom they are addressed. *Rules* are messages stipulating (or constraining) for an indefinite period the actions of (a set of) participants under specified conditions. *Organizations* consist of a set of participants who regularly interact, according to rules and orders, to accomplish a set of activities constituting the purpose of the organization. The *motivation* of a participant is a function which associates with each course of action the utility of its outcome to him. Such motivations govern responses to orders and rules within organizations. Thus, the study of a system involves the analysis of the interaction of organizations, including the composition of the organizations, the orders and rules signalling action, and the motivations affecting the participants' responses to these signals.

An *economic system*, in turn, involves the interaction of organizations of participants engaged, according to rules and orders, in the production, distribution, and use of goods and services. It may be viewed as the set of arrangements by which the community determines 1) what shall be produced ("the bill of goods"); 2) how it shall be produced, including a) the institutions and instruments to be used and b) the pattern of resource allocation; and 3) how the resulting personal income and claims to goods and services shall be distributed (and redistributed) among households.

2. Bases of Comparison of Systems

Economic systems may be compared in regard to three main aspects. 1) What forces influence the system, determining its character? 2) What is the nature of the system? How does it operate? What are the nature and extent of state intervention in economic life? 3) How well does the system perform, in regard to its own goals and in regard to additional goals which are esteemed by others if not, or more than, by the system itself? Thus, we wish to know 1) what makes systems similar or different, 2) what the similarities or differences in systems are, and 3) what differences in performance are associated with differences in systems. These three aspects will be discussed in turn in some detail.

2.1. Forces Influencing the Economic System

These forces are so numerous and their relationship so complex that a comprehensive discussion is beyond the scope of this paper. Instead, it is convenient to group them into three main categories, each of which subsumes a number of elements: 1) the level of economic development, 2) social and cultural factors, and 3) the "environment." Although these categories are not necessarily exhaustive, they illustrate how different kinds of forces shape the nature and performance of economic systems.

2.1.1. Level of Economic Development. The level of economic development can be measured and compared by various indicators, including the level of per capita income, the rate of growth of per capita income, the share of investment in GNP, the share of primary, secondary, and tertiary activities in total employment or GNP, and so forth.[1] Whichever measures are used, it is clear that economic growth alters the size and structure of the economy, and that these changes in turn modify the economic system.

[1] For an extended treatment of the subject, with a wealth of empirical data, see Simon Kuznets, *Modern Economic Growth: Rate, Structure, and Spread*, New Haven, Conn., 1966.

Thus, as Kuznets' paper points out, economic growth and development in the United States in the last 50 or 100 years has been responsible for many changes in the economic system, for instance in the nature and extent of government intervention to deal with problems of market power arising from the emergence of large firms and trade unions; problems of external diseconomies, such as water and air pollution; and problems of scientific discovery of a character and magnitude affecting survival, such as the utilization of nuclear energy.

Another example is the current economic reforms in Eastern Europe which seek to adapt the economic system to changes in the nature of the economy. This process has frequently been described as a shift from a more centralized system in the "extensive" phase of economic development, to a less centralized system in the "intensive" phase. In the earlier period, the tasks of "economic construction" were socialization of the means of production, a sharp increase in the rate of investment, rapid structural change, and revision of the income distribution. In this period, resource allocation was dominated by physical planning and administrative rationing. In contrast, the intensive phase is characterized by emphasis on greater efficiency in the use of given resources, greater responsiveness to household demand for consumer goods and services, and greater emphasis on competitiveness in international trade. This phase is seen to require a more decentralized economic system, involving greater reliance on market forces rather than administrative allocation, more need for scarcity prices, greater enterprise autonomy, and more emphasis on incentives instead of commands.

Although these examples illustrate how changes in the level of development affect the nature of the economic system, it is clear that a given level or pattern of economic development is not uniquely associated with a specific economic system. Rather, different countries at approximately the same stage of economic development exhibit a great variety of economic systems. Thus, it is not very satisfactory to classify countries into such groups as "West," "East," and "South," because some of the Communist countries in "East" are no more developed than some of the non-Communist countries in "South."

Instead, an "exclusion principle" seems useful. Although a given level of development can accommodate more than one economic system, certain levels of development may be incompatible with particular economic systems. One reason may be that the level of development alters the system. Another is that the system eschews a level or pattern of development which is incompatible with (i.e., threatens) the system. Thus, tribal or oligarchic societies may resist economic changes which will disrupt the traditional social structure.

The level of economic development is also related to the economic system in several other ways. First, it is part of the environment in which the system operates and which affects the system's performance. Second, it influences the culture, which also shapes the economic system. Finally, one of the aims of the system may be to alter the level of development. These propositions are developed further in subsequent sections.

2.1.2. Social and Cultural Forces. Many aspects of society and culture influence the economic system. One is social stratification, based on race, occupation, income, wealth, religion, or other factors; another is the customs, traditions, values, and beliefs of society. By way of illustration, I shall examine the influence of ideology, which has received considerable attention in the literature of comparative economic systems and which is the subject of papers by Gerschenkron and Hirschman in this volume.

An ideology is a set of ideas and values guiding individuals (and organizations composed of them) in interpreting their environment, choosing goals in regard to maintaining or changing the environment, and selecting the means to achieve these goals. An economic ideology is a set of ideas related to economic action. Ideology may affect the economic system in various ways. It influences both the ends and the means of the system: what its goals are, including the priorities among them; the institutions and instruments of the system and the patterns of their use; and attitudes about changes in goals and institutions and instruments. Thus, ideologies may maintain or alter systems. Koopmans and Montias suggest that ideology may be more likely to favor maintaining the system than changing it. On the other hand, Hirschman argues that "insurgent" ideologies are more important than "ruling" ideologies—that the chief role of ideology is to alter the system.

However, there are a number of difficulties in identifying the influence of ideology on the economic system, as Gerschenkron notes. First, although a single consistent ideology is sometimes ascribed to a pure model of an economic system (e.g., "rapid industrialization through comprehensive central planning based on public ownership"), in actual real-world economies there are various interest groups with different ideologies about the ends or means of the system. Second, ideologies may be misleading. The ideology may seek to rationalize what is being done rather than constitute its true motivation. Or the aim may be to deceive—to conceal what is being done by describing it in completely different terms. Thus, the explicit ideology may not be the normative guide to action. Rather, the effective ideology may be implicit in the nature and operation of the economic system, from which it must be deduced, as has been suggested for the Soviet Union.[2] Third, there is a time gap between an ideology and

[2] See, for instance, Morris Bornstein, "Ideology and the Soviet Economy," *Soviet Studies*, XVIII: 1 (1966), 74–80.

the economic system to which it relates. Gerschenkron notes how ideology can lag behind changes in the economy which it is supposed to guide, while Hirschman believes the ideology may lead the system it aims to change. The gap is narrowed in the former case when outdated ideas are finally abandoned, and in the latter case when ideology succeeds in changing the system.

In conclusion, ideology does not determine the economic system in the sense that a single consistent ideology unambiguously and effectively shapes the economic system. Rather, different ideologies—some explicit, some concealed—influence economic institutions, policies, actions, and results. For this reason, Koopmans and Montias prefer to account for the effect of ideology in terms of more specific concepts like perception, attitudes, norms (preference functions), institutions, and patterns of behavior, through which ideologies are expressed and operate.

2.1.3. Environment. The natural environment of an economic system includes such elements as the size (in area and population), location (topography, climate, access to the sea), and natural-resource endowment of the economy. These features affect the nature of the economic system indirectly in various ways. For example, they help determine the level and character of economic development. They also affect ideologies and other aspects of culture—for instance, attitudes towards the need to emphasize national unity of geographically diverse and distant regions, the desirability or feasibility of a high degree of self-sufficiency, and the like.

Another aspect of environment is contact with other economic systems which is a source of transmission of ideology and information about alternative arrangements and their results. An economic system may change as a result of its contact with another system. For example, a country may modify some facets of its economic system, such as its foreign trade arrangements, in order to accommodate international economic relations with a country having a different system. Or it may change important aspects of the economic system—indeed even the system itself—because a powerful neighboring state insists upon it.

Thus, while an economic system operates in an environment which affects its performance, the system itself may be influenced directly or indirectly by its environment.

To analyze how these various forces—the level of development, social and cultural factors, and the environment—influence economic systems, is to study how economic systems change. It is an investigation of the dynamic process, as distinct from either interspatial (transnational) comparisons at a given time or intertemporal comparisons of the economic system of the same country at different times (e.g., the United States in 1928 vs. 1968). For some purposes, it is convenient to classify these forces of change into exogenous factors, such as new technology and developments in world politics, and endogenous factors, such as the effect of increasing affluence in creating new interest groups or ideologies capable of modifying the economic system.

2.2. Nature and Operation of Economic Systems

The nature and operation of an economic system may be analyzed in terms of its social preference function, its institutions and instruments, and its patterns of resource allocation and income distribution. These three aspects are, of course, related. The social preference function determines which institutions and instruments are used in which patterns of resource allocation and income distribution to pursue which social aims. And the most useful focus of analysis for all three aspects is the nature and degree of state intervention in economic life.

2.2.1. Social Preference Function. The social preference (or utility or welfare) function expresses the community's effective aggregate preferences regarding the ends and means of economic activity. In analyzing and comparing systems, we wish to consider both how the community's decisions are reached and what these decisions are.

In regard to the first aspect, three mechanisms may be distinguished: 1) individual preferences expressed through individual choice in markets (consumer sovereignty); 2) individual preferences expressed through the political process, either by direct voting on certain issues or by indirect voting through the selection of legislators and government officials; and 3) the preferences of a ruling group not selected through the electoral process. Several questions must then be investigated. What is the relative importance of each of these mechanisms in determining the community's preference on such matters as the composition of output, the distribution of income, and so forth? How does each of these mechanisms formulate its respective preference function? What is the resulting preference function generated by each mechanism? Finally, how are the several preference functions integrated into a single (consistent?) community preference function?

In addition, we wish to compare the resulting community preferences in regard to the objectives of economic policy, the choice of institutions and instruments to achieve these aims, and the combination of these institutions and instruments in particular patterns of resource allocation and income distribution. The community's objectives will include goals in regard to the level of employment, price stability, per capita consumption, the rate of growth of national income, the distribution of income and wealth, the balance of payments, and so forth. These objectives may be expressed more precisely in specific economic policies and in quantitative terms as "targets."

2.2.2. Institutions and Instruments. *Institutions* may be defined as relatively fundamental organizational arrangements for conducting production and distribution. They are often prescribed by law and not altered as easily as instruments. Examples of institutions include firms, households, markets in which firms exchange with other firms and with households, banks, trade unions, and government economic agencies. Each of these institutions in turn has various types and subtypes. For instance, government economic agencies may be concerned with planning, regulation, redistribution (e.g., social security), or the provision of public goods. An important aspect of any institution is the motivation of its participants, because different participants may have different motivations, with their relative strength and interaction determining the motivation of the institution as such.

The institutional distinction most often made in the study of economic systems concerns the ownership of the means of production. The variants of *private* ownership include individual, partnership, cooperative, and corporate enterprises. When the means of production are *socially* owned, they may be operated by departments of government at different levels (e.g., federal, state, local), by autonomous public boards, or by the personnel of the enterprise ("workers' management"). In all of these cases, private and social, the actions of the enterprise may be restricted by other institutions, using some of the instruments noted below. However, the trend in the study of economic systems is to downgrade the significance of ownership as a critical element in the nature and operation of economic systems, on the ground that it is less important than the pattern of resource allocation and income distribution. Thus, it is now commonly held that "capitalism" and "socialism" are not very useful classifications of economic systems, and that these distinctions are more of ideological or political significance. Nevertheless, although ownership is not decisive in determining the character of the economic system, it is significant both as a factor in income distribution (an important feature of any system) and as a source of power in the formulation of the community's preference function.

Instruments refer to the tools used by the state when it intervenes to (attempt to) achieve social goals in the economic sphere. In comparison with institutions, instruments are more often subject to quantitative expression, are more easily and more frequently altered, and are used by only one kind of institution (government agencies). At least five types of instruments may be distinguished. 1) *Fiscal* instruments include taxes, subsidies, transfer payments, and government purchases. 2) *Monetary* instruments involve changes in interest rates, reserve ratios, and credit rationing; government lending and borrowing; management of existing debt; and control of consumer credit. 3) Altering *exchange rates* is another instrument. 4) Among *direct controls* are production assignments, allocation orders, fixing of prices and wages, and allocation of foreign exchange. Finally, 5) changes in the institutional framework—e.g., in property rights or rules for the operation of markets—may be considered another type of instrument.[3]

Thus, the comparison of systems involves the study of the prevalence and operation of various institutions, as well as the purposes for which, and manner in which, the state uses the possible instruments of economic policy to direct the economic activity of these institutions toward social goals.

2.2.3. Patterns of Resource Allocation and Income Distribution. The interaction of institutions and instruments generates the pattern of resource allocation and income distribution in the system. Three complementary approaches to the analysis of these patterns appear in the literature, each stressing somewhat different elements of the same economic processes.

Centralization versus decentralization involves the delineation of different hierarchies and the relationships among and within them, including 1) the locus at which different decisions are made on such matters as investment, current production, the decision rules applicable to a given unit, and changes in the hierarchical structure; and 2) the flow of information, involving the form, content, purpose, and routing of "messages." Some aspects of this complex subject are explored in Hurwicz's paper in this volume which focuses on the structure of authority and the structure of information. Although the choices along the centralization-decentralization continuum in the two cases are related, they need not be identical. For example, the flow of information could be more centralized than the decision-making process, as when the central authorities collect a great deal of information only in order to make it available to autonomous units which use it for decentralized decisions.[4]

Command versus exchange contrasts resource allocation in physical terms via administrative orders with resource allocation in response to money flows and prices in markets. Money and prices may be used in a command economy, but they perform only "secondary allocation," helping to implement plans drawn up through physical planning techniques. Although it is intended that money flows should supplement administrative orders, in practice they often conflict with them, inducing "violations" of the plan.

[3] A comprehensive analysis of these instruments is presented in E. S. Kirschen, *Economic Policy in Our Time*, Amsterdam and Chicago: 1964, Vol. I.

[4] This example was suggested by Oldřich Kýn.

Planning versus the market focuses on the manner and extent of state intervention in the economy through "planning." Thus, Levine's paper is concerned with such questions as the following: What is the coverage, in scope and detail, of the plan? How is the plan prepared—by what techniques and with what participation by lower units? How seriously is the plan implemented, and what instruments and adjustment mechanisms are used? In addition, one must be aware that some areas of government intervention may be outside the scope of what is customarily included in the "plan," and such extra-plan activities may reinforce or conflict with the plan.

In all three approaches, it is essential to investigate both the formal and the informal mechanisms and their relationship in actual operation, not merely official descriptions or theoretical models of the processes.

To summarize this section briefly: An economic system consists of a particular set of arrangements in regard to a social welfare function, institutions and instruments, and patterns of resource allocation and income distribution. Any specific economic system—whether a model or an actual case—represents a unique combination of these three related aspects. To compare the nature and operation of different systems, we must compare them in detail in all three respects, as systems are likely to be more similar or different in one respect than another. Next we want to associate differences in the nature of the system with differences in performance.

2.3. Performance of Economic Systems

Koopmans and Montias suggest that the ultimate purpose of comparing economic systems is to find ways of improving the performance of a given system (in the light of its social preference function). For this purpose, we want to compare the results of different systems, operating in similar or different environments, in regard to various performance criteria which are deemed important.

The criteria commonly considered include the following:

1. The level of output. (The objective ordinarily is a high or full-employment level, although the quantitative expression of this target depends upon assumptions or goals regarding labor force participation rates and the length of the work week.)
2. The rate of growth of output.
3. The composition of output (the shares of consumption, investment, and military programs; collective vs. individual consumption; and so forth).
4. Single-period ("static") efficiency.
5. Intertemporal ("dynamic") efficiency.
6. Stability (of output, employment, prices).

7. Economic security of the individual (security of income and/or of employment).

8. Equity (involving both an "appropriate" degree of inequality of income and wealth, and equality of opportunity).

9. Economic freedoms (of property, consumption, occupational choice).

10. A balance-of-payments situation which is satisfactory in the light of the country's economic structure.

11. Adaptability to change (in the preference function, the environment, etc.)

Other criteria may be derived from these. For example, the level of per capita consumption, sometimes suggested as an index of welfare, is a combination of 1., 3., and the size of the population. Similarly "economic justice" usually refers to goals in regard to 7., 8., and sometimes 9.

As is well known, some of these objectives are complementary, i.e., mutually reinforcing; for example, the higher the rate of growth, the greater the level of output (in the next period). Others may be competitive, i.e., mutually conflicting; for example, price stability may conflict with a high level of output and a high rate of growth.

Thus, for an aggregate evaluation of an economic system's performance it is necessary to have a utility or welfare function according to which the different criteria can be assigned appropriate weights. Different preference functions will assign different weights to the various performance criteria. Koopmans and Montias point out that the prevailing community preference function may differ in this respect from the function of some part of the community (which may be a majority or a minority of the population) which is given little weight in, or is overruled by, the prevailing function. The function prevailing in one community (i.e., country) may differ from that in another community, or in the same community at another time. It may also differ from that of the analyst of systems, who must recognize when he is using his own preference function to evaluate the system(s) he is studying.

One historically important preference function is examined in Erlich's paper in this volume which discusses the criteria given greatest weight in orthodox Soviet and East European writings. The preference function partly explicit and partly implicit in these writings emphasizes such criteria as high and rising output, stability, equity, and economic security. In contrast, recent economic reforms in the area suggest that the community preference functions now give greater weight than previously to efficiency and economic freedoms (e.g., a greater role for consumer sovereignty in determining the composition of consumption).

Thus, the comparative evaluation or ranking of different economic systems will depend on 1) the performance of the systems in regard to the various criteria considered, and 2) the preference function(s) assigning weights to the several criteria. The latter is essentially a value judgment, somehow formulated for the community as a whole, but the former is more nearly subject to objective scientific measurement.

Two steps are required for empirical comparisons of performance. First, each of the various criteria must be defined as precisely as possible to permit quantitative measurement. This is easier for some criteria than for others. For example, Lorenz curves can show the degree of inequality in the distribution of income and wealth. National accounts depict the level and composition of output. Statistics on employment (unemployment) and personal income provide a measure of economic security. Variations in output, employment, and prices indicate the degree of (in)stability of the economy. Efficiency is more difficult to quantify, but the extent of idle resources may furnish some measure of single-period efficiency, and calculations of aggregate factor productivity offer an indication of inter-temporal efficiency. It is even possible to quantify some of the differences in economic freedoms, for example to use the respective shares of output produced by private and public enterprises as some index of freedom of enterprise.

Once the criteria have been defined carefully, the next step is to measure the performance of the economies to be compared, in as uniform a way as possible. This involves many well-known problems of international comparisons, such as differences among countries in the availability, reliability, coverage, and methodology of data. An example of one of the most difficult of such comparisons is Bergson's paper in this volume. His study of the single-period (static) efficiency of the Soviet and United States economies in 1960 shows both the need for careful definition of what is to be compared, and the detailed and difficult statistical work required to achieve meaningful results.

Although such calculations are usually difficult and complex, they yield the final product toward which the comparison of economic systems is directed. They show the difference in performance—the merit of which is to be assessed in the light of one or more preference functions, and the causes of which are to be explained by the analysis of the nature and operation of the system.

3. Some Current Issues

The aim of the preceding sections has been to present a comprehensive view of the comparison of economic systems, showing the unity and coherence of the various parts of the subject. However, scholars in the field do not agree on all aspects of the methodology for studying economic systems. In this section, I shall consider four current methodological issues, suggesting how they should be resolved. I shall discuss in turn 1) the model *vs.* the case approach; 2) the study of economic systems *vs.* the study of economic development; 3) the comparative systems *vs.* the comparative economics approach; and 4) the disciplinary *vs.* the inter-disciplinary approach.

3.1. Models *vs.* Cases

Models of economic systems are simplified abstractions presenting the main institutional features and operating characteristics of different types of economic systems. They are often inspired by one or more important real-world economies, although they purport to represent general types rather than specific economies. A *case study* deals with an actual economy, which typically incorporates features from various pure models, as a result of such influences as the level of economic development, social-cultural forces, and environmental circumstances. Thus, each specific case has its own unique combination of social preference function, institutions and instruments, and patterns of resource allocation and income distribution.

The model approach to the study of systems has been criticized on the ground that it is concerned with oversimplified abstractions from reality; for example, that it is not useful to consider a pure centrally administered economy, simply because none has ever existed or is likely to exist. A second objection is that it is not possible to measure and compare the performance of models, while this can be done in regard to case studies. As a result, it is argued, the comparison of models is especially vulnerable to ideological biases in interpretation and assessment.

In turn, the case approach has been challenged on the ground that the reality of an actual economy is so complex that any case must be considered selectively, in the light of some conception of the critical variables—i.e., a model. Furthermore, it is a common pitfall to identify a case, explicitly or implicitly, as—in some sense and to some degree—representative of a group of countries with common characteristics. For example, often the United States is chosen as an example of 'capitalism, the Soviet Union as an illustration of socialism, France as a case of indicative planning, and so forth. The unsophisticated reader—student, citizen, or politician—may then erroneously assume that the features and results of the prototype country generally characterize the entire group, and that a comparison of the relative merits of the prototypes, according to one or more performance criteria, reveals the relative merits of the "families" the prototypes are supposed to represent. Thus, although in his paper Bergson is very careful to stress that the United States and the Soviet Union are, respectively, cases, rather than prototypical representatives, of capitalism and socialism, the risk exists that some readers may unjustifiably take his results to apply to capitalism and socialism generally. This may lead to erroneous conclusions, because other countries in the group may differ from the prototype in important respects; and the relative performance (merit) of the two groups will therefore depend on which member is selected as the prototype, as well as which performance criteria are chosen for comparison. In short, intragroup differences are frequently so great that prototypes are not or cannot be representative. Intragroup differences may even exceed intergroup differences in regard to certain characteristics or performance criteria.[5]

The model and case approaches should, however, be viewed as complementary rather than competitive. Models provide a framework for selecting and comparing cases. In turn, the comparison of cases with the models they are supposed to illustrate should lead to the revision and improvement of the models, for example the elaboration of various models of centrally planned socialism, or of market socialism, with different ownership arrangements and different combinations of command and exchange. In this respect, the West and East European economies offer especially promising case studies which can suggest various intermediate models between the traditional model of regulated capitalism inspired by the United States and the classic model of centrally planned socialism suggested by the Soviet Union. Hopefully, these intermediate models will generate a number of testable hypotheses about the operation and performance of economic systems to guide subsequent case studies.

3.2. Economic Systems *vs.* Economic Development

The issue here is the extent to which the comparative study of economic systems should include the less developed countries and primitive economies. For this purpose, *less developed countries* are defined as those with low per capita income levels, which are associated with differences— from the more developed countries—in various aspects of economic structure. These aspects include the distribution of national income by sector of origin, the type of enterprise, the structure of the labor force, factor shares and the size distribution of income, patterns of income use, and foreign-trade proportions. One striking characteristic of many less-developed countries is the coexistence of an important "traditional"

---

[5] Some relevant empirical evidence may be found in George J. Staller, "Fluctuations in Economic Activity: Planned and Free Market Economies, 1950–1960," *American Economic Review*, LIV: 4 (1964), 385–395; George J. Staller, "Patterns of Stability in Foreign Trade: OECD and COMECON, 1950–1963," *American Economic Review*, LVII: 4 (1967), 879–888; and Frederic L. Pryor, *Public Expenditures in Communist and Capitalist Nations*, London and Homewood, Ill.: 1968.

sector in agriculture alongside a "modern" industrial sector. *Primitive economies*, on the other hand, refer to isolated, nonmonetized tribal societies in which economic activity is guided chiefly by tradition and custom, rather than exchange or command. Although this definition may suggest some overlap with the traditional sector in the "dual" economy, the difference is that in the dual economy the traditional sector is in contact with and is being changed by the modern sector, but the primitive economy lacks such strong links to a parallel modern sector. With these distinctions in mind, I find myself in agreement with the position taken in Kuznets' paper that the study of comparative economic systems may fruitfully include the less developed countries but not primitive economies.

The major reason for including the less developed economies is that the level or stage of economic development is one of the forces affecting the nature of the economic system, as well as the conditions (environment) in which it performs. Moreover, there are large and interesting intragroup differences among the less developed countries,[6] and it is desirable to investigate how these differences in the level of development are associated with the nature and performance of economic systems. Finally, there are interesting questions about the interaction of the modern and traditional sectors in the less developed countries which do not arise in the study of more developed economies.

On the other hand, the study of primitive economies may reasonably be excluded because, as Kuznets puts it, it is not very useful to compare cases where great differences exist in material technology and the stock of useful knowledge, because the resulting differences in the economic activities of society cannot be attributed in significant measure to differences in the economic system. That is, "intra-epochal" comparisons are desirable, but "inter-epochal" comparisons are not very relevant. Of course, this position does not mean that the study of primitive societies is pointless or without interest. Rather, it suggests that the subject be considered part of economic anthropology, instead of comparative economic systems.[7]

3.3. Comparative Systems *vs.* Comparative Economics

The *comparative systems* approach encompasses the study of the entire economic system, with the broad scope indicated above in Section 2 and

[6] Kuznets believes that the variety in economic systems is probably greater among the less developed countries than among the more developed countries, because the common technology in the dominant modern component in the latter dictates considerable similarity in economic structure, organization, and goals.

[7] Some recent examples of economic anthropology are Manning Nash, *Primitive and Peasant Economic Systems*, San Francisco, 1966, and George Dalton, ed., *Tribal and Peasant Economies: Readings in Economic Anthropology*, New York, 1967.

with emphasis on the relationship among the various parts of the system. In contrast, the *comparative economics* approach is a partial or sectoral view which compares economies in relation to certain components, for example, labor markets, the nature and operation of large enterprises, agricultural organization, or the conduct of foreign trade.

It seems clear that these should be considered complementary rather than alternative approaches. On the one hand, the sectoral approach needs a view of the entire system, because the characteristics of a given sector in a particular country are determined by the system of which it is a part. On the other hand, sectoral comparisons enhance our understanding of the respective systems as a whole. Thus both approaches—and a synthesis of the results—are necessary. (If a comprehensive label embracing both the comparative systems approach and the comparative economics approach is deemed useful, "comparative economic studies" may serve the purpose.)

There are, however, some reasons for believing that it may be more fruitful to emphasize the sectoral approach in future research in the field. Most past research has stressed the systems approach, and a substantial (though by no means complete) body of "system-focused" literature is now available. Thus, at the margin the returns from research are likely to be greater in selected comparative sectoral studies. These studies can also help illuminate differences and similarities *within* the usual groupings of countries—such as East and West. Finally, such studies will hopefully enrich the United States economics curriculum by introducing a comparative dimension into courses in public finance, labor, industrial organization, and so forth. As a rule, these courses now deal solely with the United States economy, leaving consideration of the respective aspects of other economic systems to courses labeled "comparative economic systems" or "economic development."

3.4. Disciplinary *vs.* Interdisciplinary Approach

To what extent can the comparative analysis of economic systems, along the lines suggested above, be performed exclusively with the tools ordinarily found in the economist's tool box? Or must considerable use be made of the concepts and techniques of other disciplines, notably history, anthropology, political science, sociology, and psychology?

Perhaps more than other branches of economics, the comparison of economic systems requires a multidisciplinary or—better still—interdisciplinary approach. Some aspects of the subject may need this approach to a greater extent than others. For example, the comparison of ideologies involves other disciplines much more than does the comparison of growth rates.

In this field, as in others, it is incumbent upon the investigator to use all of the relevant tools. In some cases, he may acquire and use them himself. In others, the most satisfactory solution will be to secure the collaboration of appropriate scholars in other fields who possess the additional disciplinary skills. Illustrations include joint work by economists and political scientists on government resource-allocation decisions, by economists and psychologists on enterprise management, and by economists and sociologists (or anthropologists) on social-cultural forces shaping the economic system. Fortunately, current trends in other social-science disciplines are favorable to such collaboration. The comparative method has long been used in anthropology,[8] and in recent years systematic comparative studies have received increasing attention in both political science and sociology. Thus, comparative politics is concerned with transnational analysis of "the social configuration, the interest group universe, political parties, ideological attitudes as they shape and condition political behavior, and elite structure."[9] Comparative sociology is devoted to cross-societal studies of kinship, family, and marriage; polity and bureaucracy; social stratification and mobility; ecology, urban sociology, and demography; and cultural value orientation.[10] The potential for mutual assistance and cross-fertilization between these fields and comparative economic studies is clear and exciting.

4. Conclusion

The scope of comparative economic studies is broad, encompassing three main aspects. First, the field deals with the factors influencing economic systems, including the level of economic development, social and cultural forces, and the "environment." A second aspect is the nature and operation of systems, involving social preference functions, institutions and instruments, and patterns of resource allocation and income distribution. Third, the subject is concerned with the performance of systems, both empirical measurement of results for various performance criteria and aggregate evaluations in the light of the weights assigned to the various criteria by one or more social preference functions.

The broad scope of the field in turn accommodates—indeed requires—a variety of research methods and analytical approaches, disciplinary and interdisciplinary, as Ward's paper in this volume shows.

[8] Cf. A. R. Radcliffe-Brown, "The Comparative Method in Social Anthropology," *Journal of the Royal Anthropological Institute of Great Britain and Ireland*, LXXXI (1951), Parts I and II, 15–22.

[9] Roy C. Macridis and Bernard E. Brown, "Introductory Essay," in Macridis and Brown, eds., *Comparative Politics: Notes and Readings*, rev. ed. Homewood, Ill., 1964, p. 4.

[10] Cf. Robert M. Marsh, *Comparative Sociology*, New York, 1967.

Finally, comparative economic studies make a unique contribution to economics as whole, by providing the perspective to overcome the parochialism inherent in economic thinking—on both theoretical and policy questions—based on the experience of a single economic system. The comparison of systems enriches the analyst's understanding of his own system, sharpening his appreciation of its merits and demerits and suggesting organizational and operational changes to improve its performance.

Index

Actions, 29–30; the term, 33; system-bound, 54–55; informational and effective, 57–61. *See also* Interactions

Activities: technological, 50–51, 54; interdependence of, 51–52; system-bound, 54–55

"Acts of God," 60

Adaptation: to inefficiency, 19, 124–27, 131; to injustice, 20, 128–29; failure of, 110–14; and decision mechanisms, 132–33

Adjusted factor cost, 173–77

Adjustment process, 18, 86–88, 92; equation expressing, 100

Advocate ideologies. *See* Ideology; Insurgent ideologies

Africa, 247, 255, 257

Agriculturalists, Union of (*Bund der Landwirte*), 273, 274

Agriculture: Soviet output in, 161, 198; employment in, in the USSR and the USA, 190–91, 202–205; comparative valuation of Soviet and US land devoted to, 192, 197, 212; comparative output and factor inputs for, 197; comparative US and Soviet gross product of, 199–201; reproducible capital for, 207–10; Soviet rent in, 213; and efficiency, 228, 229; in German ideological conflict, 271–76

Air pollution, 75

Allocation, 117, 119. *See also* Resources, allocation of

"Allocative *vs.* X-efficiency," 113–14

Almon, Clopper, 121

"American Creed," 285n

Americas, native societies of, 247

Anarchists, 79

Anonymity, 95, 96, 101, 102

Anti-Dühring, 324

Anti-Socialist Act, 284

Antonov, O. N., 231

Arbitration, commercial, 129

Aristotle, on collective ownership, 79

Armed forces, US and Soviet employment in, 203

Arrow, Kenneth, 97, 103, 124, 125, 131–32

Asia: societies of, 247; productivity in, 255. *See also* "East"

Assets, overvaluation of, 194n

Assignment, 67, 69–70, 72

Associations, 39, 40

Atomic energy, 253

Australia, 28

Austria, labor movement in, 282–84

Autarky, organizational, 73–74

Authority: structure of, 88–92, 101–102; exercise of, 141–42; centralization of, 142,150–54,159 (*see also* Centralization)

Autonomy, 89, 92

Bacon, Roger, 79

"Balance," 111n

Barone, Enrico, economist, 92

Baumol, William, 124

Bazarov, 332

Becker, Abraham, 182, 199

Behavior, and organizational change, 116–17

Behavioral approach, 20, 127–28

Belassa, Bela, 124–25

Bergson, Abram, 2, 16–22 *passim*, 111–12, 114; discussion of paper of, 219–33, 349–51

Berliner, Joseph S., 161, 189n

Bernstein, Eduard, 283, 307n

Bolshevik party, Stalin and, 320

Bornstein, Morris, 21–22, 183n

Bourgeoisie, 274, 282

Brady, Robert, 130

Brasilia, 296

Bridgman, Percy, 285n

Budapest, 75

Bukharin, Nikolai Ivanovich, 332

Bund der Landwirte (Union of Agriculturalists), 273

Bureaucracy, 147nf

Calabresi, Guido, 125

Calvinism, 282–83

Camacho, 96

Campanella, Tommaso, 79

Capital, 15, 304, 317

Capital: income, net, rates of return on, 226; in Marxian ideology, 283; goods in post-Stalinist thought, 328–30. *See also* Reproducible capital

Capitalism, 27; organized behavior in, 104–105; efficiency of, 239; and industrialization, 279; ideologies of, 289; Marxian view of, 303–304; Lenin's views of, 306–308, 310–12; Stalin's views of, 315–17; post-Stalinist views of, 323–27; as a classification, 345

System/systems: (*cont.*)
48–49; interaction of, with norms, 48–50; organizational structure of, 55–75; interaction between, 75–78; and economic epochs, 248–49; new, 258–64; nature of, 269; convergence of, and ideology, 292–94; concept of, 339–40; economic, comparison of, 339–55 and *passim*

Tariff. *See* Protectionism
Tarn, Alexander, 183n
Taxes, turnover, sales and excise, 227–28
Taylor-Lange remedy, 92, 122
Taylor's procedure, 91
Technology: change in, 13, 165, 167; in a conceptual framework, 29–30; activities involving, 50–51, 54 (*see also* Activities); and systems, 53; knowledge in, 164, 165, 193, 239; post-Stalinist view of, 323, 330–31
Terms, system-free, 28–29
Thailand, 257
Tier, in hierarchies, 71
Tinbergen, Jan, 155
Tobin, J., 43n
Toda, Yasushi, 170
Toothless planning. *See* Indicative planning
Total Factor Productivity (Residual), 220, 225, 230, 239
Total system, 31–32. *See also* System
Trade and Industry Association for Rhineland and Westfalia, 277
Transfer price, 60. *See also* Prices
Transfer states, 52
Transformation schedules, 167, 169
Transportation costs, Soviet, 192
Tree, in graph theory, 69
Trotsky, Leon, 320

Unavailing norm, 35. *See also* Norms
Underdeveloped countries: and stage of economic growth, 254–58; Stalin's views on, 316; post-Stalinist view of, 326; economies of, 351–52
Understanding, the term, 107
Unemployment, 161, 191–92, 227
Union of Agriculturalists (*Bund der Landwirte*), 273, 274
USSR: and comparative economics, 1; incentive system of, 11; role of Marxism in, 14–15; productivity of, 16–17, 20–21, 161–62, 178–99, 201–202, 231–32, 236–40; status of study of the economy of, 22; ruling units of, 56n; planning in, 58, 137–38, 144, 149; reorganization of

industry in, 67; example of hierarchy in, 70–71; range of activities of enterprises in, 73–74; Lake Baikal dispute in, 75n; and the "command economy," 80; studies of, 109, 111, 112, 117, 127–28, 130; efficiency in, 114, 161–62, 228–30, 239; commercial arbitration in, 129; mathematical economies of, 130; economic centralization in, 145; goals of, 152; comparative valuation of workers of, 190–91; employment and workers in, 202–207, 211–12, 227; reproducible capital in, 207–10, 212; input factors of, 211–14; index for prices of, 221–23; geometric indexes for, 225; rates of return on capital for, 226; depreciation for, 226–27; services sector of, 227; private enterprise in, 252; entry of, into modern economic development, 260–63; future economic growth of, 263–67; materialist view of history in, 281n; ideology and, 286–89, 297–98, 342; civil war in, 313–14; Stalin's view of the economic system of, 317–19; and post-Stalinist thought, 329–31, 334; a case of socialism, 350–51
United Nations, 77
United States: economic experience of, 6, 8, 12, 253, 339; productivity of, 16, 20–21, 161–62, 178, 183n, 184–85, 189, 192–202 *passim*, 210, 236, 238; ruling units of, 56n; trade restrictions imposed by, 77; commercial arbitration in, 129; centralization in, 145; employment and workers in, 161, 189–91, 203–207, 212, 227; reproducible capital of, 207–10, 212; input factors of, 212–14; index for prices of, 221–23; geometric indexes for, 224–25; rates of return on capital for, 226; Bergson's analysis of, 227; efficiency of, 162, 228–30, 239; stage of economic development of, 237; ideology of, 293–94; as a case of capitalism, 350–51
Utility: function (social preference function), 30, 31, 344, 348; expected, 40; version, 43–44, 49
Utopias, 79

Varga, Eugen, 325
Values, 133
Variant. *See* Change; Systems, new
Veblen, Thorstein, 19, 108–109
Voigt, 271

Waelbroeck, J., 127
Wages, 10, 177